The Engine of Reason, the Seat of the Soul

The Engine of Reason, the Seat of the Soul

A Philosophical Journey into the Brain

Paul M. Churchland

A Bradford Book
The MIT Press
Cambridge, Massachusetts
London, England

First MIT Press paperback edition, 1996

This book was set in Melior and Helvetica by Asco Trade Typesetting Ltd., Hong Kong and was printed and bound in the United States of America.

Library of Congress Cataloging-in-Publication Data

Churchland, Paul M., 1942–
The engine of reason, the seat of the soul : a philosophical journey into the brain / Paul M. Churchland.
p. cm.
"A Bradford book."
Includes bibliographical references and index.
ISBN 0-262-03224-4 (HB), 0-262-53142-9 (PB)
1. Brain—Philosophy. 2. Neurosciences—Philosophy.
3. Cognition. I. Title.
QP376.C496 1995
612.8′2′01—dc20

94-30750
CIP

For Pat,
Who, years ago, would lie awake
And wonder with me
How the brain works.

Contents

Preface

How *does* the brain work? How does it sustain a thinking, feeling, dreaming self? How does it sustain a self-conscious *person*? New results from neuroscience and recent work with artificial neural networks together suggest a unified set of answers to these questions. If even roughly correct, those answers will have far-reaching consequences beyond the realm of pure theory. The aim of this book is therefore twofold. First, to make those scientific developments available, in a lucid and pictorial fashion, to the general reading public. And second, to begin to explore the philosophical, social, and personal consequences they are likely to have for all of us.

The book is motivated first of all by sheer excitement over the new picture that is now emerging, and over the new explanations now available for what has so long seemed mysterious. The excitement is not just mine; it is the shared mood of a half-dozen intersecting disciplines. I hope I can succeed in conveying its substance to the general reader.

The book is motivated also by the idea that this is information that the public needs to know. It is a theoretical perspective that the public needs to command. And it will fund a range of technologies whose impact the public is sure to feel. The quicker the better then, that we should make it the common property of everyone.

My philosophical research over thirty years has had many sources of inspiration, and all of them will be somehow visible here, as in my earlier writings. Concerning this book, however, four people stand out from everyone else. I wish to acknowledge their inspiration and express my affection and love for each of them. First, Francis Crick has set me—and my wife and colleague, Patricia—a marvellous intellectual and personal example of how to be a "natural philosopher." I have not entirely followed his sterling example, but my thoughts would have been poorer and my path would have been darker without it. Second, the neuroscientists Antonio and Hanna Damasio have been our neurological tutors, our philosophical students, our collaborators, and above all our friends during the writing of several books from within our regular coffee-house foursome. Their contributions have been priceless. Finally, there is the continuing inspiration of my wife and intellectual colleague, Patricia Churchland. After twenty-five years of affection and collaboration, I often feel we have become the left and right hemispheres of a single brain. Her happy influence pervades everything that follows.

La Jolla, California, April 1994

I The Little Computer that Could: The Biological Brain

1 Introduction

This book is about you. And me. And every other creature that ever measured itself in the mirror of consciousness. More broadly still, it is about every creature that ever swam, or walked, or flew over the face of the Earth. For these are *cognitive* systems also, most of whom were already perceiving and thinking many aeons before humans appeared on the scene. Clearly we need to understand them as well. It is doubtful we will ever understand our own cognition without also understanding how the various grades of cognition arise in our evolutionary neighbors.

The Newly Transparent Brain

Fortunately, recent research into neural networks, both in animals and in artificial models, has produced the beginnings of a real understanding of how the biological brain works—a real understanding, that is, of how *you* work, and everyone else like you. This idea may be found threatening, as if your innermost secrets were about to be laid bare or made public. But in one fundamental respect you should rest assured. As will be explained in chapter 5, your physical brain is far too complex and mercurial for its behavior to be predicted in any but the broadest outlines or for any but the shortest distances into the future. Faced with the extraordinary dynamical features of a functioning brain, no device constructible in this universe could ever predict your behavior, or your thoughts, with anything more than merely statistical success.

So one need not fear being reduced to a clanking robot or an empty machine. Quite to the contrary, we are now in a position to explain how our vivid sensory experience arises in the sensory cortex of our brains: how the smell of baking bread, the sound of an oboe, the taste of a peach, and the color of a sunrise are all embodied in a vast chorus of neural activity. We now have the resources to explain how the motor cortex, the cerebellum, and the spinal cord conduct an orchestra of muscles to perform the cheetah's dash, the falcon's strike, or the ballerina's dying swan. More cen-

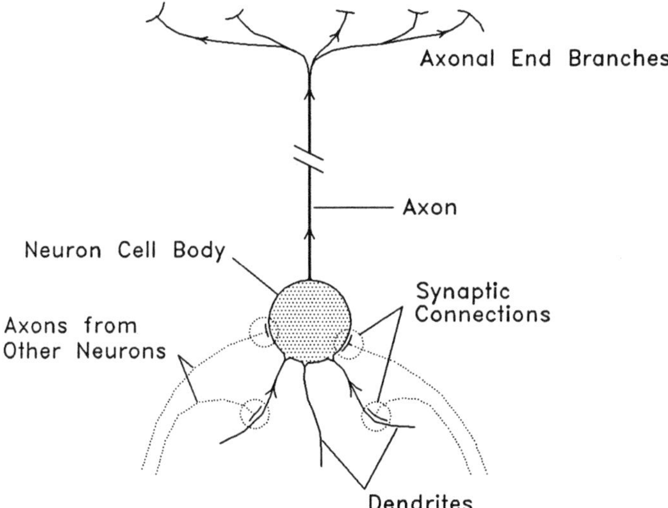

Figure 1.1 A typical neuron. It receives excitatory and inhibitory signals from other neurons by way of the many synaptic connections (circled) they make onto the neuron's cell body and its extended tree of dendritic branches. It sums those various incoming signals and emits an appropriate signal down its own axon, to make contact with further neurons.

trally, we can now understand how the infant brain slowly develops a framework of concepts with which to comprehend the world. And we can see how the matured brain deploys that framework almost instantaneously: to recognize similarities, to grasp analogies, and to anticipate both the immediate and the distant future.

On this matter of conceptual development there is especial cause for wonder. For the human brain, with a volume of roughly a quart, encompasses a space of conceptual and cognitive possibilities that is larger, by one measure at least, than the entire astronomical universe. It has this striking feature because it exploits the combinatorics of its 100 billion neurons and their 100 trillion synaptic connections with each other (figure 1.1). Each cell-to-cell connection can be strong, or weak, or anything in between. The global configuration of these 100 trillion connections is very important for the individual who has them, for that idiosyncratic set of connection strengths determines how the brain reacts to the sensory information it receives, how it responds to the emotional states it encounters, and how it plots its future behavior. We already appreciate how many different Bridge hands can be dealt from a standard deck of merely fifty-two playing cards: enough to occupy the most determined foursome for several lifetimes. Think how many more "hands" might be dealt from the brain's much larger "deck" of 100 trillion modifiable synaptic connections. The answer is easily calculated. If we assume, conservatively, that each synaptic connection might have any one of ten different strengths, then the total number of distinct possible configurations of synaptic weights that the brain might assume is, very roughly, ten raised to the 100 trillionth power, or $10^{100,000,000,000,000}$. Compare this with the measure of only 10^{87} cubic meters standardly estimated for the volume of the entire astronomical universe.

Each individual human is a unique hand dealt from this monumental deck. It is at different points within this almost endless space of connective possibilities that each individual human personality resides, that each distinct set of religious, moral, and scientific convictions resides, and that each distinct cultural orientation resides. As the child grows and learns, its myriad synaptic connections are steadily adjusted to a configuration that allows it to behave as a normal member of the local community, to a configuration that produces in that child what is locally regarded as a normal conception of the world, a conception of its general physical, social, and moral structure.

How the Brain Represents the World: General Features

As the preceding suggests, the brain represents the general or lasting features of the world with a lasting configuration of its myriad synaptic connection strengths. That configuration of carefully tuned connections dictates how the brain will react to the world. Each creature encounters similar types of circumstances, day in and day out: berries to be picked, intruders to chase away, the young to be nurtured, barriers to be walked around, dangers to be avoided, burrows to be cleaned, telephones to be answered, and so on and so on. Such standard cirumstances have more or less standard causal features and require standard, but appropriately plastic, modes of apprehension and behavioral response.

To acquire those capacities for recognition and response is to learn about the general causal structure of the world, or, at least, of that small part of it that is relevant to one's own practical concerns. That knowledge is embodied in the peculiar configuration of one's 10^{14} individual synaptic connections. During learning and development in childhood, those connection strengths, or "weights" as they are often called, are set to progressively more useful values.

These adjustments are steered in part by factors that reflect one's genetic heritage (one's nature), but they are steered most dramatically by the unique experience that each child encounters (one's nurture). Cumulatively, the connective changes made during learning are enormous. The synaptic adjustments undergone by any normal infant mark a series of conceptual revolutions that is never equaled in adult life, even in the brain of an Einstein.

To be sure, synaptic change remains possible for the matured brain: even adults can learn. But the rate of synaptic change does seem to go down steadily with increasing age. By the time we are thirty, our basic character, skills, and world view are fairly firmly in place. While conceptual change does remain possible, obvious statistics and familiar homilies about old dogs and new tricks imply that major changes are unlikely. Why this is so, and how such conceptual inertia can occasionally be overcome, is something we will explore in later chapters. There remains considerable hope here for those of us over forty: in at least one crucial respect, an old brain may be *more* plastic than a young one.

How the Brain Represents the World: Fleeting Features

To repeat, the general and lasting features of the external world are represented in the brain by relatively lasting configurations of synaptic *connections*. But what about the specific and fleeting features of the brain's immediate sensory environment? What about its ongoing experience? What about the ebb and flow of the here and now? These more fleeting facts get represented by a fleeting configuration of *activation* levels in the brain's many *neurons*, such as those in the retina and visual cortex. As we observed above, neurons do not change their mutual synaptic connections very quickly: like the wiring inside a TV set, the connections between neurons are relatively stable. But neurons can change their internal activation levels in a twinkling, and they do. Like the pixels on a TV screen, each neuron's level of activation is continuously updated by stimulations or inhibitions that stem ultimately from the external world. Like the assembled pixels on a TV screen, the overall *pattern* of neuronal activation levels at any given instant constitutes the brain's portrait of its local situation here and now. And like the TV screen once more, the temporal *sequence* of these ever-changing patterns constitutes the brain's ongoing portrait of an ever-changing world.

Brains versus TV Screens

It is worth pausing a moment to admire the capacity of a normal human brain to represent the world, for it puts a TV screen to shame. A standard TV screen boasts something like 525 × 360 pixels of resolution. These tiny dotlike elements are easily seen if you peer very closely at the screen. A grid of these dimensions yields a total of roughly 200,000 pixels, each one of which can take on a full range of brightness values. This is the representational capacity of a TV screen. But a human brain has roughly 100,000,000,000 or *100 billion* neurons, each one of which can also take on a full range of activation levels or "brightness values." Counting each neuron as a pixel then, and dividing the TV screen's capacity (200,000) into the brain's capacity (100 billion), we must reckon that the brain's representational capacity is about 500,000 times greater than a TV screen's.

To make this large advantage both vivid and visual, think of things in the following way. To get a TV display large enough to compete with the representational power of a single human brain, we would have to tile the entire outside surface of one of the twin World Trade Towers in New York City—all 500,000 square feet of it—with fully one-half million 17-inch TV screens, all glued cheek to cheek and facing outward. This arrangement would cover the entire building with an almost continuous surface of tiny pixels at the normal TV density of about 200,000 pixels for each and every square foot: in all, 100 billion dancing pixels (figure 1.2). Imagine looking up at a single unified picture displayed on that monumental scale. A wraparound screen of such heroic dimensions and extraordinary resolution could portray any situation in exquisite and spectacular detail. That is exactly the representational power that you and I already possess. And unlike the composite Trade-Tower TV screen, the brain is not limited to forming purely *visual* representations. As we will explore below, the brain portrays reality in many other sensory dimensions, and in various social, moral, and emotional dimensions as well.

Despite the modest size of the human brain, you are capable of world portrayal on a scale fit for skyscrapers for two reasons. First, your brain's pixels—your individual neurons—are much smaller than a TV's pixels (about 10 microns, or roughly one millionth of an inch across). And second, in your brain those 100 billion pixels are packed into a three-dimensional *volume* instead of a two-dimensional surface. Here it will help to imagine that the sky-

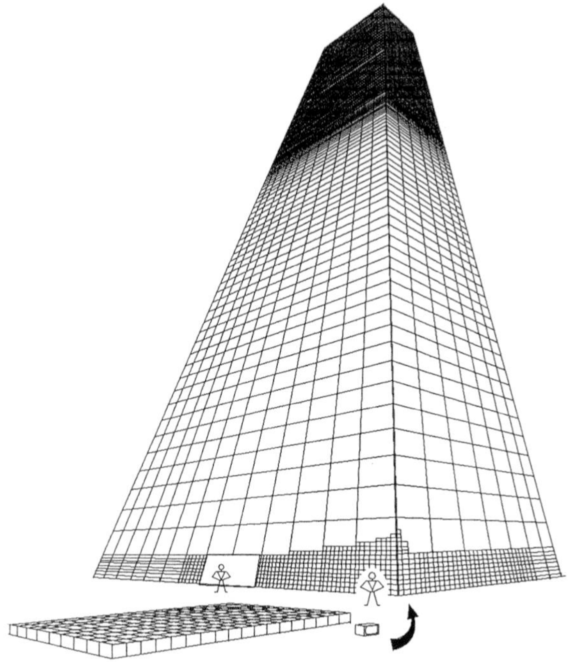

Figure 1.2 Tower One of the World Trade Center being tiled with 500,000 TV screens.

scraper's pixels are embedded in a thin sheet of aluminum foil that covers the entire building. Now grasp that great expanse of foil and scrunch it into a ball. In you, that skyscraper's pixeled surface is compacted and folded into a closely layered and tightly wrinkled volume about the size of a large grapefruit (figure 1.3). But those 100 billion dancing pixels go right on representing the world, even when they are folded out of sight.

Computation in the Brain: Pattern Transformation

But who, in that case, can be *watching* this pixilated show? The answer is straightforward: no one. There is no distinct "self" in there, beyond the brain as a whole. On the other hand, almost every part of the brain is being "watched" by some other part of the brain, often by several other parts at once. The activation patterns across the assembled retinal neurons in the eye, for example, are monitored by a distinct layer of neurons in a grape-sized cluster in the middle of the brain called the lateral geniculate nucleus, or LGN for short (figure 1.4). The retinal neurons project their collective portrait of the external world inward along a cable of ultrathin fibers

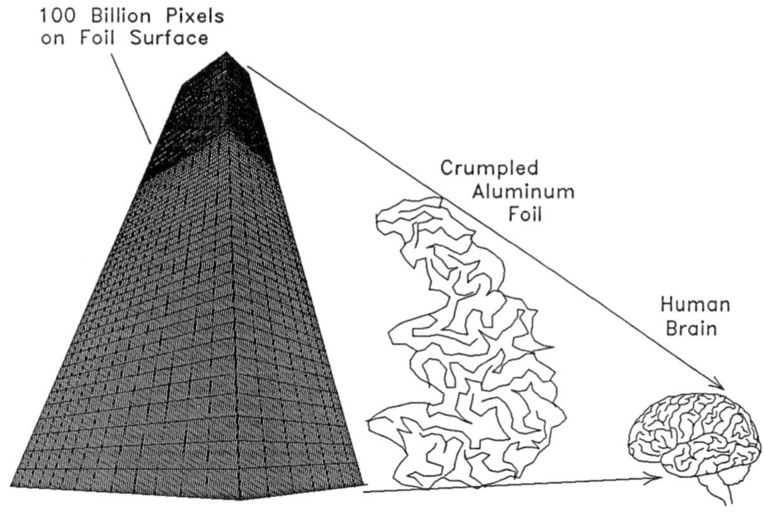

Figure 1.3 The compaction of the pixeled outer surface of the World Trade Center's Tower One into a solid volume the size of a human brain.

called *axons*. During an infant's development, each one of these wirelike axons grows multiple branches at its far end so as to make many synaptic connections with the waiting neurons in the LGN. That cable of axons is the optic nerve familiar to all of us, and it conveys to the LGN detailed information about the pattern of activation across the retinal neurons.

The LGN neurons project their axons in turn to a largish patch of neurons on the rear surface of the brain called the visual cortex. Those cortical neurons thereby receive information about the patterns of activation across the LGN's neurons. The LGN, therefore, is monitored in turn by the visual cortex. As before, the information transfer from one to the other is mediated by an intricate configuration of intervening synaptic connections, where the axons projecting from the way station of the LGN finally make contact with the neurons in the visual cortex. Such synaptic connections are of vital importance to what the brain does, because they typically *transform* the pattern of information they receive as they convey it to the next population of neurons in the chain. They modify the information, select from it, suppress within it, and in general they interpret it by a most cunning technique to be revealed in chapter 2.

These systematic connections between patches of the brain's representational surface mark a major shortcoming in our analogy

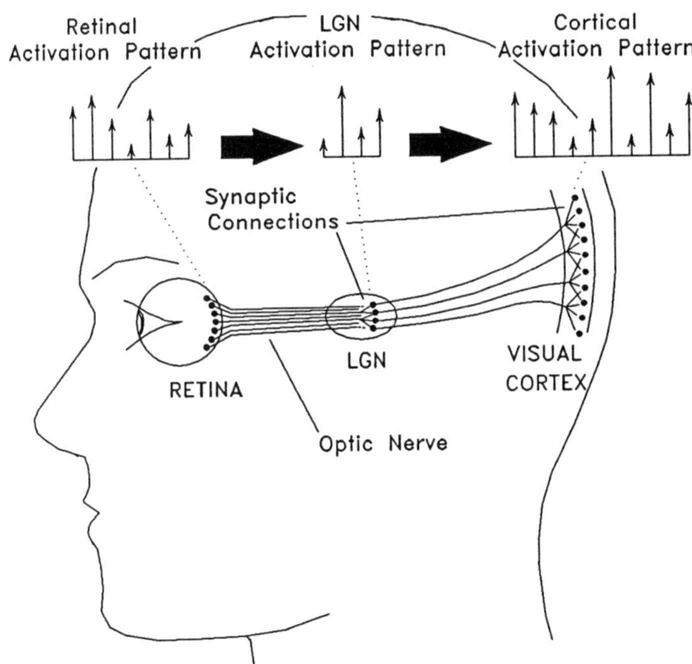

Figure 1.4 The successive transformations of neuronal activation patterns produced by passing them through a matrix of many synaptic connections.

with the skyscraper TV screen. The yard-square patch of pixels on the right-most window at the 103rd floor, for example, has no way to talk to or influence the behavior of the large patch of pixels on the left-most window at the 57th. There are no causal interactions whatever between the parts of this system.

To introduce such causal interaction, we would need to add, for example, a massive cable of optical fibers emerging from the 103rd-floor patch of pixels, a drooping cable stretching across the face of the building to make suitable contact with the patch of pixels at the 57th. Even better, put all such cables *inside* the building to minimize cable length. Better still, take the microthin outside surface of the TV-tiled building—the surface containing the 100 billion pixels—and scrunch that entire surface into a tinfoil ball the size of a grapefruit, as discussed above. Now we can really minimize cable length. Practically every pixel patch will be pressed surface-to-surface against several others, and the longest straight-line cable traverse inside the ball is now only six inches. With this arrangement, we finally have something whose physical organization resembles the physical organization of the brain.

To approximate the brain's *functional* activity, however, we need one further wrinkle. If the target patch of receiving pixels is to do anything more than simply repeat or re-present the original activation pattern across the transmitting patch of pixels, then the cable's many connections to the receiving patch had better *modify* the arriving pattern in some way so that a new pattern results at their destination. In the brain, this is precisely what happens.

This means that the process I have loosely characterized as monitoring or "watching"—strictly, the process of re-representing the activation patterns of earlier populations of neurons—is not a passive process at all. It is dramatically active. As the original pixilated pattern across the many retinal neurons gets passed inward from one specialized neural population to the next, and to the next and the next, the original pattern is progressively transformed at each stage by the intervening configuration of synaptic connections. This is where the bulk of the brain's *computation* takes place. This is where past learning shows itself, where character and insight come in, and where intelligence is ultimately grounded. You can see the process at work in figure 1.4: each successive patch of neurons displays a new and different pattern of activation. That diagram is of course a cartoon: the retina, LGN, and visual cortex each have many *millions* of neurons. But the computational point is clear.

The Cunning of Reason: Parallel Distributed Processing

This style of computing—transforming one pattern into another by passing it through a large configuration of synaptic connections—is called *parallel distributed processing*, or PDP for short. It is standard throughout the animal kingdom, and for good reasons. It has a number of absolutely decisive advantages over the more familiar but rather different style of computing, called *serial processing*, displayed in conventional desktop and mainframe computing machines. In the chapters to follow we will explore those advantages at length, but two of them deserve immediate mention.

Speed and Power

First and foremost, a PDP computer is much faster than a serial computer, at least for the large range of problems that typically confront a living creature. It is faster because it performs hundreds of millions of individual computations *simultaneously* instead of in laborious sequence. To illustrate with an example you already understand, consider once again the axonal pathway from the LGN to the visual cortex. When the LGN's collective activation pattern arrives at the visual cortex, that pattern is filtered through roughly 100 billion (100,000,000,000) tiny synaptic connections, as a whole and all at once. Each cortical synapse performs its own tiny part of the overall transformation of the activation-pattern-at-the-LGN into the activation-pattern-at-the-visual-cortex.

If the LGN is thought of as a starting gate, the race to the visual cortex is over in about 10 milliseconds (msec), with all of the axonal impulses crossing the cortical finish line together. This time scale—10 msec—is typical for a single layer-to-layer transformation within the brain. The typical result of such a transformation is a new pattern of activations across the neurons in the visual cortex, a pattern that might now explicitly portray, for example, the *three-dimensional* structure of the visual world. That 3-D information was only implicit in the two retinal activation patterns at the sensory periphery; it was buried in the subtle pictorial disparities between them. But two or three transformations later, at the visual cortex, that buried information has been made explicit. (Part of what the human visual system is computing is stereo or 3-D vision. We will see how it works in the next chapter.)

One hundred billion elementary computations at one blow is a fair feat. It takes a typical desktop computer, running at 12 MHz, about a quarter of an hour to perform 100 billion elementary computations. But a single stage of the human visual system does all this in only 10 msec—that is, in 1/100th of a second—because it performs the many computations required independently and all at the same time. Kitchen lore contains a humble analog of this time-saving trick. Faced with the problem of cutting the stem ends off each and every one of a large bag of green beans before tossing them into the pot, the wise cook lines them all up in parallel, stem ends together, and lops them all off with a single stroke of the knife.

Looking now beyond the relatively small visual cortex to the brain as a whole, let us note that the brain can perform altogether 100 *trillion* elementary computations in that same interval, since that is the total number of synaptic connections you possess, and each one performs its own tiny computation independently. A desktop computer, running day and night, would spend over a week on such a task. Clearly, evolution hit upon a winner when it stumbled across parallel distributed processing.

Functional Persistence

It gets better. A PDP computer can suffer the malfunction, inactivation, or outright death of large numbers of its synaptic connections, and yet suffer only a marginal degradation in its performance. If we shrank a rampaging Rambo down to the size of a neuron and turned him loose with a tiny machine gun inside your visual cortex, he could blow away at random perhaps 10 percent (about 10 billion) of the synaptic connections meeting your cortical neurons, and yet you would notice hardly a thing. Your basic visual capacities might be reduced by some small margin, as revealed by some careful test, but that is about all.

The reason is simple. Each synapse contributes such a tiny amount, to the overall pattern-to-pattern transformation in which it participates, that the random loss of every tenth connection leaves the system performing approximately the same transformation that it performed in its undamaged state. Any large subset of the overall population of connections, if chosen at random, has pretty much the same transformational character as any other large subset. This means that, at any given instant, a fair proportion of one's synapses can be inactive, overactive, or just plain dead, and yet the remaining majority will collectively display the same input-output behavior that makes one a functional human.

This most fortunate feature is called functional persistence or fault tolerance, and in this respect PDP computers differ profoundly from serial computers. The loss of a single connection inside the central processor of a desktop computer is almost certain to produce a profoundly dysfunctional machine. Given the endless minor accidents we suffer, humans and other animals cannot afford such a perilous arrangement. Even normal aging itself involves the loss, without replacement, of roughly 10 thousand neurons every day of one's life. (This rate is not quite so appalling as it seems. One starts life with 100 billion neurons, so a lifetime at this rate of loss steals less than one percent of one's initial capital.)

Since a biological brain is composed of highly unreliable components, evolution had no choice but to explore parallel distributed processing, and to exploit the fault tolerance and functional persistence that PDP automatically confers. Unlike the well-behaved electronic components in a modern serial/digital computer, biological neurons and their mutual synaptic connections are all rather noisy and unreliable citizens. This poses a problem for any serial machine made of real neurons. A serial machine is fault *in*tolerant because its chainlike sequence of computations can be only as strong as its weakest link. Accordingly, it is flatly impossible to make a successful serial computer using only biological components. On average, it might work properly for only two or three seconds a week—on those rare and fleeting occasions when all of its components happened to be working properly at exactly the same time.

This is not just a theorist's joke. Computer engineering has had real and frustrating experience with this sort of problem. Unreliability was a potentially fatal feature of the earliest serial computers, since they used thousands of vacuum tubes—like the ones in early radios—for the many high-speed switches required. A vacuum tube is like an ordinary light bulb in many respects, most relevantly in its annoying tendency to burn out at unpredictable moments. With thousands of vacuum tubes in constant operation, and every one crucial to the serial computer's function, sheer statistics guaranteed endlessly repeated down time for any machine so constructed. And of course the problem got exponentially worse as computers were made more powerful and the number of such components increased.

Fortunately for the future of serial computing, Bell Labs invented the transistor, a high-speed electronic switching device that did not tend to burn out. It could also be made arbitrarily small. Save for the appearance of this extraordinarily reliable electronic valve, computer technology would still be in the dark ages.

Except, of course, for that marvelous alternative technology humming happily away inside the nervous system of any living creature. That technology has been highly developed for millions of years and does not depend on perfection in its components. It gets its computational speed from the massively parallel nature of its information processing. And it gets its functional persistence from the massively distributed nature of its information coding and storage. The inevitable scattered failures are thus swamped by a surrounding sea of robust success. Jointly, these two features allow the biological brain to outperform any existing supercomputer, on a wide range of problems, despite being constructed out of components that, taken individually, are both slow and unreliable. An army of fumbling tortoises, by an artful strategy, manages to outrun the hare.

Toward More Lifelike Cognitive Capacities

Blinding speed and functional persistence are important, but they merely begin the list of fascinating cognitive properties displayed by PDP computers. That list includes all of the distinctive cognitive properties displayed in living creatures, such as

- the capacity for recognizing features or patterns through a veil of noise and distortion, or given only partial information;
- the capacity for seeing complex analogies;
- the capacity for recalling relevant information, instantly, as it bears on novel circumstances;
- the capacity for focusing attention on different features of one's sensory input;
- the capacity for trying out a series of different cognitive "takes" on a problematic situation;
- the capacity for recognizing subtle and indefinable sensory qualities such as your own child's voice or the smell of pine needles;
- the capacity for moving one's body with coherence and grace through the physical environment; and
- the capacity for navigating one's social self with purpose and responsibility through the social and moral environment.

These capacities, and others like them, have long been claimed to be beyond the power of any material computing system. This is a profound mistake. Such capacities may be beyond the power of a conventional serial computer functioning in real time, although that is still debatable. But they are by no means beyond the power of a PDP computer. To the contrary, it will be argued below that such biologically salient capacities are the characteristic signature of a functioning PDP system. They are the surest behavioral sign that we are dealing with a parallel distributed processor. To paraphrase A. A. Milne's ever-eager Tigger, "Seeing relevance and analogy through noise and confusion is what PDP computers do best!"

How can this be so? In the next two chapters we will see how it can be so. But those chapters are still preamble, and I wish to reassure the reader at the outset that we are not embarking on a book that is primarily about computer technology, technology either artificial or biological. This book is first and foremost about human beings and human activities. I wish to explore the character of human cognition in all of its familiar dimensions: perceptual knowledge, practical skill, scientific understanding, social perception, self-consciousness, moral knowledge, religious conviction, political wisdom, and even mathematical and aesthetic knowledge.

Most of these cognitive areas are seldom if ever discussed by researchers either in artificial intelligence or in neuroscience, at least until recently. Usually they have been left to philosophers to mull over as best they could, often in ignorance of both computers and brains. Researchers in AI or neuroscience have quite rightly tended to address more narrow and more tractable problems, such as how a machine can be made to play high-grade chess, or how the hungry frog's brain detects moving flies. But both the theoretical and the experimental situations have changed dramatically in the last decade, and especially in the last five years. With new theories and new experimental techniques it is now possible for us to begin to address the full range of animal and human cognition. It is now possible to bring testable artificial models and detailed neurobiological information to bear on what used to be purely philosophical questions.

Theory and Experiment: Historical Parallels

When an opportunity like this arises, it is essential that we seize it. The combined appearance of Nicholas Copernicus's rough theory of the solar system and Galileo Galilei's crude telescope led to the downfall of a myopic and spiritually repressive theory of the cosmos: the old earth-centered view of Aristotle, Ptolemy, and the Renaissance Roman Church. This dramatic episode launched us on a journey of cosmological discovery that is still unfolding. Similarly, Robert Hooke's seventeenth-century observations of teeming microorganisms through the newly invented microscope led quickly to a new theory of the origins of disease, one that overturned the unintentionally cruel theological conviction that disease was the punishment of God or the torment of the devil. Simple discoveries such as "If you boil your drinking water, you kill the disease bacteria within it" launched a process that brought us the many comforts of modern medicine and public health policy. More recently still, Charles Darwin's account of the origin of species, plus the emerging fossil and geological record, plus modern protein and DNA analysis, have freed us from a quaint myth about the age of the Earth and the privileged status of humankind.

In all of these cases, testable theory and systematic experiment brought new and potentially decisive light to what previously had been a purely philosophical or theological matter. And in all of these cases, we were freed from some unfortunate nonsense or other, nonsense that was not obviously nonsense beforehand. On the contrary, it was often widespread and unquestioned conviction, conviction whose defects were invisible in advance of the new developments, even to highly reasonable people. But as we slowly digested the new conceptual framework held out to us in each of these liberating episodes, and as we saw its cognitive virtues unfold in practice, the world in which we lived was changed forever, including our social and moral world.

If we can be so evidently and so wildly wrong about the structure of the universe, about the significance of disease, about the age of the Earth, and about the origin of humans, we should in all modesty be prepared to contemplate the possibility that we remain deeply misled or confused about the nature of human cognition and consciousness. One need not look far for potential examples of deep confusion. A hypothesis that still enjoys broad acceptance throughout the world is the idea that human cognition resides in an immaterial substance: a soul or mind. This proposed nonphysical substance is held to be uniquely capable of consciousness and of rational and moral judgment. And it is commonly held to survive the death of the physical body, thence to receive some form of reward or punishment for its Earthly behavior. It will be evident from the rest of this book that this familiar hypothesis is difficult to square with the emerging theory of cognitive processes and with the experimental results from the several neurosciences. The doctrine of an immaterial soul looks, to put it frankly, like just another myth, false not just at the edges, but to the core.

This is unfortunate, since that hypothesis is still embedded, to some depth or other, in the social and moral consciousness of billions of people across widely diverse cultures. If that hypothesis is false, then sooner or later they are going to have to deal with the problem of how best to reconceive the nature of an individual human life, and how best to understand the ground of the moral relations that bind us together. Such adjustments, to judge from the past, are often painful. The good side is that they just as often set us free, and allow us to achieve a still higher level of moral insight and mutual care. In exploring the lessons of cognitive neurobiology, I will proceed at all times on this hopeful assumption.

Reworking the Mirror of Our Self Conception

Pointing to primitive religious beliefs does not, however, find the most interesting location for theoretical conflict and potential conceptual change. The religious hypothesis of mind-body dualism has been in deep trouble with evolutionary biology, and with several other sciences as well, for more than a century. It didn't need any special input from artificial intelligence or neuroscience to make it scientifically implausible. I bring it up here only because it is a clear example of a popular and important belief currently under siege by modern information. And because its example may be repeated. The fact is, there is a much more intriguing area of current conceptual commitment, one more likely to be affected by emerging cognitive theory in particular. It lies even closer to home and is even more widespread, if that is possible, than mind-body dualism. It is our current self-conception: our shared portrait of ourselves as self-conscious creatures with beliefs, desires, emotions, and the power of reason.

This conceptual framework is the unquestioned possession of every normal human who wasn't raised from birth by wolves. It is the template of our normal socialization as children; it is the primary vehicle of our social and psychological commerce as adults; and it forms the background matrix for our current moral and legal discussions. It is often called "folk psychology" by philosophers, not as a term of derision, but to acknowledge it as the basic descriptive and explanatory conceptual framework with which all of us currently comprehend the behavior and mental life of our fellow humans, and of ourselves.

Suddenly we are looking in a mirror. Not into the distant heavens nor down the halls of evolutionary time nor into the teeming microworld, but squarely at ourselves. Is our basic conception of human cognition and agency yet another myth, moderately useful in the past perhaps, yet false at edge or core? Will a proper theory of brain function present a significantly different or incompatible portrait of human nature? Should we prepare ourselves, emotionally, for yet another conceptual revolution, one that will touch us more closely than ever before?

The Aim of This Book

As will become plain, I am inclined toward positive answers to all of these questions, and toward an optimistic estimate of our future prospects, both scientific and moral. But I am uncertain of my position here, and it is not the primary purpose of this book to urge or establish any particular philosophical doctrine. Its primary aim is to make available to the thinking public, in vivid and comprehensible form, the character and potential significance of the developing theory and the recent experimental results. I hope to make available here a conceptual framework of sufficient richness and integrity that you will be able to reconceive at least some of your own mental life in explicitly neurocomputational terms. You will then be able to judge for yourself the potential conflicts and turmoil we confront. And you will be better able to participate in the inevitable debates about appropriate public policy concerning medical care, psychiatry, the law, moral responsibility, our correctional system, education, private morality, and the nature of freedom. These are matters of preeminent importance. In a democratic society they will require from all of us as much wisdom as we can muster. It is therefore crucial that relevant information be made widely available.

Much has been written about what computers cannot do. From Descartes and Leibniz in the seventeenth century, to my colleagues Dreyfus and Searle and Penrose in the closing decades of the twentieth, computation has repeatedly been judged inadequate to account for the full range of human cognition. Not all of this writing has been wasted, since there are indeed types and classes and styles of computers that Can't. But this book is not about them. This book is about the Computer that Could. Let us turn finally to examine how it Can.

2 Sensory Representation: The Incredible Power of Vector Coding

Humans are famously bad at describing their sensations—of tastes, of aromas, of feelings—but we are famously good at discriminating, enjoying, and suffering them. Indeed, becoming familiar with the great space of sensory characters is part of what makes a life worth living. And yet, while we all participate in the richness of sensory life, we struggle to communicate to others all but its coarsest features. Our capacity for verbal description comes nowhere near our capacity for sensory discrimination.

This disparity arises from a fundamental difference between the coding strategy employed in language and the coding strategy employed in the nervous system. Language employs a set of discrete names, decidedly finite in number, and it falls back on lame metaphor when the subtlety of the sensory situation outruns the standard names, which regularly it does. By contrast, the nervous system employs a combinatorial *system* of representation, one that permits a fine-grained *analysis* of each of the sensory subtleties it encounters. This allows us to discriminate and recognize far more than we can typically express in words.

Taste Coding

Although the system is powerful, there is no great trick to how it works. We may see it in action in the sense of taste. Tastes are complex and various, but the system that codes them is simple. We have exactly four types of taste sensors on the tongue, sometimes called the sweet, sour, salty, and bitter receptors (figure 2.1). (There are some recent hints of a fifth type, but having noted this possibility, I'll put it aside.) These names are not entirely appropriate, as we are about to see, but they do have a point. If a given taste is to answer honestly to any one of the four names listed, it must produce a fairly high level of activation in the receptor type so named.

Consider a familiar example: a ripe peach, bitten into and savored. As the juice hits the receptors on the tongue, it affects their

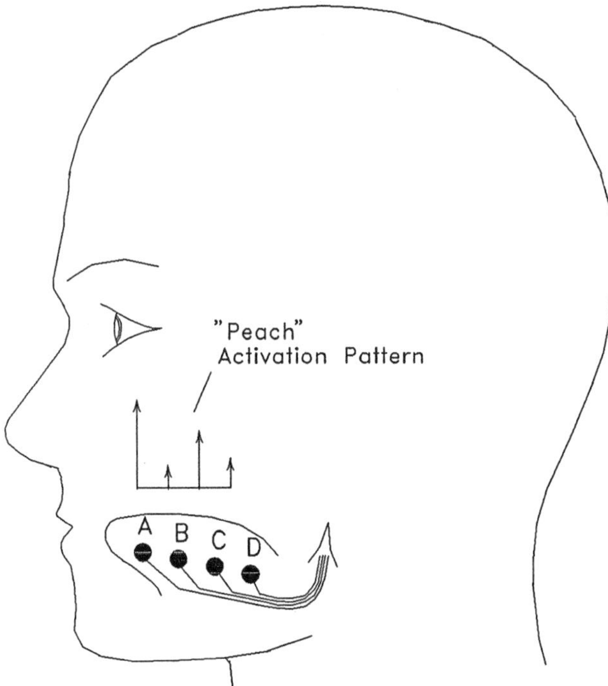

Figure 2.1 Schematic: four types of taste receptors on the human tongue.

levels of excitation—their activation levels—but it does not have the same effect on each of the four types. Cells of type A, for example, respond strongly, almost maximally, to the presentation of a peach. Type B hardly respond at all. Type C respond robustly, although not so much as A. And type D cells react politely, but without much enthusiasm.

What is important here, for the business of recognizing a peach, is not the reaction level at any single receptor type, but rather the collective *pattern* across all four of these receptor types (note the bar graph above the tongue). Any peach, at a comparable stage of maturity, will produce almost exactly the same pattern of activation. That pattern is a kind of signature or fingerprint, specific to peaches in particular. It is not a "mixing together" of four "basic" tastes, as one might be tempted to suppose. Rather, any taste at all, even one of the so-called basic tastes, is a unique pattern of activations across all four of the four cell types. A sweet taste does require a high activation level in the type A cells, but it also requires a low level of activation in cell types B, C, and D.

Such patterns or signatures are special in a further respect. The word "peach" is not at all similar to the word "apricot," but the corresponding four-dimensional neural activation pattern for a peach *is* closely similar to the pattern produced by an apricot. This is why the tastes of those two fruits are so similar: the subjective taste just *is* the activation pattern across the four types of tongue receptors, as re-represented downstream in one's taste cortex, and the peach pattern differs from the apricot pattern by only a few percentage points in each of the four dimensions.

In this way are the brain's representations of the various possible tastes arranged in a systematic "space" of similarities and differences. Closely similar tastes, like those of peaches and apricots, are coded as very close together in that space of possible codings. Vastly different tastes, such as those of peaches and black olives, for example, are coded as quite far apart in that space of possible codings. Compared to the signature for a peach, a black olive will produce a very different pattern of activations across the four types of receptors, as will a spoonful of mustard or a pinch of sauerkraut.

We can see how familiar tastes cluster and diverge by representing them graphically in a "taste space", a space with a proprietary dimension for each of the four cell types on the tongue (figure 2.2). (I here suppress one of the four axes, since I can't draw a 4-D space on a 2-D surface, but the visual point still comes through.) Sweetish things are clustered at the top rear; bitter things are near the origin (the bitter axis is the one we dropped); salty things are at the lower right; and sour things cluster at the right rear. As you might expect, the four so-called simple tastes are each located toward the extreme periphery. But every taste possible for the human sensory system is located at some point within this space of possible patterns across the four cell types.

Such a simple system hides an unexpected strength. If one can usefully discriminate, say, only ten distinct levels of activation along each of the four axes, then the total number of four-element *patterns* one can discriminate will be $10 \times 10 \times 10 \times 10 = 10{,}000$. That is to say, with only four distinct types of chemical receptors on the tongue, one will be able to discriminate 10,000 different tastes. Vast representational power thus results from very modest resources; that is the first major payoff we derive from coding sensory inputs with a pattern of activation levels across a population of neurons. The combinatorics of the situation are here working for

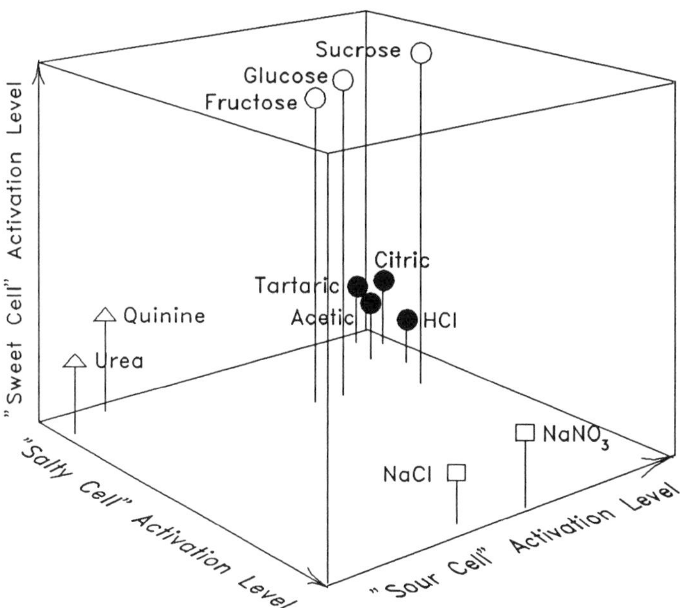

Figure 2.2 Taste space: the position of some familiar tastes. (Adapted from Jean Bartoshuk.)

the brain, rather than against it, as was so often the case in classical approaches to AI.

Color Coding

The technique used in the coding of tastes is too fertile not to be repeated elsewhere, and other instances are quickly found. It appears that the visual system uses the same trick to code colors. The retina contains three distinct kinds of cone-shaped photosensitive cones, each of which is tuned to one of three distinct wavelengths of light. Those photosensitive cone cells collectively project their stimulation levels to a different population of neurons, also composed of three cell types. These downstream cells embody our true color space, a space with three dimensions this time, one for each of the three cell types. One axis of the brain's color space represents the result of a tug-of-war between two of the cone types back at the retina: it is called the Blue-versus-Green axis. A second axis, representing the result of a different conal tug-of-war, is called the Yellow-versus-Blue axis. And the third axis represents the local relative brightness levels falling across all three retinal cone types. Any humanly perceivable color, therefore, will be a distinct pattern

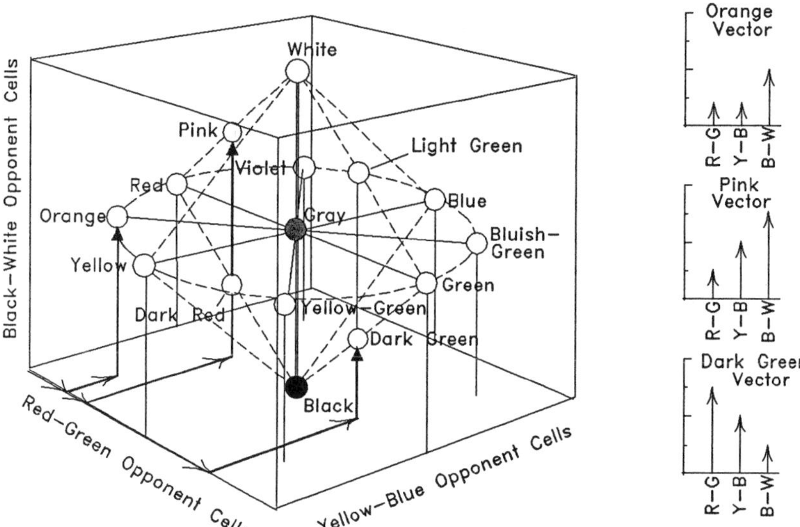

Figure 2.3 Human color space

of activations across these three types of downstream *opponent process* neurons.

You can see from figure 2.3 that such a coding strategy locates all of the familiar colors or *hues* in a continuous circle around a central vertical axis. Their *vividness* is represented by their horizontal distance from the central axis: as they get closer to that axis, the hues fade into a colorless gray. As one moves upward in this space from any point, the lighter or more pastel the color at that point becomes. Moving downward makes it steadily darker, heading toward black.

We get a combinatorial benefit with color coding, a benefit similar to that displayed in the coding of tastes. If the brain is able to discriminate, say, ten different positions along each of the three opponent-process axes, then the number of distinct *patterns* it can discriminate will be $10 \times 10 \times 10 = 1000$ distinct colors. (In fact, we can discriminate at least 10,000 distinct colors, so a better guess for each axis would be the cube root of 10,000, which equals about 20 discriminable positions along each of the three axes.) Once again, a small number of distinct receptor types, collectively deployed, yields a wide range of detectable properties.

Notice a further feature, clearly evident in this example. Coding each color with a unique triplet of neural activation levels provides not only for phenomenological similarities, as we saw in the case of taste, but for other phenomenological relations as well. Intuitively, orange is *between* yellow and red, as pink is *between* white and red. And that is exactly how they are positioned within the coding space described (see again figure 2.3). These and many other familiar relations are direct consequences of the simple coding scheme the brain employs.

Smell Coding

Along with taste, the sense of smell (olfaction) is perhaps the most primordial of all the senses, a fact reflected in its curious ability to stir even the most distant memories. After many years in the ocean, a mature salmon sniffs out the river of its childhood and, using the same olfactory sense, follows the appropriate branching tributaries to the very site of its birth: a quiet pool, distinctive in its mineral composition and biochemical whiff. Although olfactory navigation is largely beyond *Homo sapiens*, even a human will feel a cathartic flood of familiarity upon breathing in the aroma of one's first-grade schoolroom, or grandmother's kitchen, or the valley of one's childhood.

The capacity for such subtle discriminations resides again in the combinatorics of vector coding. Humans possess at least six distinct types of olfactory receptors, and a particular odor is coded as a pattern of activation levels across all six types. The capacity to discriminate only ten positions along each of these six axes would yield the overall capacity to discriminate 10^6, or fully one million, distinct aromas.

What is interesting here is the welcome exponential *explosion* of one's overall discriminatory capacity, as the number of dimensions in one's coding vectors (and one's acuity along each dimension) increases. Presumably this is a major part of the explanation of why animals such as mice and bloodhounds have such spectacular senses of smell. The actual figures for these animals are not known, but should a dog have merely seven types of receptor cells where a human has six, and only three times the human acuity along each of its seven olfactory axes, then it would be able to discriminate 30^7 or 20 *billion* distinct odors. It is small wonder then, that a bloodhound can distinguish between any two people on the planet by smell alone.

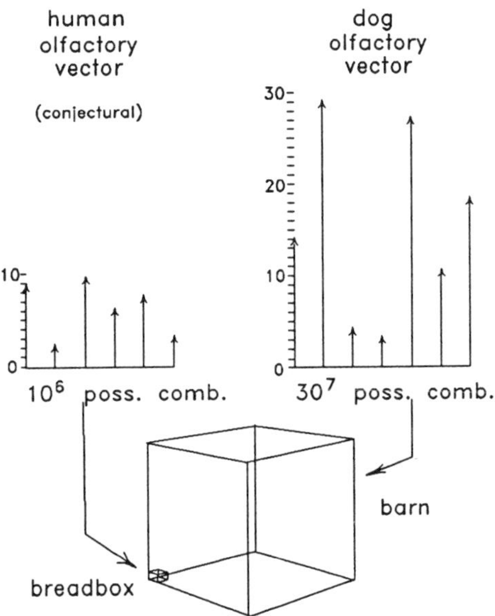

Figure 2.4 The relative volumes of human and canine olfactory spaces.

Figure 2.4 attempts to portray the difference between the human and the bloodhound olfactory spaces. Remember that the number of distinct possible *combinations* of activation levels is the critical measure of the difference between us, so the relevant contrast is portrayed in the two olfactory spaces underneath the sample smell vectors. If the canine olfactory space were a cube the size of a large barn, then, comparatively speaking, the human olfactory space would be a cube about the size of a small breadbox tucked away in one corner. To dogs, humans must appear to be almost "blind" in the olfactory domain, and to be bumbling klutzes in consequence. We should be thankful anew for canine good nature. Who knows how much patience they expend on us, and how much caprice our benighted behavior must seem to display?

Face Coding

If dogs are especially good at distinguishing odors, humans excel at discriminating faces and their changing emotional expressions. A human face is a complex thing, but a familiar face will be recognized from almost any angle in less than 250 milliseconds. Unlike tastes, colors, and odors, faces are commonly the subject of at least some description of their constituent parts—the length of a nose, the fullness of the lips, the distance between the eyes, the heaviness of the brow, and so forth. But as with those simpler sensory qualities, our capacity for verbal description again falls far short of our capacity for direct sensory analysis. The bank teller's determined but inevitably vague description of the face of the bank robber will likely fail to distinguish that face from a hundred thousand others, and yet the teller might be able to recognize and discriminate the robber's face exactly, when she finally lays eyes on him again.

This capacity apparently reflects another instance of vector coding. The brain seems to represent faces with a pattern of activations in a special cortical area somewhat farther along in the visual system (the occipito-temporal region), a pattern whose elements correspond to various canonical features or abstract "dimensions" of observed faces. It is not known exactly what those dimensions are, nor even that they are identical for all of us. But it is known that the various features of the *eyes* and their immediate surround are of overwhelming importance for facial discrimination, followed by the several characteristics of the mouth and then the overall shape of the face. The nose, it seems, matters little, at least in frontal views.

By way of illustration, figure 2.5 depicts a face-coding space with only three dimensions of variation: eye separation, nose width, and

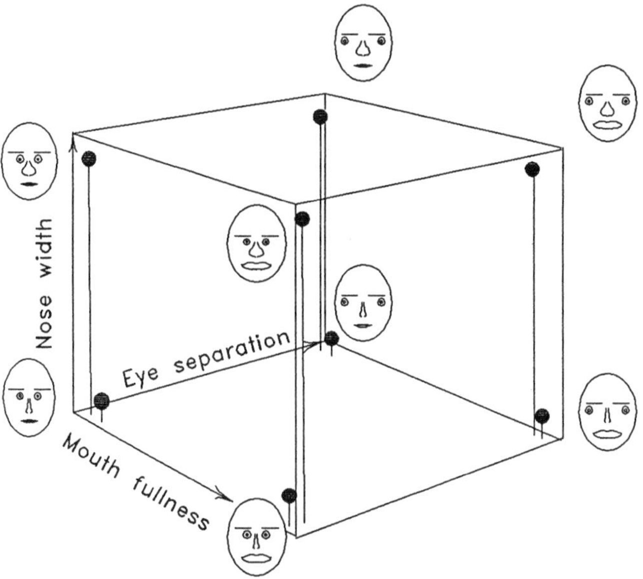

Figure 2.5 A rudimentary face space of three dimensions.

mouth fullness. This is highly unrealistic—our coding space for faces probably has at least twenty dimensions—but it does evoke the wide range of faces one can discriminately code with only a few resources. Some familiar mugs are already coded, even in this cartoon. They are drawn next to their positions in face space. At the bottom rear corner of the cube, for example, I think you will find the English model Twiggy, or perhaps it is the actress Michelle Pfeiffer. At the nearest upper corner you may find the familiar face of the boxer Mike Tyson. George Bush is at the lower left. Perhaps you will find some of your friends in there.

The vector coding of faces yields the same combinatorial advantages displayed in other domains. If humans represent faces with a ten-dimensional vector, with only five increments of discrimination along each of its ten dimensions, then we should be able to discriminate 5^{10}, or roughly 10 million different faces. And so, it seems, we can.

The other virtues of vector coding are also present here. Members of the same family will tend to be coded in the same general region of face space, a consequence of—or better, the ground of—their facial similarities. As well, children will often be coded at some point that is roughly between the two coding points for their parents, a consequence of their "splitting the difference" between diverse parental contributions.

The familiar case of human faces also allows us to illustrate two further virtues of vector coding: average or *prototypical* representations and *hyperbolic* (exaggerated) representations. Both ideas have a natural and obvious expression within the sort of multidimensional face space we have already introduced. Let me explain.

The human family displays a wonderful diversity of faces, but each one strikes out in its own idiosyncratic direction from what might be called the standard, average, or prototypical human face. We can recover this prototypical face by taking pictures of a largish random sample—male and female, white, black, and oriental, large and small, young and old—and averaging the lot of them.

That part is straightforward. Code each one of, say, a hundred faces with its own twenty-dimensional vector, which vector simply lists the appropriate values for that face's nose width, eyebrow position, eye separation, and so on. For each one of these salient dimensions, add all one hundred of the examples together and then divide by one hundred to get an *average* nose, an *average* pair of eyebrows, and so forth. Stringing these average elements together

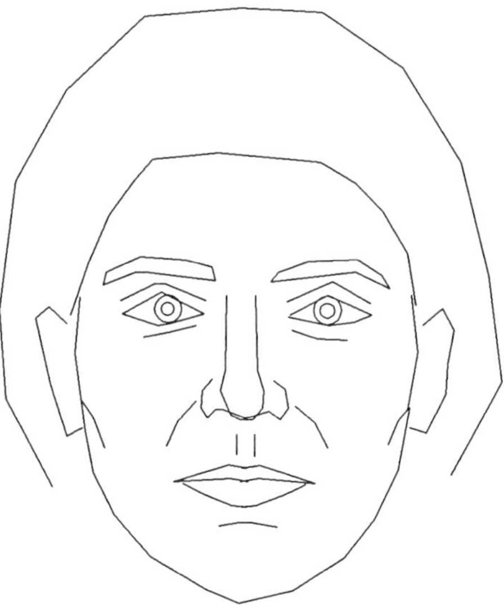

Figure 2.6 The vector-average or prototypical human face. (Adapted from Susan Brennan.)

in the proper order gives us a vector that codes the overall average of the sample faces. Once given that vector, we can simply draw the face that matches this vectorial recipe.

Figure 2.6 portrays a face constructed by just such a process. Notice that it is curiously ambiguous as to sex, race, or age. This is your androgynous, multiracial, dead-center, plain-vanilla human face. It is not even bad looking.

One can do the same thing for male faces only, or female faces only. One thus recovers the prototypical male face or the prototypical female face. The essential differences between them are just the differences between the corresponding elements of the two prototype vectors. Most important, apparently, is the lower and heavier brow sported by males, their heavier jaw, and the larger relative distance between the bottom of the nose and the upper lip.

The existence of quantifiable prototypes also makes possible a bit of fun: wicked caricature. Consider the (partial) face space of figure 2.7, in which the coding point for the prototypical human face vector is marked with a solid circle. (This figure suppresses all but three of the relevant dimensions for facial recognition, for reasons now becoming familiar.) Where is your own face in this space? It is not coded at the prototypical point, because you do not look exactly like the prototypical face. Somewhere else then. Perhaps your coding point is the second solid circle, for example.

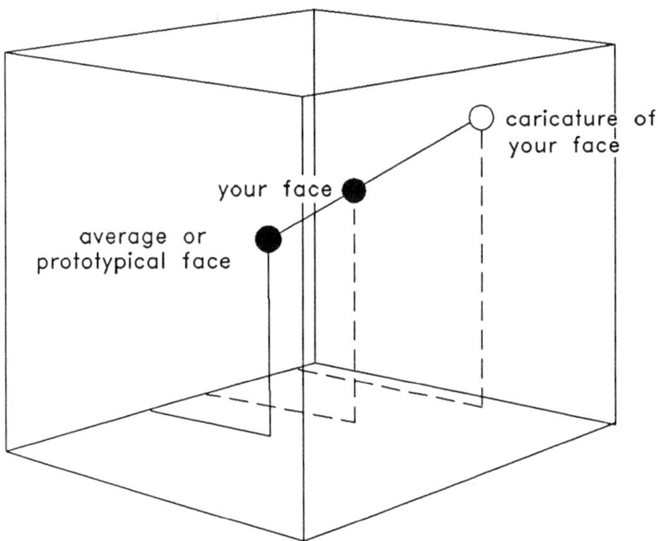

Figure 2.7 A facial vector space: divergence from the prototypical face.

Figure 2.8 Faithful tracing of a Reagan photograph. (Adapted from Brennan.)

Figure 2.9 Reagan caricature 1. (Adapted from Brennan.)

Consider now a straight line drawn directly from the prototypical point to your facial point and extended some distance beyond. What do the points on that extended portion represent? Faces, of course. Every point in this space represents a corresponding face. But what kinds of faces does that line segment define? The answer is clear: faces that differ from the prototypical human face in the same ways that yours does, only more so. They are all caricatures of your face. They are what political cartoonists would strive to create, were you unfortunate enough to become their target.

A real example will illustrate the point. (Thanks here to Susan Brennan, *Scientific American*, 1985.) Figure 2.8 portrays the familiar face of Ronald Reagan, as coded in a multidimensional space of the kind at issue. Figure 2.6, recall, codes the prototypical human face within the same space. Brennan's simple computer program, *Face Bender*, computes the straight line from that prototypical point out through the coding point for Ronald Reagan to a third point somewhat beyond it. One can then command the program, "Draw me the face that corresponds to that third point." Using the information present in that third coding vector, the program returns to us, on screen, the face of figure 2.9.

This welcome caricature is more easily or more quickly recognizable as Reagan than was his original, nonhyperbolic, entirely faithful portrayal in figure 2.8. This is because the caricature of Reagan is "less ambiguous than"—is even farther away from any

Figure 2.10 Reagan caricature 2. (Adapted from Brennan.)

alternative real faces in face space than—Reagan's *own* face. The caricature "couldn't be anybody but him."

The hyperbolic figure 2.9 also has that slight element of cruelty that we all like to see in a good caricature. Which immediately suggests that we reach out a little farther on the hyperbolic line segment in search of a still crueler point. Upon entry of this more extreme coding vector, the computer program displays the distorted face of figure 2.10.

It is hard not to like vector coding. On a whim, and to test Brennan's technique, I generated a similarly hyperbolic caricature of my wife. She won't let me show it to anyone.

Finally, an example illustrating once more the ideas of similarity and qualitative betweenness. Let us plot the respective positions, in some facial vector space, of Jack Kennedy's face and Bill Clinton's face (figure 2.11). Consider the straight line, within that space, that connects those two coding points. Consider four additional points on that line, carving its length into five equal segments, and consider the faces that must correspond to those four intervening points. They are presented in portraits 1–6. As you can see, they constitute a sequence of faces, almost indistinguishable when taken pairwise, faces that span the space of facial character between the two familiar end points. Although it is difficult or impossible to articulate *in language* the changes that are taking place across

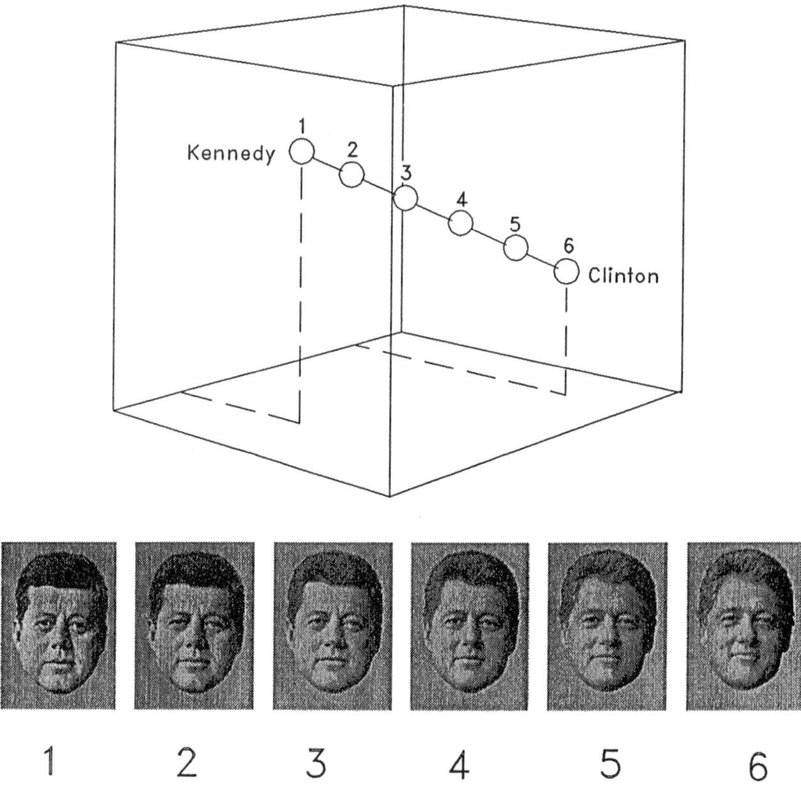

1 2 3 4 5 6

Figure 2.11 (Top) A facial state space coding six faces along a straight line. (Bottom) The six faces that those points represent. Kennedy at the left is slowly transformed into Clinton at the right, and vice versa. (Thanks to James Beale and Frank Keil.)

the sequence of six faces, the technique of facial representation with high-dimensional vectors allows us to capture the otherwise uncapturable.

The four faces between Kennedy and Clinton were in fact generated by a vector-coding system of exactly the type under discussion. The technique is called "morphing," and the trick involved is easily grasped. We start by vector-coding the two objects to be morphed. We then construct the straight line between those two points in vector space. We finish by converting the sequence of points along that line back into a sequence of corresponding faces, just as in figure 2.11. For graphic artists, the technique of vector coding is new, and filled with interesting possibilities. For the biological brain, however, the technique is old, far older than the dinosaurs. And yet, as the following chapters will show, it remains a font of endless possibilities.

3 Vector Processing: How It Works and Why It Is Essential

The vector-coding account of human facial recognition, appealing as it is, must surmount a serious objection. Humans do not possess twenty or so distinct types of sensory cells, each sensitive to one specific aspect of any perceived face. We have no sensory analog to the four types of taste receptors or the six types of smell receptors. We have only eyes to code faces at our sensory periphery, and the cells on the retina are sensitive to color and brightness and changes therein, but they couldn't care less about faces. How then do we manage to represent and recognize faces?

Where and How Are Faces Coded?

The account to be outlined below is still conjectural rather than proven, but it is a plausible account of how humans recognize faces and, equally important for our purposes here, it is a highly *accessible* example of how vector processing works. The first part of the idea is this. Although no retinal cell is responsive specifically to any of the various aspects of a face that are relevant for facial recognition, collectively the retinal cells do contain information about perceived faces as an implicit part of their overall pattern of cellular activations. Moreover, they do send that implicit information forward to subsequent populations of neurons—to the LGN cells, to the visual cortex, and ultimately to a special area in the temporal lobe that is crucial for facial recognition. Is it possible that the cell types that code faces explicitly are to be found not at the body's sensory periphery, as with taste and smell, but farther along in the chain of cell populations?

Not only is it possible; apparently it is actual. Isolated physical damage to a specific area of the brain's temporal lobe—the result of a tumor, perhaps, or a stroke (a burst blood vessel)—produces a strange condition known as *facial agnosia*. Familiar to neurologists working the hospital wards, the occasional patients with this odd affliction show a highly specific loss of the normal ability to recognize *faces*, even those previously well known to them. Nor can the patient learn to recognize any new faces. Surprisingly, there is nothing wrong with the patient's eyes, and he can visually recognize most nonfacial objects without any pause or difficulty. But the face of his brother, or his wife, or even his own face in a mirror, evokes no recognition. He may easily identify these people by their voices, by their dress, or by some other cue. But the distinctive character of their faces, and of all other faces, is now and forever beyond his visual grasp.

So there does appear to be a distinct population of neurons specialized for the coding of faces, a population perhaps five or six synaptic steps downstream from the retina.

The second part of the idea is this. The many synaptic connections, between the retinal cells and the distant "facial cells" in the temporal lobe, filter and transform the incoming information in such a way that the "facial" cells respond to, and only to, the important dimensions of facial structure implicitly coded in the overall retinal-activation pattern. The retinal cells collectively contain oceans of information, of course: about trees and benches and stoplights and doors. But the special connective path, leading stepwise from the eye to the facial area described above, suppresses or ignores all of that information, except for such *facial* features as may happen to be retinally represented along with everything else. To exactly these features, diffuse and implicit though their retinal representation may be, the downstream population of neurons responds vigorously.

Simple Pattern Recognition

How is such selective magic possible? A fully general answer is impossible to state in a few sentences, but a first approximation to the correct answer is easily given. Indeed, we can display it visually. Let us take, for our example, something a little simpler than a face. Suppose we wish to discriminate the occasional registration of the letter "T" on a small screen of exactly nine light-sensitive cells or pixels. (See figure 3.1. For ease of visual apprehension, we shall suppose that the blackened areas are the ones receiving illumination.)

We can achieve this goal by funneling the nine output axons of those small retinal cells to a single large target cell, there to make nine synaptic connections all of the same size or "weight," but differing in their several polarities. The job is completed by making

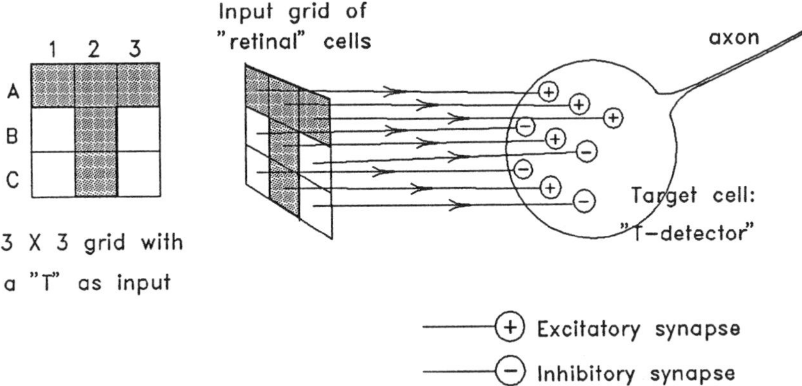

Figure 3.1 A simple arrangement for pattern recognition. The cell at the right is maximally activated when, and only when, a T is projected onto the grid of "retinal" cells at the left.

the connections from cells A1, A2, A3, B2, and C2 all positive or excitatory, and by making the connections from cells B1, C1, B3, and C3 all negative or inhibitory. The only possible way to activate the target cell, then, is to activate one or more of the first group of cells: the T-element cells. As each one of those five cells becomes activated by illumination, the excitatory effect on the target cell goes up. Maximum activation is achieved when all of the T-element cells are illuminated, *unless* one or more of the non-T cells is also illuminated. That would have the effect of inhibiting the target cell to the appropriate degree, and of reducing its level of activation.

What we have here is a simple tug-of-war between the excitatory effects of the T-element cells and the inhibitory effects of the non-T cells. So long as there are conflicting messages reaching the target cell, its activation level will be below its maximum level. The inhibitory messages will always cancel out a corresponding number of excitatory messages, if any there should happen to be. Only when the entire retinal grid is unanimous in its collective message—the T-element cells are all on, and the non-T cells are all off—will the target cell reach its maximum level of activation.

The target cell has thus become a T-detecting cell. Although none of the individual retinal cells knew or cared about the projection of a T across their population, the target cell *does* care. It cares most about perfect Ts, complete in every respect and unmarred by additional illuminations elsewhere in its "visual field." There is a technical term for the input pattern that a cell likes best: that pattern is called the *preferred stimulus* of the cell in question. This term allows us a convenient way of talking about the discriminatory focus of an individual cell. We simply specify its preferred stimulus.

It is important to notice that our artfully tuned target cell will also respond fairly strongly to patterns of illumination that are very close to a perfect T: to a T with a single pixel missing, for example, or to an otherwise perfect T marred by the illumination of some pixel outside the perfect pattern. The target cell's response will be suboptimal, but it will still be considerable. Accordingly, our target cell will indicate not only the occurrence of the occasional bull's eye, it will give a graded indication of the occurrence of anything closely *similar* to a perfect T.

Notice further that we could just as easily have made the target cell a detector of U-shaped patterns, or of L-shaped patterns, or of O-shaped patterns, and so on. Simply arrange appropriately the pattern of excitatory and inhibitory synaptic connections projecting from the retinal grid to the target cell (see again figure 3.1), and you can have it detect any of the 2^9 distinct patterns possible for our nine-element retinal grid.

More important still, we can put in place an entire population of downstream target cells, each one of which receives a complete set of axonal end-branches from the projecting retinal axons, and each one of which has a configuration of excitatory and inhibitory synaptic connections that makes it a detector of exactly one of the possible patterns. This downstream population of target cells will thus constitute a well-informed committee, with each member responsible for the detection of some specific pattern. Complex patterns that were lost on the individual retinal cells will thus be registered with keen and focused concern by the cells at the downstream population. In this way can distributed features at the input level be unerringly "picked out" at subsequent levels of neurons, thanks to the filtering activity of an artfully arranged set of synaptic connections. This is an important reason—the first of many reasons—why coding vectors at the sensory periphery often need to be processed and transformed by passing them through a matrix of synaptic connections.

Face Recognition

We were talking about face recognition. Let us now return. The lessons just learned about pattern recognition apply equally well

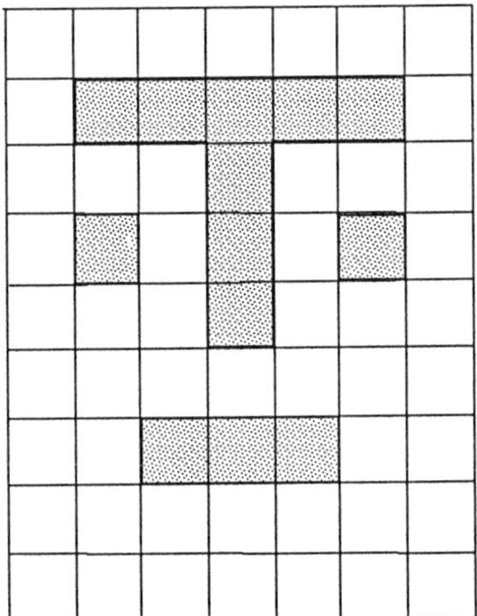

Figure 3.2 A rudimentary face pattern in a 9 × 7 grid.

here. See the slightly more complex pattern displayed in figure 3.2. Here again we have a T pattern, this time flanked by a pair of eyes and underlined by a mouth. The T thus appears as eyebrows bisected by a nose. This facelike pattern is as readily detectable by some downstream target cell as was the letter T in our earlier example. The retinal grid is now nine cells by seven, rather than three by three, but the principle of downstream detection is the same. We need axonal projections, from all sixty-three of these sensory cells, to an appropriate target cell. The retinal cells darkened in figure 3.2 will need excitatory projections to the target cell, and the undarkened cells will need inhibitory projections. A target cell thus connected will serve as a primitive *face* detector as neatly as you please. Its preferred stimulus—the specific input pattern that produces its maximum level of activation—is precisely the face of figure 3.2. Notice finally that this system will register the occurrence of that face, or of something similar to it, in no more time than it takes the information to traverse the axons and the synaptic connections involved: in this case, about 1/100th of a second.

Admittedly, this is still pretty thin fare. The face of figure 3.2 is rudimentary in the extreme, and the downstream target cell can indicate little more than its presence or absence. It cannot hope to recognize real faces, much less discriminate your brother from your sister. We need something more. Most obviously, we need to consider input grids with many thousands of pixel cells, and we need

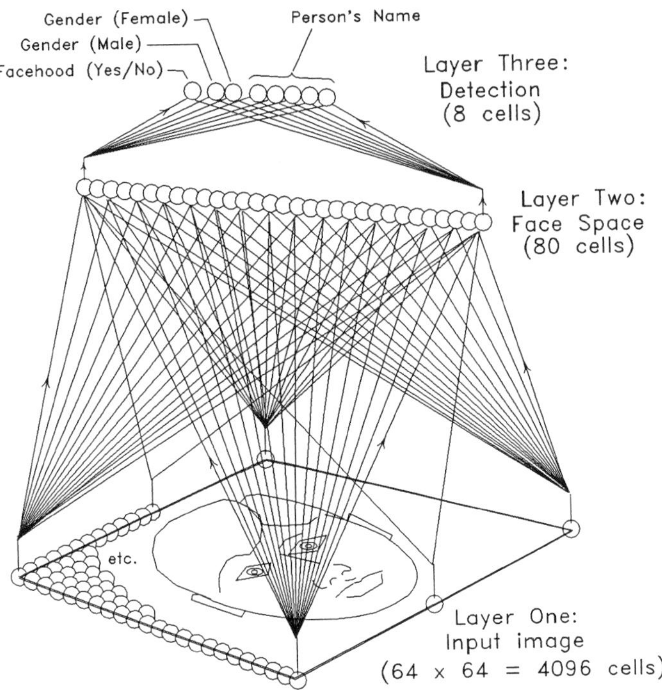

Figure 3.3 An artificial neural network for recognizing real faces.

pixels that will admit of a smooth variety of brightness levels rather than just "on" and "off." Less obviously, we need a largish *committee* of downstream cells that can detect a variety of distinct facial features within that larger retinal canvas. This would permit the coding of diverse faces within a set of proprietary dimensions; that is, within a "face space" of the general kind we explored in the previous chapter (figure 2.5). There we played with only three dimensions of variation across faces, and we could code only cartoons. A system adequate to represent and discriminate among real faces will need a good deal more.

This is precisely what some neural-net researchers have recently succeeded in modeling. (Thanks here to the work of Garrison Cottrell's group at the University of California, San Diego.) Their three-stage artificial network is schematically portrayed in figure 3.3. Its input layer or "retina" is a 64 × 64-pixel grid whose elements each admit of 256 different levels of activation or "brightness." This higher resolution, both in space and in brightness, allows the network to code recognizable representations of real faces. Figure 3.4 shows several of the many input photographs on which the net-

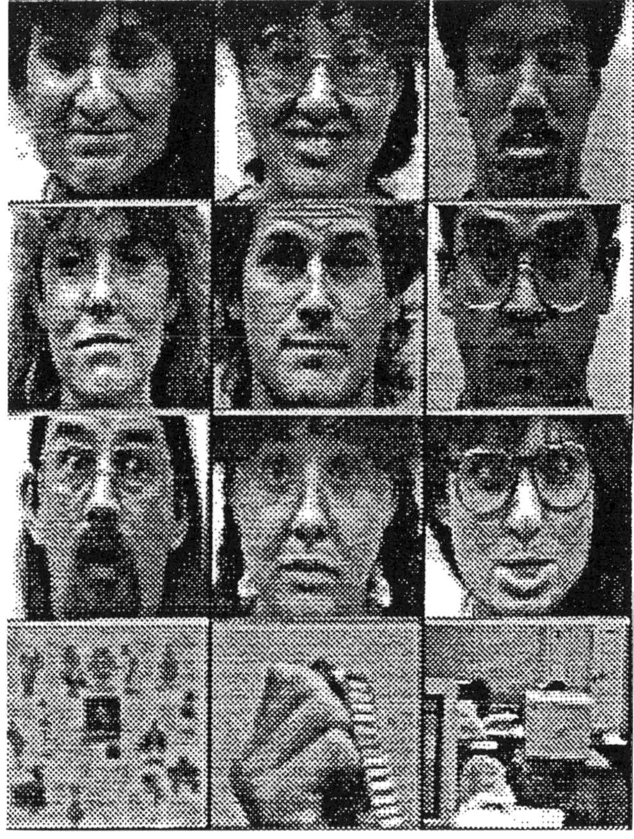

Figure 3.4 Selected input images for training the face-recognition network. (Thanks to Gary Cottrell.)

work was actually trained. That *training set* contained 64 different photos of 11 different faces, plus 13 photos of nonface scenes. Cottrell himself is the bespectacled face at the lower left.

Each input cell projects a radiating set of axonal end branches to each and every one of the 80 cells in the second layer, which layer represents an abstract space of 80 dimensions (rather than just three) in which the input faces are explicitly coded. This second layer projects finally to an output layer of only eight cells. These output cells have had their synaptic connections carefully tuned to discriminate, first, between faces and nonfaces; second, between male and female faces; and third, to respond with the person's "name" (an arbitrarily assigned numerical code) to the re-presentation of any face that the network "got to know" during its training period.

As with the simple T-pattern recognition system of figure 3.1, what actually does the work in Cottrell's face-recognition network is the overall configuration of synaptic connections—positive and negative, weak and strong. It is these, and only these, that progressively transform the initial 64 × 64-element pattern or vector into a second and finally a third vector that exactly represents the input photo's facehood, gender, and name explicitly. But while it was obvious how to configure the nine synaptic connections of the simple two-layer T-pattern recognizer, it is not at all obvious how to configure the connections in this much larger network. After all, it contains $(64 \times 64) + 80 + 8 = 4184$ cells, and a grand total of 328,320 synaptic connections!

Network Learning: Repeated Synaptic Adjustment

In fact, Cottrell's group had no idea how the synaptic connections should be configured. That was part of the problem they had to solve. Fortunately, there exists a general technique for finding synaptic solutions to transformational problems, a technique widely used by neuromodelers. It is biologically realistic in the single respect that it involves the steady adjustment of a network's synapses in response to the pressures of experience. Sadly, it is biologically unrealistic in just about every other respect. But beggars can't be choosers. Until we sleuth out the brain's actual learning procedures, we have to use whatever is available. This interim technique is called "synaptic adjustment by the successive backpropagation of errors," or just *backpropagation* for short. It has two outstanding virtues. It works like the dickens, at least for smallish networks. And the procedure can be administered by a conventional serial computer, which takes the extraordinary drudgery of the procedure out of the neuromodeler's hands. It works roughly as follows.

What does one wish one's network to do? To transform each one of a wide range of possible input vectors into an output vector that is somehow appropriate (depending on the particular skill being taught) for that input. And how does one do that? One sets the weights of the synaptic connections so that collectively they will perform the desired transformation. And if one does not know what weights to impose to achieve this end? One sets all of the synaptic weights at random values, both positive (excitatory) and negative (inhibitory), not too far from zero on either side. This constitutes an utterly blind stab in the dark at the desired configuration of weights. By itself, this gets us nowhere, but have faith for a second.

What this stab permits is the discovery of just how *mistaken* it is, at least in the output vectors it is prone to produce. Let us therefore present one of the relevant input vectors to the input layer, and then observe the transformed result at the output layer. Given that the weights were set at random, almost certainly that particular output is gibberish, and not at all what we want the network to produce for that input. But at least we know what the appropriate output *should* have been. If the input face was Janet's, and Janet's name code is ".5, 1, .5, 0, 0," then the output vector ideally should have been {1; 0, 1; .5, 1, .5, 0, 0}. The first "1" codes that the input is indeed a face; the following "0, 1" codes "No" for male and "Yes" for female; and the rest identifies the face as Janet's.

Unfortunately, that is not the result we got. What we got was, say, {.23; .8, .39; .2, .03, .19, .66, .96}. But let us compare the desired to the actual output. Specifically, let us subtract each element of the actual vector from its corresponding element in the desired vector (figure 3.5). This gives us a third vector that represents exactly the *error* committed by the network for the input on this occasion. Now let us simply square each of these eight errormeasures. The point of doing this is to exaggerate somewhat the relative importance of the larger errors over the smaller ones. (The little ones we can tolerate; the big ones demand immediate attention.) The average of these eight squared errors is called the *mean squared error*. It is this number that we are determined to reduce.

And reduce it we can. We have to settle for a series of small, incremental reductions, but here is how it is done. Let us hold *all but one* of the network's synaptic weights *constant*, at their initial (randomly set) values, and then examine the contribution that this

```
   ⟨  1,   0,   1,   .5,   1,   .5,   0,   0  ⟩   Desired output vector
 - ⟨ .23,  .8, .39,  .2,  .03, .19, .66, .96  ⟩   Actual output vector
   ----------------------------------------------
 = ⟨ .77, -.8, .61,  .3,  .97, .31,-.66,-.96  ⟩   Error vector
   ⟨ .59, .64, .37, .09,  .94, .09, .44, .94  ⟩   Squared-error vector
                   .5125  ←-------------------   Mean of squared errors
```

Figure 3.5 The calculation of the mean squared error at the output layer.

single isolated connection weight makes to the mean squared error. Since the network's transformational activities are entirely determined by its connective configuration, this smaller question is one we can answer decisively. In particular, we can determine whether a tiny change, up or down, in that isolated connection weight, would lead to an output vector *slightly* closer to the one desired. That is, we can determine whether a tiny change in that weight would reduce the mean squared error at the output. If it would make no detectable difference, we leave the weight as it is. If a tiny change upward (or downward) would improve things slightly, then we make that change, a change whose very small size is proportional to the degree of improvement promised.

The resulting change in the network's overall performance is of course minuscule. But having nudged one weight in a profitable or error-reducing direction, we shift our attention to the connection weight immediately next door and repeat the entire process just described. Now we have two weights successfully nudged to error-reducing values. Proceeding stepwise in this fashion, through every one of the network's connections, produces a "new" network, new in having a slightly different connective configuration than the net with which we began, and an ever-so-slightly better performance at the output vector. Now we repeat this lengthy procedure with a second input-output pair, then a third, a fourth, and so on.

This sounds like a tedious undertaking, and it would be, if we had to do it ourselves. Fortunately, we can assign the entire business of vector presentation, error calculation, and repeated weight adjustments to a conventional serial computer, and then just stand back and watch the process unfold automatically. All of the input vectors in the training set are paired with their proprietary output vectors and stored in the computer's memory, and the computer is programmed to present each one to the student neural network, compute the error involved in each output, and adjust the weights according to the principles just outlined. After each presentation of each input-output pair, the computer nudges all of the network's weights to a slightly happier configuration.

We instruct the computer to keep repeating this procedure, for all of the input-output pairs in the training set, until the mean squared error of the student network's output performance is made as small as possible; until, that is, its performance on the training set has "topped out." Depending on the complexity of the network, this can take hours, days, or even weeks of furious computing on the best available machines. But it regularly leaves us with a network that has genuinely *learned* the skill or transformational capacity in question.

Once this goal has been achieved, the training ends and the network's weights are frozen at their final values. We then have a network whose cognitive capacities and internal coding strategies we can begin to explore.

Performance in the Trained Network

Cottrell's face-recognition network topped out at an impressive level of performance. It achieved 100 percent accuracy, on the training set of images, with respect to faceness, gender, and the identity of the face presented. In itself, this is not necessarily impressive, since the network may just have "memorized" the finite set of input-output pairs presented to it during training, rather than acquired some truly general understanding of how to represent faces. A more severe and more relevant test occurs when we present the network with photos it has never seen before, that is, with various photos of the same people drawn from outside the training set. Here again the network comes through. It identified correctly 98 percent of novel photographs of the people encountered in its training set, missing the name and gender of only one female subject.

A second and even more severe test of its ability to generalize involved asking it to discriminate the faceness and gender of completely novel scenes and people. Here it was 100 percent correct on whether or not it was confronting a human face, and it was roughly 81 percent correct in its verdicts on the gender of the novel faces presented. (It got the male faces mostly correct, but showed a decided tendency to misclassify some of the female faces as male.)

A third and highly intriguing experiment tested the network's ability to recognize and identify a "familiar" person when one-fifth of the person's face was obscured by a horizontal bar across the input image (figure 3.6a). Surprisingly, the network's performance was hardly impaired at all. Subjects were identified correctly despite the obstruction, save in the one set of cases where the bar was placed so as to obscure each subject's forehead. For those inputs, performance fell to 71 percent correct, indicating that characteristic variations in hair position across the forehead must have

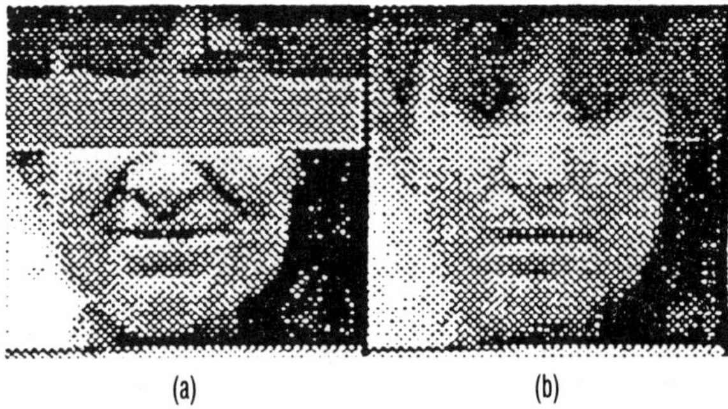

(a) (b)

Figure 3.6 (a) An input image of a face one-fifth obscured by a bar. (b) How the representation at the middle layer of Cottrell's compression network fills in the obscured input area with coherently related facial features. (Thanks to Gary Cottrell.)

played a relatively large but far from exhaustive role in shaping the network's learned classification of individuals.

A fourth and final experiment trained a closely similar network to identify a number of typical emotional states, as they were feigned in the facial expressions of the same group of subjects. But we will postpone discussion of such acquired social-psychological skills until the chapter on *social* perception and action.

Internal Coding and Distributed Representations

How on earth does the trained network do all of this? What is going on inside it to make these surprising skills possible? It is all very well to be told that a zillion synaptic weights have been "suitably configured," but is there any more informative or illuminating description of what has happened to the network during training?

Yes, there is. For starters, let us focus our attention on the 80 cells at the second layer of the network (see again figure 3.4). We might suspect that, as in the cartoon example, the cells at this layer constitute an 80-dimensional face space, a space in which each discriminable face will occupy a unique position, a position specified by a unique pattern or vector of activation levels across that cell population. And that suspicion is entirely correct. As we are about to see, the representational trick used in so many other cases is hard at work here as well, not just in theory, but in fact.

What we now want to know is this: exactly *what* facial features are being coded by the cells at this level of the network? What effective coding strategy was gradually discovered by the network during the relentless pressure of its training period? To put the same question in a third and final form, what is the *preferred stimulus*, at the input layer, of each of these many cells?

With an artificial network, as opposed to a living brain, we can obtain an absolutely determinate answer to this question, for each and every one of the 80 cells at issue. This is because the serial computer that conducted the network's training knows the exact value of the synaptic connection between any two cells in the entire network. In particular, it knows the pattern of connection weights onto each of the 80 face-dimension cells. As with the connection pattern onto the simple T-detection cell of figure 3.1, such connection-weight patterns uniquely determine the retinal input pattern to which a given face cell will give its maximum response. By reading out the training computer's memory—of the network's final configuration of weights for that cell—we can reconstruct the retinal input pattern that constitutes its preferred stimulus. Indeed, we can reconstruct it in the form of an image that we can look at ourselves.

The result of doing all this, for each of the 80 cells, yields a bit of a surprise. We might have expected each of these cells to become focused on some localized facial feature such as nose length, mouth width, eye separation, and so forth. But reconstructing the actual preferred stimuli of the 80 face cells reveals that the network settled into a coding strategy quite different from this.

Figure 3.7 reconstructs the preferred stimulus of six typical face cells from layer two of Cottrell's network. One can see immediately that each cell comprehends the *entire surface* of the input layer, and represents an entire facelike structure, rather than just an isolated facial feature of some sort or other. Neither do these preferred stimuli correspond to individual faces in the original training set. (There are 80 cells, recall, but only eleven distinct faces in the training set.) Rather, they seem to embody a variety of decidedly *holistic* features or dimensions of facehood, dimensions for which ordinary language has no adequate vocabulary. And yet, a given face presented at the input layer will variously activate each of these 80 holistic features, thus producing an activation vector at the second layer, a vector unique to that face. And different photographs of the same person presented to the input layer will produce essentially the same activation vector across the cells of layer two, thus allowing the output cells at layer three to identify that individual correctly.

Figure 3.7 Six of many *holons*: the preferred stimuli of some of the cells in layer two of the face-recognition network in figure 3.3. Note that each preferred pattern spans the entire input space. (Thanks to Gary Cottrell.)

Janet Metcalfe, Cottrell's co-worker on this and other networks, coined the term *holon* for a preferred stimulus or feature of this diffuse, input-spanning sort. As we will see, it is a coding strategy that networks quite regularly discover during training. This is presumably because it is an efficient and effective way of coding the information needed to solve the problem of finding the right input-output transformation. But it has a vitally important virtue beyond its efficiency: it helps to make the trained network functionally persistent against scattered cell damage and synaptic malfunction.

Since each pixel segment of the input image has some small effect on—that is to say, its information is *distributed* across—every cell at the second layer, and since every cell at the second layer contains at least some important information about the entire input layer, the scattered loss of cells and connections throughout the network leaves us with a network whose function is somewhat degraded, but still closely similar to its function in its undamaged state. With both the coded representations *and* their transformations being widely distributed across the entire network, there is no "bottleneck," neither representational nor transformational, whose isolated failure would bring the network suddenly to its knees.

Beyond this distributed wrinkle, we are still in familiar territory so far as coding goes. As with taste, color, and smell, neural representation here still consists in an activation vector across the representing population of neurons. What is changing in these increasingly complex examples is the size of the neuronal popu-

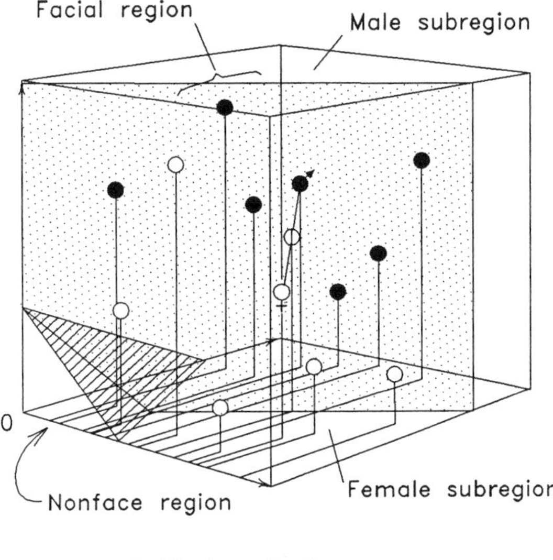

Figure 3.8 The hierarchy of learned partitions across the neuronal activation space of layer three (schematic).

lation, and thereby the dimensionality of the vectors involved. Most important, there is the increasingly holistic character of the features assigned to each dimension. Here also we begin to see something important and very welcome emerging: a hierarchical structure of recognizable *categories*.

The Emergence of Categories

Figure 3.8 attempts to portray the eighty-dimensional space of the cells in layer two of the trained network. It suppresses seventy-seven of them, of course, and settles for three of its typical dimensions so we can comprehend the point visually. Notice that, thanks to the network's training, this space now shows a primary partition into two regions: a large region in which all faces tend to be coded, and a smaller one close to the origin in which all nonfaces tend to be coded. This latter region is smaller because the cells at layer two respond hardly at all to any input that is not a face. The connection weights have been configured so that the dynamic range of layer two is primarily spent on discriminating among faces. That is why the facial region is the larger of the two subspaces. If something isn't a face to begin with, it is hardly noticed, it barely even exists, so far as layer two is concerned. Notice also that there is no particular cutoff value, on any dimension, below which the coded subject must fail to be a face. A given face may produce a zero activation level in dimension 1, and yet still be coded as a face in virtue of having a sufficiently high value in dimensions 2 and 3. The vector {0, .5, .5}, for example, still codes a point well within the facial region.

Within that facial region is a secondary partition into male faces and female faces. These two regions are roughly equal in volume, reflecting the network's rough parity of discriminatory power within each class of faces. This is no surprise: it was trained on roughly equal numbers of male and female faces. Had the training set been biased in either direction, the resulting partition might well have been lopsided, as we will shortly see.

At the female subregion's "center of gravity" is the coding point for the prototypical female face. The prototypical male face occupies a complementary position next door. Scattered throughout these two subregions are the proprietary coding points for each of the several faces in the training set. These partitions across the activation space of the cells at layer two—these *categories*, for there is nothing else to call them—slowly emerged and stabilized during the course of the network's training. And it was to these partitions, and to the eleven "familiar face" points within them, that the cells at layer three slowly became tuned as well.

The appearance of these hierarchically divided regions provides us with a further way of describing and explaining the network's acquired skills of recognition and discrimination, a way beyond the austere vocabulary of synaptic connections. Not to put too fine an edge on it, what the network has developed during training is a family of rudimentary *concepts*, concepts that get variously activated by sensory inputs of the appropriate kind. This way of talking has yet to be fully justified, but you can already see the point of introducing it. The suggestion we are exploring is that the appearance of concepts in living cognitive creatures consists in the same sort of learned partitioning of neuronal activation spaces.

Return your attention to the partitions of figure 3.8. What is the significance of the dividing "walls" themselves? They certainly do not represent barriers of any sort. Rather, they represent planes of indecision or uncertainty on the part of the network. An input image that produces a layer-two activation vector whose coding point lies on the basic face-nonface partition plane is an input image that the network is unable to discriminate as either a face or a nonface. Coding points at the boundaries between regions are coding points where the network, in effect, throws up its hands. Such coding points represent maximally *ambiguous* input images.

We can even generate them on purpose. Let us construct an input image that is the vector average of two images—the prototypical male face and the prototypical female face (see again the face of figure 2.6). When presented to the face network, it will produce an activation vector at layer two, a vector whose coding point lies midway between the two prototypical face points and precisely on the partition between the two subregions. Of course, the face of figure 2.6 is not the only face that is exactly ambiguous as between male and female—there are zillions of other possibilities elsewhere on the relevant partition—but it is an example quickly grasped.

And quickly experienced, too. If you wish to "hit" your own male-female partition across your own facial activation space, simply gaze again at figure 2.6. Individual reactions differ, it seems, as people's partitions are slightly idiosyncratic. But if your reaction is anything like mine, the face of figure 2.6 is highly ambiguous so far as its gender is concerned.

Is all of this really how humans recognize faces? Is the facial network at all realistic, biologically? Well, certainly not in the character of its third or output layer. That small population of cells is there only to provide the researchers with a convenient means of monitoring the network's performance. It is not intended to correspond to anything in the brain. But the gross anatomical outlines and the functional activity of the network connecting layers one and two may be a different matter.

On the anatomical issue, it must be said that the face-coding region in the human brain is at least five synaptic steps and five neuronal populations downstream from the retina, not one step, as with the crucial eighty-cell layer two in the artificial network. However, this need not be a significant contrast between reality and the model. The human visual system is concerned with many cognitive tasks in its first several layers, not just facial recognition. It must discriminate borders, shapes, typical objects, three-dimensional spatial relations, changes over time, physical movements, object trajectories, and more, all of it based on input vectors at the retina.

It would be no surprise if it takes such a busy network five, six, or even ten layers before it starts devoting proprietary processing resources to some special task such as face recognition.

There are many other known respects in which the artificial network is at best a clumsy and partial model of the intricate neuronal reality, and no doubt many more as yet unknown. But remember that we have reached the present stage of functional success in our artificial networks by trying to be as faithful to the neural reality as presently we can be. It is an empirical question whether deeper faithfulness will yield yet deeper success. At the very least, it is a question richly worth pursuing.

On the purely functional issue, we continue to find realistic aspects of the network's behavior beyond those already outlined. For example, networks of the kind at issue show what psychologists call "familiarity effects" in the profile of their discriminations. Alice O'Toole's group at the University of Texas, Dallas, trained facial-discrimination networks similar to Cottrell's on a training set that contained a relatively large number of Oriental faces plus a small number of Caucasian faces. The trained network showed a success level similar to Cottrell's, but it was less able to discriminate among, or to determine the sex of, novel faces that were Caucasian as opposed to Oriental. Although it performed just fine on Oriental faces, all Caucasian faces "looked pretty much the same" to it.

A second training experiment, this time with African faces in the majority over Oriental, yielded a network that performed fine on novel African faces, but poorly on Oriental faces. To the network, this time all of the Oriental faces looked pretty much the same. A third experiment, this time with a few African faces scattered among a large number of Caucasians, yielded a similar result. None of this is surprising. A network's acquired discriminatory capacities are maximally tuned to solving the recognition problems that it typically or most frequently encounters. If, during training, it encounters faces of type *A* much less frequently than faces of type *B*, then, if there are any systematic differences between faces of types *A* and *B*, the network will ultimately suffer a performance deficit where faces of type *A* are concerned.

The phenomenon is not only robust among the differently trained networks, it is familiar from human experience. Those who grew up in anything close to a monotonic racial environment have small but real discriminatory deficits for faces outside their racial group. Those who didn't, don't. Such deficits are of course avoidable, even correctable, both in artificial networks and in humans. Simply pile on a training set that contains an equable distribution of the full range of human facial diversity. A healthy network adjusts its holons slightly, re-metrizes its face space accordingly, and the deficit disappears.

There is of course nothing essentially racial about this phenomenon. Had we trained the network on a preponderence of young faces over old ones, the network would have acquired a relative deficit in discriminating among old faces. Had we trained it on a preponderence of female over male faces, it would have acquired a relative deficit in discriminating among male faces. The basic point is that a common human failing appears to be a simple and explicable consequence of how neural networks partition their activation spaces in response to their ongoing experience.

Inductive Inference, Network Style

A related wrinkle in the profile of network learning yields a very advantageous property. Recall the ability of Cottrell's network to identify a familiar face hidden behind a horizontal bar. This ability to identify familiar faces correctly despite the loss of 20 percent of the information in the input vector illustrates a marvellous property of neural networks, a property with far-reaching consequences. This property is their capacity for what is called *vector completion.* Since the output layer identifies the input person correctly as Jane, it must be responding to a facial coding vector at the second layer that is very close to the proper coding point for Jane. At the least, that second-layer coding vector must be closer to Jane's point than to any other person's coding point, else the output layer could not have identified her correctly.

How is it that something very close to a complete Jane-vector at layer two can result from a 20 percent incomplete image vector of Jane at the input layer? The answer, in part, is that the information in the remaining 80 percent of the input image is still strictly sufficient to distinguish Jane's face, if not from *every* other possible face, at least from each of the other ten faces in the training set. Although there might exist other faces identical to Jane's face save for that portion of her face hidden behind the bar, certainly none of the other faces in the training set meet this condition.

The second part of the answer is that the network's second layer, having been trained primarily on faces, tends to fill in any empty portion of an input facial image with generic facelike features, features roughly consistent, however, with the unobscured features of the input image. Figure 3.6b illustrates the informational content of layer two given the obscured image of a face (3.6a) as input. Compare that filled-in face to the face of the original and unobscured subject, the very first or upper-left female face in figure 3.3. The reconstruction isn't perfect, but it isn't half bad, either.

The third and most important part of the answer is that, during its training on the original eleven faces, the network has partitioned its activation space at layer two into a set of eleven "basins of attraction," each one centered on the prototypical coding point generated for each of the eleven faces. After all, it was not trained on all possible faces, only on these eleven. It was not asked to discriminate a million faces, just these eleven. The pressures thus exerted on the network during its training period forced it to become extremely sensitive to any and all input features that happen to point, even feebly, toward any one of exactly these eleven faces. This hypersensitivity regarding certain features of the input vector, and this forced concern with eleven specific individuals, means that the trained network has a strong tendency to "jump to conclusions" about the identity of an input face, even when the input is missing some standardly available information. To put the same point in another vocabulary, the network has acquired an especially strong tendency to activate, at layer two, some one or other of the eleven face-vectors to which it was so carefully trained, even when the input vector is partial or degraded. It tends to activate, at layer two, the specific facial vector that is most probable—*among the favored eleven*—given the "evidence" of the input vector received.

What we are observing here, in the phenomenon of vector completion at layers two and three, is a primitive form of *inductive inference*. Indeed, it may be that vector completion is the basic form that inductive inference takes in living creatures generally. We will address this issue in chapter 7 when we examine the nature of scientific reasoning. For now, let us just note that vector completion or inductive inference appears as a natural and inevitable cognitive phenomenon in the very simplest of neural networks.

With these points in place, we here leave the topic of face recognition, at least for now. I have spent a large portion of this chapter explaining how a specific network can achieve facial recognition because I wished you to have a detailed understanding of how at least one multilayered network performs a familiar cognitive task. The face-recognition network is especially useful as an instructional example because it displays together, in a simple and intuitively accessible form, so many of the special features characteristic of neural networks and their style of operation. The lessons learned here are mostly repeated in the further examples explored in chapter 4. This will allow us to move through them rather more quickly.

Entering the Third Dimension: Stereoscopic Vision

Stereo vision, as a distinct and isolable perceptual skill, is familiar to anyone who has ever peered into a nineteenth-century stereoscope or twentieth-century Viewmaster®, read bicolored comic books with flimsy red-green glasses, or donned polarized plastic glasses and settled in for a 3-D movie. To our delight, stereo perception stands out sharply in such cases, because photographs, slides, and movies typically *deny* us the 3-D vision we standardly have when viewing the real world. When viewing a photograph or movie screen, each of one's eyes sees exactly the same thing. But when viewing the real world, with objects scattered at different depths, the two eyes always see systematically *different* scenes, because they are invariably viewing those objects from two different vantage points about two and a half inches apart. The point of each of the four playful technologies mentioned is to recreate this original situation by somehow directing a quite different visual image to each of one's two eyes.

Just how substantial those differences are is immediately apparent if one looks at the bowls, milk carton, and cereal boxes scattered across the breakfast table while quickly and repeatedly closing alternate eyes. Nearby objects seem to jump back and forth to the left and right, and the nearer they are, the larger the apparent shift they display. We are usually unaware of these chronic left-right image disparities because the brain converts them effortlessly into a powerful sense of depth in three-dimensional space. How does the brain do this? How does it recover depth information from left-right disparities, and how does it code that information as part of our visual experience?

Let us begin with a vivid example of stereo perception. Remove the cardboard stereo viewer from its pocket on the inside back cover of this book and fold it into its operating configuration according to the instructions printed on its bottom side. (Make sure all the folds make neat right angles.) With the two lenses facing you, place the other end of the viewer so that the vertical piece

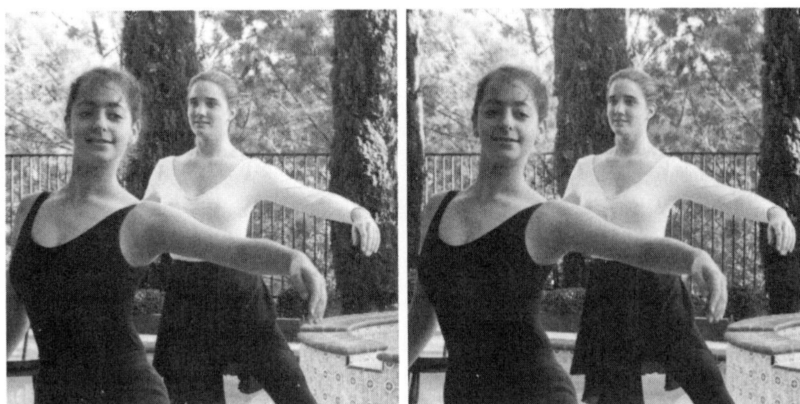

Figure 4.1 A stereoscopic pair of images.

beyond the two lenses lies exactly between the two photographs of figure 4.1, and the horizontal part lines up with their bottom borders. Make sure the page lies flat and that both pictures are brightly illuminated and free of shadows. Also, you may have to rock the eyepiece a degree or two, clockwise or anticlockwise, in order to bring the two images into mutual register, but experimentation will bring you success. Within ten or twenty seconds the two images will fuse into a single image rich in three-dimensional structure. (The subjects are my daughter, Anne, and in the foreground her soulmate, Debra, back in their early teens, all dressed up before heading off to a ballet lesson. Two 35mm SLR cameras were taped together, base to base, and the two images were captured simultaneously.)

Notice that, once fusion is achieved, one can explore the third dimension thus revealed, in the sense that one can fixate first on Debra, then look past Debra to fixate on Anne, and then look past Anne to fixate on the cypress trees in the background. What one cannot do is fixate at all three depths at once, since each fixation depth places one's eyes at a unique angle of convergence. For each momentary fixation, however, one has a vivid sense of the other, currently *un*fixated objects as being either fore or aft of, as being either in front of or behind, that momentary plane of fixation. This sense of relative distance is what we want explained. Let us approach it indirectly.

The Neuroanatomy of Stereoscopic Vision

Many animals lack stereo vision entirely. This is because their eyes are placed on opposite sides of their heads, and their left and

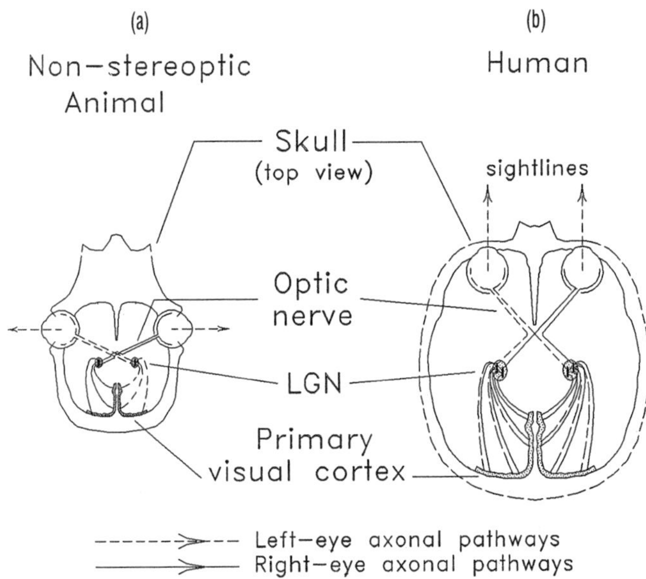

Figure 4.2 (a) The visual system of a schematic nonbinocular mammal. Note the complete separation of left-eye and right-eye image representations at the visual cortex. (b) The human visual system. Note that every point in the visual cortex receives input from corresponding parts of both the left and right eyes.

right visual fields overlap little or none at all. They are thus in no position to exploit, as we do, the subtle differences between two simultaneous images of the same thing. Their two eyes always comprehend distinct, nonoverlapping images.

In such animals those two images, the left and the right, are separately projected via the animal's optic nerve and LGN to its visual cortex. The left side of the visual cortex receives the image from the right eye, and the right side receives the image from the left (figure 4.2a). The information is separately taken in, separately projected, and it ends up represented in separate areas of the visual cortex.

In monkeys, the great apes, and humans, however, both the optical and the neuronal arrangements are different. Only the intervention of the nose prevents complete overlap of the left and right visual fields, and the overlap is 80 percent even so. More important, in the crucial foveal center of our visual fields where our vision is sharpest, the overlap between the left and right images *is* complete.

To exploit this situation, evolution has shaped humanity's internal wiring so that one's two eyes share a *common* target at the visual cortex. As figure 4.2b illustrates, the whole left-eye image is represented across almost the whole of the visual cortex, and the

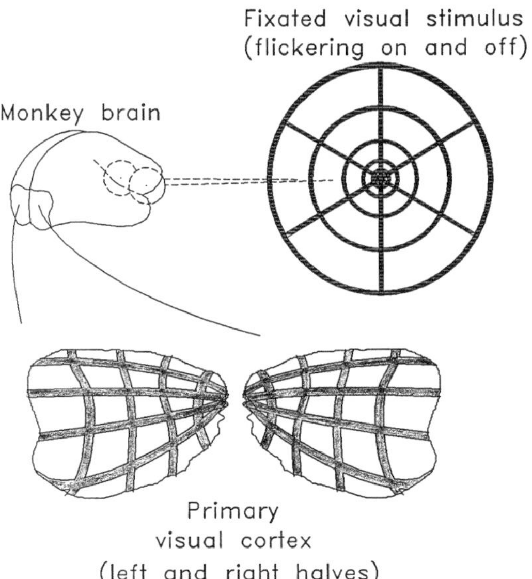

Figure 4.3 Neuronal activity across the monkey's visual cortex as the monkey views a simple pattern. (Adapted from Tootell.)

same is true of the right-eye image. Notice that the left half of the visual cortex still represents the world on the righthand side of the body, and the right half of the cortex represents the world on the left, as was the case in figure 4.2a. But in us, each half of the cortex is driven by two eyes rather than just one. That common movie screen at the rear of the brain is "illuminated" simultaneously by two projectors instead of one.

The metaphor of the preceding sentence is not entirely idle. The visual cortex is a thin, two-dimensional sheet of neurons, and the neuronal activity across its surface is a fairly faithful projection of the neuronal activity across the retina. A literal image at the one place reappears as a neuronal "image" at the other. Figure 4.3 shows how literally this is true. If one injects a radioactively labeled form of glucose into a monkey's bloodstream and fixates the monkey's eyes on some simple external image, an internal copy of that image, painted in radioactive glucose, will build up at the monkey's visual cortex. X-ray film will then reveal it.

So your cortical surface is indeed a sort of projection screen, and your two eyes are the projectors. But here is where a serious problem begins to show itself. For recall: these two projectors are projecting significantly *different* images onto exactly the same screen. This means that the image across the cortex is doomed to be confused and full of doubled images. The nature of this problem

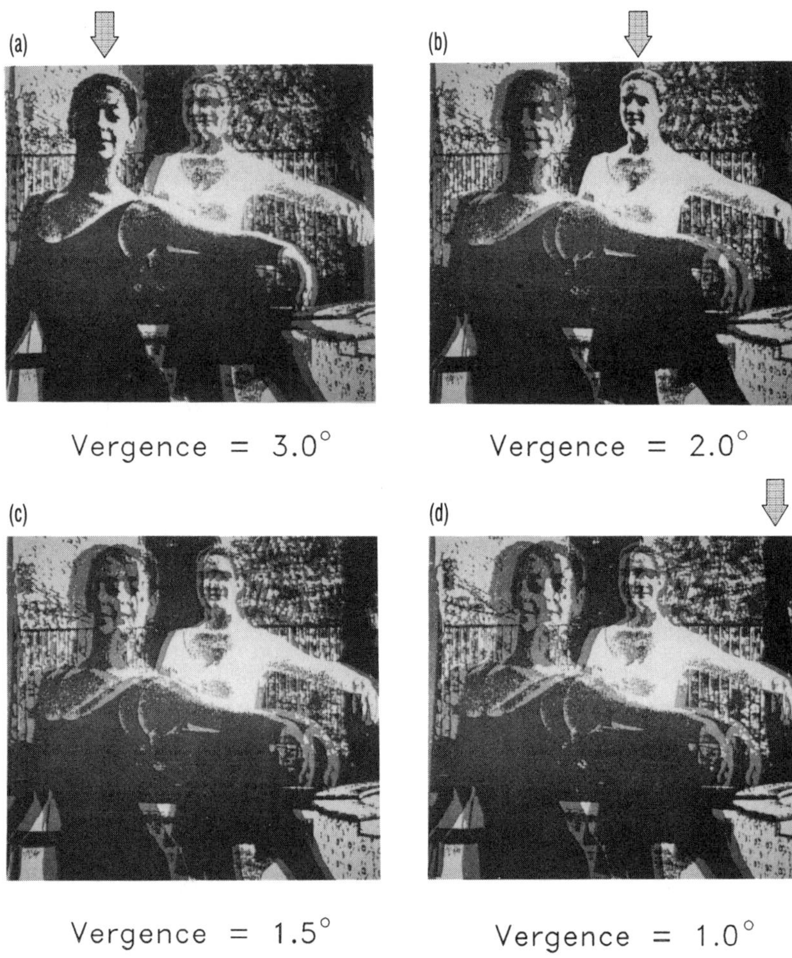

Figure 4.4 Four different superpositions of a stereo pair of images, corresponding to four different eye vergences or fixation depths. Notice the partial correspondences in superpositions (a), (b), and (d). The dancer in black is undoubled (fused) in (a); the dancer in white is fused in (b); and the rightmost tree and iron fence are fused in (d).

becomes graphically apparent when we superimpose the left photographic image of the two dancers over the right photographic image, as in figure 4.4a. Whatever left-right alignment we choose, the two images fail to "fit" each other completely, because the objects portrayed in them are all at slightly different left-right positions relative to each other.

This confusion or failure of mutual fit between the left and right eye images is called "binocular *rivalry*." It is the unavoidable fate of any creature—like you and me—whose eyes project their separate and different images to the same area of visual cortex. If this is

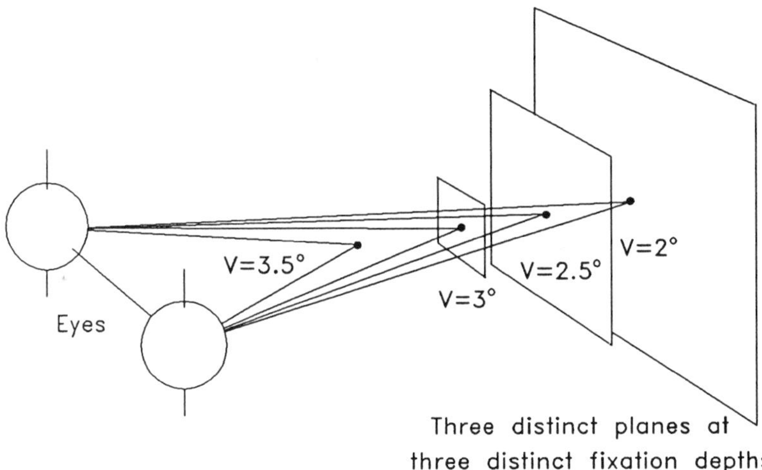

Figure 4.5 Increasing vergence angles yield successively closer fixation depths.

what makes stereo vision possible, it is very puzzling, because at first consideration it seems to pose a serious problem, one that the simple bison, for example, is spared.

How Stereoscopic Vision Works

The problem of chronic right-left image disparities is entirely real. Human newborns are universally flummoxed by it, at least for a while. At eight weeks, however, they suddenly hit on some partial ways around it. What they begin to discover is close control of their eye muscles and, most especially, of the degree of convergence of their eyes' two sightlines.

This allows them to fixate their gaze at various desired depths by turning their eyes inward slightly so that the two sightlines converge exactly at the fixation depth. When fixating at infinity, the sight lines are parallel and the *vergence angle* of the two eyes is zero (figure 4.5). When fixating at successively nearer depth planes, the sight lines now converge and the successive vergence angles are increasingly larger. Looking with crossed eyes at a fly on the tip of one's nose is the near end of this spectrum of cases.

Consider now what happens at the visual cortex during vergence changes at the two eyes. Fixating at successive depth planes while looking at the two dancers, for example, has the effect of sliding the two superimposed images slowly past each other at the visual cortex. It may be useful here to imagine holding two transparencies upright on a smooth table, one in each hand, while sliding one of them slowly back and forth behind the other. In effect, this is what figure 4.4 displays.

As is evident from the four examples in figure 4.4, at *some* of these fixation depths a significant *part* of each image finds itself matched perfectly with the corresponding part of the other image. More specifically, the two images of Debra are in perfect correspondence in 4.4a; the two images of Anne are in perfect correspondence in 4.4b; and the right-most cypress tree and the iron fence are in perfect correspondence in 4.4d.

The significance of a broad area of perfect correspondence at any given vergence is obvious: *object discovered at this fixation depth!* Only when the eyes are jointly fixated at exactly the same depth as a given object will the two images of that object be in exactly the same relative position on each of the two retinas. And only then will those projected images be in perfect register or correspondence when they finally reach the surface of the visual cortex at the back of the brain. Such a cortical correspondence, when it occurs, is therefore a robust indicator of the existence of an object positioned exactly at the current fixation depth of the eyes. (If there were no object at that depth, the sight lines for the two eyes would cross at that fixation point, continue on in space, and eventually make contact with two quite distinct objects. A perfect correspondence between the two image elements, in that circumstance, would be highly unlikely.)

Plainly, what the brain needs is something to detect those highly informative correspondences when they occur. And what it needs, in this case it has. They are called *fixation cells* and they are liberally peppered across the surface of the visual cortex. Their activity in live animals can be detected by a microthin electrical probe, and they have the singular feature that any given fixation cell is maximally active only when the spot of cortex where it lies is receiving *identical* input activity from each of the two eyes. Otherwise it is quiet. The fixation cells, when active, thereby code the presence of an object at the eyes' current fixation depth. They neither know nor care what the object contained in the relevant images might *be*—only that the left and right images match perfectly. That is the crucial information so far as object detection is concerned.

Prepare yourself now to be the subject of a neuropsychological experiment. We are about to activate a sizable patch of your own

Figure 4.6 A random-dot stereo pair. A simple geometric figure (not the circle) is perfectly camouflaged in each image. But at the appropriate vergence, our fixation cells will reveal its existence clearly. (Thanks to Bela Julesz, who pioneered the study of random-dot stereograms.)

fixation cells at the back of your brain, and the experiment will show that you need not *recognize* any object, or shape, or antecedent borders in order to detect clearly an area of right-left correspondence. Your fixation cells will "light up" the relevant area for you without any prior recognition of what it is you are seeing, and you will notice, quite plainly, when they do. Prepare then, in effect, to "look into" your own brain.

Retrieve the cardboard stereoscope you used earlier for fusing the stereo pair of ballet dancers. Place it this time between the stereo pair of figure 4.6, and prepare to fuse the two images into one, as before. Here I ask you to fixate on and fuse the tiny circle. The purpose of this (strictly inessential) reference point is just to help you find the relevant vergence angle quickly—the vergence angle at which the left and right image parts that make up the camouflaged object will be reproduced in perfect register at your visual cortex. When they are so reproduced, your fixation cells should detect that area of correspondence, and they should become highly active across precisely that area of cortex. The perceptual result, from your subjective point of view, is that a small square region, about one-ninth of the area of the background square, suddenly pops out at you. You see a distinct object, isolated at your current fixation depth, that was completely invisible before your stereo network got ahold of it. Its sudden visibility, at a critical vergence angle, is entirely owed to the relevant fixation cells all buzzing furiously at that local correspondence between the left and right eye images. You can even turn them on and off at will by winking one eye while maintaining the correct vergence angle.

In addition to revealing clearly the activity of your fixation cells, this experiment reveals the capacity of stereo vision to *break the camouflage* of hidden objects. This is a useful capacity, especially for predatory creatures such as cats, wolves, foxes, and owls, all of whom have their eyes placed facing forward, and all of whom have excellent stereo vision. A speckled gray lizard basking motionless on a speckled gray boulder might be safe from a monocular hunter, but like the hidden square you have just discovered, the lizard will stand out clearly to a predator armed with stereoscopic vision.

The capacity for stereo vision has an earlier and deeper purpose than catching mice and lizards, however, since to the profoundly ignorant newborn infant the entire *world* is little better than a random-dot stereogram. In order to get a grip on what sorts of objects the world contains, the infant needs to overcome the binocular rivalry inherent to her visual system. Gaining control over the vergence angle of her eyes is the first step. Once she learns to assume and then hold a particular vergence angle, she can respond to the signals of her fixation cells and finally get a clear, unambiguous, nonrivalrous look at *some* of the objects the world contains. Thanks to her fixation cells, she can break the camouflage of what is initially a profoundly confusing visual world.

Neither does the story end here. This critical forward step, which most humans infants make at eight weeks, is just the beginning. For we possess not only "fixation cells" scattered throughout the visual cortex, but also "near cells" and "far cells." These latter are cells that respond, respectively, to left-right correspondences slightly *in front of* and slightly *behind* one's current fixation depth. Just as the fixation cells signal the presence of an object *at* the current fixation depth, the near and far cells give notice of objects just fore and just aft of that primary planelike locus. This allows us to have a simultaneous awareness of the presence of several objects at several different depths simultaneously. This is what finally brings us the full-fledged stereo vision that most humans enjoy.

You may observe your fixation, near, and far cells at work simultaneously in the stereogram of figure 4.7. Fixate again on the tiny circle, and you will find yourself viewing a smallish raised square, as before. But here you will also sense a very small square raised in front of that middle-sized square, with the larger background

Figure 4.7 A random-dot stereo pair containing three distinct, camouflaged square planes.

square behind them both. As you fixate on the middle object, whose existence is coded by your fixation cells, your near cells are coding the closest square and your far cells are coding the most distant square.

Notice that the squares above and below the middle square are not perceived with the same sharpness or acuity as the middle square, at least while that middle square has the honor of fixation. This is because the foreground and background objects are then both projected onto your visual cortex *out of perfect register.* Both the foreground and background squares are clouded by a small amount of binocular rivalry. This repeats the lesson we learned earlier: *only* the objects at current fixation depth are seen in a way that is completely free of binocular rivalry or doubled images.

You can quickly surmount this residual problem by refixating your vergence angle on the closest of the three squares. Then *it* will be the clear, unambiguous, nonrivalrous target of your fixation cells. Accordingly, the details of the middle square will then be slightly indistinct, and the background square will be one notch muddier yet. This vergence-steered control over a movable plane of visual clarity, plus a reliable system of coding for objects somewhat fore and aft of that plane, is what constitutes the core of human stereoscopic vision.

A summary illustration is found in the original stereo pair of the two dancers. When you fixate on Anne (the ingenue in white), your fixation cells will light up within the cortical area of Anne's image, your near cells will light up within the cortical area of Debra's

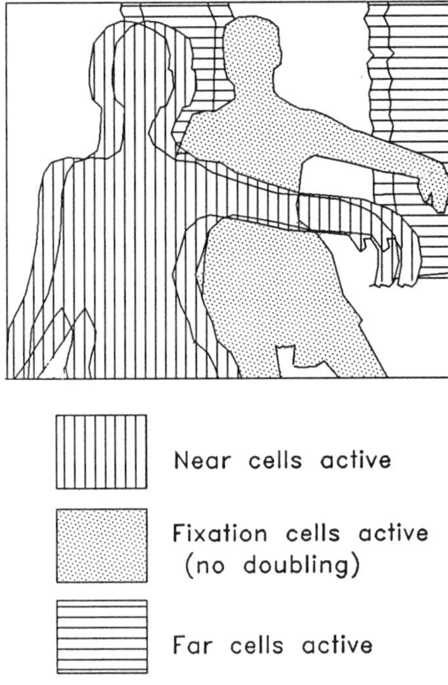

Figure 4.8 The left and right images of the dancers as projected onto the surface of the visual cortex while fixating on the background dancer, Anne. Anne's nonrivalrous image is here painted over with faint dots to indicate local activity of the fixation cells. Debra's slightly-doubled image is painted over in vertical lines to indicate local activity of the near cells. The slightly-doubled images of the two cypress trees are painted over with horizontal stripes to indicate local activity of the far cells.

image, and your far cells will light up the areas of the two cypress trees (figure 4.8). In this way is the independently existing visual image across your visual cortex selectively "painted" for relative depth by the appropriate activity of your scattered stereo cells.

Expanding One's Visual Grip on the World

If an understanding of how stereo vision works permits us to look inward and detect something internal that we have never been aware of before—namely, the activation of our fixation cells in visual cortex—it will also permit us to look outward and see the external world as we have never grasped it before. I continue this exploration of stereo vision with two examples of something that has brought me endless delight and astonishment since its possibility first occurred to me about fifteen years ago: *long-baseline stereography*. Let me explain.

With our eyes barely two and a half inches apart, human stereoptic discrimination of relative depth fades steadily as the objects in question are placed farther and farther from us, and it disappears entirely at about 100 yards. Beyond this fairly paltry distance, we might as well be monocular. Beyond 100 yards, relative distances must be judged by nonstereoptic visual cues such as relative angular size, the occlusion of more distant objects by nearer ones, texture gradients, and so forth. That is because the left-right disparities between retinal images always shrink steadily as the distance of objects increases (this is, after all, why stereo is possible in the first place!). Those disparities become undetectably small for scene elements located beyond 100 yards. Our stereoptic discrimination of relative depth is therefore confined within a sphere barely 100 yards in radius. The very-large-scale 3-D structure of the world—its structure beyond 100 yards, that is—is therefore chronically hidden from human stereoptic apprehension.

Is there any way to make that sphere larger? Well, surgery comes to mind. If we could somehow move our eyes *farther apart*—double their separation to five inches, say—then, all else being equal, our stereoptic discrimination would reach out to 200 yards. Hmmmm. Move one's eyes to a position ten inches apart, and stereopsis would reach out to 400 yards! And so on.

But we must be serious. Facial reconstruction (with eye stalks?) seems a bit extreme. Fortunately, there is an easier way to achieve the same end. Take two simultaneous photographs of the relevant large-scale scene, from two positions 200 *feet* apart. Then present the left photo to the left eye and the right photo to the right eye, as in any stereoscope. What the eyes will then see is exactly what they would see if they were actually 200 feet apart. Thus the expression, "long-baseline stereography."

Think of this as "virtual surgery." More accurately, think of it as "virtual giantism," for what it delivers is the stereoptic perspective that a giant would enjoy, a giant with a head large enough to have its eyes fully 200 feet apart (figure 4.9). Such a behemoth would boast stereoptic discrimination out to fifty-six miles! Would you like to know "what it would be like" to be such a creature? Retrieve the cardboard stereoscope once more and use it to fuse the stereo pair in figure 4.10. These two images were taken from an altitude of 2000 feet, roughly 200 feet apart. When viewed stereoptically they will provide you with exactly the visual experience of the giant described, an experience that is impossible for normal humans save by the subterfuge here employed.

Figure 4.9 A giant 2000 feet tall, with eyes 200 feet apart, approaching lower Manhattan.

Figure 4.10 A long-baseline stereo pair of Manhattan Island. The altitude is 2000 feet and the interocular baseline is about 200 feet. (Thanks to pilot Mike Garcia of MacDan Aircraft in New Jersey, and to his Cessna 172, for placing me and my camera where the giant's two eyes would be.)

What is noticeable immediately is the 3-D structure evident all the way up Manhattan, to midtown and beyond. You may notice also that it is difficult to fuse the entire scene simultaneously: you have to choose your fixation point somewhere and then resign yourself to a slightly doubled-up foreground or background image relative to that point. This is a familiar and easily handled problem when one is viewing a dinner-table setting, but it is completely novel in a scene on the scale of a city. Finally, you may notice that the whole scene has somehow the character of an intricate little *model* of Manhattan, of a fastidiously constructed *toy* city. My wife, Patricia, coined the expression "the Lilliputian effect" on first experiencing this phenomenon. It occurs because the only objects for which you ever experience anything like the high-disparity stereo perspective at issue are objects that are much smaller than you, and never more than several yards away. The brain automatically interprets the high-disparity scene as toylike, because truly large objects are *never* seen in that perspective.

Until now. With long-baseline stereography you can bring almost any scene, no matter what its scale, within stereoptic reach of the human visual system. In fact, you can take your own photographic pairs at suitable baselines, trim them with scissors to fit the format familiar from these pages, and expand your visual grasp to almost any horizon. The only practical limit involves placing your two cameras at the required baseline. To gain stereoptic discrimination out to a distance of 30,000 feet (almost six miles), for example, you will need to place the two cameras 20 feet apart and on a baseline lying at right angles to the photographic line of sight. One unit of baseline employed per 1500 units of stereoptic discrimination achieved is the relevant and universal ratio. If your photographic subjects will hold completely still for you, you can even get by with a single camera. Take the left photo from one end of the desired baseline, and then run quickly along it and take the right photo from the other end. If nothing moves in the interim, your stereo pair should be perfect.

The longest baseline and the deepest stereo I can provide you is buried in figure 4.11. The baseline here is about 40 million miles and it provides the viewer with stereoptic discrimination 60 billion miles out into space, far beyond the edge of the solar system. Some years ago, there was a gorgeous conjunction of the outer planets that placed them high in the sky in the middle of the night for several winter months. The right and left photos were taken about 50 days apart, during which time the planet Earth moved in its orbit

Figure 4.11 A *very* long-baseline stereo pair of the outer solar system: Jupiter, Saturn, and Mars against the stars of Virgo.

about 40 million miles. This provided the necessary baseline. In the distance is the constellation Virgo, still far beyond stereoptic reach. Its stars are tens, even hundreds, of *light-years* away. The three bright foreground objects, however, are well within stereoptic reach, and they are none other than the planets Jupiter, Saturn, and Mars. To use the metaphor of the giant once more, your head is now roughly the diameter of the Earth's orbit, your eyes are 40 million miles apart, and the three outer planets are just within reach of your arm. And therefore within easy reach of your stereopsis. With a mere cardboard toy to your nose and a couple of frost-bitten photos, you have gained visual command of the three-dimensional structure of the outer solar system.

Fusion.net: A Network with Stereo Vision

There is rough agreement among researchers on the basic principles of how stereo vision works. But it remains an open question how the brain is wired up so as to execute those principles. What follows is no more than a theoretical conjecture on my part. But the proposed solution will at least illuminate the problem, and it does have testable consequences. What we wish to know now is exactly how the fixation, near, and far cells manage to extract their invaluable information about depth from the two images arriving from the eyes. The network described below offers a possible account of that extraction. As will be evident, it does indeed have the perceptual capacities described in the preceding sections. Whether its physical organization reflects the true details of the neuronal connections in the brain remains to be determined.

The gross structure of the network is displayed in figure 4.12. Aside from being binocular instead of monocular, it is not radically different from the face-recognition network you already know. It has two 60 × 60-cell input layers or "retinas" that project to a common second layer of 120 × 120 cells. These project in turn to three distinct output layers: a 60 × 60 layer of fixation cells, a 30 × 60 layer of near cells, and a 30 × 60 layer of far cells. These final cells, the stereo cells, are artificially divided into three separate layers so that we can more easily discern their separate functions, but of course their biological analogs in real visual cortex will all lie within the same cortical surface.

Put the near and far cells aside for a moment and focus attention on the vitally important fixation cells. What stereo vision requires

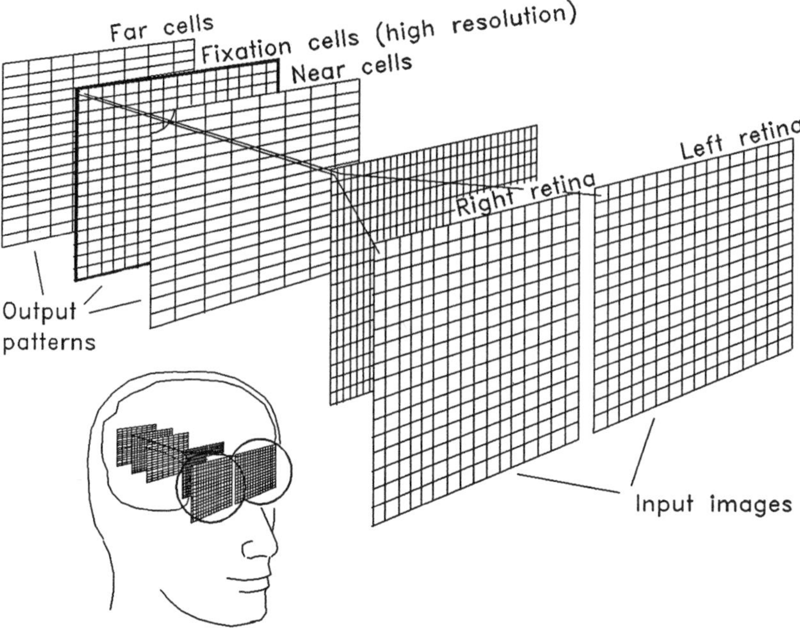

Figure 4.12 Fusion.net: an artificial network for stereoscopic vision.

is that each fixation cell in that final grid be active exactly when the two input cells at the two corresponding points at the retinal grid are sending identical signals, when they have identical levels of excitation. We can achieve this goal immediately with the connective arrangement displayed in figure 4.13.

You can see pretty quickly how it works. The fixation cell at the output is the subject of a tug-of-war between two competing influences. The first is a chronic excitatory influence arriving from the so-called "bias" cell, whose activation level is constantly at maximum. The second is a pair of strongly inhibitory influences from the two cells at the second layer. Those two cells receive inputs from both of the retinal cells, whose connection weights are as indicated. Notice that they are deliberately contrived so as to cancel each other out—whatever the strength of the incoming signals—exactly when the inputs from the two retinal cells are identical in strength. Since in that case they cancel each other, the net effect on the cells in the middle layer is zero. Which means that they are not activated at all. Which means that no signal at all goes to the fixation cell via the two inhibitory connections. Which means that the tug-of-war is won by the never-resting bias cell, and the fixation cell gets strongly activated.

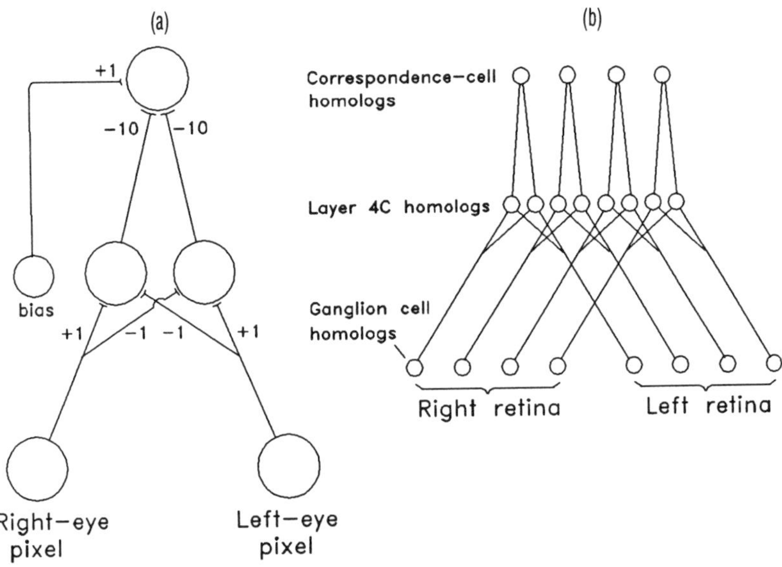

Figure 4.13 (a) The elementary correspondence-detecting subnetwork whose repetition makes up Fusion.net. The output "fixation" cell is activated when, and only when, the two input cells have identical levels of activation, whatever that level might happen to be. (b) A plan view of the pattern of repetition of the basic subnetwork. Note that each cell in either "retina" projects to a cell at the cortex that occupies a corresponding relative position within that target population.

On the other hand, if the signal strengths from the two retinal cells are even slightly different from each other, then the incoming influences at the middle-layer cells do not cancel one another. This means that at least one of those two cells does get activated, if only slightly. That activation, when projected along its axon, has a strongly inhibitory effect on the fixation cell (notice the large negative weight of minus 10), an effect sufficient to outweigh the constant excitatory effect of the bias cell. The fixation cell is thus shut down. And it will remain shut down by such inhibitory influences until such time as the activation levels at the two corresponding retinal cells once again fall into a perfect balance. The fixation cell, as desired, detects left-right correspondences at the input layer, and does so across the entire range of possible input signals.

Let us therefore wire up the entire network in this fashion, repeating the inverted-V configuration 3600 times so as to connect up each of the corresponding left-right cell pairs at the retina with its corresponding cell at the 60×60-cell output grid.

That takes care of the fixation cells. Now for the near cells. We want them to become active exactly when there is a doubled

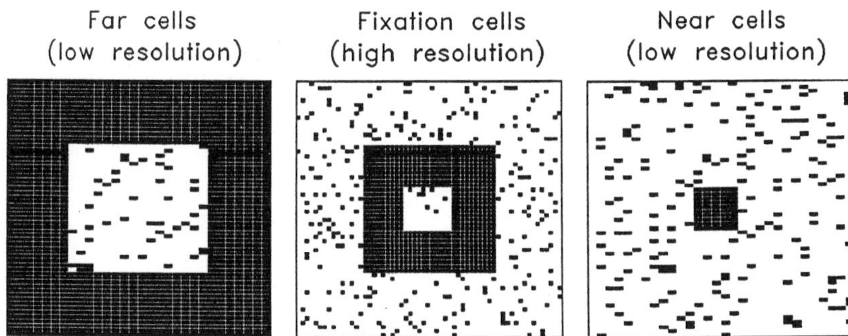

Figure 4.14 The activation patterns across the far cells, fixation cells, and near cells of Fusion.net when presented with the camouflaged stereo pair of figure 4.7 at a vergence angle that fixates on the middle-size or first raised square.

image element that is only one-pixel-to-the-*left* away from being in perfect register. No problem. For the near cells, let us use the same inverted V configuration as before, but run the output axons not to exactly corresponding cells at the two retinas, but rather to a pair of cells that are exactly one-pixel-to-the-left away from exact correspondence. While the fixation cells are busy detecting objects at the current fixation depth, the near cells will thus be busy detecting objects at a depth that is one notch *closer* than fixation depth.

The same trick will connect up the far cells appropriately, only this time the inverted V configuration must connect left-right cells at the two retinas that are one-pixel-to-the-*right* away from perfect correspondence. While the fixation cells are busy with objects at fixation depth, the far cells will thus be busy detecting objects at a depth that is one notch *farther* than fixation depth.

That is all there is to it. Fusion.net has rather more cells—36,000—than Cottrell's face-recognition network. But it has many fewer synaptic connections—only 50,400—because its transformational task is much simpler. Indeed, it is almost trivial. But the network delivers the desired capacity. If we present the random-dot stereo pair of figure 4.7 to the network's retinas at the same vergence you assumed for that figure, the network returns, as output, the three activation patterns shown in figure 4.14. Each of the three classes of stereo cells correctly detects the hidden object at its proprietary relative depth.

Testing Fusion.net's performance on real scenes, such as the two dancers, requires that we first chop up the two photos into a 60×60 grid, compute the average brightness level across each

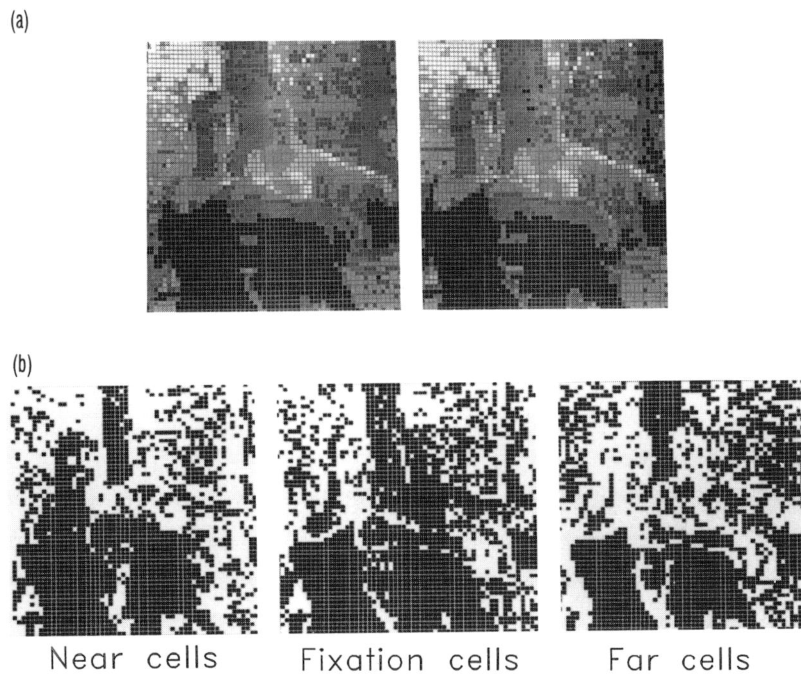

Figure 4.15 (a) A digitized version of the original stereo pair of the two dancers (figure 4.1). Resolution is reduced to 60 × 60, and brightness levels are averaged and normalized to ten distinct levels for presentation to Fusion.net. (b) The activation patterns across the near cells, fixation cells, and far cells of Fusion.net when presented with the digitized stereo pair of (a).

square pixel, and express each pixel's brightness level with a convenient one-place decimal between 0 (dark) and 1 (bright). This yields the stereo pair of figure 4.15a, which rather grainier picture is what Fusion.net actually "saw." Its output for that graded input appears in figure 4.15b. It will help to view this figure from about six feet away in order to appreciate what the network is and is not discriminating.

It is evident that with real scenes instead of computer-generated ones (i.e., the random-dot pairs), the artificial network does less well, since neither its spatial resolution (a coarse 60 × 60) nor the gray-scale discrimination of the digitized input image (only ten distinct levels in this experiment) is equal to the complexity and smooth subtlety of the original photo of the two dancers. But as figure 4.15b reveals, Fusion.net performs appropriately even so, despite the graininess, and plus or minus some false correspondences registered across some now uniformly black articles of clothing. (Use the cardboard stereoscope to fuse this grainy pair yourself. See if your visual system does much better than the network.) The deficits reflect the rudimentary nature of the model network and the low quality of my digitized input image. Greater faithfulness to our biological reality in either of the two digitized dimensions would yield immediate improvements in the quality of the stereopsis achieved.

Greater realism or biological fidelity would require a variety of further things from this network. For starters, the bias cells need to be eliminated entirely. They are merely a network modeler's quick and easy trick for simulating the behavior of cells that are intrinsically active to some degree or other. Second, the network will need a *variety* of near cells and far cells tuned to a variety of depths fore and aft of the fixation plane: human stereo vision comprehends a continuous variety of depths, not just three. Third, the criss-cross inhibitory connections to the middle layer need to be mediated by small inhibitory interneurons, since it is biologically implausible to have any given cell type project both excitatory *and* inhibitory connections. And fourth, we must remember that a depth-discriminating system of the kind here represented is but a small subsystem of the visual system in general, a subsystem with a very narrow function.

With these several qualifications in place, Fusion.net may capture both the structural and the behavioral reality of human stereo. As illustrated in figure 4.16, among the many cells at the special input-receiving layer of the visual cortex, layer 4C, there are special cells with exactly the response profile of the model's middle-layer cells. (That is, they are excited by inputs from one eye and inhibited by exactly corresponding inputs from the other. I think of these cells as "Pettigrew cells", after the neuroscientist, J. D. Pettigrew, who first identified their curious dual sensitivity.) The very next layer of visual cortex, layer 3, contains as a subset of its vast population the experimentally detected fixation, near, and far cells. (Thanks here to my colleague Simon LeVay.) If we now look back to the sensory periphery, we find that the human retina is completely tiled with so-called "ganglion cells," cells that code the changes in brightness levels across the retinal image. And the projections, from those retinal ganglion cells to the cells in visual cortex, do indeed display the careful preservation of left-right correspondences required in the model (see again figure 4.13b).

Finally, I should mention that the brightness levels of the pixels in the stereo pair in figure 4.15a were not presented, just as they

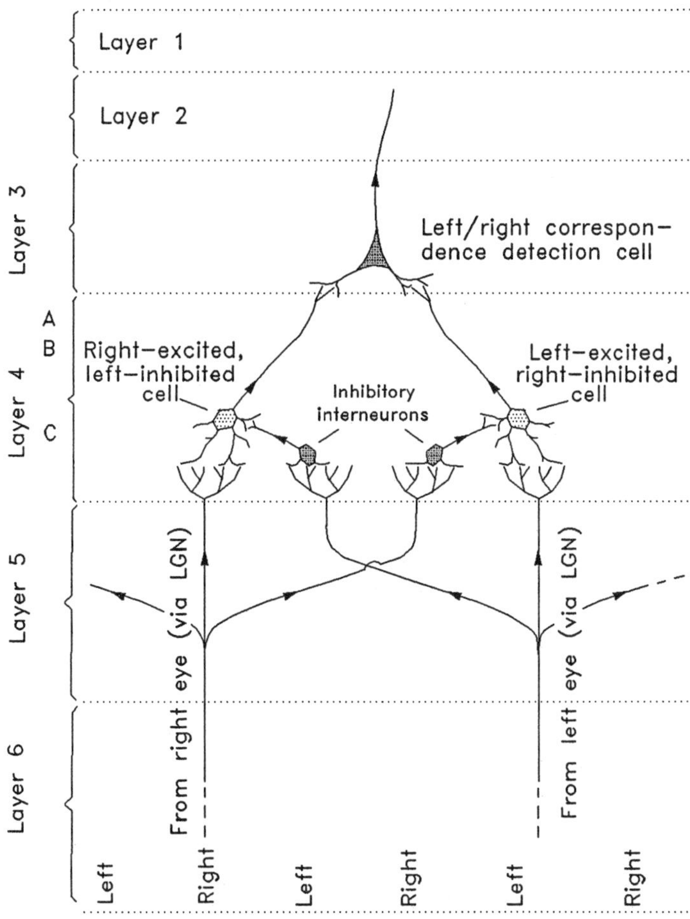

Figure 4.16 A blown-up cross section of human visual cortex, showing its several layers and some of the cell types they are known to contain. The connections illustrated are conjectural.

stand, directly to Fusion.net's input cells. Instead, the experiment took a leaf from the human eye's own book and I first did the following. Each pixel in the pair, except at the edges, has an enclosing square of eight other pixels immediately surrounding it. Choosing a pixel at random, let us take the *average* of the brightness values of the eight pixels in its surrounding square, and then subtract that average from the brightness value of the centered pixel itself. This gives us a value for the amount by which that center pixel's brightness level *differs* from the average of its immediate neighbors. (Honest, this is really what gets computed at the retina of the human eye.) This critical difference is called a *delta*-brightness level, and *this* is what finally gets coded, both at the ganglion cells at the back of the human retina, and at each cell of Fusion.net's input layer.

Doing this for every pixel in the digitized image gives us a portrait of how the light levels go up and down as we move across the picture; it provides a portrait of the overall structure of the locally *relative* brightness levels across each of the two input images. In the end, what the fixation cells at the output layer actually detect is *correspondences in structure* between the right-eye and left-eye images, rather than correspondences in absolute brightness levels themselves.

This apparently arcane procedure has a payoff. In fact, it has two payoffs. The first is noteworthy, but a little dull: taking the *average* of the surrounding cells helps to smooth out the inevitable "noise" that biological cells always display. The second is striking: since each retina sends forward a structure description rather than a simple brightness-level description, the fixation cells at the visual cortex can continue to detect left-right correspondences in structure even when one of the two stereo images is systematically lighter or darker than the other!

To see this point for yourself, look once again at the original stereo pair of the two dancers with the cardboard stereoscope, but this time interpose a pair of sunglasses over the right eyepiece. (Or, if you don't wish to leave your chair to fetch some sun-glasses, just look at a bright light for a few moments with the left eye closed, before looking again at the stereo pair. That will shrink your right pupil for a minute or so, restricting the light it can admit.) This effectively makes the right image much darker than the left image across its entire surface.

Now, if correspondences in absolute *brightness levels* at the retina were what mattered, your fixation cells would then find no correspondences whatever. There would be no left-right brightness-level matches at all! Your stereopsis should then disappear completely, but in fact, it is impaired little if at all. The picture's 3-D structure remains richly evident. Thanks to the fact that brightness-structure descriptions are what get sent forward from your retinal ganglion cells, your stereopsis is largely immune to global variations in left-right brightness levels. Fusion.net's stereopsis is also thus immune, and for exactly the same reason.

Finally, the network's behavior has two further quirks displayed in human stereo vision. First, it is subject to the stereo illusion of *false correspondences* (see again the black clothing in figure 4.15).

Second, it can detect depth only when the input images have detectable *variations* in brightness levels (recall the *delta*-brightness coding function of the ganglion cells). As experiments have shown, a stereo pair of images that is entirely kosher in its mutual disparities, but that is composed of different but equally bright *colors*, will produce no stereoptic response whatever in humans. Such an isoluminant stereo pair fails to get any rise out of Fusion.net either. Both the brain and the artificial network need color-independent *brightness* variations to kick their stereopsis into gear. This may reflect the fact that, evolutionarily speaking, stereopsis appeared millions of years before color vision developed. Color differences always were and still are plain invisible to our stereoptic subsystem. (My thanks here to Richard Gregory, for two decades the director of the Brain and Perception Laboratory at Bristol. It was he who introduced me, as a young man, to both of these stereoptical quirks during a most memorable visit to his laboratory in the late 1970s.)

Submarine Intrigue: A Network for Sonar Perception

Bring your thoughts now back from the Manhattan skyline, back from the outer solar system. Relocate them about 300 feet below the surface of the Pacific Ocean, in the silent realm of the stealthy submarine. You are the commander of a modern attack sub with a sophisticated sonar detection system. Your problem-of-the-week is to find a way to distinguish the sonar echoes that bounce back from harmless rocks lying on the sandy ocean floor from sonar echoes that bounce back from the occasional explosive underwater mines scattered among those rocks by your cunning adversary. The rocks are small and you can pass over them without incident, but the mines are armed with magnetic proximity fuses that can detect the steel hull of your sub. They will detonate if you come within 100 yards of them. Distinguishing, from a safe distance, between the sonar returns from each type of object is therefore of some importance.

The difficulty is, there is considerable variety among each of the two types of echoes, depending on the size, shape, and orientation of the ocean-floor object detected. Moreover, a typical example of both types of echo sounds pretty much the same: ka-pwinggg, or thereabouts. Sonar operators, after years of experience listening to such echoes, start to feel they can sense the difference between mine echoes and rock echoes. Careful tests on both mines and rocks show that the sonar operators are indeed performing at some level above chance, but nowhere near the level of reliability required to risk your sub and crew in a mine-strewn environment. What to do?

Give the job to an artificial network whose sole function in life is to make the desired discrimination. We may begin by taking a lesson from the human auditory system, whose sensory cells—the so-called "hair cells"—are arrayed in sequence the entire length of a narrow conical tube called the *cochlea*. In fact, the tube is coiled into a Nautilus-like shape well inside the head, but we will here straighten it out graphically so we can see what is going on (figure 4.17).

As the diameter of the sounding tube steadily narrows toward its far end, each successive cross-section of the tube is subject to a resonance that is specific to a particular frequency of sound wave entering through the diaphragm at the opening end. Low-frequency sounds resonate at the small end and high-frequency sounds resonate at the large end. A given hair cell responds only to resonances that occur exactly at the cross-section where the cell is located. Collectively, they provide a frequency analysis of the distribution of received sound energy across the acoustic spectrum. In the language with which you are by now familiar, they produce a *vector of activation levels* that uniquely characterizes the input sound.

In a fashion that recalls the visual system described earlier, the cochlear cells project their collective activation vector to a way station called the medial geniculate nucleus (MGN), which projects in turn to an area of the cortical surface called the primary auditory cortex.

From here the story is familiar, at least in its general outlines. Let us assemble a simple network with thirteen input cells strung out in single file. Each input cell codes the total energy contained in the sonar echo at exactly one of the thirteen sampled frequencies. Each echo is thus characterized by a distinct activation vector across that input population. The cells at the input layer all project to a second layer, which projects in turn to a third. The third layer has only two cells, whose job it is to signal a mine or a rock, respectively. The output cell with the higher activation level wins (figure 4.18).

As with the face-recognition network, we have no idea how to configure the connection weights of this network. In fact, we cannot yet be sure that a solution to our discrimination problem even

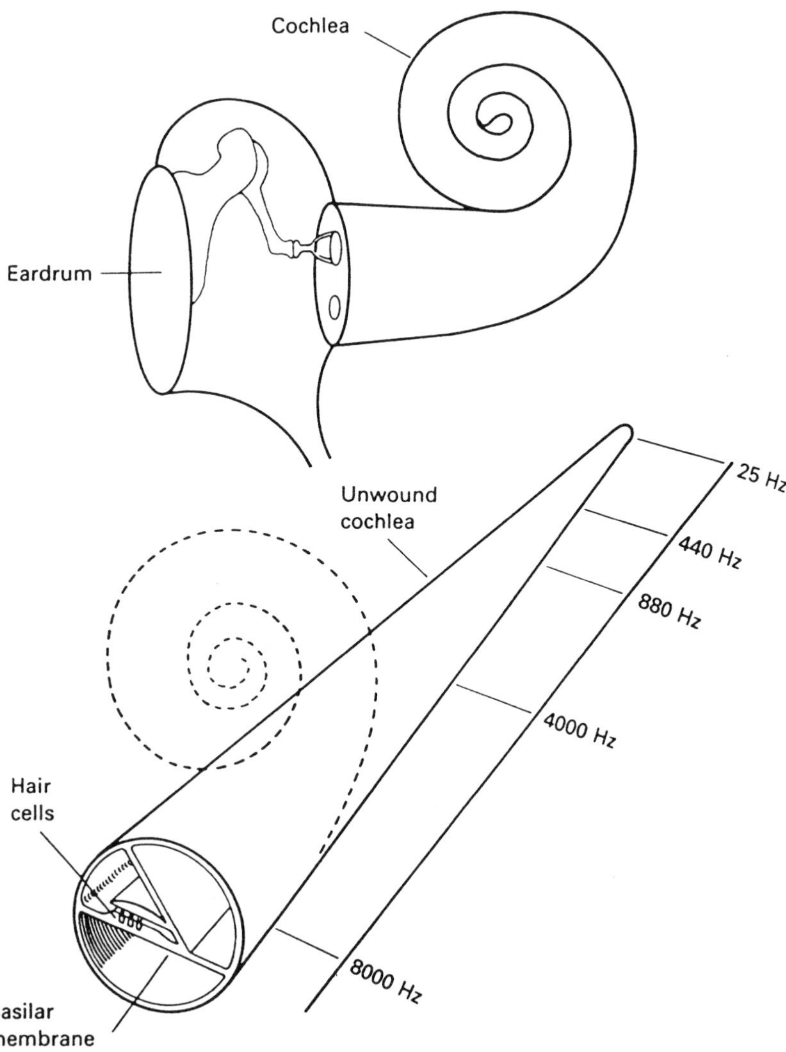

Figure 4.17 The human cochlea: a structure for detecting acoustical energy levels at many different frequencies simultaneously.

exists. Hoping to get lucky, we set the weights at small random values and prepare to teach the network on a substantial training set of recorded sonar echoes, half of them returned from real mines placed by us on the ocean floor, and half of them returned from visually identified rocks. Using the backpropagation technique of synaptic weight adjustment, as before, we cycle repeatedly through the training set until the network has assumed an overall synaptic-weight configuration that minimizes the mean squared error at the output layer. That is to say, we continue to instruct it until it has learned to make the mine-rock distinction as reliably as it possibly can.

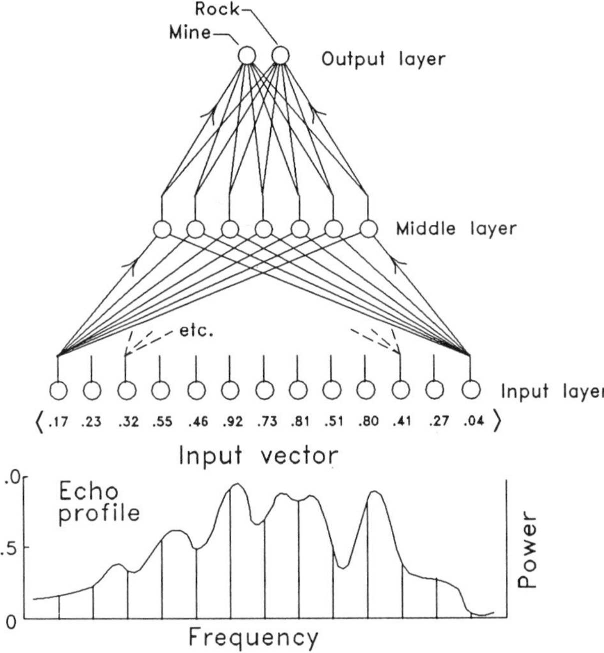

Figure 4.18 A simple acoustical network for distinguishing explosive-mine echoes from harmless-rock echoes.

Despite the fictional setting of the preceding paragraphs, the network described is quite real. Paul Gorman (Grumman Corp.) and Terry Sejnowski (University of California at San Diego and the Salk Institute) are its creators, and it topped out at a performance level of 100 percent on the training set. When tested on echoes drawn from outside the training set, it generalized to these novel examples very well, identifying better than 90 percent of them correctly. Plainly, it has learned to ignore or filter out the irrelevant variations across the two kinds of echoes, and has become tuned to some thirteen-dimensional feature buried in the input vectors but made explicit at the middle layer of cells.

An examination of the activation vectors across the middle layer, in response to the input of mine and rock echoes respectively, reveals that this is indeed the case. To appreciate the point graphically, see the familiar activation space of figure 4.19. (Ten of the relevant thirteen dimensions have been suppressed.) As a result of the net's training, this space has been partitioned into two subspaces, one for mine-echo vectors and the other for rock-echo vectors. Moreover, the central region of each contains a sort of

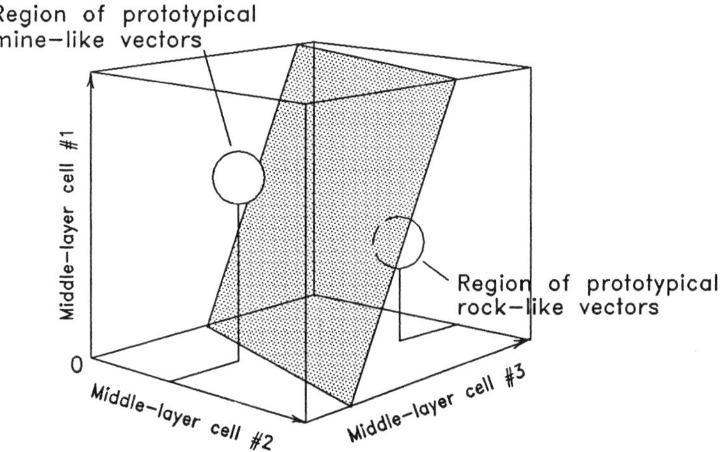

Figure 4.19 The activation-vector space of the middle layer of the acoustic network for sonar analysis. Note the partition into two exclusive categories: mine echoes and rock echoes. Note also the two prototypical hot spots where typical and uncompromised examples of each category are routinely coded.

"prototypical hot spot," a spot at which a five-star or prototypical instance of the relevant type gets coded. Less typical, incomplete, or noise-degraded echoes end up coded at various distances from the relevant prototypical hot spot. Utterly ambiguous echoes get coded, as in earlier networks, on the "curtain of uncertainty" that separates the two regions.

A pattern is emerging here, and I want to emphasize it before exploring its next instance. The training of a network, to some discriminatory skill or other, regularly produces a partitioning of its higher-level activation spaces into a hierarchical structure of categories and subcategories. It produces a framework of *concepts* that subserve the skill acquired. The sonar network displays two categories with prototypical cores; the face network displays two major categories (faces and nonfaces), plus two *sub*categories (male and female) with appropriate prototypical cores. The next network we will examine takes the business of hierarchical subdivision to new heights, and it requires a new graphical technique to display its learned partitional structure adequately. Drawing planes and subplanes across a 3-D space, as we have been doing, while conceptually correct, is visually feasible for only the simplest cases. Let me here introduce the "dendogram"—so named for its treelike branching structure—to represent the categorial structure of two familiar networks (figure 4.20). We can now approach a further example.

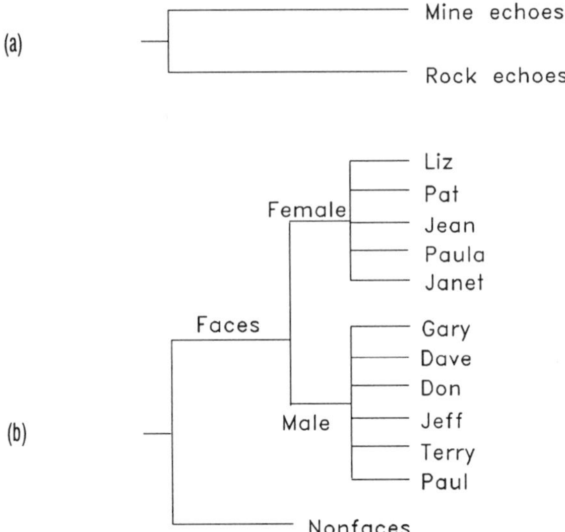

Figure 4.20 Two dendograms: (a) The categorial partitions within the middle-layer activation space of the sonar network. (b) The categorial partitions and subpartitions within the middle-layer activation space of the face network.

NETtalk: A Network that Reads Aloud

Some years ago, the Digital Equipment Corporation (DEC) released a product designed to make the world's libraries accessible to the blind. It is called "DECtalk", and it does just what its name suggests. You place a book or magazine into its optical scanner, and its input system determines the sequence of letters, spaces, and punctuation marks that make up the lines and pages being scanned. A computer program, following a complex set of rules, then computes an output for each of those input letters, an output that codes the phoneme or audible sound that is appropriate to the letter received as input. That phonetic output code is then fed into a speech synthesizer, a device that actually produces the sound in question. The running scan of letters thus produces a running output of audible sounds. In sum, DECtalk is a machine that will read printed text aloud.

The tricky part of this system is neither the input scanner nor the output synthesizer. It is the hidden computer program that takes each input letter and computes the appropriate phoneme for production at the output module. The difficulty is plain enough: there are seventy-nine different phonemes displayed in English speech, but only twenty-six letters in the English alphabet. Each letter is thus, on average, at least three ways ambiguous. Consider "c," for example. It can be hard, as in "carrot," but it might also be soft, as in "circuit," or something else again, as in "cherry." Similar ambiguities plague the vowels, and vowel combinations and consonant combinations as well. Recall, for example, the infamous phonemic diversity displayed by both "ou" and "gh" in the words "cough," "tough," "dough," and "through." Not to mention "bough" and "thought."

Although native anglophones fail to appreciate it, English has the most inconsistent and tangled spelling system on the planet. (Compare Spanish or Italian, for example. *Much* more rational.) This posed a severe problem for the poor programmers at DEC. In order to find the right output phoneme for any input letter, their program would have take into account the surrounding context in which the letter appears, just as you and I do when we read printed text. We look not just at a single letter, but also at the several letters or empty spaces preceding and following that letter. DECtalk used a "context window" of seven spaces: three in front and three behind the letter currently in question. Inevitably, this meant a long and very complicated program, full of complex conditional rules, subrules, and files of exceptions to them. Its size and intricacy were hidden, in the end, by the lightning speed of the computer chip that executes its commands when the system is up and running. But it took several man-*years* of programming labor to produce that program in the first place.

In 1986 Terry Sejnowski (then at Johns Hopkins) and his student Charles Rosenberg (now at Princeton) asked themselves whether a neural network—using just a configuration of synaptic weights instead of a complex system of explicit rules expressed in a programming language—could learn the complex input-output transformation embodied in DECtalk's laborious program. They used the same input and output modules found in DEC's system, but they effectively replaced its intervening serial-computer-plus-program with the neural net depicted in figure 4.21. The network's job was to produce an output phoneme for the input letter in the center of a seven-letter input string. The three letters on either side of the focal letter provided the necessary context, just as with DECtalk.

The network was trained on an arbitrarily chosen English-language text of about 1000 words. Once the text was chosen, the corresponding *phonetic* script for that text was carefully written out, and this provided the target output. The text was gone over by

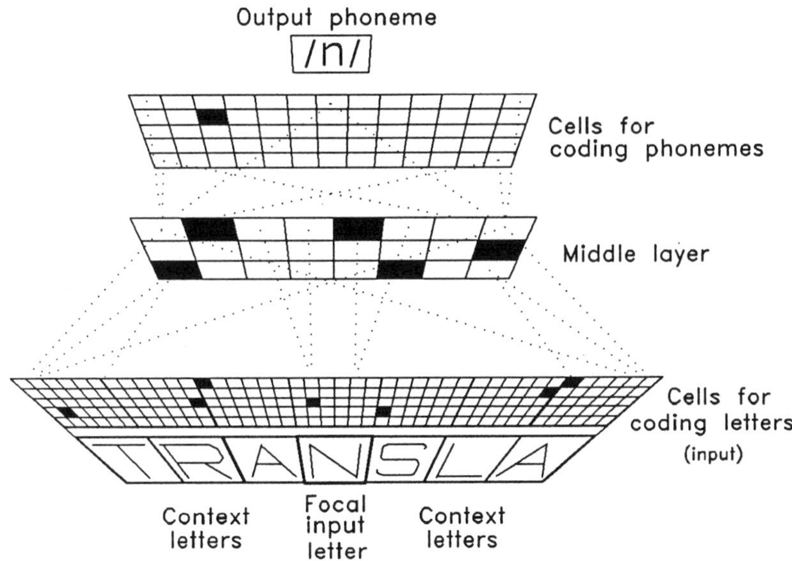

Figure 4.21 NETtalk: a feedforward network for transforming scanned letters into voiced phonemes appropriate to the English-language text being scanned. (Adapted from Terry Sejnowski.)

hand, seven letters at a time, shifting to the right exactly one letter each time, and the phoneme corresponding to the centermost letter was specified as the proper output for that seven-letter string. All of these input-output pairs were then stored in a large file, on the disk of an auxiliary computer, to serve as the training set for the student network. The network's synaptic weights were set at small random values and, using the backpropagation procedure described above, the training process was begun.

NETtalk, as this network was named by its authors, took a mere ten *hours* of steady synapse nudging to top out at a performance level of 95 percent on the original training set. (This network-modeling success was achieved in 1986 on a computer no better than the high-end desktop machines available anywhere today.) Subsequent testing on novel text—text the network had never seen before—produced an impressive performance level of 78 percent correct phonetic output. And despite the 22 percent error rate, the output speech was still quite intelligible to anyone listening, since the network's errors were typically what we would count as small ones. For example, it would pronounce "flood" as rhyming with "food" instead of with "mud"; or it would pronounce "therapy" as having the same voiced "th" as "there" and "then." But unless you were listening for such errors, you might not even hear them.

Where the network made mistakes on novel text, and often enough it did, it regularly came close enough to the mark to preserve the intelligibility of its speech. Moreover, many of these residual failings should be blamed on the small and not fully representative training set, rather than on any computational limitations possibly intrinsic to the network. Several tests explored this issue. Subsequent training on much larger training sets pushed performance up to 97.5 percent.

The output module shared by both DECtalk and NETtalk made use of the lucid phonemes in the recorded voice of a fourteen-year-old boy dubbed "Kit the Kid." The computationally driven output in both cases lilts along in a charming fashion faintly reminiscent of a Jamaican accent. It sounds unusual, but it effectively avoids the impression of a mere machine.

Sejnowski and Rosenberg tested the steadily improving output of NETtalk at several stages during its initial training. This provided a recorded sequence of distinct and progressively more intelligible speech samples, a sequence that began with monotonous cooing and babbling when the weights were set at random, and ended with coherent English speech at the end of training. The impact of that recording on academic audiences at technical conferences was profound and lasting. I remember Sejnowski playing that tape to our own weekly cognitive science seminar at UCSD just before he moved his lab here from Hopkins. The diverse audience of perhaps two dozen people, ranging from philosophers to electrical engineers, was bowled over. We loved it. In all, Sejnowski had a high time on the lecture circuit, outlining the architecture of his network and playing the audio tape of its phonetic output to slightly stunned audiences everywhere, including, at one point, the national television audience of ABC's "Good Morning America." Neural nets had made it into the media.

NETtalk, of course, has absolutely no *comprehension* of what it is reading, no grasp whatever of word *meaning*. In that respect it is as dumb as a post. What is intriguing, however, is that it manages to do the job of a complex set of explicit pronunciation rules, several man-years in the formulation, with a single pass through a few hundred neurons knit together by a pattern of connection weights. After all, NETtalk was never given any explicit rules, nor did it have the resources to express them in any case. Repeated exposure to the examples in the training set was its only source of instruction, and readjusting its weights was its only form of response. The prime question then is, how does NETtalk pull it off? How does the network manage to embody the general letter-to-phoneme transformation desired?

Once again, it is the middle layer of cells that holds the key. Recall that the network had to master seventy-nine distinct transformations. If we look at the activation patterns across the middle layer during the trained network's mature operation, we find that each of those seventy-nine transformations is mediated by a standard and proprietary activation vector across the middle layer. (This is a slight oversimplification. Each of the seventy-nine "canonical cases" is actually a small *cloud* of diverse points closely clustered around an average or "prototype" vector. The contextual variation on either side of the focal input letter is what gives rise to this residual diversity.) Each of those seventy-nine vectors can be thought of as one point in the eighty-dimensional activation space of the cells at the middle layer (figure 4.22). Yet again do we find a network coding its learned categories with a set of points in the space of possible activations. To perform the job required, NETtalk had to learn to discriminate seventy-nine distinct cases. It had to configure its weights so as to funnel a wide diversity of input vec-

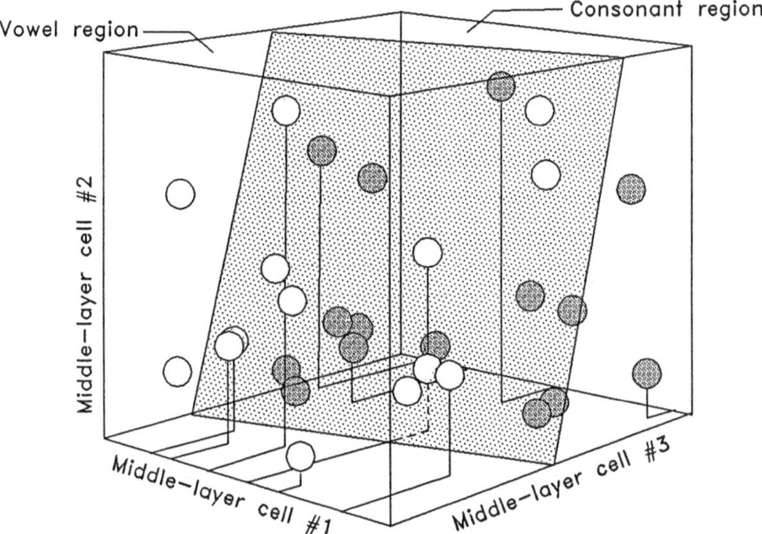

Figure 4.22 The activation space of the cells at the middle layer of NETtalk. Note the seventy-nine distinct points corresponding to the seventy-nine distinct letter-to-phoneme transformations. Only three of the eighty dimensions are shown. Some of the points overlap because the dimensions that would separate them have been suppressed.

tors into exactly seventy-nine distinct output vectors. The appearance of seventy-nine distinct points in figure 4.22 shows that it succeeded.

But there is more. Those points are not scattered at random within the activation space. Analysis revealed an intricate structure that unites them as much as it divides them. Sejnowski and Rosenberg were curious about the mutual proximity of the many points in figure 4.22. In particular, they wanted to know, for each such point, what is its *closest neighbor* in that 80-dimensional vector space? A quickly written program computed all of the mutual distances and identified the thirty-eight pairs of points that were closest together. These represent pairs of input-output transformations that the trained network regards as *most similar* to each other.

The network's pairings are highly intuitive. The middle-layer vector displayed during the "k"-to-/*kuh*/ transform (as in "*k*ick") is very similar to the middle-layer vector displayed during the "c"-to-/*kuh*/ transform (as in "*c*at"). Similarly, the middle-layer vector displayed during the "s"-to-/*zzz*/ transform (as in "bu*s*y") is very similar to the middle-layer vector displayed during the "s"-to-/*sss*/ transform (as in "si*s*sy"). Neither pairing is surprising, since, in written English in general, and in the training text in particular, "k" and "c" usually do appear in orthographic situations that are highly similar, at least when a /*kuh*/ is the appropriate pronunciation. Statistically speaking, "s" and "z" also occur in similar orthographic surroundings. It is precisely such orthographic contexts, and the phonetically relevant similarities between them, that the network becomes sensitive to during the course of its training. A similar lesson is displayed for all of the other pairings as well. You can see them displayed down the rightmost side of the dendogram of figure 4.23.

But there is still more. We can repeat the clustering procedure that produced thirty-eight vector pairs, in order to find out which pairs are closest to which other pairs. This produces about nineteen clusters of four vectors, where each cluster is united by some "family resemblance" or other among its members, a resemblance the network found relevant to performing its task. Repeating this clustering procedure, until all seventy-nine vectors are encompassed, reveals the hierarchical structure of figure 4.23. Notice in particular the fundamental division the network has discovered between the vowels and the consonants. No such distinction was

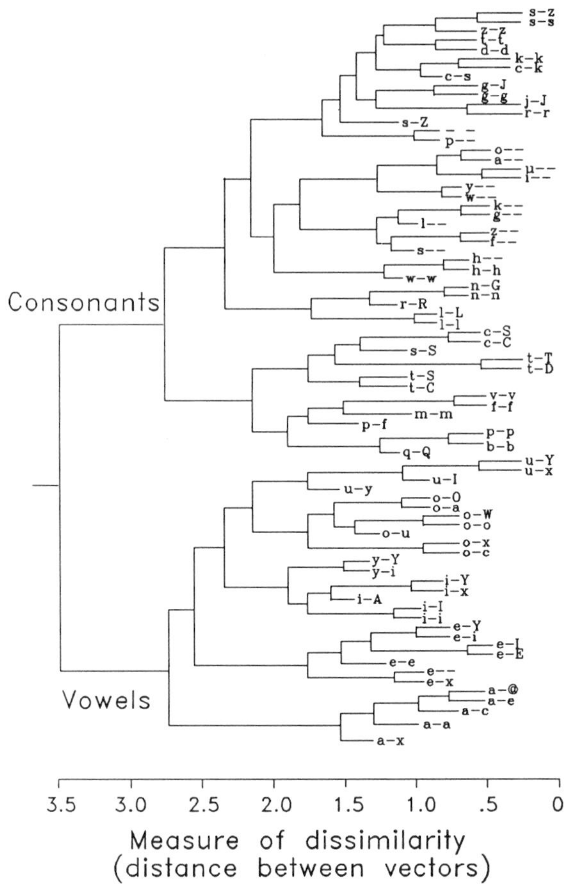

Figure 4.23 A dendogram showing the categorial hierarchy within the middle-layer activation space of NETtalk. The letter-to-phoneme transform for each end branch is indicated at the right. Note the spontaneous and uninstructed division into consonants and vowels. (Adapted from Terry Sejnowski.)

ever made *for* the network. Rather, it discovered that basic distinction on its own, with no source of information beyond the statistical features implicit in its training text and the steady pressure of the backpropagation procedure, a procedure that slowly forced the network to become sensitive to the orthographic features involved.

What we are looking at in figure 4.23 is the *conceptual framework* that learning has produced within NETtalk. It displays the *system* of interrelated categories or *concepts* whose activation is responsible for NETtalk's sophisticated input-output behavior. If you wanted to glimpse some of the fundamental features of the mind's cognitive activity made visible in some aspect of a physical brain's activity, you are starting to see them clearly in figure 4.23.

This example extends the simple pattern noted in the sonar network and the face-recognition network, where the nets' activation space was partitioned into two categories, or into three. NETtalk's space has been partitioned into seventy-nine distinct categories, and you can begin to see how such categorial sophistication can further explode in networks boasting millions of cells per layer instead of a mere eighty, networks facing still more complex transformational problems. NETtalk's example is instructive for the final reason that it embodies a genuine *skill*. It is not just an abstract model. When hooked to a speech synthesizer, it produces actual *behavior* in the form of voiced speech. This highlights an important fact. After all, the ultimate point of having a conceptual framework, for humans as well as animals, is to produce and steer well-tuned behavior.

Vector Coding at the Output End: Sensorimotor Coordination

Picture a traditional wooden puppet, all hinges, floppy joints, and many supporting strings. Without those strings, or without a skilled puppeteer to guide them, the puppet must collapse, lifeless, into an angular heap. The human body's situation is little different from the puppet's. Without the continuous tension of the thousands of muscles attached to its many bones, and without the brain's continuous direction of those changing tensions, we too would collapse in a heap. So how does the brain keep us upright? By sending neural activations down the very long axons of the motor nerves in the massive spinal cord. Those axons synapse onto the many ventral neurons that project out between the doughnut-like bones stacked on top of each other to make up the spinal column. Those long axons eventually synapse in turn onto the individual muscle fibers deep in the muscles themselves. Here the arriving neural activations cause each muscle to increase or decrease its level of tension.

This accounts for the causal connection, but it leaves open the most important questions. How does the brain manage to coordinate the thousands of muscles it controls? How does it produce a *coherent* configuration of the body, such as taking aim at a distant target with a bow and arrow? And how does it direct a coherent *sequence* of bodily configurations, so as to produce walking, talking, catching a fly ball, and playing the flute?

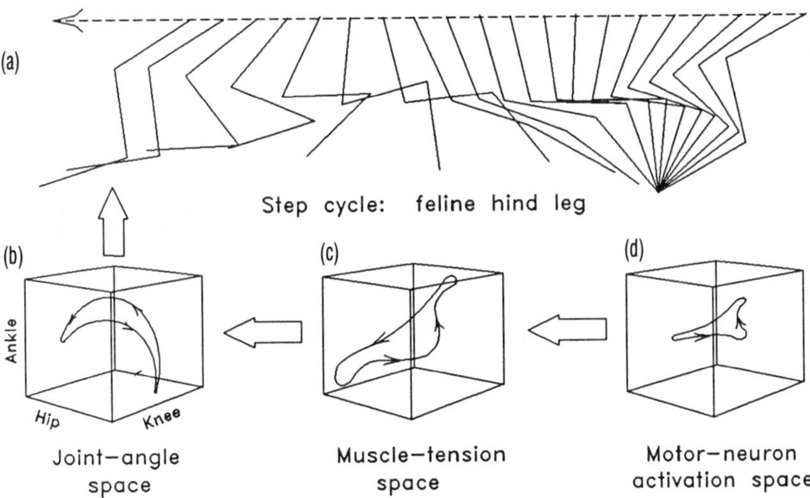

Figure 4.24 (a) The sequence of hind-leg positions, in real space, of a loping cat through one step cycle. (b) A joint-angle configuration space for a cat's hind leg. The closed loop represents the sequence of configuration-space positions through one step cycle. (c) A muscle-tension space for a cat's hind leg: one complete cycle. (d) A motor-neuron activation space for a cat's hind leg: one complete cycle. Note that (d) causes (c), which causes (b), which looks like (a).

By *vector coding,* of course. What has proved to be so spectacularly useful at the sensory-input end of the system proves to be just as useful at the motor-output end. In order to control a large population of distinct muscles, the brain uses a vector-coding system that sends to them, all at once, a pattern of activation levels. Each element in that activation pattern arrives at the appropriate muscle fiber within the larger population of muscles, and dictates its tension according to the magnitude of that one arriving element. The result is that an entire population of muscles is simultaneously orchestrated to assume a collective configuration of tensions, such that the body draws back the bow, reaches up for the fly ball, or touches its finger to the tip of its nose.

This means that you and I can deploy the same descriptive resources already familiar from the preceding pages: coding spaces, vector similarity, and vector-to-vector transformations. We can see the first two of these resources at work immediately in figure 4.24. A loping cat's hind leg moves through the sequence of real-space positions depicted in (*a*). That same sequence, represented in an abstract "joint-angle" space, appears as the closed loop in (*b*). The cat's leg configuration "moves" along that loop because the leg is driven by a set of muscles, whose ongoing tension behavior appears as a closed loop in (*c*). That muscle behavior is driven in turn by a sequence of motor-neuron activation vectors, whose path in activation space appears in (*d*).

That sequence originates in the brain, of which more in a moment. For now, notice that *similar* things, whether they be leg positions or activation patterns, are again represented by points that are *close together* in the relevant coding space. Notice also that the cat's leg has many more muscles than can be represented with only three dimensions, and there are many more motor neurons as well. This is our familiar graphical problem, encountered way back with the introduction of taste coding, of having too many dimensions to portray adequately in a picture. But the brain doesn't care about our graphical problems. It commands millions of motor neurons and orchestrates thousands of muscles, almost effortlessly. Because high-dimensional vector coding is the perfect solution to a complex problem.

Just how perfect a solution it is emerges when we address the problem of how to tune a creature's physical behavior to suit the creature's current perception of the environment. The problem is how to produce behavior that is appropriate or intelligent relative to a perceived situation. To give it a final description, this is the problem of *sensorimotor coordination*.

You can probably see what is coming. If the external environment is represented in the brain with high-dimensional coding vectors; and if the brain's "intended" bodily behavior is represented in its motor nerves with high-dimensional coding vectors; then what intelligence requires is some appropriate or well-tuned *transformation* of sensory vectors into motor vectors!

What sort of mechanism might perform such a task? We already know the answer: a multi-layered neural network, with a well-configured matrix of synaptic connection weights. But just to drive the point home, let us observe the answer in action.

Let us take a deliberately simple creature confronting a very basic coordination problem. The crab in figure 4.25 has two eyes that rotate only about their vertical axes. It represents the location of visually fixated edible tidbits by an internal activation vector that has only two elements: one activation level for each eye's position angle. This maximally simple sensory vector represents the joint positions of both eyes, and thus their two sightlines, and thus their

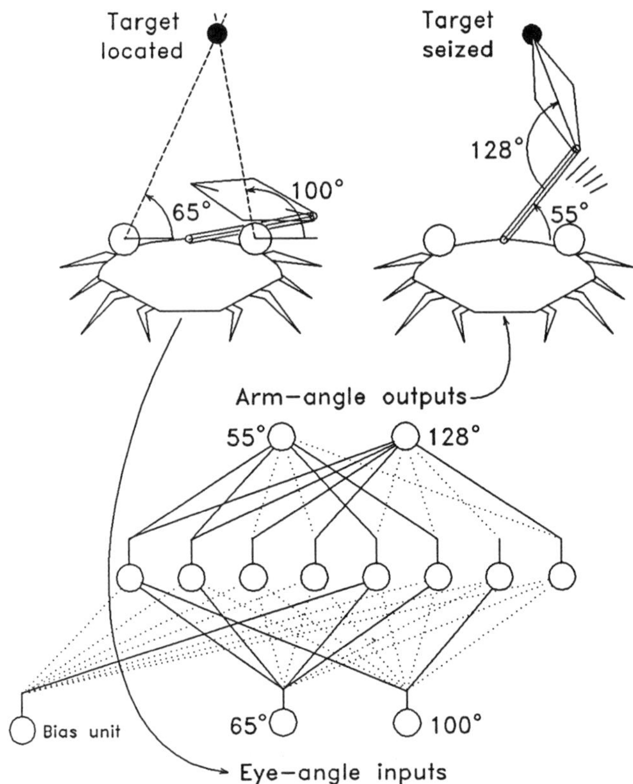

Figure 4.25 A network for coordinating the crab's motor output with its sensory input. (a) The crab's eye-angle representation of an edible target's spatial position is the input vector to (b) a simple network that transforms the input into a joint-angle motor vector specifying (c) the arm configuration that will successfully seize the target object at its perceived location. In (b), the excitatory connections are shown with solid lines. The inhibitory connections are shown with dotted lines.

intersection point, where lies the edible tidbit. That is how the crab represents the position in space of any external object: with a two-element eye-angle activation vector.

The crab also has a two-jointed arm with a pincer forearm. For the pincer to do him any good, he must be able to position his arm so as to locate the end of his pincer at the spot where the edible tidbit resides, namely, the spot where his two sightlines currently intersect. That arm position requires a unique pair of angles at the shoulder joint and the elbow joint. Let us suppose that the crab can position his arm by sending an appropriate two-element *motor* activation vector down its motor nerves. The elements of this vector must each represent, and through the crab's muscle spindles must actually produce, one of the two joint angles required.

The problem now is how to *transform* any incoming sensory vector into its appropriate outgoing motor vector, into a motor vector that will position the crab's arm so that its pincer tip meets the intersection point of his eyes' two sightlines. Can a feedforward network solve this sort of problem? Very easily. The tiny network pictured in figure 4.25 was trained on a hundred representative input-output pairs, and it topped out at an average error level of plus or minus 7 percent in the joint angles it produced for a broad sample of visual targets. This level of performance, note well, yields what is still a very clumsy crab. But the important point is that even a small and rudimentary neural network can successfully *approximate* the desired input-output function. And a rough approximation may be all a living creature needs. In any case, a larger network can approximate the desired function as closely as you please.

We are here observing our first example of coordinating the behavior of movable limbs in order to respond intelligently to some perceived environmental circumstance. The crab reaches out for a perceived object. It assumes a position in its "motor space" that corresponds to the position of an object in its "sensory space." This is a cartoon example, to be sure, both in the creature coordinated and in the network performing the transformation. But the lesson it contains is highly general and reaches far beyond the cartoons at hand. Whether a creature's sensory space has two dimensions or two million; and whether a creature's motor space has two dimensions or two thousand; the coordination of its behavior with its perception will require that the creature's brain execute principled transformations of sensory vectors into motor vectors.

This is where intelligence begins: in the brain's capacity for executing principled sensorimotor transforms, in its capacity for doing the right thing in its perceived circumstance. Here is where skills reside, where know-how is embodied, where smarts are buried. And as we know well from the preceding pages of this essay, this know-how is embodied in the personal configuration of the brain's synaptic weights. Even if the creature is too small or too primitive to have a well-defined brain, whatever intelligence it has will nevertheless be embodied in the configuration of synaptic weights within its scattered neuronal clusters or "ganglia." The vector-processing model here illustrated is as appropriate to ants, sea slugs, and crabs as it is to humans. A large and well-defined brain is just evolution's latest and highest achievement in sensorimotor coordination, not its earliest or only example.

Can this really be all there is to it? Is intelligence nothing more than the capacity for sophisticated vector transformation? That may seem to have been the slant of my argument. But no. At least one major piece of the puzzle has so far been left out of the account. I have worked hard at explaining and praising the virtues of purely feedforward networks, because their extraordinary power should not be underestimated, and because a clear appreciation of what they do and how they do it is essential if we are to appreciate the next step in the story. But they have a profound shortcoming that is simplicity itself: they are ill suited to represent *time.* No creature that lacks a sense of unfolding time can enjoy the peculiar form of cognition and consciousness that animals and humans possess. We must explore how this limitation can be overcome.

5 Recurrent Networks: The Conquest of Time

The Temporal Dimension of Behavior

Behavior is typically extended in time. Actions such as reaching, running, and talking each involve a closely orchestrated *sequence* of distinct bodily positions. A real brain guiding a real body must generate, not a single motor vector for one-time delivery to its many muscles, but an ongoing sequence of motor vectors whose changes over time will produce the right bodily changes over time.

In this respect, the nervous system never rests. In repose, one might think, or perhaps in sleep, we would be relieved of the necessity to emit a constant stream of motor vectors. But even here the activity is ceaseless. The nervous system must keep the muscles of the diaphragm oscillating faithfully, lest we suffocate. It must keep the heart beating, lest we expire. Generating vector sequences is not an occasional or late-developing luxury in a nervous system. It's a primordial necessity.

And a necessity beyond that. The story of the artificial crab's coordination, completed just a few moments ago, is plainly a scam where time is concerned. The story of the cat's hind leg was much closer to the mark, since it portrayed a sequence of positions for all three systems: neural, muscular, and skeletal. The crab's coordination, while genuine, was importantly unrealistic. The little network of figure 4.25 will indeed compute an appropriate *target* configuration for the crab's arm. But getting that arm, from wherever it presently might be, *to* that target configuration was an issue quietly finessed in the story provided. I there gave the impression that a single motor vector would suddenly induce a set of continuing tensions in the relevant muscles, a set of tensions such that—sproing!—the arm would simply spring to a new position, a position that was stable relative to those tensions.

To be sure, one could make a little robot crab to work in precisely that way. But after its spring-driven arrival in the target region, the slightly massive arm would probably oscillate around the target configuration before settling down. Most important, it would probably knock the edible tidbit completely out of reach with its first spastic lunge. If we wish to spare our little crab a lot of frustration and social embarrassment, we would do well to give it some more genteel skills to bring to the dinner table. In particular, we need to provide it with the means to compute, not just target positions in joint-angle space, but also appropriate *trajectories* in joint-angle space, trajectories that lead safely and without overshot to the ultimate target position.

But what about NETtalk? Isn't that a purely feed*forward* network? And doesn't it produce a *sequence* of output vectors, the vectors that make the speech synthesizer produce coherent speech? Yes it is, and yes it does. But whereas each phonetic output is generated within the network, the sequence in which the outputs appear is owed not to any computation within the network itself, but entirely to the spatial order among the input letters, and to the temporal order in which they are presented to the network. Present them to the net in reverse order, and the net will respond by talking backwards! It doesn't know anything about temporal order. It responds to each seven-letter input completely independently of whatever other seven-letter strings might precede or follow it, and it produces a single phoneme as output independently of whatever other phonemes might precede or follow it. As Immanuel Kant would put it, were he with us today, NETtalk displays a temporal sequence of computations, but no computation of any temporal sequences.

What is it that feedforward networks are missing? What needs to be added to bring time into representational reach? Two things: some form of sensitivity to specific events in the recent past, and some mechanism by which that information can shape current cognitive activity. Bluntly, we need some form of *short-term memory.*

The model networks already possess one form of memory, of course: the knowledge or skill embodied in their overall synaptic-weight configuration. But that form of memory is blind to the details of specific past events. A stone worn hollow by an endless sequence of falling water droplets bears dramatic witness to its many encounters over the years. But the specific shape, size, rotation, temperature, pH, and timing of any *individual* water droplet is information that is utterly lost in the record of the stone's final shape. The synaptic shaping of a neural network is a similar process. Its final configuration contains no record of individual inputs and outputs, nor of the zillion synaptic nudgings that brought it to its current configuration. It needs some additional mechanism if it is to grasp explicitly specific events in its recent past.

How might a feedforward network be given this capacity? On this matter, let us look at the biological brain itself, and ask what prominent features of the brain are missing in the model networks examined so far? The question, once asked, is immediately embarrassing, since there are so many respects in which the models fall short of the reality. Yet one prominent feature stands out from all the rest, if only because it is a large-scale structural feature.

In the model networks to this point, the distinct neural populations or layers are connected in a spatial sequence of axonal projections that feeds forward, always forward. The brain shows this pattern prominently enough, but it also displays massive axonal projections from "later" or "higher" populations back to "earlier" populations. The familiar feedforward pathways are called "ascending" pathways. The *feedbackwards* pathways are called "descending" or "recurrent" pathways.

The brain must love them: it grows so very many of them. It is a rare neural population that sports no descending projections at all. In some cases, the descending pathways that connect two neuronal populations even outnumber the ascending pathways. You will recall that your LGN projects a massive cable of ascending axons forward to your visual cortex. Curiously, the neurons in your visual cortex project back roughly ten times as many *descending* axons to make synaptic connections within the LGN. If the behavior of one's cortical neurons is dictated by the behavior of the LGN neurons, as projected up the ascending pathways, the anatomical and functional reverse is also true, and to an even greater degree. The pattern evident here is widespread throughout the brain.

Very well. So descending pathways are there in the brain in droves. So how do they solve the problems of short-term memory and of representing sequences of events in time? As follows.

A feedforward system is a pipeline, a pipeline of information. The farther along in the pipeline one samples the flow of information, the farther back in the past must that sampled information have first entered the pipeline, and the farther back in the past must lie the events that the sampled information depicts. Since a recurrent axon originates in a cell farther along in the pipeline, a descending or recurrent pathway therefore makes information about the

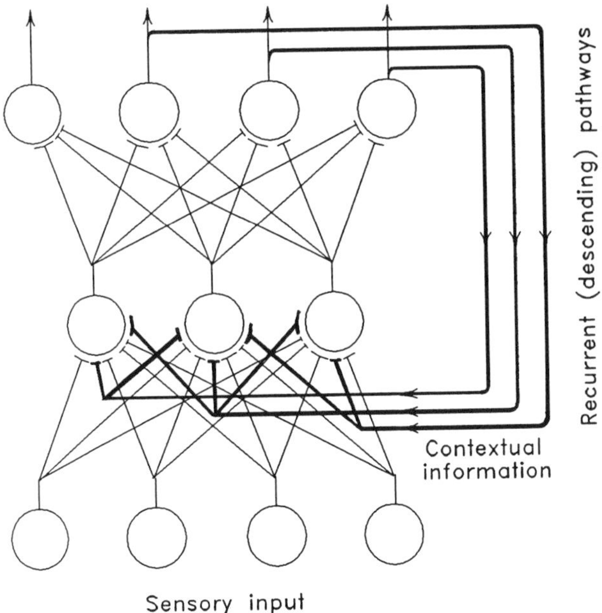

Figure 5.1 A simple feedforward configuration with three descending pathways added. The neuronal activation levels at layer 2 are thus controlled, not only by the activation vectors arriving from the input layer, but also by the activation vectors arriving from layer 3, which vectors contain (processed) information about the prior state of layer 2, and, indirectly, about the prior state of layer 1 as well.

network's *past* activity available for *current* processing, specifically, at the layer of neurons where the descending pathway touches down for a landing.

Recurrent pathways thus sustain a rudimentary form of short-term memory. They make the creature's immediate cognitive past continually available to it for processing together with incoming sensory information about the present. Information that passed by layer 2 just a split second ago can be brought back to layer 2, usually in modified form, to be added into the current mix. This allows the creature to represent its current situation in a way that takes into account the situation that immediately preceded it. As figure 5.1 illustrates, layer 2 is continuously in receipt of information both from its sensory periphery at layer 1 *and* from layers farther along in the pipeline, most obviously, from layer 3.

With these descending pathways added, the network is no longer a prisoner of the infinitely thin Plane of the Present. Its cognitive grasp now extends at least a few fractions of a second into the Extended Past.

This is good, but it gets much better. Let us turn to the second question: how does the brain actually *represent* sequences of specific states-of-affairs in time? This question probably does not have a single answer: almost certainly there is more than one way in which the brain codes temporal information. And yet, one of those ways is obvious, and you have known the answer to this question ever since you first contemplated the TV-screen analogy in the opening chapter. Just as a temporal sequence of pixel-patterns on a TV screen represents some temporal sequence of events in the world, so does a temporal sequence of activation vectors in the visual cortex, for example, represent an unfolding sequence of events in the world.

But then how is this different from NETtalk? It too displays a sequence of activation vectors, at least so long as we continue to pump text in at its input layer. This last qualification locates the crucial difference. A purely feedforward system such as NETtalk cannot generate any vector sequences on its own. It is wholly dependent on its input. But a recurrent network can *generate* complex sequences of activation vectors all by itself, even if and even when its input layers fall silent.

It is not hard to see how it might do this. If the network of figure 5.1 can supply its own input to the cells at layer 2, there is no clear reason why it should *ever* stop cycling vectors around that (partially) closed circuit, even when the input cells are quiet. In fact, that is precisely what many recurrent networks do, if you configure their weights just so and then kick them into activity with some suitable input vector. They quickly fall into some stable cycle of activation vectors and then repeat that cycle endlessly, or at least until some new vector at the input layer jars them out of it. Such periodic behavior is called a *limit cycle*. (The adjective "limit" just means that such a cycle is stable around its path, that any cyclical behavior very close to it will tend to converge on exactly that cycle as its limiting form.)

Limit cycles are vital for orchestrating one's muscles to perform many familiar behaviors. At first, such cyclical monotony may strike one as a maniacal defect, but it looks different when you realize that this is what keeps your heart muscle pumping, faithfully and without pause, for three score and ten. Breathing has a similar source. So do swimming, crawling, walking, running, flying, chewing, and almost every other repetitive or periodic behavior you can think of.

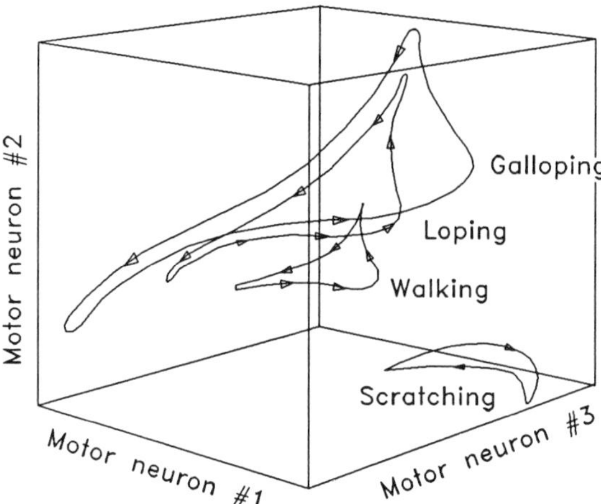

Figure 5.2 A (partial) activation space for the motor neurons that control a cat's left hind leg. Note the four distinct limit cycles or activation sequences that produce walking, loping, galloping, and scratching.

As a coding device, the limit cycle is a direct extension of an idea already familiar to you. From the many examples already explored, you know how a *point* in an activation space can represent some complex sensory reality, or code for some complex configuration of muscle tensions as output. A limit cycle is just a continuous *sequence* of exactly such points, an ongoing *line* in an activation space, a line that bends around and returns to its starting point to make a closed loop.

You observed a limit cycle several pages back, in figure 4.24d, where the closed loop in neuronal activation space depicts the special sequence of motor vectors that drive the collected muscles of the loping cat's left hind leg. Let us reprise that little activation space here, blown up a little, and take a deeper look at its occasional and quite various contents (figure 5.2).

The limit cycle that produces loping is there as before, but the figure now illustrates several other possible limit cycles. The smaller and slower cycle (as indicated by the closer spacing of the arrowheads) is the cycle that produces the cat's slow, sauntering walk—or anyhow, the left hind leg's contribution to that walk. The larger and much faster loop is the limit cycle that produces a terrified, flat-out gallop, as when the cat flees a pursuing dog. Finally, the smallest and most quickly repeating limit cycle is what produces a scratching-behind-the-left-ear motion.

There are many other behaviors possible for a cat's hind leg, but each one of them will be produced by a characteristic path or sequence of activations in the output space of the relevant recurrent network. We may also note, at last, that these useful paths need not always be closed loops. Not all behavior is periodic. Not all actions are immediately repeated. And not every movement ends where it started.

In fact, most actions are produced by an open line, by a nonreturning trajectory in motor-neuron activation space. For example, you swat a fly on your ear. Where your hand might happen to go after it makes contact is irrelevant to that action. Or you pick up a fork and spear a drumstick from the picnic table. Which child's plate then gets the booty is irrelevant to that action. During the course of a day, an individual's continuous vectorial path in its overall motor-neuron activation space may frequently fall into various prototypical cycles—brushing one's hair, sharpening a pencil, riding a bike. But just as often that path will follow a jerky series of *short prototypical line-elements*, zig-zagging here and there across activation space as one puts on the oven gloves, opens the oven door, takes out the sizzling chicken, puts it on the counter, shuts the oven door, takes off the gloves, puts them by the sink, rips off a sheet of aluminum foil, folds it around the chicken, ... well, you get the point. Motor competence requires the production of many prototypical *lines* as well as prototypical loops.

Of course, no recurrent network can do all of this, or any of it, unless its synaptic weights have somehow been shaped into an appropriate global configuration. The good news is that recurrent networks can be trained as surely as feedforward ones. Backpropagation is applicable here also. And when they are, they open a new universe, at least to neural network modelers. For the nets can be trained not just to discriminate a timeless or unchanging physical pattern, such as a snapshot of a face. They can also be trained to discriminate a standard sequence of physical configurations such as might make up a wink, a handshake, a bouncing ball, a cat stalking, or two people dancing. And they can be trained not only to compute an appropriate motor end-point given some perceptual opportunity. They can also be trained to compute a smooth sequence of limb positions, such as will take those limbs deftly and gently to that end-point configuration without overshot or intervening collision.

With the addition of *descending* pathways to the basic feedforward architecture, the nature of the game is fundamentally changed. The external structures graspable by a recurrent network include the endless patterns in *time* as well as the endless patterns in space. Despite the fact that its short-term "memory" reaches only a fraction of a second into the past, a well-trained recurrent network can nonetheless represent temporal sequences of arbitrary length. It has this capability because it can generate, by recurrent modulation of its own vectorial activity, long sequences of activation vectors all on its own.

Recognizing Causal Processes

This introduction just completed, to the *temporally extended* activity of recurrent networks, was focused primarily on motor activity and on the role of vector sequences in the production of bodily behavior. There were at least two reasons for starting there. The problem of motor control is an easy place to make the basic properties of recurrent architectures clear. Beginning with motor control also reflects the evolutionary primacy of this salient role of recurrency. Making a heart beat, making water pulse past the gills, making a serpentine body swim, these are primordial functions indeed. But the various motoric functions of a recurrent network are far from being its only functions. Recurrent pathways and vectorial sequences have just as dramatic a role to play at the input end of the system, specifically, in the domain of perception. Let us see.

If having a feedforward neural architecture is what allows one to discriminate instances of prototypical *things*, then having a recurrent neural architecture is what provides one with the further capacity to discriminate instances of prototypical *processes*. In the former case, recognition occurs when something close to a prototypical activation vector is caused to appear across the relevant population of neurons. In the latter case, recognition occurs when something close to a prototypical sequence of activation vectors unfolds across the relevant population of neurons, when the activation vectors carve out, over time, a special line or path in the relevant space. Figure 5.3 highlights the relevant contrast.

We have already seen how recurrent networks can generate a wide variety of behaviors. But they are clearly just as necessary if one is to perceive and *recognize* those sorts of behaviors when they are displayed by other creatures. To return to the ocean floor,

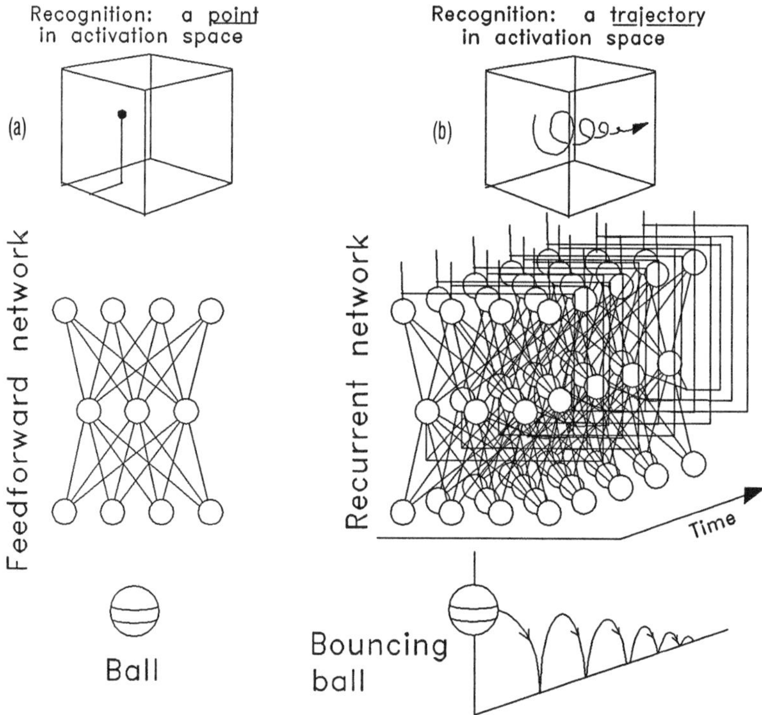

Figure 5.3 (a) Recognizing a ball, *qua* instance of a type of static object. (b) Recognizing a bouncing trajectory, *qua* instance of a type of causal or law-governed process.

almost any aquatic creature will need to be able to recognize a swimming behavior, and to discriminate its leisurely and non-threatening instances from its more frantic fleeing and attacking modes. In a world of systematic camouflage, each predator must be able to recognize the characteristic pace or gait of its typical prey's locomotion. And whether one is predator or prey, it is characteristic *movement* that gives one's adversary away at least as often as does characteristic shape or markings. Think of cases where a creature's spatial structure is mostly hidden in the murk or the faint light, for example, but where its special form of movement allows immediate identification.

The recognition of prototypical sequences in the world, however—any sequences at all—requires the possession of recurrent pathways in the recognizing network. Those pathways are essential for the production of an appropriate vectorial sequence within the network. Recognition requires prior training as well, or prior synaptic configuration of some sort, in order to produce the framework of waiting categories whose selective activation constitutes the network's recognition of the perceived sequence of behavior. Just as feedforward networks have their activation spaces configured into a richly structured hierarchy of categories, so also do recurrent networks. The difference is that, in their case, the categories often have a temporal dimension: the categories are often lines instead of mere points. And just as perceptual discrimination in feedforward networks consists in the perceptually initiated activation of an appropriate activation vector, perceptual discrimination in a recurrent network often consists in the perceptually initiated activation of an appropriate vectorial sequence; a sequence whose unfolding, however, is owed primarily to the recurrent activity of the trained network itself rather than to the external stimuli it receives.

This allows us to recognize so much of what is important in real life: the gait of an approaching toddler, the flow of liquid from a tilted container, the arc of a drumstick arriving to your plate, the swing of a baseball bat, the envelopment of an embrace, the rolling of an eye, the blinking of a left-turn signal, and a hundred thousand other prototypical movements that come to have a place within the conceptual library of any normally socialized human.

I mentioned earlier that recurrent pathways provide access into the network's immediate past. You will now appreciate that a recurrent network's capacity for generating prototypical event sequences gives it a window onto the *future* as well. For unlike the case of motor generation, perceptual recognition does not require that the internal vectorial sequence unfold at the same pace as the external process represented. To the contrary, the more the creature can accelerate or foreshorten its internal representational sequences, the sooner it can anticipate the future events that are about to befall it.

As long as the world displays a learnable variety of law-governed behaviors or causal processes, and as long as the network can generate a foreshortened representational sequence from its perception of the early stages of those behaviors or processes, then so long will the network be able to predict future events. Once trained to initiate such internal sequences, it can begin *now* to generate behaviors, such as flight or interception, that will serve its interests in the immediate future.

How *far* into the future its cognition can reach is dependent on at least two things: the temporal length and reliability of the prototypical causal processes actually contained in the world, and the capacity of the network to learn them and subsequently to discriminate their early stages. A boxer's appreciation that he is about to be struck by an incoming left jab lies close to one end of the anticipatory spectrum. An astronomer's appreciation that the Sun will stop shining in about 5 billion years lies close to the other. In between these extremes lies most of a normal human's practical anticipatory life.

In all three cases, however, the temporal insight has the same source: the vectorial sequences generated within a well-trained recurrent network. Without these, we would have no concept of temporal extension or of causal processes at all. We would be oblivious to one of the most fundamental and important dimensions of reality. With them, however, a cognitive creature can aspire to see just as far into Time as it can into Space.

Ambiguous Figures and Recurrent Modulation

We are not yet done with recurrent pathways, nor with the cognitive skills they make possible. Descending neural pathways play a major role in a further type of cognitive capacity, one essential to our getting by in a confusing and ambiguous world. It is also the source of much entertainment and amusement, as we will see. Consider the pair of ambiguous figures in figure 5.4. Each one can be interpreted or seen in two quite different ways. The first can be seen as a rabbit facing right, or as a duck facing left. The two finger-like appendages then appear as a pair of ears or as an open beak,

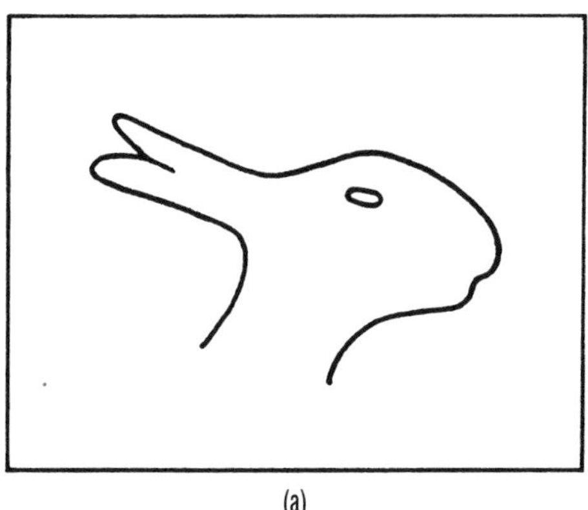

(a)

(b)

Figure 5.4 Ambiguous perceptual figures. (a) The duck/rabbit. (b) The old/young woman.

respectively. The second figure can be seen as an old woman's face in close portrait, looking left; or as a young woman's head and upper body, with her head turned largely away from us. The young woman's left ear and jaw line confront us, and her tiny nose is just visible past her left cheek. These two figures illustrate what a million other examples might have illustrated equally well: that the way an object is perceived is not determined solely by the external stimulus it presents to our senses. It is determined, at least sometimes and at least in part, by the antecedent cognitive state, educational background, or frame of mind of the perceiver.

This phenomenon of alternative recognitions of the very same perceptual situation poses a severe problem for purely feedforward networks. Here's why. To train up a feedforward network to any cognitive capacity is, as we saw, to impose a general input-output function upon it. But a function, by definition, always has a *unique* output for any given input, not a variety of them, depending on how it happens to feel that day. A purely feedforward network, therefore, cannot possibly display the kind of interpretive plasticity that we humans display in confronting ambiguous inputs.

Recurrent networks, however, most certainly can. And quite possibly their recurrency holds the explanation of our own systematic tolerance of perceptual ambiguity, and of our considerable skills in surmounting it. Certainly we have descending axonal pathways in abundance, in all of the perceptual modalities, and most especially in vision and hearing. Let us explore how they might contribute to the capacity at issue.

Glance back at the elementary recurrent network of figure 5.1. That figure shows how the coding vectors produced at layer 2 are a function of the input received from *two* quite distinct sources: the coding vectors at the network's sensory periphery, and the simultaneous coding vectors across the network's neuronal population(s) at some higher level(s) of processing. Given our earlier description of the problem posed, you can see that this is at least in the neighborhood of what we need. Let's pursue it further.

If the recurrent activity arriving at layer 2 is such as to tilt its vectorial activity *already* in the general direction of a rabbit vector, then the input of figure 5.4a will be much more likely to result in the activation of a rabbit vector over any other. Alternatively, if the recurrent activity tilts layer 2 toward a duck vector, then the input of figure 5.4a will almost certainly result in that activation pattern instead. Here the cognitive activity at layer 2 is steered by information (or *mis*information) from sources other than the sensory periphery. There is thus no mystery that identical sensory inputs should occasionally result in quite different vectorial representations farther up the hierarchy of visual processing. In a recurrent network, evidently, the hidden hand of prior cognitive bias will occasionally play a nontrivial role.

These classically ambiguous figures, however, illustrate only part of our capacity for handling ambiguity. These examples are nicely bimodal; they have exactly two equally salient and equally stable interpretations. Other examples are more daunting. Sometimes we look at something and see nothing at all. Then, after mulling for awhile, we suddenly recognize what is before us. Can recurrency throw any light on this phenomenon? It can indeed. Watch.

Suppose now that the perceptual vector arriving at layer 2 from layer 1 happens to be degraded or confused in some way or other, sufficiently degraded that it fails to activate, at layer 2, the prototypical pattern for which the network has been thoroughly trained, the pattern that an *un*degraded perceptual vector would most surely activate. You may remember (from Cottrell's face-recognition example) that a trained network, even a purely feedforward network, has a strong tendency to "complete" input vectors that are slightly degraded (remember the occluded face of figure 3.6). But here I am asking you to suppose that the input on this occasion is too degraded to be rescued by this feature alone.

Despite all this, the degraded input might still be rescued, and might still result in the activation of the appropriate prototype vector at layer 2, if the recurrent activity arriving via the descending pathways can in some way make good the deficit in the original perceptual input. And plainly it can. It need only provide a background vectorial input to layer 2 that, independently of the input from layer 1, would produce a feeble activation pattern across layer 2 that is *already* leaning in the direction of the appropriate prototype. That recurrent activity would thus "tilt the playing field" in a certain cognitive direction. It might tilt it sufficiently that even the degraded input from layer 1 would then be adequate to push layer 2 the rest of the way toward the appropriate prototype vector.

Plainly there is danger in this process. By thus biasing the vectorial activity at layer 2, the recurrent activity may lead to the production of prototype vectors that are flatly *in*appropriate to the external reality. The recurrent activity may represent a wholly false

Figure 5.5 A highly degraded perceptual input. See the text for the correct interpretation.

take on the situation. On the other hand, if the higher levels of the network happen to contain *accurate* information about the network's current situation, they can provide relevant and valuable information to layer 2 that might be missing in the sensory signal alone. Let us look at some real examples.

Prepare once more to be the subject of a neuropsychological experiment. This time we will examine the effect, on your visual perception, of collateral information arriving at your visual layers by way of pathways that descend from higher, *non*visual cognitive layers. We start with an easy example, so easy, in fact, that you may not *need* any descending information to achieve activation of the right prototype.

Take a look at the scattered splotches in figure 5.5 (now, that is, before reading any further). Most people initially see nothing at all in this figure. But I will now provide you with some collateral information of a nonpictorial kind, information that will initially get represented in your discursive or linguistic cognitive centers rather than in your visual centers. This information, or some distillation thereof, will make its way down the relevant descending pathways to your visual centers. And it will there make good the deficit in the degraded input of the figure. Here goes.

You are looking at a Dalmatian dog—the white-with-black-spots breed associated with hunters and fire stations—walking across a sun-lit field. The dog is smack in the center of the picture, with its head down sniffing at the ground, walking to the left and slightly away from you. You can just see its left ear hanging down, and its

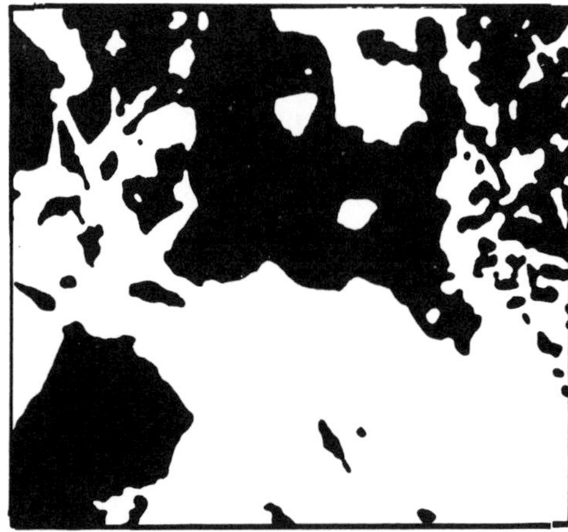

Figure 5.6 A highly degraded perceptual input. See the text for the correct interpretation. (Adapted from Russell Hanson.)

black collar. In the left background is a small ornamental tree with a shadow underneath it.

After a few moments perusal, very likely the sniffing dog will pop out of the chaos and the scene will display a structure and a coherence that was utterly lacking in its initial presentation. The figure's appearance will then be dramatically different, and it will be difficult or impossible to see it again in its initial confusion. You have managed to activate your spotted dog vector, despite the marginal input. Behold your recurrent pathways at work, and marvel at the perceptual transformation they can effect.

This example introduces a multitude. Consider a slightly harder one. But let me first give you some misdirection. Look at the snowy mountain scene in figure 5.6. (Right now, before reading any further.) Of course, there is no snowy mountain scene there at all, but very likely I have succeeded in tilting your visual centers *away* from the correct interpretation. Probably you see nothing at all save a bunch of black splotches. Let us now supply the proper background information in hopes of activating your recurrent pathways and tickling the relevant population of cells in your visual system toward a prototypical pattern. (I don't know which of the several candidates *is* the relevant population, but it is unlikely to be any earlier in your processing hierarchy than the visual cortex at the rear of your brain, and unlikely to be much later.)

You are looking at a picture of a bearded man, rather Christlike in his dress and general appearance. His head is at the top-most center

Figure 5.7 A highly degraded perceptual input. See the text for the correct interpretation. (Adapted from Irvin Rock.)

one-sixth of the picture area, looking directly at you, and his forehead is cropped across the middle by the top border. Bright sunlight is streaming down from the upper right, highlighting one side of his nose and leaving both eye cavities in shadow. The other side of his nose and face is also in shadow, except for a small spot of his right cheek. The bottom half of the picture contains his shoulders and upper body, which is facing slightly to your right. (If even extended perusal of this figure fails to find the face, it may help, as a last resort, to isolate the small facial region by placing your fingers on either side and underneath it. But this would be cheating, relative to our experiment, because it would strictly speaking change your sensory input vector.)

Once again, collateral information tilts the cognitive playing field to which the sensory input arrives, and the resulting activity yields a quite different cognitive result. Look now at a final example (figure 5.7), harder still to make any sense of at first, but easiest of all to recognize once the collateral information makes its way down the descending pathways and tilts your visual centers in a specific vectorial direction. If fact, you will kick yourself for not recognizing the scene earlier, despite its initial chaos.

You are looking at a man on a horse. The horse's head is visible at the upper left, facing left, with its two small ears sticking up. Its neck extends almost straight down below it, with the line swelling slightly at its chest. Its right front leg is lifted up while the left is planted. You can see the outline of the bottom of the rider's right boot sticking out from beyond the horse's chest. The rider's left boot is in a corresponding position on this side of the horse. The bushy tail droops down at the lower right of the picture, just behind the animal's hind legs. And you may see the rider's left forearm and elbow just to the right of the horse's neck, holding the reins, or perhaps it is a drooping lance. In the end, and from all this scatter, there emerges Don Quixote on Rocinante!

The point here illustrated is once again the brain's descending control of, or influence over, the vectorial activity occurring at the neuronal layers close to its own sensory periphery. Bluntly, it has some nontrivial control over how it sees and hears things. I emphasize this point with three examples because the phenomenon is of paramount importance for understanding human cognition, as we will see repeatedly in the coming chapters.

Recurrent networks also display a feature mentioned briefly on my opening page: the feature of being predictable only within statistical limits. The cycling sequences of vector-to-vector transformations within a recurrent network are *nonlinear* in the intuitive sense that they do not "follow a straight line." A recurrent network's unfolding path in activation space is a winding path—sometimes curving gently, sometimes zig-zagging sharply—a path that is at times stable against small perturbations, and at other times shows an exquisite sensitivity to infinitesimally small influences from any quarter. That is to say, a nonlinear system is one in which, at least occasionally, even the tiniest of differences in its current state will quickly be magnified into very large differences in its subsequent state. Since we can never have *infinitely* accurate information about the current state of any physical system, let alone a system of the complexity of a living brain, we are doomed to be forever limited in what we can predict about such a system's unfolding behavior, even if there are, and even if we happen to know, the inviolable laws that govern the system's behavior. Such systems are strictly deterministic, in the sense of being law governed, but they are nevertheless unpredictable, beyond their statistical regularities, by any cognitive system within the same physical universe.

It would be foolish to mistake such (genuine) unpredictability for what philosophers and theologians have often hoped for in the way of free will. That term was typically meant to apply to a human capacity that *transcended* the causal order, whereas the dynamical picture here presented keeps us firmly embedded within the causal order. But it is legitimate to see it as the ground of something extremely important: our capacity, at least occasionally, for genuinely spontaneous activity, for endless and strictly unpredictable variety in the behavior that we display and the cognitive activities that we undergo. This point is as true for the ways in which we perceive the world as it is for the ways in which we behave within it.

Recognition, Theoretical Understanding, and Scientific Progress

In the course of this chapter we have gone from the simplest forms of sensory coding, and the simplest forms of feedforward processing, to vector coding at the scale of many thousands or even millions of neurons, to the emergence of categories and their central prototypes as carefully crafted areas of activation space, and finally to recurrent processing at the level of animal locomotion and even high-level visual interpretation in humans. In part, the climb up this ladder of complexity was motivated as a strategy of useful instruction. It is best to take the simple cases first and then work upward. But it has a deeper motivation. The account of cognition outlined in this chapter deliberately depicts our specifically human cognitive activities as lying on a smooth continuum with the cognition of creatures generally. On the account proposed, we are not playing a different cognitive game from all of the "lesser" creatures. Rather, we are playing the same game, but playing certain aspects of it very much better than other creatures.

There is much about human cognition that remains to be discussed, and future chapters await our attention. In the meantime, however, and in the closing section of this chapter, I hope to underscore my statement of the Continuity Thesis by showing, very briefly, how one of humankind's crowning glories—the activity of scientific theorizing—can also be understood as just a high-level instance of the cognitive activities already examined.

The central phenomenon to be explored here is the brain's *vector completion* of partial or degraded inputs, a completion often aided by the brain's recurrent manipulation of the relevant population of representing neurons. In plain English, it is the phenomenon of your recognizing—perhaps slowly at first, but then suddenly—some unfamiliar, puzzling, or otherwise problematic situation as being an instance or example of something well known to you. The preceding section provided three fairly humble examples of this phenomenon. It outlined how a neural network with recurrent pathways would naturally give rise to both a plasticity in its perceptual processing, and to sudden interpretational successes when the cycling system finally activates some vector close to one of its antecedently learned prototypes. Let us now look at some rather grander and historically more celebrated examples of the same thing.

Consider looking up at the stars, on a clear, moonless night, from some pastoral vantage point free of the occluding haze and background light of the city. Thousands of stars are visible, scattered carelessly both in space and in brightness. Here is a "degraded perceptual input" indeed! For sheer unstructured chaos, it surpasses any of the random-dot figures or splotchy photos presented so far.

And yet, all human cultures impose a structural order of some kind or other on the contents of the night sky, interpreting one group of stars as a dipper, another as a flying swan, a third as a hunter with dogs, a fourth as a scorpion, and so on. Few of these interpretations are very compelling, visually. And certainly none of them yielded any useful predictions of stellar behavior, despite the elaborate mythologies in which they were often embedded. The scorpion never stung anything; the dogs never caught anything; the dipper never poured out any water. In this respect, these interpretations of the visual chaos were not "good theories" about stellar phenomena.

The absence of any such action in the sky reflects the fact that the positions of the stars, relative to each other, remained *constant* over time. With the marginal exception of a puzzling handful of *planetes* or "wanderers," every star had a fixed and utterly permanent position relative to every other star in the sky. This constancy allows any nighttime observer to notice that, *collectively*, the stars do display a very regular form of behavior.

An hour's peaceful attention reveals that the stars at the eastern horizon are climbing into the sky at the rate of fifteen degrees (thirty moon diameters!) every hour. In the same period, the western stars have been sinking below their horizon at the same brisk rate. Indeed, the entire framework of stars, the *planetes* included, moves as a single unified object relative to the circle of the earthly horizon, as if the stars were all permanently positioned on the inside surface of a vast sphere surrounding all of terra firma, a

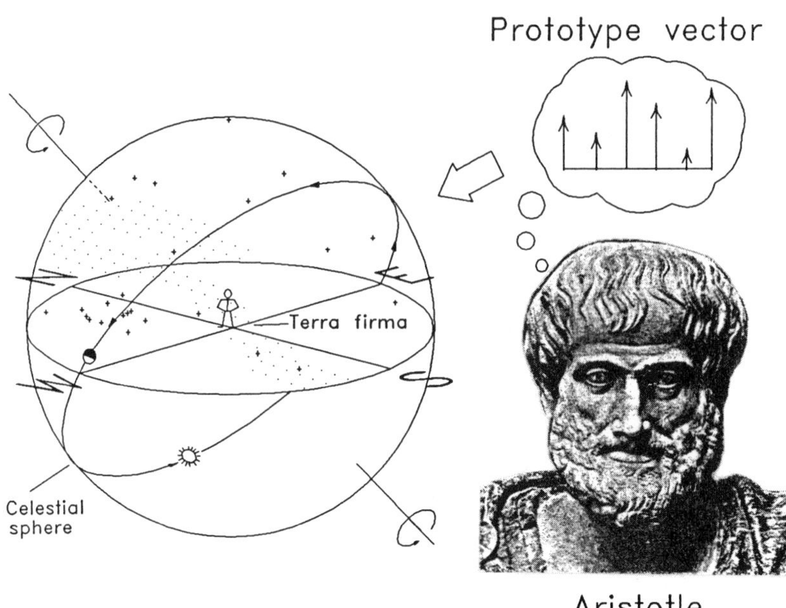

Figure 5.8 Interpreting the night sky as revealing a solid sphere of fixed stars, a sphere that rotates around the observer at a rate of roughly one revolution per day.

sphere that rotates in a most magisterial fashion about a gargantuan axis that cuts the sphere at Polaris, the pole star (figure 5.8).

Here, in the last clause of the preceding sentence, is the interpretation that suddenly unites the scattered elements of the night sky as visible manifestations of a familiar object: *a rotating sphere*. What is unusual about this particular sphere is its vast size, its utterly regular rotation, and the fact that we are viewing it from the inside, from somewhere close to its center. Beyond these notable novelties, and given a clear view of the night sky's behavior, it is close to being visually *obvious* that we are here dealing with a large sphere. Moreover, and unlike the animistic mythology of the individual constellations, this rotating-sphere interpretation of the whole sky allows us to predict the motions and future positions of all of the stars with great accuracy. Its ultimate truth or falsity aside, this interpretation of the initial chaos was a very *successful* theory. That is partly why it was, in some version or other, the accepted theory of the cosmos in almost every culture from the ancient Greeks until post-Newtonian Europe.

I am here representing the cognitive achievement of an ancient cosmological theory as being similar to the cognitive achievement involved in recognizing a familiar sort of object or process in any other problematic context—any context that involves incomplete or degraded input, for example, or an unusual sensory perspective, or other novelty sufficient to produce the kind of confusion encountered in figures 5.5, 5.6, and 5.7. This assimilation of "theoretical insight" to "prototype activation" has the further advantage that prototypes, especially temporal prototypes, typically represent far more information than is present in the sensory input that activates them on any given occasion. Those prototypes were originally acquired during training over many and varied instances thereof. This means that a prototype carries a substantial predictive content about what further or subsequent features will be perceptually discovered in addition to those already observed. This content can go uncorroborated, or be flatly contradicted, by subsequent experience. In this way are "theoretical" interpretations, just like interpretations generally, subject to empirical criticism.

Consider another historical example of a theoretical insight: Descartes' dynamical account of the motions of the Sun and planets. Why do the planets all circle the Sun? Why do they all revolve in the same direction? Why are the revolutions slower the more distant the body is from the Sun? What *is* the solar system?

For one who held, as Descartes did, that space must everywhere be continuously occupied by some sort of rarefied and translucent fluid matter, the circling behavior of the planets suggested nothing so much as a giant *vortex* in this universal fluid medium. That was exactly Descartes' hypothesis. He saw the planets as being like leaves swept around in a giant whirlpool, with those leaves that are closer to the center—Mercury and Venus—being carried around much faster in consequence.

Here is a dynamical interpretation that makes familiar and unitary sense of the many motions at issue. Descartes knew that the Sun was by far the largest of the bodies in the solar system, and so it was only natural that it be stable at the center of all this rotating fluid. And he also knew (from Galileo's sunspot observations) that the Sun itself rotated, in the same direction as the planets, only faster than any of them, just as the center of a whirlpool would display. The secondary motion of the Moon about the Earth, and of the Jovian satellites about Jupiter, were clearly small subsidiary whirlpools being carried around within the larger. The axial rotations of both the Earth and Jupiter matched the direction of rotation of the tiny moons at issue, and they matched the rotational direc-

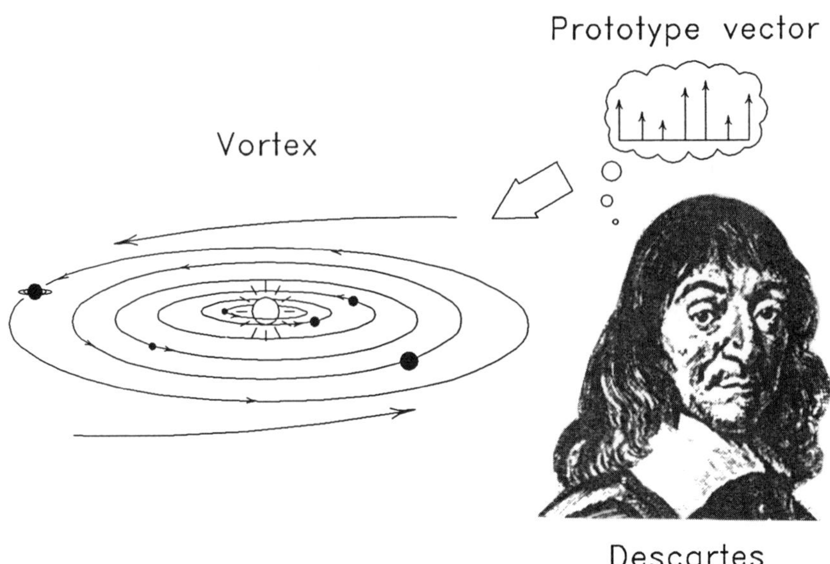

Figure 5.9 Descartes' "whirlpool" interpretation of the various planetary motions.

tion of the principal vortex as well. Altogether, it was a compelling interpretation of the substances, forces, and observable motions involved. Once again, a puzzling phenomenon was apprehended as an unusual instance of something familiar (figure 5.9).

And once again, the interpretation was false. Or, at least, Isaac Newton came up with a much better one. Instead of interpreting the Moon's circular motion around the Earth as the consequence of the Moon's being carried around by a swirling liquid medium, Newton saw the Moon as being more like a circling stone at the end of a centrally attached string, where the force of the Earth's gravity played the role of the endlessly tugging string (figure 5.10). The Moon's motion was therefore an instance of a *body endlessly falling* toward the Earth. The combination of (*a*) this steady accelerated motion Earthward, plus (*b*) the Moon's tangential, straight-line, inertial motion away from the Earth, produces the roughly circular orbit we observe. What would otherwise be a uniform, straight-line motion for the Moon gets continually deformed into a closed elliptical path by the centrally directed force of the Earth's gravity. The same interpretation was imposed for the much larger orbits of the six known planets, only this time it was the massive Sun that provided the central attraction. The planets too were endlessly falling *away* from their natural inertial path outward, and *toward* the attracting Sun. With the further assumption of an inverse-square

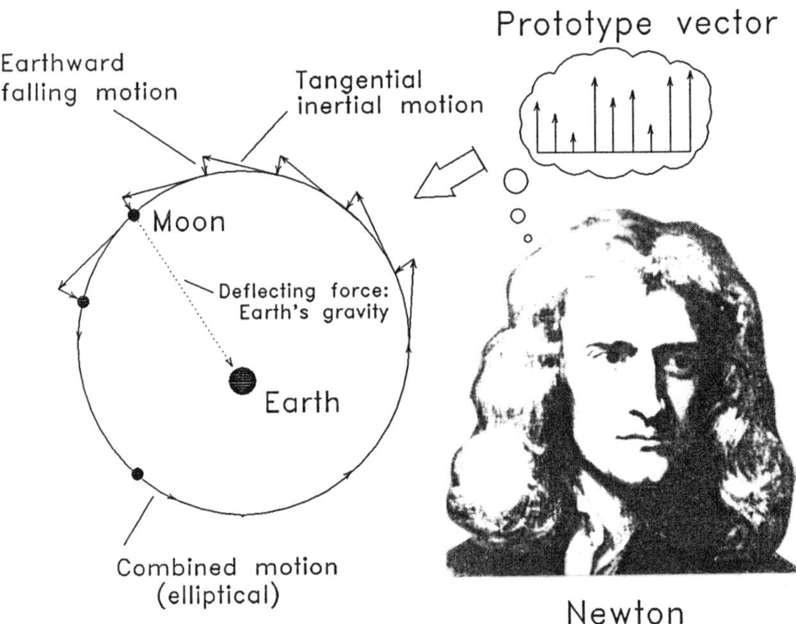

Figure 5.10 Newton's "deflecting force" interpretation of the Moon's elliptical orbit around the Earth.

law concerning the fading *strength* of gravity as one recedes from its central source, Newton was able to account exactly for the relative revolutionary periods of the six known planets, for their elliptical shape of their orbits, and for their individual variations in orbital velocity to boot. In all, the "central force" interpretation gave us a much more detailed and accurate model of the various lunar and planetary motions. Newton's interpretation of the situation made systematic sense of even the subtlest of planetary behaviors. A body moving under exactly those influences would display exactly the sort of motions observed, at least to the limits of our ability to measure them. Once again, a familiar form of order—a form familiar to Newton, anyhow—can be seen in what is initially a puzzling diversity of planetary behaviors.

Intriguingly, this brilliant interpretation eventually proved false as well. Or at any rate, Albert Einstein came up with a still better one. The so-called "force of gravity" is an illusion, said Einstein. A planet's curved path in three-dimensional *space* is in reality a *straight* path (a so-called "geodesic" or "shortest path") within the non-Euclidean geometry of the *four*-dimensional *spacetime* continuum that surrounds the "attracting" body. Since the planet's

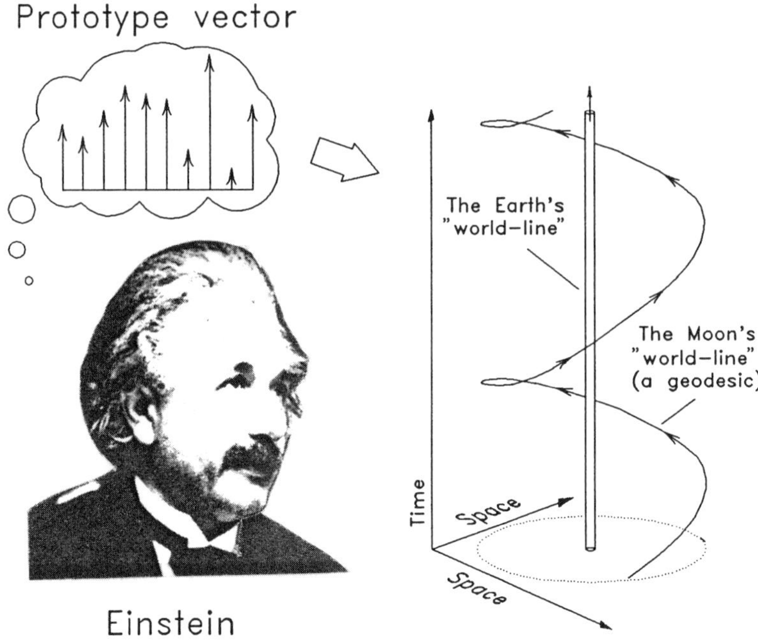

Figure 5.11 Einstein's "straight line in non-Euclidean spacetime" interpretation of the Moon's elliptical orbit around the Earth.

path is a straight line in four dimensions, there is no "deflection" in need of a deflecting force for its explanation. What the Sun does is not to exert a *force* on anything; rather, its great mass just deforms the local geometry of space-time. Given that geometrical deformation, the familiar prototype of an inertial or "straight line" path takes care of all the rest (figure 5.11).

This prototype—geodesic paths in a non-Euclidean space-time—is admittedly arcane to most of us. But that is beside the point here being made. It *was* a prototype with which *Einstein* was at least moderately familiar. And it was the contextual activation of that very prototype, as an interpretation of the planetary motions, that constituted Einstein's novel insight into the nature of gravitational phenomena.

That prototype involved a family of observable planetary behaviors that were closely similar to the behaviors involved in Newton's earlier prototype. It was therefore and automatically an alternative possible interpretation of the same domain of phenomena. But it also involved some subtle *deviations* from Newtonian behavior—such as the advancing major axis of any highly elliptical orbit—deviations that astronomers had already observed in Mercury's orbital behavior, and quite independently of Einstein's theoretical musings. Further divergences between the two prototypes were also investigated empirically, and it was always the Newtonian expectations that went disappointed. Once again, an ever more penetrating interpretation displaced an earlier one.

Einstein's theory of gravity has some more recent competition of its own, but I will close the series of illustrative examples here. The point of this brief and highly selective excursion into the history of science has been to portray some of the most sophisticated of our intellectual achievements as involving the very same activities of vector processing, recurrent manipulation, prototype activation, and prototype evaluation as can be found in some of the simplest of our cognitive activities, such as recognizing a dog in a low-grade photograph. What distinguishes scientific cognition is just the unusual ambition of its interpretive enterprise, the sophistication of many of the prototypes deployed, and the institutional procedures that govern the evaluation of the competing interpretations proposed. At its core, scientific cognition involves the very same cognitive mechanisms as define cognition generally. And those mechanisms, according to the theoretical interpretation under exploration in the present chapter, are precisely the mechanisms embodied in a large and highly trained recurrent neural network.

6 The Neural Representation of the Social World

Social Space

A crab lives in a submarine space of rocks and open sand and hidden recesses. A ground squirrel, in a space of bolt holes and branching tunnels and leaf-lined bedrooms. A human occupies a physical space of comparable complexity, but in our case it is overwhelmingly obvious that we live also in an intricate space of obligations, duties, entitlements, prohibitions, appointments, debts, affections, insults, allies, contracts, enemies, infatuations, compromises, mutual love, legitimate expectations, and collective ideals. Learning the structure of this social space, learning to recognize the current position of oneself and others within it, and learning to navigate one's way through that space without personal or social destruction, is at least as important to any human as learning the counterpart skills for purely physical space.

This is not to slight the squirrels and crabs, nor the bees and ants and termites either, come to think of it. The social dimensions of their cognitive lives, if simpler than ours, are still intricate and no doubt of comparable importance to them. What is important, at all levels of the phylogenetic scale, is that each creature lives in a world not just of physical objects, but of *other creatures* as well, creatures that can perceive and plan and act, both for and against one's interests. Those other creatures, therefore, bear systematic attention. Even nonsocial animals must learn to perceive, and to respond to, the threat of predators or the opportunity for prey. Social animals must learn, in addition, the interactive culture that structures their collective life. This means that their nervous systems must learn to represent the many dimensions of the local social space, a space that embeds them as surely and as relevantly as does the local physical space. They must learn a hierarchy of categories for social agents, events, positions, configurations, and processes. They must learn to recognize instances of those many categories through the veil of degraded inputs, chronic ambiguity, and the occasional deliberate deception. Above all, they must learn to generate appropriate behavioral *outputs* in that social space, just as surely as they must learn to locomote, grasp food, and find shelter.

In confronting these additional necessities, a social creature must use the same sorts of resources used elsewhere. The job may be special, but the tools available are the same. The creature must configure its synaptic weights within some special neuronal populations so as to represent the structure of the social reality in which it lives. Further, it must learn to generate vectorial sequences that will produce socially acceptable or socially advantageous behavioral outputs. As we will see in what follows, social and moral reality is also the province of the physical brain. Social and moral cognition, social and moral behavior, are no less activities of the brain than is any other kind of cognition or behavior. We need to confront this fact squarely and forthrightly if we are ever to understand our own moral natures. We need to confront it if we are ever to deal both effectively and humanely with our too-frequent social pathologies. And we need to confront it if we are ever to realize our full social and moral potential.

Inevitably, these sentiments will evoke discomfort in some readers, as if, by being located in the purely physical brain, social and moral knowledge were about to be devalued in some way. Let me say, most emphatically, that devaluation is not my purpose. As I see it, social and moral comprehension has just as much right to the term "knowledge" as does scientific or theoretical comprehension. No more right, but no less. In the case of gregarious creatures such as humans, social and moral understanding is as hard won, it is as robustly empirical and objective, and it is as vital to our well-being as is any piece of scientific knowledge. It also shows progress over time, both within an individual's lifetime and over the course of many centuries. It adjusts itself steadily to the pressures of cruel experience. And it is drawn ever forward by the hope of a surer peace, a more fruitful commerce, and a deeper enlightenment.

The issue of moral realism will be addressed again, at the close of this chapter and once more at the close of the book. Its philosophical defense will be more readily pursued then. With the patient reader fairly forewarned, let us put this issue aside for now and approach the focal issue of how social and moral knowledge, whatever its metaphysical status, might actually be *embodied* in the brains of living biological creatures.

It can't be too difficult. Ants and bees live intricate social lives, but their neural resources are minuscule: for an ant, 10^4 neurons, tops. However tiny those resources may be, evidently they are adequate. So how demanding can the job be? In an ant's case, perhaps not very. Ant society displays a robust caste system, and a given caste's behavioral role may be fairly narrow. Even so, a worker ant's neural network must be able to recognize a wide variety of socially relevant things: pheromonal trail markings to be pursued or avoided; a vocabulary of antennae exchanges to steer one another's behavior; the occasions for general defense, or attack, or fission of the colony; fertile pasture for the nest's aphid herd; the complex needs of the queen and her developing eggs; and so forth.

Presumably the challenge of social cognition and social behavior is not fundamentally different from that of physical cognition and behavior. The social features or processes to be discriminated may be subtle and complex, but as before, a high-dimensional vectorial representation can capture them successfully. The environment in which those features appear may be filled with noise and distraction, but as before, a network's capacity for vector completion and recurrent modulation will regularly lead to their successful discrimination. To see how this might be so, let us start with a simple case: the principal emotional states as they are displayed in human faces.

EMPATH: A Network for Recognizing Human Emotions

Cottrell and Metcalfe trained a minor variant of the face-recognition network (pp. 38–53) on eight familiar emotional states, as they were willingly feigned in the cooperating faces of twenty undergraduate subjects, ten male and ten female. Three of these charming subjects are displayed eight times in figure 6.1, one for each of the eight emotions. In sequence, you will there see astonishment, delight, pleasure, relaxation, sleepiness, boredom, misery, and anger. (Cottrell and Metcalfe weren't too pleased with their acting skills either.) The aim was to discover if a network of the modest size at issue could learn to discriminate features at this level of subtlety, across a real diversity of human faces.

The answer is yes, but it must be qualified. On the training set of (8 emotions × 20 faces =) 160 photos in all, and after 1000 presentations of the entire training set, the network reached high levels of accuracy on the four positive emotions (about 80%), but extremely poor levels on the negative emotions, with the sole exception of anger, which was correctly identified 85% of the time.

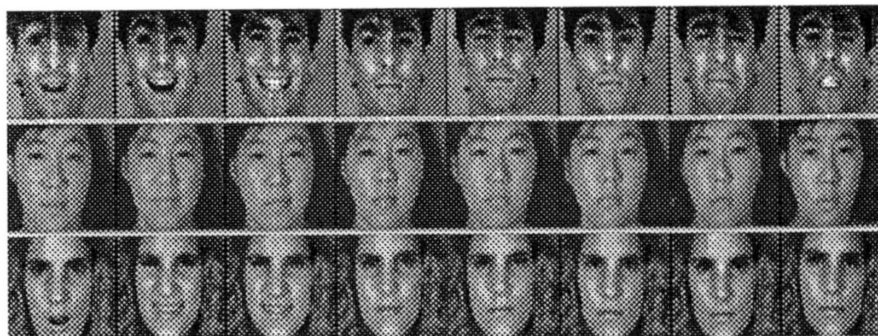

Figure 6.1 Eight familiar emotional states, as feigned in the facial expressions of three human subjects. From the left, they are astonishment, delight, pleasure, relaxation, sleepiness, boredom, misery, and anger. These photos, and those for seventeen other subjects, were used to train EMPATH, a network for discriminating emotions as they are displayed in human faces. (Thanks to Gary Cottrell and Janet Metcalfe.)

Part of this marginal performance can be ascribed to the poor acting abilities of the student subjects and to the close expressive similarity of three of the four negative emotions. (See how well you can discriminate sleepiness, boredom, and misery in the photos at issue.) To test this alibi, the same set of photos was shown to a sample of normal human subjects, who were asked to make the same discriminations required of the network. Not surprisingly, the humans also did poorest on the negative emotions, anger once more sharply excepted. But comparatively, they did a great deal better than the network. So perhaps some of the network's shortfall can be blamed on the clumsy student actors, but clearly not all of it. Several additional factors confirm that the network is operating at the outer limits of its discriminatory capacity.

For example, further training on the same 160 photos (an additional 2000 presentations of the set) yielded some genuine improvement in the network's recognition of the negative emotions. Unfortunately, this was purchased at the expense of some *loss* in its original accuracy on the several positive emotions. This robbing of Peter to pay Paul indicates that a network of the size at issue does not have enough resources to capture fully the entire range of features displayed.

Second, the more highly the network was trained on the original set, the poorer became its ability to generalize to *novel* faces, an important test of any network's real achievement. EMPATH's capacity for generalization peaked at about 1000 presentations of the training set, and it actually fell off with further training on that set. This indicates that, after the first 1000 presentations, the struggling network was merely learning the minor and accidental discriminatory features peculiar to the specific photos in the training set, rather than learning, as was intended, the important features common to an emotion as displayed in faces generally.

Withal, it did learn, and it did generalize. Its performance was robustly accurate for five of the eight emotions, and its weakest performance parallels a similar performance weakness in humans. This means that the emotional expressions at issue are indeed within the grasp of a neural network, and it indicates that a larger network and a larger training set might do a great deal better. EMPATH is an "existence proof," if you like: a proof that for some networks and for some socially relevant human behaviors, the one can learn to discriminate the other.

Social Features and Prototypical Sequences

EMPATH's level of sophistication is of course quite low. The patterns to which it has become tuned are timeless snapshots. It has no grasp of any expressive sequences. In stark contrast to a normal human, it will recognize sadness in a series of heaving sobs no more reliably than in a single photo of one slice of that telltale sequence. For both the human and the network, a single photo might be ambiguous. But to the human, that distressing sequence of behavior certainly will not be. Lacking any recurrent pathways, EMPATH cannot tap into the rich palette of information contained in how perceivable patterns unfold in time. For this reason, no network with a purely feedforward architecture, no matter how large, could ever equal the recognitional capacities of a human.

Lacking any grasp of temporal patterns carries a further price. EMPATH has no conception of what sorts of causal antecedents typically *produce* the principal emotions, and no conception of what *effects* those emotions have on the ongoing cognitive, social, and physical behaviors of the people who have them. That the discovered loss of a loved one typically causes grief; that grief typically causes some degree of social paralysis; these things are utterly beyond EMPATH's ken. In short, the prototypical *causal roles* of the several emotions are also beyond any network such as EMPATH. Just as we discovered in the realm of purely physical cognition, sophisticated social cognition requires a grasp of patterns in time, and this requires that the network be richly endowed with recurrent pathways.

An important subset of causal sequences is the set of *ritual* or *conventional* sequences. To take some prototypical examples, consider a social introduction, an exchange of pleasantries, an extended negotiation, a closing of a deal, a proper leave-taking, and so on. All of these mutual exchanges require, for their recognition as well as for execution, a well-tuned recurrent network. And they require of the network a considerable history spent embedded within a social space already filled with such prototypical activities on every side. After all, those prototypes must be learned, and this will require both instructive examples and plenty of time to internalize them.

In the end, the acquired library of social prototypes hierarchically embedded in the vast neuronal activation space of any normally socialized human must rival, if it does not exceed, the acquired library of purely natural or nonsocial prototypes. One need only read a novel by someone such as Henry James to appreciate the intricate structure of human social space and the complexity of human social dynamics. More simply, just recall your teenage years. Mastering that complexity is a cognitive achievement at least equal to earning a degree in physics. And yet with few exceptions, all of us do it.

Are There "Social Areas" in the Brain?

Experimental neuroscience in the twentieth century has focused almost exclusively on finding the neuroanatomical (i.e., structural) and the neurophysiological (i.e., activational) correlates of perceptual properties that are purely *natural* or *physical* in nature. The central and programmatic question has been as follows. Where in the brain, and by what processes, do we recognize such properties as color, shape, motion, sound, taste, aroma, temperature, texture, bodily damage, relative distance, and so on? The pursuit of such questions has led to real insights, and we have long been able to provide a map of the various areas in the brain that seem centrally involved in each of the functions mentioned.

The discovery technique is simple in concept. Just insert a long, thin microelectrode into any one of the cells in the cortical area in question (the brain has no pain sensors, so the experimental animal is utterly unaware of this telephone tap), and then see whether and

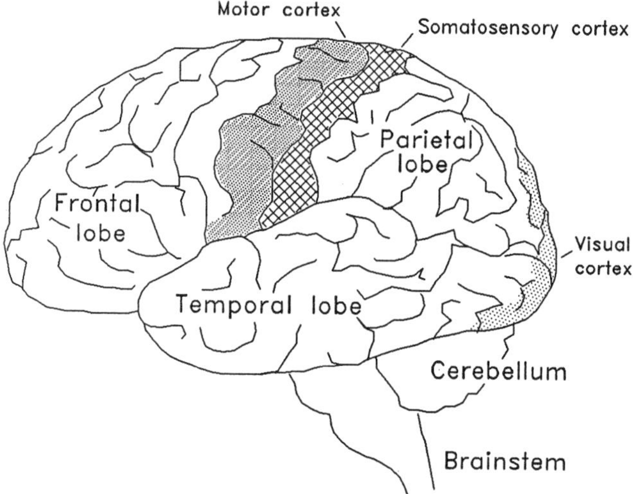

Figure 6.2 The location of some of the primary and secondary sensory areas within the primate cerebral cortex. (Subcortical structures such as the LGN and MGN are not shown.) The motor output cortex is also shown. Note the broad cortical areas that lie outside these easily identified areas.

how that cell responds when the animal is shown color or motion, or hears tones, or feels warmth and cold, and so on. In this fashion, a functional map is painstakingly produced. Figure 6.2 provides a quick look at the several primary and secondary sensory cortices and their positions within the rear half of a typical primate cerebral cortex.

But what about the front half of the cortex, the so-called "premotor" cortex? What is it for? The conventional but vague answer is, "to formulate potential motor behaviors for delivery to and execution by the motor cortex." Here we possess much less insight into the significance of these cortical structures and their neuronal activities. We cannot manipulate the input to those areas in any detail, as we can with the several sensory areas, because the input received by the premotor areas comes ultimately from all over the brain. It comes from areas that are already high up in the processing hierarchy, areas a long way from the sensory periphery where we can control what is and isn't presented.

On the other hand, we can insert microelectrodes as before, but this time *stimulate* the target cell rather than record from it. In the motor cortex itself, this works beautifully. If we briefly stimulate the cells in certain areas, certain muscles in the body twitch, and there is a systematic correspondence between the areas of motor cortex and the muscles they control. In short, the motor strip itself constitutes a well-ordered map of the body's many muscles, much as the primary visual cortex is a map of the eye's retina. Stimulating single cells in the *premotor* areas, however, produces little or nothing in the way of behavioral response, presumably because the production of actual behavior requires smooth sequences of large activation vectors involving many thousands of cells at once. *That* kind of stimulation we still lack the technology to produce.

A conventional education in neuroscience thus leaves one wondering exactly how the entire spectrum of sensory inputs processed in the rear half of the brain finally gets transformed into some appropriate motor outputs formulated in the front half of the brain. This is indeed a genuine problem, and it is no wonder that researchers have found it so difficult. From the perspective we have gained from our study of artificial networks, we can see how complex the business of vector coding and vector transformation must be in something as large as the brain, especially given the existence of massively recurrent pathways all over the place.

Plainly, sleuthing out the brain's complete sensorimotor strategy would be a daunting task even if the brain were an *artificial* network, a network whose every synaptic weight were known and all of whose neuronal activation levels were open to continuous and simultaneous monitoring. But a living brain is not so accommodating. Its weights are mostly inaccessible, and monitoring the activity of more than a few cells at a time is currently impossible.

This is one of the reasons why the recent artificial network models have made possible so much progress. We can learn things from the models that we might never have learned from the brain directly. And we can then return to the biological brain with some new and better-informed experimental questions to pose, questions concerning the empirical faithfulness of our network models, questions that we do have some hope of answering. Accordingly, the hidden transformations that produce behavior from perceptual input need not remain hidden after all.

If we aspire to track them down, however, we need to broaden our conception of the problem. In particular, we should be wary of the assumption that perception is first and foremost the perception of purely physical features in the world. And we should be wary of the correlative assumption that behavioral output is first and primarily the manipulation of physical objects.

We should be wary because we already know that humans and other social animals are keenly sensitive, perceptually, to *social* features of their surroundings. And because we already know that humans and social animals manipulate their *social* environment as well as their purely physical surroundings. And above all, because we already know that infants in most social species begin acquiring their *social* coordination at least as early as they begin learning sensorimotor coordination in its purely physical sense. Even infants can discriminate a smile from a scowl, a kind tone of voice from a hostile tone, a humorous exchange from a fractious one. And even an infant can successfully call for protection, induce feeding behavior, and invite affection and play.

I do not mean to suggest that social properties are anything more, ultimately, than just intricate aspects of the purely physical world. Nor do I wish to suggest that they have independent causal properties over and above what is captured by physics and chemistry. What I do wish to suggest is that, in learning to represent the world, the brains of infant social creatures focus naturally and relentlessly on the social features of their local environment, often slighting physical features that will later seem unmissable. Human children, for example, typically do not acquire command of the basic *color* vocabulary until their third or fourth year of life, long after they have gained linguistic competence on matters such as anger, promises, friendship, ownership, and love. As a parent, I was quite surprised to discover this in my own children, and surprised again to learn that the pattern is quite general. But perhaps I shouldn't have been. The social features listed are far more important to a young child's practical life than are the endlessly various colors.

The general lesson is plain. As social infants partition their activation spaces, the categories that form are just as often social categories as they are natural or physical categories. In apportioning neuronal resources for important cognitive tasks, the brain expends roughly as much of those resources on representing and controlling social reality as it does on representing and controlling physical reality.

In light of these remarks, look once again at the brain in figure 6.2. Note the unmapped frontal half and the large unmapped areas of the rear half. Might some of these areas be principally involved in *social* perception and action? Might they be teeming with vast vectorial sequences representing *social* realities of one sort or other? Indeed, once the question is raised, why stop with these areas? Might the so-called "primary" sensory cortical areas—for touch, vision, and hearing especially—be as much in the business of grasping and processing social facts as they are in the business of grasping and processing purely physical facts? These two functions are certainly not mutually exclusive.

I think the answer is almost certainly yes to all of these questions. We lack intricate brain maps for social features comparable to existing brain maps for physical features, not because they aren't there to be found, I suggest, but rather because we have not looked for them with a determination comparable to the physical case.

The Human Capacity for Language

That comparative neglect of the brain's social areas is not hard to understand. Put yourself in the scientist's shoes. Controlling and manipulating a social environment, for perceptual presentation to an experimental subject, is far more difficult than controlling and manipulating colors, shapes, tones, and so forth. This is doubly true when the social environment is alien, poorly understood by humans, and somewhat disrupted in any case, as it surely is in the typical colony of laboratory macaques or rhesus monkeys.

It is hard, but not impossible. In fact, some entry-level research has already been done in this area: as it happens, on facial recognition in monkeys. Monkeys, it turns out, have a small cortical area that is implicated in the recognition of other monkeys' faces. Their "facial cortex," if we may call it that, enjoys a position in the monkey brain roughly analogous to the position of the facial region already discovered in humans (recall pp. 35–36).

Social regions are more commonly revealed, however, in human subjects, and in cases that originate outside the laboratory. Accidents of many sorts yield patients that display a variety of fairly well-defined cognitive or social deficits, and these can be correlated with damage to specific parts of the brain. The extent and profile of the cognitive deficits can be probed behaviorally. And post-mortem examination of the patient's brain, or a detailed imaging of the living brain with one of the new noninvasive scanning devices, tells us what areas were actually injured. Putting these two kinds of information together, over a large population of patients, allows us to construct a map of the various neuronal areas

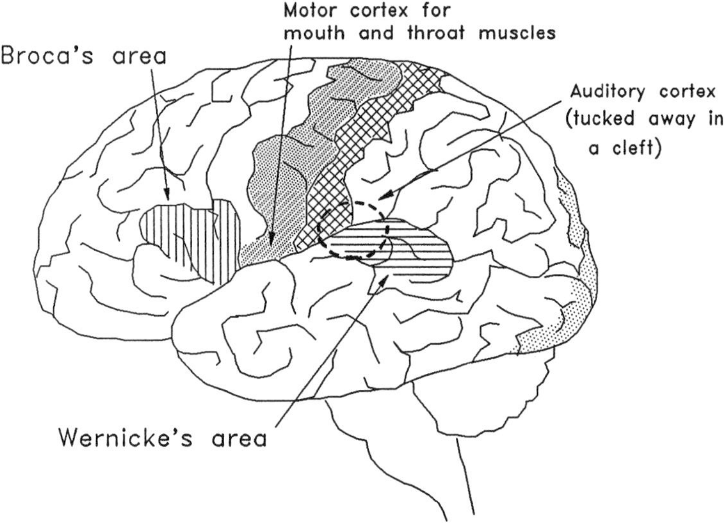

Figure 6.3 Some human cortical areas implicated in the comprehension and production of language.

that, in humans, are specialized for specific cognitive functions. And this is achieved without ever putting an electrode into a single human brain.

The lessons of that research are the subject of the next chapter, but one case may be usefully discussed here. Humans possess an interconnected family of cortical areas, typically although not universally on the left side of the brain, areas that are profoundly important for the comprehension and production of speech. Damage in these areas typically produces a profound loss in the capacity for producing speech and/or for comprehending the speech of others. Two of the more salient of these areas are called "Broca's area" and "Wernicke's area" respectively, after the nineteenth-century physicians who first identified them (figure 6.3).

Their importance for speech is not hard to appreciate, given their locations in the brain. Broca's area is next to, and is axonally just upstream from, the lower part of the primary motor cortex, the part that exercises general control over the muscles of the mouth and throat. Broca's area is evidently a crucial part of the broader cortical system that constructs the abstract vectorial sequences that, when processed through the motor cortex, generate fluid, grammatical, and semantically coherent speech. The job is clearly not done by the motor cortex alone. An undamaged motor cortex will continue to exercise detailed control over the muscles of the mouth and throat, but if Broca's area is severely damaged, the motor cortex will no longer give voice to normal, coherent speech.

Damage to Wernicke's area also produces an intriguing range of defects in speech behavior, as we will see in the next chapter. So it is evidently part of the speech-production system as well. But it is next to the primary auditory cortex (which area is entirely tucked away inside the horizontal "sulcus," or cleft, that separates the temporal and parietal lobes) and it is axonally downstream from it, so it is no surprise that Wernicke's area is also crucial for speech *comprehension*. With an undamaged primary auditory cortex, one's basic hearing is unimpaired. But if there is significant damage to Wernicke's area, or to the larger temporal lobe of which it is a part, then one's comprehension of heard speech will be seriously impaired or destroyed.

Human language is perhaps the most spectacular of social skills in any species, and some localized areas of the human brain appear almost totally devoted to its administration. Yes, there are indeed "social areas" in the brain; two or three, for certain, and there are more to come just ahead. The case of the language areas, however, is of special interest relative to the aims of this book. This is because the current orthodoxy in the science of linguistics explains our command of language, of its grammatical part at least, in terms of our possession of a rigorous set of generative grammatical *rules*, rules whose iterative application is essential for speech production and comprehension alike. The basic outline of the possible forms that such rules can take is claimed to be biologically innate and universal to all normal humans. The human brain, in short, is said to contain a "language organ" with the basic form of all human languages already built into it at birth.

This is, in sketch, the Chomskean approach to understanding language, and it has dominated theoretical work in linguistics for the last three decades. The emerging conflict with the more recent neural network approach is not hard to see. Chomsky's approach postulates the existence, within any linguistically competent human, of a set of *rules* for the formation of admissible or grammatical sequences of words. And it assumes that the brain *applies* or *follows* those rules in order to comprehend and produce actual sentences. By contrast, the neural network models we have been exploring in this book certainly do not function by applying any rules that they have come to represent internally. They have no representation whatever of any specific rules. And the transformations they effect are made by a different sort of process entirely: by the embodied multiplication of a vector by a large matrix of synaptic connections to yield a new vector as product.

In the end, a trained network can indeed produce highly "regular" behavior, in that the network has come to *embody* a specific input-output function. And some set of explicit rules may accurately specify or recreate that input-output behavior. But the claim that the network actually produces its input-ouput behavior by some internal representation and application of those rules is typically false of the neural network architectures at issue. They are playing a different sort of computational game entirely. The point at issue between the generative grammarians and the neural networkers is simply this: in which of these two ways is language competence realized in humans?

The issue has a simpler analog in a case already familiar to you from chapter 4. Recall the sophisticated computer program written by the software engineers at Digital Equipment Corporation in order to realize the complex letter-to-phoneme input-output function embodied in DECtalk. That program consisted of a large set of rules explicitly represented in the memory chip of the computer. In executing that program to produce audible sounds, the computer was literally applying or following those stored rules. A Chomsky-like hypothesis, to explain DECtalk's underlying competence, is *correct* in this case. DECtalk does represent and follow rules.

Contrast with this the case of NETtalk, whose input-output competence is effectively identical with DECtalk's. The means by which NETtalk realizes this competence, however, is very different from the rules-and-application technique employed within the classical computing architecture of DECtalk. That is why NETtalk caused such a sensation. It showed that there is a completely different way to realize a complex input-output competence, a way that makes no use of rules at all, neither in the network's initial instruction nor in its mature performance. A Chomsky-like hypothesis, to explain NETtalk's underlying competence, is flatly *false* in this case. Although it embodies intricate regularities, NETtalk neither represents nor follows rules.

Return now to our human competence for our native language, a competence, let us remind ourselves, that is orders of magnitude more complex than the simple "get the sound right" competence of DECtalk or NETtalk. The still dominant position among linguists is that linguistic competence is realized in humans in a fashion much closer to the case of DECtalk than to the case of NETtalk. To that audience, the picture of stored rules remains the more appealing.

There are important reasons for this beyond the sheer inertia of three decades' dominance. For one thing, the Chomskean tradition has accumulated systematic and detailed explanations of grammatical phenomena across many different languages. These achievements are not about to be dismissed as insignificant; not, at least, until some alternative approach succeeds in duplicating them. Neural net research here has several decades of ground to make up, and there is no use pretending otherwise.

A second reason often cited is the fact that any natural language contains a potential infinity of legitimate or grammatical sentences. This is because grammatical sentences of arbitrary length and complexity can always be constructed. The only plausible way to explain this "productivity" of language, argues Chomsky, is by appealing to a set of rules, internal to each of us, whose repeated or iterated application can continue to generate new and more complicated sentences without end.

Here the orthodox tradition is mistaken, at least in thinking that it has the *only* possible explanation of grammatical productivity. A sentence, after all, is a temporal sequence of words. We already know that recurrent neural networks can be trained to produce well-behaved sequences of behavior, and sequences of sequences as well. Recall my example, in chapter 5, of the long sequence of more elementary actions that began with putting on the oven gloves and ended, eight or nine steps later, with wrapping the hot chicken on the countertop with a square of aluminum foil. In fact, given examples such as this, motor behavior *in general* starts to look "productive" in something like the sense at issue. For consider: There are an indefinite number of distinct actions one might perform, ranging from scratching one's chin to cooking an elaborate dinner to launching the Allied invasion of Normandy. Such actions can be of arbitrary temporal length, and they are constituted from a finite repertoire of suitably variable elementary actions. Must we adopt a Chomsky-style explanation for this all-inclusive capacity too?

Presumably not. But now our linguistic capacity no longer looks so utterly unique, and it may no longer demand a unique form of explanation. Perhaps it might be explained in terms of the underlying capacity of recurrent neural networks to learn a finite "library" of prototypical sequential behaviors to the exclusion of zillions of others, and in terms of the indefinitely many possible variations and entrainments of those elemental sequences. This is possible in principle. Is it possible in fact?

That is a pretty question, and its answer is not known. However, it certainly will be known before another three decades slip behind us. Network modeling of linguistic capacities will tell us whether a recurrent network can truly be taught the intricate functions at issue. And brain research on the structure and activity of human language areas will tell us whether those artificial linguistic networks are biologically realistic.

On the former matter we already have some early results. A recurrent network trained to discriminate between grammatical and ungrammatical word sequences of arbitrary length is something that already exists. Its acquired skills encompass only a small part of a standard English speaker's grammatical skills, but the example is both instructive and encouraging.

Recurrent Networks for Grammatical Discrimination

Jeff Elman, Director of UCSD's Center for Research in Language, is a pioneer in the application of neural network models to the theory of language. The networks described below are examples of what are now called "Elman nets," one of the simplest possible forms that a recurrent network can take. Elman wanted to know, first, if a network could abstract, from a large corpus of simple sentences, grammatical categories such as *noun*, *verb*, and *direct object*. Second, he wished to know if such a network could learn, from a large corpus of rather more complex sentences, to discriminate *grammatical* sentences from ungrammatical sentences, including novel sentences of arbitrary length. These two questions had a certain bite to them, since researchers in the orthodox Chomskean tradition had argued vociferously that artificial neural networks of the kind we have been exploring could not possibly show the sophisticated knowledge of abstract structures required for grammatical productivity. Or, if they did show such knowledge, it was because they were somehow managing to represent exactly the Chomskean rules favored by the orthodox account. In either case, it was concluded, the orthodox account had nothing to fear.

Let us see if it does. Elman and David Zipser addressed the first question with a simple recurrent network (figure 6.4a), a list of 29

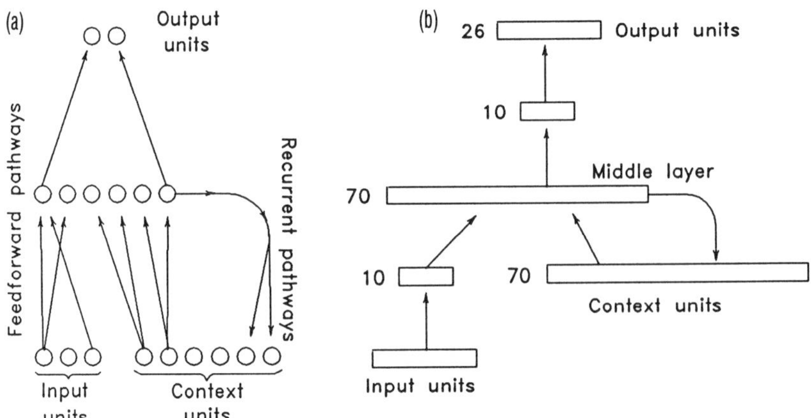

Figure 6.4 (a) The simplest form of Elman net. The activation pattern across the middle layer is conveyed backward at each cycle, so that the total input to the network at each step includes that "contextual" information about its immediately prior state. The network can thus evaluate each new input word in light of the sequence of words in which it appears. (b) A somewhat larger and more elaborate Elman net used to discriminate grammaticality in sentences with iteratively nested relative clauses. (Adapted from Jeff Elman.)

humdrum nouns and verbs, and a training corpus of 10,000 two- and three-word sentences composed therefrom, sentences such as "Man eats bread", "Lion chases cat", "Boy sleeps", "Monster smashes car", and so on. The network was given such sentences as input, one word at a time, and its task was to try to predict, from the prior word or words already given it, the *next* word in the sequence.

Perfect prediction in this task is impossible, since there is usually more than one grammatically admissible answer. The two words, "Monster smashes . . . ," could equally well be followed by "car", "cookie", "plate", or "glass", for example. Even so, the network did learn to predict correctly as often as the local statistics would permit. And where its predictions were mistaken, the word predicted was almost always of the *right grammatical category.* Given "Monster smashes . . . ," for example, it would never predict a *verb* as the next word. In general, after training it generated only sentences that we would find acceptable.

How does it do it? An analysis of the activation vectors occurring across the network's middle layer during each of the twenty-nine possible predictions revealed a hierarchical pattern whose outlines will be familiar to you. The dendogram of figure 6.5 displays all of

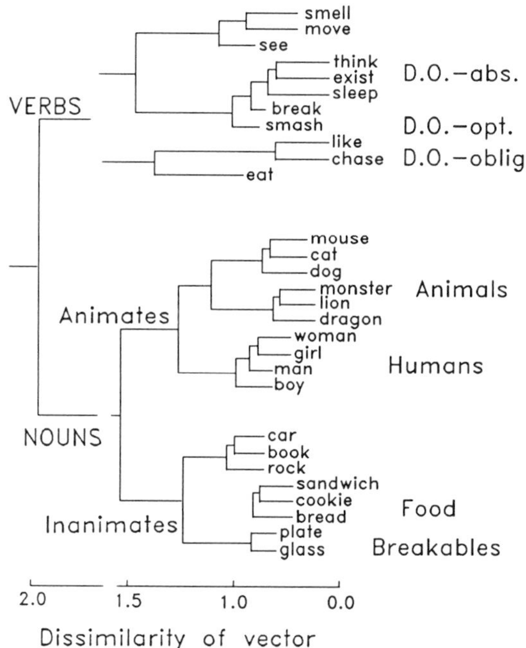

Figure 6.5 The hierarchical set of partitions across the activation space of the network's middle layer. Note the groupings into various grammatically relevant categories, including the three-way distinction between verbs that must be followed by a direct object, verbs that cannot be so followed, and those for which an object is optional. (Adapted from Jeff Elman.)

the twenty-nine words from which the 10,000 training sentences were constructed. The dendogram groups them according to the similarity of their learned activation vectors, just as the seventy-nine vectors of NETtalk were grouped earlier. You can see directly that the network has successfully abstracted, from the large corpus of grammatical sentences in the training set, the categories that determine whether and where a given word can properly turn up in a sentence.

This modest result is encouraging, but it does not yet meet the real challenge of the Chomskean tradition: can a network internalize the highly *abstract* structure of nested relative clauses and multiple subject-verb agreements that underlies the genuine *productivity* shown in human language? To address this question, Elman generated a miniature version of the problem at hand: a small lexicon of eight nouns, twelve verbs, the relative pronoun "who," and a sentence-ending period. (To make things simpler, the lexicon contained no "the" or "a.") These selected elements were governed by a simple but genuinely productive grammar, prepared by Elman, of some dozen or so rules. That grammar was used to generate, from the lexicon described and in orthodox Chomskean fashion, a no-nonsense training set of 10,000 grammatical sentences of various lengths and degrees of complexity. Unlike the previous network, this one had to confront sentences containing relative clauses such as, "Boys [who chase girls] chase cats." This training set was fed to the network of figure 6.4b—the simple sentences first and the complex sentences later—while backpropagation was used to gradually reconfigure the network's many synaptic weights.

The recurrent network's task was to predict, for each input string of words, all of the grammatically permissible *next* types of words, such as, relative pronoun, plural verb, singular noun, and so on. To make a long story short, the network learned like the dickens. To pick a relevant example, it learned to distinguish correct subject-verb agreements, even through the complexity of multiply embedded relative clauses, as in "Boys [who kiss girl {who feeds dog}] chase cats." Note that the plural verb "chase" agrees with the plural subject "Boys" despite being separated from it by six words, two nested relative clauses, and two distracting *singular* nouns. The trained network gets those agreements right. (And it does so without the help of any added parentheses. I put them in just for you and me.) In general, the network learned to discriminate, as grammatical, almost exactly the same set of sentences generated as grammatical by the original set of genuinely productive Chomsky-like rules.

But now comes the pretty part. How does the network do it? What kinds of *representations* are being employed inside the successfully trained network in order to sustain these sophisticated skills? Here, finally, cluster analysis—as in NETtalk and in Elman-and-Zipser's earlier net—begins to fail us. For that procedure deliberately averages out all contextual variations, and thus obliterates all information concerning how input words get differently coded, from occasion to occasion, as a function of their varying temporal or sequential position within a sentence. Now that we are looking at sentences of nontrivial length, we need to take exactly such information into account.

The crucial perspective is not far to seek. (You know it already from modeling walking behavior in cats.) Instead of blindly *averaging* the vectors that occur at various times, look at the *sequence*

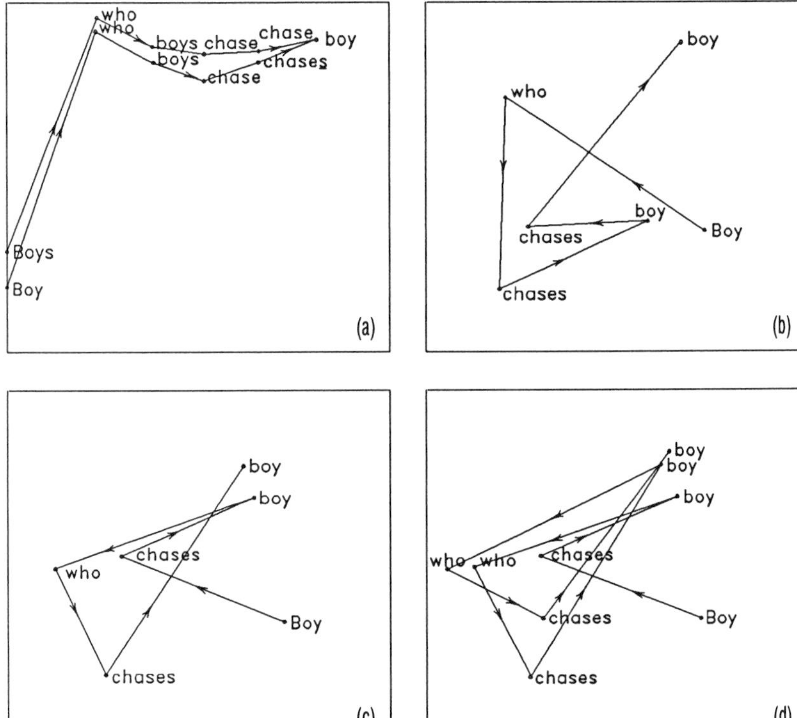

Figure 6.6 The trajectories of different sentences within the activation space of Elman's grammatically competent recurrent network. (a) Grammatically similar sentences have similar trajectories in vector space. (b) and (c) Grammatically diverse sentences have quite different trajectories. (d) Successively nested relative clauses are coded as similar but spatially distinct cycles within the activation space. (Adapted from Jeff Elman.)

of such word vectors over time and ask what the resulting vector-space *trajectory* might signify. With this approach, we strike gold almost immediately.

Elman had to do a bit of work—called *principal components analysis*—to find the crucial hyperplanes within the seventy-dimensional vector space of his network's middle layer; to find, that is, the particular tilted planes most active in coding what the network learned to regard as important. But once these planes were identified, each grammatical sentence turned out to have a signature trajectory within those special planes. Figure 6.6 illustrates the unique paths in hyperspace that represent some typical sentences.

Note that grammatically similar sentences have closely similar vector-space trajectories, as in figure 6.6a. The sentences,

(1) Boy who boys chase chases boy.

(2) Boys who boys chase chase boy.

differ only in the number of their subject and the number of the corresponding final verb. Their trajectories begin in slightly different places and that small difference is preserved, through three identical words in common, until the main subject's agreeing verb is finally reached, after which point the two trajectories converge. The network's tactic in this example illustrates its tactics in general. It codes small grammatical differences as slight but dynamically relevant differences in vector-space trajectory. What the network has learned is how to represent not just a *word*, but rather a *word-in-specific-grammatical-context.* It represents this abstract and context-laden linguistic entity with a dynamically-relevant point in activation space, a point that reflects what has gone before, and that responds to subsequent word inputs in a grammatically appropriate way.

Grammatically diverse sentences, on the other hand, have quite different trajectories. The sentences,

(3) Boy who chases boy chases boy.

(4) Boy chases boy who chases boy.

have different relative clause structures, such as to modify the subject in the first case and the direct object in the second. And they display very different coding trajectories, as shown in figure 6.6b and 6.6c. Finally, sentences with repeated center-embedded relative clauses, such as

(5) Boy chases boy who chases boy who chases boy.

get coded in such a fashion that those nested clauses show up as similar but spatially distinct cycles within activation space, as shown in figure 6.6d.

Concerning the *productivity* of the network's capacity for discriminating grammatical sentences, it is evident that the network has it. In principle, nothing limits the length of the sentences that may be coded: the network is recurrent and knows no upper bound on input sequences. And in practice, only the inevitable decay of relevant grammatical information over repeated recurrent cyclings prevents the network from living up to the ideal of perfect (i.e., infinite) productivity. In Elman's net, for example, performance fell to chance after three nested center embeddings of the sort seen in sentence 5) above. But humans have a similar limitation. Consider the famous sentence,

(6) The cat that the dog that the man kicked bit jumped.

Most of us reach the end of this sentence in a state of severe confusion, despite the fact that it is perfectly grammatical. If one rewrites it as follows, however,

(7) The cat—that the dog (that the man kicked) bit—jumped!

then one is much more likely to have comprehension dawn. The dashes and parentheses magnify or make good the information that tends to get lost in an activation-space trajectory with too many closely similar cycles.

The productivity of this network is of course a feeble subset of the vast capacity that any normal English speaker commands. But productivity is productivity, and evidently a recurrent network can possess it. Elman's striking demonstration hardly settles the issue between the rule-centered approach to grammar and the network approach. That will be some time in working itself out. But the conflict is now an even one. And I have made no secret of where my own bets would be placed.

Moral Perception and Moral Understanding

We saw earlier, when discussing the nature of scientific understanding, that the role of learned prototypes and their continual redeployment in new domains of phenomena was central to the scientific process. Specific rules or "laws of nature" play an undeniably important but nonetheless secondary role, mostly in the social business of communicating or teaching scientific skills. One's scientific understanding is lodged primarily in one's acquired hierarchy of structural and dynamical prototypes, not primarily in a set of linguistic formulas.

In a parallel fashion, we have just seen how our knowledge of a language may well be embodied in a hierarchy of prototypes for verbal sequences that admit of varied instances and indefinitely many combinations, rather than in a set of specific rules-to-be-followed. Of course we can and do state grammatical rules, but a child's grammatical competence in no way depends on ever hearing them uttered or being able to state them. It may be that the main function of such rules resides in the social business of describing and refining our linguistic skills. One's grammatical capacity, at its original core, may consist of something other than a list of internalized rules-to-be-followed.

With these two points in mind, let us now turn to the celebrated matter of our *moral* capacity. Let us address our ability to recognize cruelty and kindness, avarice and generosity, treachery and honor, mendacity and honesty, the cowardly way out and the right thing to do. Here, once again, the intellectual tradition of Western moral philosophy is focused on *rules*, on specific laws or principles. These are supposed to govern one's behavior, to the extent that one's behavior is moral at all. And the discussion has always centered on which rules are the truly valid, correct, or binding rules.

I have no wish whatever to minimize the importance of that ongoing moral conversation. It is an essential part of mankind's collective cognitive adventure, and I would be honored to make even the most modest of contributions to it. Nevertheless, it may be that a normal human's capacity for moral perception, cognition, deliberation, and action has rather less to do with rules, whether internal or external, than is commonly supposed.

What is the alternative to a rule-based account of our moral capacity? The alternative is a hierarchy of learned prototypes, for both moral perception and moral behavior, prototypes embodied in the well-tuned configuration of a neural network's synaptic weights. We may here find a more fruitful path to understanding the nature of moral learning, moral insight, moral disagreements, moral failings, moral pathologies, and moral growth at the level of entire societies. Let us explore this alternative, just to see how some familiar territory looks from a new and different hilltop.

Early in this book we noted that one's capacity for recognizing and discriminating sensory properties usually outstrips one's ability to articulate or express the basis of such discriminations in words. Taste and color sensations were the leading examples, but the point quickly showed itself to have a much broader application. Faces, too, are something we can discriminate, recognize, and remember to a degree that exceeds any verbal articulation we could possibly provide. The facial expression of emotions is evidently a third example. The recognition of sounds is a forth. In fact, the cognitive priority of the preverbal over the verbal shows itself, upon examination, to be a feature of almost all of our cognitive categories.

Consider the humdrum category, "Cat", for example. A reasonable commonsense definition of this category might go, "Cat: a smallish, furry, four-legged predatory mammal with small, sharp teeth, a serpentine tail, a fondness for chasing mice, and a 'meow'-like cry." To be sure, a biologist could give a more penetrating definition, but that is here beside the point: children and ordinary folks neither know nor depend on a biologist's scientific definition. Human familiarity with cats antedates modern biology by thousands of years. But neither, it turns out, do we depend on any commonsense definition in order to recognize cats. A mute, three-legged feline amputee with a bobbed tail, dull teeth, and all the predatory instincts of a couch pillow will still be quickly and reliably identified as a cat by any normal person, even by a child. Plainly, our commonsense grasp of cathood must outstrip, and by some margin, the commonsense "definition" at issue, if we can still make such identifications, effortlessly, in the face of outright violations of almost every one of its conditions.

At best, such definitions merely list some salient features of the standard or prototypical cat: they capture only a small part of one's actual grasp of the category. That more comprehensive grasp is embodied in some well-tuned partition within the high-dimensional activation space encompassed by one's brain. That special feline partition embodies a portrait of the difficult-to-describe facial configuration peculiar to cats, and of the ways in which it can vary, from fluffy Persian to lean Siamese for example. It embodies a portrait of typical cat-style behaviors such as grooming, yawning, stretching, purring, stalking, and running. And it embodies a similarity gradient along every one of its many dimensions that will allow one to recognize novel examples of cats, even cats that are plainly nonstandard or atypical in some one or more respects.

This, after all, is the point of having concepts: to allow us to deal appropriately with the always novel but never-*entirely*-novel situations flowing endlessly toward us from an open-ended future. That same flexible readiness characterizes our social and moral concepts no less than our physical concepts. And our moral concepts show the same penetration and supraverbal sophistication shown by nonmoral concepts. One's ability to recognize instances of cruelty, patience, meanness, and courage, for instance, far outstrips one's capacity for verbal definition of those notions. One's diffuse expectations of their likely consequences similarly exceeds any verbal formulas that one could offer or construct, and those expectations are much the more penetrating because of it. All told, moral cognition would seem to display the same profile or signature that in other domains indicates the activity of a well-tuned neural network underlying the whole process.

If this is so, then moral perception will be subject to same ambiguities that characterize perception generally. Moral perception will be subject to the same modulation, shaping, and occasional "prejudice" that recurrent pathways make possible. By the same token, moral perception will occasionally be capable of the same cognitive reversals that we saw in such examples as the old/young woman in figure 5.4b. Pursuing the parallel further, it should also display cases where one's first moral reaction to a novel social situation is simply moral confusion, but where a little background knowledge or collateral information suddenly resolves that confusion into an example of something familiar, into an unexpected instance of some familiar moral prototype.

On these same assumptions, moral learning will be a matter of slowly generating a hierarchy of moral prototypes, presumably from a substantial number of relevant *examples* of the moral kinds at issue. Hence the relevance of stories and fables, and above all, the ongoing relevance of the parental example of interpersonal behavior, and parental commentary on and consistent guidance of childhood behavior. No child can learn the route to love and laughter entirely unaided, and no child will escape the pitfalls of selfishness and chronic conflict without an environment filled with examples to the contrary.

People with moral perception will be people who have learned those lessons well. People with reliable moral perception will be those who can protect their moral perception from the predations of self-deception and the corruptions of self-service. And, let us add, from the predations of group-think and the corruptions of fanaticism, which involves a rapacious disrespect for the moral cognition of others.

People with unusually penetrating moral insight will be those who can see a problematic moral situation in more than one way, and who can evaluate the relative accuracy and relevance of those competing interpretations. Such people will be those with unusual moral *imagination*, and a critical capacity to match. The former virtue will require a rich library of moral prototypes from which to draw, and especial skills in the recurrent manipulation of one's moral perception. The latter virtue will require a keen eye for local divergences from any presumptive prototype, and a willingness to take them seriously as grounds for finding some alternative understanding. Such people will by definition be rare, although all of us have some moral imagination, and all of us some capacity for criticism.

Accordingly, moral disagreements will be less a matter of interpersonal conflict over what "moral rules" to follow, and more a matter of interpersonal divergence as to what moral prototype best characterizes the situation at issue; more a matter, that is, of divergences over what kind of case we are confronting in the first place. Moral argument and moral persuasion, on this view, will most typically be a matter of trying to make salient this, that, or the other feature of the problematic situation, in hopes of winning one's opponent's assent to the local appropriateness of one general moral prototype over another. A nonmoral parallel of this phenomenon can again be found in the old/young woman example of figure 5.4b. If that figure were a photograph, say, and if there were some issue as to what it was *really* a picture of, I think we would agree that the young-woman interpretation is by far the more realistic of the two. The old-woman interpretation, by comparison, asks us to believe in the reality of a hyperbolic cartoon.

A genuinely moral example of this point about the nature of moral disagreement can be found in the current issue over a woman's right to abort a first-trimester pregnancy without legal impediment. One side of the debate considers the status of the early fetus and invokes the moral prototype of a Person, albeit a very tiny and incomplete person, a person who is defenseless for that very reason. The other side of the debate addresses the same situation and invokes the prototype of a tiny and possibly unwelcome Growth, as yet no more a person than is a cyst or a cluster of one's own skin cells. The first prototype bids us bring to bear all the presumptive rights of protection due any person, especially one that is young and defenseless. The second prototype bids us leave the woman to deal with the tiny growth as she sees fit, depending on the value it may or may not currently have for her, relative to her own long-term plans as an independently rightful human. Moral argument, in this case as elsewhere, typically consists in urging the accuracy or the poverty of the prototypes at issue as portrayals of the situation at hand.

I cite this example not to enter into this debate (I will do that in chapter 11), nor to presume on the patience of either party. I cite it to illustrate a point about the nature of moral disagreements and the nature of moral arguments. The point is that real disagreements need not be and seldom are about which explicit moral rules are true or false; the adversaries in this case might even agree on the obvious principles lurking in the area, such as, "It is prima facie wrong to kill any person." The disagreement here lies at a level deeper than that glib anodyne. It lies in a disagreement about the boundaries of the category "person", and hence about whether the explicit principle even applies to the case at hand. It lies in a divergence in the way people perceive or interpret the social world they encounter, and in their inevitably divergent behavioral responses to that world.

Whatever the eventual resolution of this divergence of moral cognition, it is antecedently plain that both parties to this debate are driven by some or other application of a moral prototype. But not all conflicts are thus morally grounded. Interpersonal conflicts are regularly no more principled than that between a jackal and a buzzard quarreling over a steaming carcass. Or a pair of two-year-old human children screaming in frustration at a tug-of-war over the same toy. This returns us, naturally enough, to the matter of moral development in children, and to the matter of the occasional failures of such development. How do such failures look, on the trained-network model here being explored?

Some of them recall a view from antiquity. Plato was inclined to argue, at least in his occasional voice as Socrates, that no man ever knowingly does wrong. For if he recognizes the action as being genuinely *wrong*—rather than just "thought to be wrong by others" —what motive could he possibly have to perform it? Generations of students have rejected Plato's suggestion, and rightly so. But Plato's point, however overstated, remains an instructive one: an enormous portion of human moral misbehavior is due primarily to *cognitive* failures of one kind or another.

Such failures are inevitable. We have neither infinite intelligence nor total information. No one is perfect. But some people, as we know, are notably less perfect than the norm, and their failures are systematic. In fact, some people are rightly judged to be chronic troublemakers, terminal narcissists, thoughtless blockheads, or treacherous snakes; not to mention bullies and sadists. Whence stem these sorry failings?

From many sources, as the next chapter will show. But we may note right at the beginning that a simple failure to develop the normal range of moral *perception* and social *skills* will account for a great deal here. Consider the child who, for whatever reasons, learns only very slowly to distinguish the minute-by-minute flux of rights, expectations, entitlements, and duties as they are created and canceled in the course of an afternoon at the day-care center, an outing with one's siblings, or a playground game of hide-and-seek. Such a child is doomed to chronic conflict with other children—doomed to cause them disappointment, frustration, and eventually anger, all of it directed at him.

Moreover, he has all of it coming, despite the fact that a flinty-eyed determination to "flout the rules" is *not* what lies behind his unacceptable behavior. The boy is a moral cretin because he has not acquired the skills already flourishing in the others. He is missing skills of recognition to begin with, and also the skills of matching his behavior to the moral circumstance at hand, even when it is dimly recognized. The child steps out of turn, seizes disallowed advantages, reacts badly to constraints binding on everyone, denies earned approval to others, and is blind to opportunities for profitable cooperation. His failure to develop and deploy a roughly normal hierarchy of social and moral prototypes may seem tragic, and it is. But one's sympathies must lie with the other children when, after due patience runs out, they drive the miscreant howling from the playground.

What holds for a playground community holds for adult communities as well. We all know adult humans whose behavior recalls to some degree the bleak portrait just outlined. They are, to put the point gently, unskilled in social practices. Moreover, all of them pay a stiff and continuing price for their failure. Overt retribution aside, they miss out on the profound and ever-compounding advantages that successful socialization brings, specifically, the intricate practical, cognitive, and emotional commerce that lifts everyone in its embrace.

This quick portrait of the moral miscreant invites a correspondingly altered portrait of the morally successful person. The common picture of the Moral Agent as one who has acquiesced in a set of explicit rules imposed from the outside—from God, perhaps, or from Society—is dubious in the extreme. A relentless commitment to a handful of explicit rules does not make one a morally successful or a morally insightful person. The price of virtue is a good deal higher, and the path thereto is a good deal longer. It is much more accurate to see the moral person as one who has acquired a complex set of subtle and enviable skills: perceptual, cognitive, and behavioral.

This was in fact the view of Aristotle, to recall another name from antiquity. Moral virtue, as he saw it, was something acquired and refined over a lifetime of social experience, not something swallowed whole from an outside authority. It was a matter of slowly developing a set of largely inarticulable skills, a matter of *practical* wisdom. Aristotle's perspective and the neural network perspective here converge. From this perspective, the traditional question posed by the moral skeptic, namely, "Why should I be moral?", looks peculiar and uncomprehending. As well ask, "Why should I acquire the skills of swimming?" when one is a fish. In both cases, the short answer is, "Consider, dear creature, the environment in which you have no choice but to live." To be sure, this answer leaves open the question of exactly what motor skills will make one the *best possible* swimmer, and likewise the question of exactly what social skills will make one the *maximally successful* social agent. But that is as it should be. Only experience can answer that question—one's own experience, and the accumulated experience of all mankind.

7 The Brain in Trouble: Cognitive Dysfunction and Mental Illness

Diagnostic Techniques: The Literally Transparent Brain

Nature herself regularly performs experiments, on human as well as animal subjects, in a variety and with a blind cruelty almost beyond human imitation. The neurology sections of modern hospitals manage a constant traffic in people whose brains have suffered damage, or what physicians call "lesions", to some area or other. These can result from a growing tumor, a burst or blocked blood vessel, a skull injury, a toxic drug, a genetic or developmental misfortune, or a runaway viral infection. In this unhappy domain, modern science enters almost exclusively in its nurturing and curative mode. Its primary aims are to arrest the assault, to minimize the damage, and to promote whatever degree of cognitive recovery remains possible for the patient. Ethical considerations preclude genuinely hazardous experimentation on human subjects, save in rare cases and only to the degree that it is essential to providing the best possible treatment for the individual involved.

Despite such limitations, it is here in the world's hospitals that we have learned the bulk of what we know about the localization or regional specialization of cognitive functions in the *human* brain. Until the last third of this century, access to brain damage was limited to postmortem dissections. One then tried to find, in a large population of deceased patients, regular correlations between the location of the brain damage thus discovered and the type of cognitive or behavioral deficit displayed prior to death. This produced some real understanding of which brain areas are specialized for which cognitive functions, but it was rarely of benefit to any living patients.

The widespread availability of X-ray machines finally allowed us to look past the skull of live patients. Even so, little was revealed beyond the occasional bullet. The brain is entirely soft tissue, and therefore almost completely and uniformly transparent to X rays. One's skull might as well have been empty, for all that standard X-ray machines revealed.

CAT Scans

The spread of computer technology in the 1970's improved things dramatically. Special X-ray scans that exploited computerized axial tomography—*CAT scans* or *CT scans*, for short—took many thinly sliced X-ray shots of the brain rotated around an axis through the patient's head. A computer program processed the subtle differences in transparency that are practically invisible in ordinary X-ray pictures, and then assembled the results into a useful picture of the patient's brain. One could finally see major lesions and swelling tumors in advance of surgery or death, and plan one's surgery or therapy to suit. The resolution, or sharpness of focus, of the early CAT scans was poor, but fuzzy data were better than none. Modern versions do much better, resolving anatomical structure down to a millimeter. These work-horse machines are relatively inexpensive and easy to use, and they are still the brain-scanning machines most likely to be encountered in any modern hospital.

PET Scans

Positron emission tomography, or *PET*, opened a further window, this time onto the brain's ongoing physiological *activity* instead of its static physical structure. When the neurons in some specialized brain area are unusually active because the person is engaged in some specialized cognitive task, those neurons consume extra energy. That energy is ultimately drawn from the breakdown of chemicals in the bloodstream, and the local blood flow increases in response to that increased demand for energy. If one could somehow monitor the local elevations in blood flow within the brain, one could thereby monitor the increases in neural activity in the specific areas that underlie specific cognitive functions.

The PET technology allows us to do exactly that. The trick is to label the blood to make it detectable from outside the skull. This is done by injecting it with a form of water containing a short-lived radioactive isotope of oxygen, O 15. This specially labeled water arrives fresh from bombardment in an on-site cyclotron, which makes it slightly radioactive for a very short period, no more than ten or twenty minutes so as not to present a danger to the patient. The water is then injected into the patient's bloodstream, where it quickly diffuses.

During the water's brief radioactive period, each labeled water molecule sooner or later radiates a special particle called a positron, the antimatter version of the electron. Each emitted positron immediately encounters a local electron, and their mutual annihilation produces a gamma ray with a signature wavelength. These rays are detected as they leave the brain and skull, both of which are transparent to gamma rays.

The detector is a large ring about the size of a truck tire, with many gamma-ray detectors tuned to the signature wavelength. The patient's head is placed within the ring, and the many small detectors pick up the locations in the brain where the labeled water molecules have become concentrated due to an increased local blood flow caused by an elevated energy demand. As with CAT scans, the ring is moved through a number of distinct planes or "cuts" (hence "tomography"). A computer program processes the data collected in this fashion, and assembles a visual image of the brain for us to see, an image that is color-coded for relative levels of O 15, and hence for elevated neural activity.

The spatial and temporal resolution of a PET scan is fairly poor. A hot spot of neuronal activity smaller than a cubic half-centimeter will generally go undetected, as will a hot spot that lasts for less than thirty seconds. Only large and perseverant activity gets picked up. Even so, PET's ability to reveal the hidden profile of ongoing brain *activity* rather than just brain structure makes it invaluable. Since PET is noninvasive, in contrast to a probing microelectrode, it permits research on live, normal, cognitively active humans. Simply have the subject engage in some well-defined cognitive task while relaxing in the scanner, and then see which areas of her brain show heightened levels of activity during her execution of that special task.

The various functional specializations of human brain areas revealed in PET experiments agree more or less closely with the earlier maps constructed by correlating behavioral deficits with post-mortem discovery of the injured patient's brain-lesions. With PET scans, however, we can explore the many dimensions of cognitive activity in much greater detail, and we can explore them in brains that are entirely normal.

Knowing the activational profile of a normal brain puts us in a position to use PET scans to locate and recognize an abnormal profile. This returns us to the medical domain and to patients with neurological and psychiatric disorders. Because PET makes visible the previously invisible. It permits the physician to discover and locate neurological problems whose cause is too subtle or too diffuse to show up in a CAT scan or other technique designed to detect large-scale structural problems such as brain tumors or lesions. For example, if a patient's problem lies in an abnormal distribution of some important neurochemical, or in the scattered deterioration of individual neurons, a CAT scan of the brain's purely structural condition will show nothing out of the ordinary. But a PET scan, being sensitive to the activation levels of the brain's many neurons, will reveal activational abnormalities vividly, however subtle or diffuse might be their underlying cause. We will encounter such cases shortly.

MRI Scans

The final imaging technique in the modern armory is perhaps the most spectacular of all. It is called magnetic resonance imaging, or *MRI.* Like the CAT scan, its original function is structural imaging, but its spatial resolution is rather better, reaching down to fractions of a millimeter. It is also more sensitive to subtle differences in the character of soft tissue, and so the brain's internal anatomy is easily seen. Moreover, dead or damaged areas within the brain stand out quite dramatically, and bone is no longer the occluding problem it is with CAT.

Superficially, an MRI machine looks much like a PET machine: the patient's head is placed in a massive ring containing the many detectors. But no radioactive substances need be injected nor need any X rays be directed at the brain. The only thing that enters the patient's body is a powerful pulsating magnetic field generated by large electromagnets in the enclosing ring. That magnetic field has the effect of forcing the nuclei of the brain's water atoms to line up all in the same direction, rather like iron filings lining up on a sheet of paper with a magnet placed underneath, only on a subatomic scale. But when the magnetic field is then turned off, the nuclei snap back to their original positions, thus losing their acquired energy and releasing it in the form of a signature photon, to which the brain is transparent but the surrounding detectors are sensitive. With many such magnetic pulses produced per second, an image of the brain's interior slowly accumulates. Given the variations in water content of the different kinds of brain tissue, especially inac-

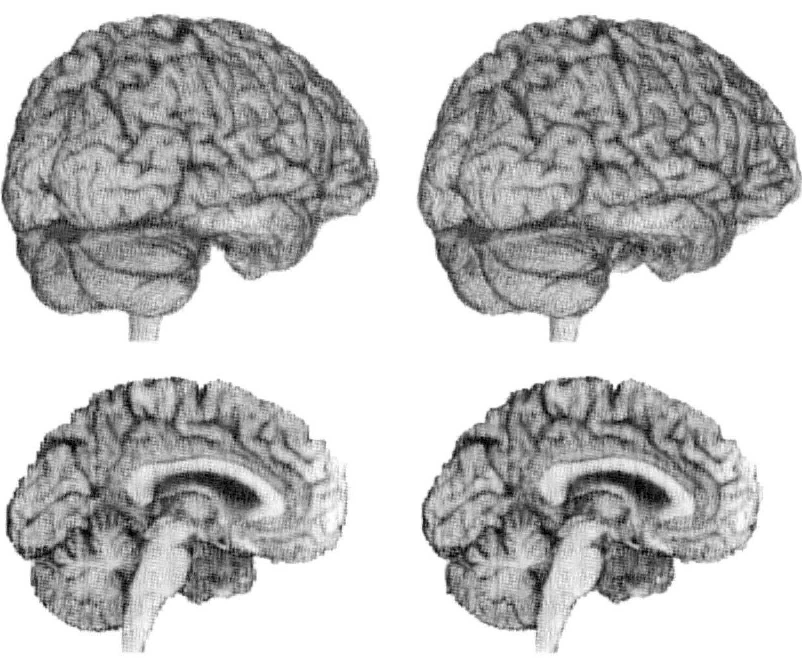

Figure 7.1 (Top) An MRI image of a normal human brain, alive, conscious, and thinking furiously. A computer was used to manipulate the accumulated data and present the image from two different perspectives so that it can be viewed as a stereoscopic pair. Retrieve once more the cardboard stereoscope from the inside back cover of this book. (Bottom) The same living brain, as "sectioned down the middle" by computer processing of the MRI data. (Thanks to H. Damasio, T. Grabowski, et al for the MRI images.)

tive scar tissue, an MRI scan reveals a wealth of structural detail through the brain's entire volume.

A simple example of a brain image produced by MRI appears in figure 7.1 (top). This particular brain is in fact well known to me via more conventional informational pathways. It is the brain of my wife and colleague, Patricia Churchland, and it is very dear to me. (Thanks here to our colleagues, Drs. Hanna and Antonio R. Damasio of the University of Iowa College of Medicine, for providing the MRI, the computing facilities, and much mirth.)

Since a complete MRI scan provides us with information about every cubic millimeter throughout the brain's entire volume, which information is stored in a computer file for pictorial reconstruction by a computer program, we are not limited to surface-only views of the brain. The computer programs now in use at the Damasio's laboratory allow us to cut through the brain's image at any place and at any angle, and then rotate the revealed section for direct inspection, as in figure 7.1 (bottom)—once again, Pat's brain.

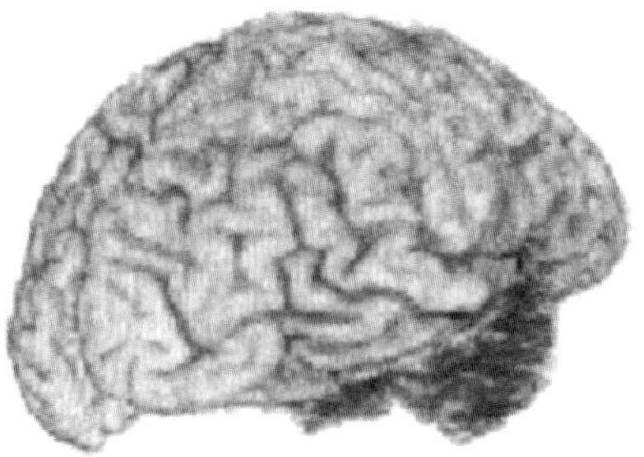
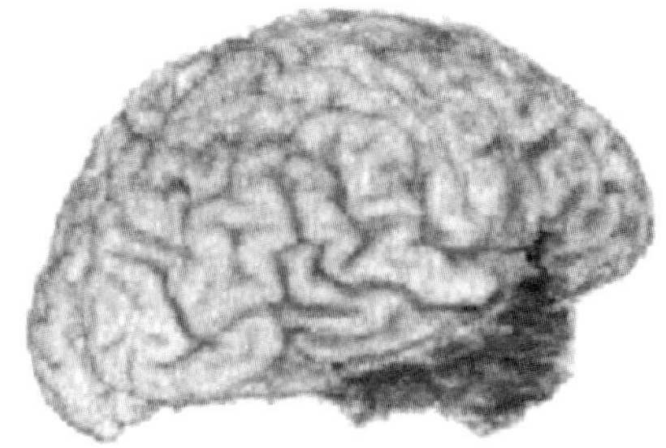

Figure 7.2 An MRI-computer-produced stereo image of the live brain of the patient known as "Boswell", a brain that has suffered extensive lesions. The lesioned or dysfunctional areas show up in black. Note the damage to the frontal pole of both temporal lobes, and to the underpart of the frontal cortex. (Thanks to H. Damasio, T. Grabowski, et al for the MRI images.)

Repeated application of this procedure can reveal the idiosyncratic details of any individual brain's physical structure, and the exact shape, location, and extent of any lesions or tumors it may contain. In short, this technique allows the physician or the neuroscientist to do detailed *exploratory brain surgery* on any patient or subject without ever leaving the computer console's video screen, and without ever lifting a scalpel.

Figure 7.2 shows an MRI-produced stereo pair of the the brain of one of the Damasios' more celebrated subjects, referred to in the medical literature as "Boswell," a man with a memory that never reaches back more than thirty seconds into the past. We will discuss him later in this chapter. For now, notice the extensive lesion in the under part of the frontal cortex on both sides, reaching into both of the two flanking or so-called "temporal" lobes as well. The damage shows in black.

Putting MRI and PET scans together allows us to match in detail any person's idiosyncratic brain structure with her idiosyncratic activational profiles during cognitive activity. It is important to match them in this way, since each person's brain is unique in its physical details. This was in fact the motivation behind Pat's sitting for an MRI. The Damasios used Pat's MRI results to help interpret the data from a subsequent PET scan of her brain activity during several carefully contrived cognitive tasks (figure 7.3). The idea was to observe and compare localized elevations in her neuronal activity during (1) a purely visual observation task, (2) a purely auditory observation task, and (3) an extended task, with no perceptual input, involving only her visual *imagination*.

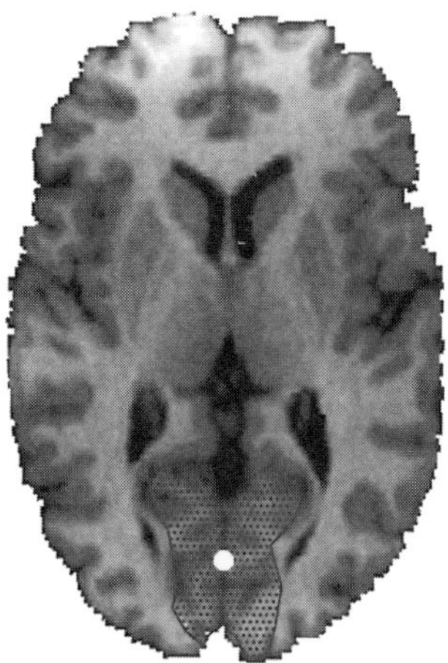

Figure 7.3 A PET scan of neuronal activity in the primary and secondary visual cortex, averaged over five subjects, during a cognitive task involving visual imagination, but no external visual input. The area of elevated activity is cross-hatched and superimposed on the image of Pat's brain. (Thanks to H. Damasio, T. Grabowski, et al for the MRI and PET images.)

The MRI allowed the Damasios to determine the exact location and extent of Pat's visual cortex, and of her auditory cortex as well. The PET allowed them to identify any elevations in neural activity in those areas. As was entirely expected, the visual and auditory tasks produced increased activity within her visual and auditory cortices, respectively. These were merely baseline tests. What was interesting was what PET revealed about her visual cortex during the visual imagination task: that familiar area at the back of her brain showed an elevated level of activity exactly during the period of that task. The activity level was not as high as during externally stimulated visual perception, but it was clearly higher than the quiescent level shown during the purely auditory tasks. Visual *imagination*, it would appear, involves heavy use of the same brain areas that sustain visual *perception* in the first place.

What kind of input could stimulate such pronounced activity across the neurons in Pat's visual cortex? Her eyes were closed and fully masked during that visual imagination task, so nothing came from her retinas. And yet her cortical cells were continuously active. If this result immediately suggests to you the possibility that the process of visual imagery involves the systematic stimulation of the visual cortex by way of *recurrent* axonal pathways descending from elsewhere in the brain, then you share the same hypothesis advanced by the Damasios. Evidently, you are also starting to redeploy some neurocomputational prototypes, prototypes learned in chapter 5, in novel explanatory situations. If so, this realizes one of my aims in writing this book: to enable the reader to begin to think spontaneously in neurocomputational terms.

Apraxia and Motor Dysfunction

Praxis is the ancient Greek term for acquired skills, for learned abilities, for practical knowledge or knowledge of how to do things. "Apraxia" is thus an appropriate term for any localized loss of skills or loss of practical know-how due to brain damage. In practice, neurologists tend to restrict the use of that term to deficits in voluntary movement, but I here advert to its original and more general meaning in order to remind the reader that the dysfunctions we are about to survey all involve the failure of real neural networks to discharge or display their acquired skills.

A language-loss condition called *aphasia* is a too-frequent example of the general category. It is commonly produced by a stroke (a blocked or burst blood vessel in the brain) or other localized loss of normal blood flow, which starves the local neural network to death within minutes. Aphasia involves an isolated loss of the ability to produce *speech*, even though the patient might still comprehend the speech of others, and even though he retains basic motor control of his mouth and larynx. He can still chew normally, for example, pronounce a few nouns without difficulty, perhaps even sing at some length. His basic control over that complex muscle system is evidently intact.

But the higher neural system for language—the recurrent system that in normal people produces the complex vectorial sequences that result in coherent speech—is in him destroyed. A PET scan reveals a lack of neural activity in the left frontal area (often called Broca's area) adjacent to the mouth and throat areas of the primary motor strip. It often reveals, in addition, a lack of activity in the area of the temporal lobe indicated in figure 7.4 (often called Wernicke's area), an area crucial for speech *comprehension* as well. In such a case, the patient will also suffer *comprehension aphasia*. The joint condition is called *global aphasia*. An MRI scan of such a patient reveals a dark patch of morbid scar tissue in one or both areas. The individual's mouth may still be his to command. But the

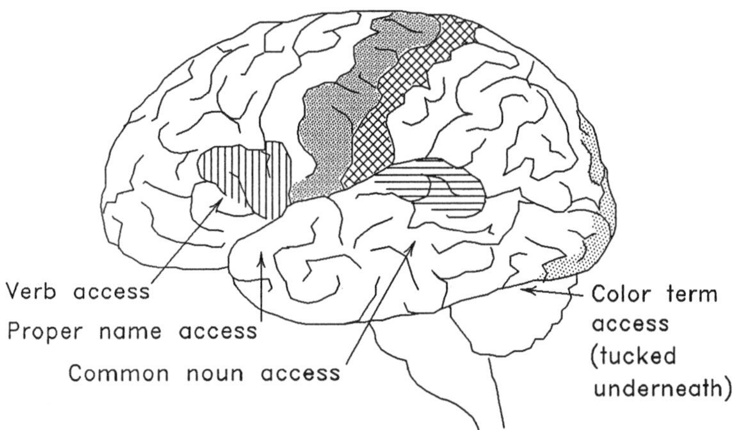

Figure 7.4 The areas of absent activity and neuronal death associated with the selective loss of normal command over distinct parts of speech, as revealed by both PET and MRI scans. (Adapted from A. and H. Damasio)

specially trained "conductor" that could coax coherent speech from that instrument has simply been destroyed.

In some patients, that special conductor is spared or only slightly injured; Broca's area may be intact. But owing to lesions just upstream from that speech-production area, its normal connections to the rest of the patient's cognitive activity are lost or severely compromised. The resulting language deficits vary, and they are sensitive to just where the damage is located. Empirical studies by the Damasios have revealed that it is not just Wernicke's area that is important for normal language competence, but practically the entire temporal lobe from front to back.

For example, if a lesion or other damage should occur at the bottom rear of the temporal lobe, close to the visual cortex, the patient loses the ability to apply his *color* vocabulary, although he can still discriminate colors perceptually. If the damage occurs in the middle part of the temporal lobe, underneath the primary auditory cortex, then the patient's command of *common nouns* is lost. If the damage is farther forward, highly *specific nouns* disappear from his speech. Finally, damage at the frontal tip steals *proper names*, the most specific terms of all, from his speech. (Boswell has this last deficit, and substantial loss of specific nouns, as we are about to see. Figure 7.2 shows the damage to his left temporal lobe: the front end is dead and the damage reaches back slightly farther than that.)

In all of these cases, it appears that the victim's command of the relevant prelinguistic *concepts* is not significantly impaired. For example, when shown a picture of Marilyn Monroe, one of the Damasios' name-impaired patients said, "Don't know her name, but I know who she is; I saw her movies; she had an affair with the president; she committed suicide; or maybe somebody killed her; the police, maybe?" Such patients have no deficit in facial recognition, the failing discussed in chapter 2. But they can no longer deploy proper names to express their recognitions. The same point goes for people whose language deficit concerns common nouns. No failure of recognition need be evident, but the standard categories can no longer be named in speech, although the patient's speech is otherwise normal.

This loss of functional vocabulary is often partial. Boswell, for example (of figure 7.2), has an extensive loss where common "natural-kind" terms are concerned. When shown simple pictures of natural objects, he is unable to apply terms such as "raccoon", "peach", "pine tree", "carrot", "lion", etc. But he has no deficit for common "functional-kind" terms, such as "fork", "car", "radio", "hammer", "toothbrush", and the like. When shown pictures of these items, he identifies them all without difficulty. There is one exception for only one group of functional kinds: musical instruments! For some reason, Boswell's command of terms such as "trumpet", "guitar", etc., got wiped out along with his natural-kind terms.

Looking at these broad divisions in what is and isn't lost, one may be reminded of the sometimes unexpected hierarchical partitions across the activation spaces of many of the model networks discussed earlier, networks trained to perform complex discriminatory tasks. Recall NETtalk's binary division of its conceptual space into Vowel transformations and Consonant transformations.

In such a network it is possible to create artificially a cognitive deficit, a partial one similar to Boswell's, by selectively removing, or cutting the connections to, those neurons at the middle layer whose activation plays a more crucial role in coding the vowels. Since they are quiescent or invariant anyway during the coding of consonants, their destruction or disconnection leaves intact the network's ability to respond appropriately to consonants, while it cripples its performance on vowels. Might partial damage to the neuronal populations in *living* brains occasionally reveal, in the curiously selective survival of certain cognitive skills, comparable partitions across our own activation spaces? The idea is conjectural, but it provides food for thought. Boswell's case is not unique.

Let us now look beyond specifically linguistic skills. A much more common apraxia, and one more gradual in its onset, is Parkinson's disease. In older people—beyond sixty or seventy—one frequently sees chronic oscillations in the movements of their arms and hands, at a frequency of perhaps three or four cycles per second. One later sees a marked deterioration in the quality or coordination of their walking, and in advanced cases, a curious inability to initiate motor behavior, or to arrest it once initiated.

Parkinson's disease is one example of the slow degeneration of a robust and fault-tolerant neuronal system, as opposed to the sudden and catastrophic demise of an entire network as in a stroke-induced aphasia. Parkinson's patients typically show some degeneration in their *substantia nigra* (literally, "black bodies"), two tiny midbrain areas whose neurons produce and use the neurotransmitter chemical dopamine. A standard treatment for the symptoms of Parkinson's disease is a substance called L-dopa, which metabolizes to form dopamine inside the body. This intervention does nothing to cure the original condition—the patient's intrinsic dopamine deficit is so far irreversible—but the steady administration of L-dopa does reduce the tremors and other motor abnormalities, at least for a time.

Among younger adults, who are typically still innocent of either strokes or parkinsonian degeneration, a frequent frustration is *multiple sclerosis*, or *MS*. (This affliction has already touched more than one, indeed, more than two, of my own dear friends.) MS attacks and slowly destroys the many millions of peculiar pancake-shaped cells that normally wrap themselves tightly around the axons of almost all neurons.

During childhood, those self-wrapping cells slowly come to encase most of the nervous system's longish axons with a thin layer of insulation known as a *myelin sheath*. An axon thus encased gains a real advantage: the velocity with which its signal gets transmitted along its length goes up by at least a factor of ten. Accordingly, the well-tuned recurrent motor network of any adult will have its synaptic weights configured to suit the dynamic features of that network. Thus does it achieve sensorimotor coordination, as we observed in chapter 5.

Alas, should the conduction velocities of the many axons within that recurrent motor network ever change significantly, as inevitably they must if the layers of myelin insulation are slowly and randomly being destroyed by MS, then the quality of the sensory information that the brain gets from its own body will be degraded, and the existing configuration of synaptic weights will sustain an increasingly inadequate regime of sensorimotor coordination. The subject will begin to notice a numbness in his limb extremities, and will find himself increasingly clumsy. He will retreat into "safe" but visibly plodding modes of walking and manual behavior, modes that leave plenty of room for the ever-growing background of motor error. And he will often suffer a gathering muscle weakness due to the muscle atrophy that stems from the ever-shrinking energy and complexity of his motor exercise.

The agent responsible for the demise of those insulating myelin sheaths remains mysterious. It may be viral. Or it may be some autoimmune disorder, where one's immune system wrongly identifies one's own myelin cells as alien and methodically sets about destroying them. In either case, it is no surprise that randomly and progressively reducing the velocity and the integrity of one's axonal communications should impair one's perception and carefully tuned motor coordination.

In the domain of motor deficits, MS has a more rapacious cousin, *amyotrophic lateral sclerosis*, or *ALS*, more widely known as Lou Gerhig's disease after the baseball star who died of it in the 1940s. With ALS, it is the motor neurons themselves that are attacked, rather than the myelin cells that enfold them. With the progressive death of the long motor neurons in the spinal cord, motor control is not just disrupted, it is destroyed. The end result is comparable to cutting the strings that guide a puppet: the puppet becomes limp and incapable of bodily motion. In the long run, the only motor control to survive is control over the eye muscles and the bladder and bowels. These exceptions are mysterious, and perhaps significant, for we are uncertain what causes this selective assault on or degeneration of the body's motor neurons. Nor have we any treatment. Recent research results indicate, however, that ALS has a genetic component, so our helplessness may be temporary.

The more common disease discussed earlier, MS, proceeds fairly slowly, and it regularly pauses in its incremental advance for years at a time, allowing a strong soul some time in which to adjust. With ALS, by contrast, the loss of motor control proceeds more swiftly and relentlessly, and it tests severely even the most resilient of characters. Within five years or so, depending on where in the peripheral motor system the degeneration first began, motor control of the entire body, speech included, may disappear almost completely. And yet, all the while, the nonmotor systems of the brain remain unaffected, and thus the victim's sheerly cognitive faculties survive untouched.

The gifted and imaginative physicist Stephen Hawking is a compelling example of this latter point. Struck by ALS as a young adult, he persevered in his professional pursuit of physics. At this writing, his motor control has shrunk to a tiny window, and without modern computer technology he would be unable to communicate at all. And yet his theoretical imagination is as free as yours or mine—and stronger. Hawking is the celebrated author of some of the most important and original ideas in current cosmology and modern physics. Evidently, a massively recurrent network does not require motor control in order to explore new possibilities for the understanding of old phenomena. With one's perception and memory of intriguing problems intact, and with one's recurrent pathways humming, there is endless space to explore. Where voluntary movement in physical space has become impossible, conceptual space remains open to unimpaired and purposeful flight.

We have so far seen two general sources of motor deficits: outright network destruction caused by stroke, trauma, or autoimmune disease; and the disruption of normal axonal communication caused by the demyelinization of axons. These do not exhaust the possibilities, but they will serve to give us a preliminary feeling for the space that contains them.

Perceptual and Cognitive Dysfunction

In the light of what earlier chapters have presented concerning the brain's coding of visual information, it will come as no surprise that massive destruction of the primary visual cortex produces a profound and permanent blindness, even though the eyes themselves might remain healthy. The condition is called *cortical blindness* to distinguish it from the more common forms of blindness that result from damage to the eye or optic nerve. What is more likely to surprise is that occasionally such patients are *unaware* that they are blind, especially if their cortical destruction has occurred suddenly and all at once. Indeed, some deny their blindness quite stoutly, often for some days or weeks after the internal accident has occurred. Though they stumble into things and cannot see your hand in front of their face, they smoothly confabulate excuses for their clumsiness, continue speaking about their environment as if nothing had changed, and they become evasive, confabulatory, and eventually quite annoyed if pressed about what they are manifestly unable to see.

Such *blindness denial* is one instance of what is called *anosognosia*: the curious lack of awareness that some major cognitive or motor subsystem has simply disappeared. Perhaps this phenomenon is not so surprising. In a brain-normal person, if her eyes are covered, or somehow lost due to accident, then "everything looks black." Her visual cortex will correctly represent a complete absence of incoming light. However, when the visual cortex itself has been entirely destroyed, there is no cognitive system left to represent either the presence *or* the absence of incoming light. In that case, her cortex does not represent "blackness". Rather, it has ceased to represent entirely. It is now out of the representation business. So it cannot actively represent a visual problem, as it can when undamaged. Such a patient will therefore have to learn that she is blind from some source other than her own visual system. Hence the initial period of confabulation and denial.

A similar loss of awareness concerns one's own body and limbs. If one loses, on the right side of the brain only, both the motor cortex and the adjacent somatosensory cortex (see again figure 7.4), one has thereby lost the capacity to represent or control the entire left-hand side of one's body. (In all of us, the relevant axons connecting the limbs with the brain *cross* on their journey to and from the cortex.) Such a patient is chronically unaware of that disconnected half of his own body. When dressing, he will dress only the right half of his body, leaving the left pant leg and the left shirt sleeve dangling. When shaving, he will shave only the right side of his face. When bathing, only the body's right half gets washed. And so on.

Quite regularly, these hemineglect patients will adamantly deny that a limb on the neglected side of their body even *belongs* to them, and they do so without hesitation or evident embarrassment, despite the fact that they can see that the limb is still firmly attached to them. Hemineglect patients will occasionally become annoyed at the presence of such an alien object in such close proximity and attempt to throw their own limb out of bed! Such robust alienation of major elements of one's own body is indeed hard to credit or imagine, but the syndrome is familiar to neurologists. Perhaps it is not so hard to comprehend if we remember that an intimate part of the patient's original self—specifically, the part of his brain responsible for directing commerce with the now-neglected limbs—has indeed disappeared as a functioning cognitive entity. And it has taken all awareness of those limbs with it. Although his entire body may remain, a part of the patient's inner *self* has vanished.

These examples all involve a spatial loss of some kind. Given that humans are massively recurrent networks, we might also expect disorders in temporal cognition. Once again, Nature delivers a wide variety. The Damasios' subject, Boswell, is an example of a rare but striking memory deficit called *anterograde amnesia*. The viral infection that destroyed the front ends of Boswell's temporal lobes and the underpart of his frontal lobe, also destroyed a pair of finger-size bodies that flank the midbrain on either side, just inside the wrinkled "helmet" of the cerebral hemispheres. These bodies are called the left and right *hippocampus*. They do not show up well in figure 7.2 (Boswell's brain), but they are to be found toward the rear of the badly lesioned areas in the underpart of his frontal cortex, and they are completely destroyed on both sides.

The hippocampus plays a critical role in converting the fleeting contents of one's ongoing short-term memory into the permanent contents of one's long-term memory. How it does this is not yet known. But for Boswell, the result of his hippocampal loss is a complete inability to recall anything in his experience that happened more than about thirty or forty seconds earlier than the present. His window of consciousness and short-term memory reaches back no farther than forty seconds into the past. Once any event recedes beyond that narrow limit—as in forty seconds, of course, absolutely everything does—it is then lost to Boswell forever.

Boswell can still learn new skills, such as how to solve certain puzzles, and these acquired skills will persist in the normal fashion. But Boswell will completely forget the learning episode, and even forget that he now has that skill. Implausible as it might seem, in the eighteen years since his injury, Boswell has not laid down a single new memory of the episodic or autobiographical sort. Moreover, he is completely unaware of his cognitive loss. You can tell him, explain it to him, of course. But in thirty seconds he has forgotten your explanation without a trace. In fact, if he loses sight of you for more than forty seconds, he will forget *you* just as completely as your doomed explanation. On one occasion, after observing the Damasios perform an experiment on Boswell's category-recognition skills for about an hour, I left the lab for a few minutes. When I returned, Boswell had no idea who I was, and the original introductions and opening pleasantries had to be completely reperformed before we could all return to the testing at hand.

Boswell has come to the Damasios' lab for tests once a month for each of the eighteen years since his injury. Antonio and Hanna have gotten to know Boswell—a forthright and cheerful man—rather well. And yet, each time he is brought from his care facility to the university's hospital, he meets his long-term physicians as if for the first time. They appear to him to be perfect strangers. And when taken back home in the late afternoon, he will meet his long-term care givers as if he'd never seen them before either. With Boswell, social introduction is a never-ending activity. In all, his condition may seem nightmarish. The mercy is that Boswell himself has no inkling of it.

A small qualification is necessary here, reflecting the earlier point about skill acquisition. Over time, Boswell does show some discrimination in his emotional reactions to and preferences for specific people, a subconscious or preconscious reflection of his past experiences in their company. Although his autobiographical memory has been abolished, plainly there is residual learning somewhere in his brain.

With brain dysfunction, mercies are rare. More often, it is confusion, frustration, and even terror that beset the lives of the afflicted. Nowhere is this more evident than in the several types of *schizophrenia*, the second most common and absolutely the most disabling form of major mental illness. This is the disorder that involves delusions—lasting factual beliefs of a bizarre nature, such as the belief that the CIA and the KGB are both spying on you, or that the Martians have implanted a radio receiver inside your brain. This is the disorder that involves hallucinatory experiences—such as seeing people who are not there, or hearing voices inside your head—not always, perhaps, but at least occasionally.

More chronically, schizophrenia is marked by a growing incoherence in the victim's conversation and trains of thought. The afflicted individual is unable to stick to or follow a unified chain of reasoning, either practical or theoretical. As the disorder progresses, schizophrenics can no longer be trusted with any position of practical responsibility. They are chronically distracted. Their attention wanders chaotically, and they are given to mumbling to themselves. Last but not least, their emotions become disconnected from what normal people would regard as their appropriate occasions. Most commonly, the schizophrenic's emotional tone is curiously flat and unresponsive. But often they will spontaneously display a fear, grief, or rage that is wholly out of keeping with their actual circumstances. Schizophrenics, to use a familiar phrase, are "out of touch with reality," both physical reality and social reality.

Schizophrenia is still deeply puzzling to us, but it appears to involve the global and comparatively gradual degeneration of a robust and fault-tolerant brain, rather than the sudden and catastrophic demise of a specialized cognitive subsystem, as happens in local and stroke-induced lesions. (Overt schizophrenic symptoms can often appear suddenly, in young adults, for example, but this would seem to mark the passing of a critical point rather than the beginning of the basic problem.) The presumed nature of that broad degeneration introduces a new dimension to our discussion of neural networks, a dimension so far deliberately suppressed by me for reasons of expositional simplicity.

The fact is, a biological neural network spends its entire working life submerged in a complex biochemical soup. That soup serves not only to nourish the hard-working neurons, as one might expect. It is also part and parcel of almost everything a neuron does. In particular, the microprocess by which a given neuron's activation level is conducted across any synaptic gap, in order to stimulate or inhibit its target neuron at the next population, is a microprocess that is biochemical through and through. It actually consists in a dance of specialized molecules called *neurotransmitters* that are released through the surface of the synaptic end-bulb in proportion to the strength of the axonal signal that reaches it. Once released, those molecules diffuse almost instantly throughout the liquid medium within the synaptic cleft, to be taken up on the other side by the waiting "receptor sites" on the surface of the target neuron. Figure 7.5 presents, at last, a close-up look at the microphysical details of a synaptic connection, and a cartoon sketch of the chemical dynamics of its operation.

Note that the chemical flow goes in both directions. Once a neurotransmitter molecule is taken up by the receptors of the target neuron, there to stimulate or inhibit that neuron, the neurotransmitter is broken down and its parts are released back into the liquid me-

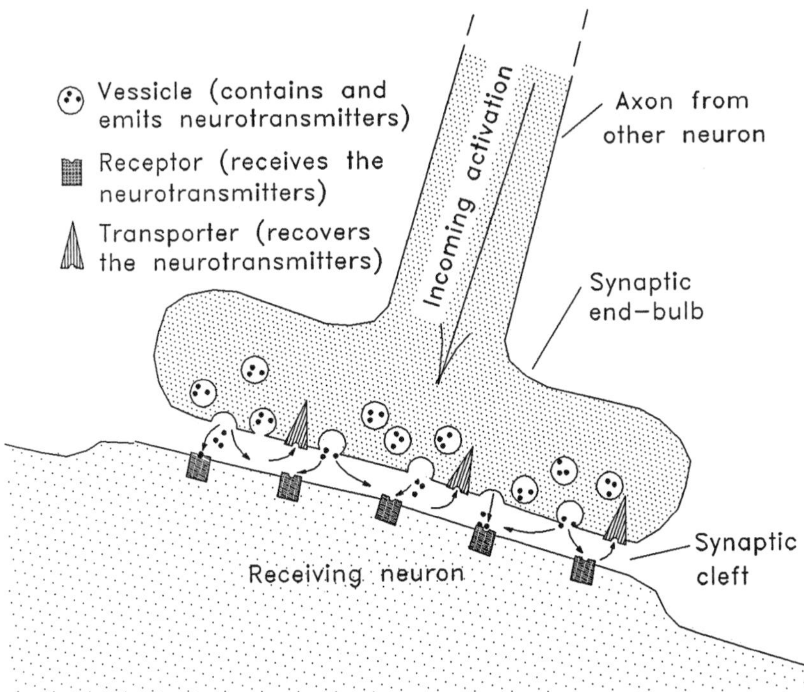

Figure 7.5 A schematic synaptic connection.

dium of the synaptic cleft. Those molecular parts are quickly taken up again by the original synaptic end-bulb, where they are used to resynthesize more of that neurotransmitter for the next round of synaptic communication. All of this microactivity happens in milliseconds.

Compare this situation with the artificial models of the preceding chapters. In a neural-network model that exists solely as an abstract simulation within a conventional computer (in truth, this is most of such models), the all-important process of synaptic transmission is simply a matter of the local hacker's program multiplying together a pair of numbers. One number represents the value of the "synaptic weight", and the other represents the value of the arriving "activation level". Their product equals the impact on the target cell. And that's it. No other factors are relevant. In neural-network models that exist as real systems of electronic hardware—networks etched on a microchip, for example—synaptic transmission is once more very simple: a matter of an encountered Conductance multiplied by an impressed Voltage. Only occasional variations in the local thermal or optical environment might complicate or modulate this process of "synaptic" transmission.

With real neurons and biological synapses, by contrast, the transmission process can be modulated, enhanced, degraded, or even arrested entirely by a host of biochemical factors. Some of these factors operate on a time scale of milliseconds, others on a scale of minutes, hours, or days. This means that, in biological brains, cognitive activity has rather more dimensions than have so far been displayed in our artificial network models. Further variety arises from the fact that different subsystems of the brain use different and proprietary types of neurotransmitter chemicals, of which there are dozens. The selective modulation of any one of them can therefore have highly selective cognitive effects.

You can see immediately some of the possibilities here, any of which will produce short-term or long-term changes in the effective weight of the synaptic connection involved. The presynaptic end-bulb may chronically produce too much, or too little, of its appropriate neurotransmitter. The receptors at the target cell may become hypersensitive to that neurotransmitter; or they may become blocked, for a time, by some alien neurotransmitter-like chemical that the target cell is unable to break down. Alternatively, after leaving the target cell, the recyclable breakdown products of the local neurotransmitter may be intercepted by some predatory chemicals before they can be taken up again by the presynaptic end-bulb for resynthesis and reuse.

It is typically here—in and around the synaptic cleft—that the various psychoactive "street drugs" do their work. Given that they can change profoundly, and often permanently, the ways in which our normal coding vectors are transmitted and transformed, it is no surprise that normal cognition is at least temporarily corrupted or bent out of shape when those chemicals are introduced into the soup. At a minimum, they have the effect of temporarily reweighting every synaptic connection in the affected neural subsystems. And at maximum, they can serve to stimulate the relevant neurons directly, in a widespread indiscriminate rush.

The effects of psychoactive drugs are many and various, but I will make no attempt to canvass them here. I raise the topic because the cognitive and emotional phenomena produced by some of them, especially after prolonged use, closely resemble the cognitive and emotional phenomena displayed in the major forms of mental illness, phenomena such as hallucinations, chaotic thought processes, paranoia, mania, and depression. Partly for this reason, it is a working assumption of much current research that mental illnesses such as schizophrenia may arise from characteristic chemical disorders in the neurochemical environment of the brain's 10^{14} synapses, chemical disorders closely similar to those produced by some of the drugs at issue.

This assumption suggests a line of treatment or control for the major forms of mental illness. If we can manipulate the neurochemical processes intrinsic to the patient's brain, we may be able to repair the underlying chemical disorder. Failing that, we may at least be able to compensate for the chemical problem by the daily administration of a chemical that will make good the chronic chemical deficit, or eat into the chronic chemical surfeit, depending on the type of illness at hand.

Schizophrenia has for some time been suspected of being a diffuse neurochemical disorder of some kind, one treatable, perhaps, by chemical countermeasures. The theory is still conjectural, but it has some plausibility. For one thing, postmortem dissections or MRI scans reveal no "smoking gun" in the form of unambiguous, localized anatomical damage to the brain. Although marginally reduced in total volume, a schizophrenic's brain looks pretty much like yours or mine. For another, it was discovered in the 1950s that the faintly psychoactive drug *chlorpromazine* produced a robust reduction in the hallucinations, incoherence, and chaotic emotions of people with schizophrenia.

Chlorpromazine, it turns out, is antagonistic to a very common type of neurotransmitter called *dopamine*, a neurotransmitter characteristic of many neuronal systems, especially in the frontal part of the brain's more primitive core and in the frontal lobe of the cerebral cortex. The daily administration of chlorpromazine, or of some related dopamine antagonist such as clozapine, tends to break down and to slow the resynthesis of dopamine in these "dopaminergic" neural subsystems. It thus depresses the activity of these frontal subsystems, which for some reason reduces—although it does not truly abolish—the crippling psychological symptoms characteristic of schizophrenia.

The discovery of chlorpromazine transformed the nature of psychiatric care in North America, and also the institutions that deliver it. Within two decades of its discovery, our many "insane asylums" were largely emptied, at least of their schizophrenic patients; not because those patients were cured, but because the drug had made it possible for them to return to the care of their own homes, and in some cases even to work. They were not yet normal, but many were functional once more.

Overall, it should be said, the shift in medical practice was as much economic as it was psychiatric: it was much cheaper to maintain these people on an inexpensive pill as outpatients, than to confine them permanently within heavily staffed institutions. In consequence, many of the old asylums and sanitariums eventually closed their doors for good. We no longer have the extensive physical facilities we used to have, and incarceration is for the truly helpless or truly violent only. This is a good thing, although it has its down side. Many abandoned, untreated, or irregularly treated schizophrenics, people who would surely have been institutionalized forty years ago, now add to the ranks of the chronically homeless. Our city streets carry openly the burden once carried discreetly by unobtrusive institutions. For obvious reasons, concerning both civil rights and continuity of treatment, health care delivery on the streets is very difficult, even when we possess a cheap and useful treatment.

How is it that chlorpromazine reduces the offending symptoms? And what is responsible for the cognitive chaos of schizophrenia in the first place? We don't know the answer to either of these questions. The pace of speculation, however, has quickened recently, thanks to our growing comprehension of how recurrent networks can sustain cognition-like processes, and of how they can occasionally *fail* to function optimally. The speculation is preliminary, so we must be duly skeptical. On the other hand, such speculation is now constrained by empirical data from neural network experiments, neurophysiological experiments, and neuropharmacological experiments, data that take us far beyond the long-familiar data on the behavior of schizophrenics. We may hope, therefore, that our speculative flights of theory will be better guided than in the past. In any case, here follows an example of such speculation.

What is responsible for the coherent and reality-sensitive cognition of a *normal* person? How is it produced? According to the general model of cognition being explored in this book, normal cognition consists in the following. The brain's global trajectory, through its own neuronal-activation space, follows the well-oiled prototypical pathways that prior learning has carved out in that space; and the brain's global trajectory shifts from one prototype to another as an appropriate function of the brain's changing perceptual inputs. This is a stick-figure description, in our new neurocomputational vocabulary, of normal cognitive function.

Using that same vocabulary, how might we describe the several cognitive pathologies of schizophrenia? Perhaps as follows. Instead of following the well-tuned prototypical pathways of normal function, the afflicted brain finds those pathways lacking in their usual stability. The brain wanders uncertainly through its activation space, only loosely and fleetingly tied to its familiar causal prototypes. It thus follows a path that is less firmly guided by its normal prototypical pathways, and less firmly corrected by its sensory inputs. That is to say, the brain is degraded in both its internal grasp of *typical* reality, and also its perceptual touch with *external* reality, at least in part because of the gathering corruption of its recurrent modulation of its own perceptual activity.

In such a compromised system, the distinction between imagination and perception must become blurred. The distinction between internally generated stories and externally generated sequences must become unclear. What were well-oiled prototypical transitions before, become noisy and unpredictable transitions afterward. What was merely shaped by recurrent modulation before becomes largely tyrannized by recurrent prejudice and confusion afterward. Owing to the widespread but unprincipled reweighting of entire networks, the landscape of normal cognitive function has been deformed from its well-trained topography. The brain's unfolding path in that activation space is therefore ill governed and incoherent.

What *physical* conditions might degrade a network's cognitive behavior in these ways? A great many. For example, anything that causes widespread changes in the network's effective synaptic weights will degrade the network's behavior in these general ways, especially in a recurrent network, where small errors can quickly become magnified in nonlinear ways. Such corruption in vectorial sequencing will be further magnified by anything that changes the normal balance of sensory versus recurrent control over one's primary sensory cortices. If vectorial activity in those basic visual and auditory areas should come to be dominated inappropriately by recurrent or "top-down" signals, as opposed to purely sensory or "bottom-up" signals, then prejudiced perception, a dream-like consciousness, and outright hallucinations are only to be expected. Both of these very general pathologies—effective synaptic reweighting, and abnormal stimulation or inhibition of entire neural subsystems—can and do result from abnormal levels of one's own neurotransmitters.

What we have, then, is a possible account of schizophrenic cognitive dysfunction in neurocomputational terms, and a possible location at the neurochemical level for the underlying cause of such computational dysfunction. More than this we do not have, and most of the real work remains to be done.

One might be tempted to think, on the strength of chlorpromazine's antagonism to dopamine, that the brains of schizophrenics are simply awash in their own dopamine, a dysfunctional condition that chlorpromazine corrects. Would it were so simple. But when pressed, this story doesn't hang together. The PET scans of schizophrenic patients receiving chlorpromazine show levels of neural activity in the brain's frontal regions that are significantly below the activity levels of normal people. This is entirely to be expected, of course, given the drug's strongly depressive effect on all of the dopaminergic frontal subsystems. It would be amazing if those systems were not substantially depressed.

But these people are still schizophrenic, even though they now have *sub*normal dopamine levels. Their pathological symptoms have been markedly reduced, but they have not been abolished. In any case, if a dopamine surfeit were the central culprit, one would expect normal cognition to return exactly when dopamine levels and consequent frontal activity were returned to *normal* levels, not when they are depressed to subnormal levels, as is required to suppress schizophrenic symptoms. Finally, the few PET-scan studies on schizophrenics who have never taken any dopamine-antagonist drugs show levels of frontal activity that are vigorous but not obviously hypernormal. This does not mean that the frontal activity of these patients is normal (almost certainly it isn't), but it does suggest that sheer level of activity is not their primary problem.

There is a different and slightly deflationary explanation of why chlorpromazine and its dopamine-antagonist cousins are so useful. A massive reduction in the brain's dopamine levels may compensate for deeper cognitive disorders in something like the way that reducing an automobile's speed from sixty miles per hour to twenty can compensate for an unbalanced rear wheel, a misaligned steering system, loose kingpins, and worn roller bearings at all four wheels. Dynamical defects that set the car oscillating dangerously and veering unpredictably at normal highway speeds can cease to be so evident at lower speeds, even though the defects remain. A slower speed simply reduces the dynamical impact of the background defects. It doesn't cure them. Still, if you drive such an unstable car, speed suppression is a well-advised compensation. And if you are schizophrenic, dopamine suppression is a well-advised compensation, for similar reasons. As the analogy suggests, however, the real neurochemical locus of the disorder is likely to lie elsewhere.

The good news is that we now have a fighting chance of finding that crucial locus. And in the meantime, we have a measure of control over schizophrenia, imperfect though it is. The widespread suppression of frontal activity produced by dopamine antagonists can be carefully tuned, and if need be it can be reversed, at least in the early stages, simply by suspending the medication. In this respect it forms a welcome contrast with an earlier technique of frontal suppression called the *frontal lobotomy.* This is a surgical technique, now rarely if ever performed, in which a scalpel is used to lesion or disconnect large areas of the patient's frontal cortex. The "pacifying" effects of such surgical assaults were indisputable, whatever the patient's initial disorder. Those frontal areas are essential for planning practical activities. A patient who is thus rendered indifferent or blind to all but the simplest of practical opportunities is a patient unlikely to cause further trouble to anyone, whatever tangles might afflict the brain remaining. Given murderously violent and emotionally uncontrollable patients, people otherwise unreachable, one can even sympathize with that surgical decision. But it is a decision we no longer have to confront. We have already entered a wiser and more humane era.

Mood Disorders and Emotional Dysfunction

The two major mood disorders here to be discussed are not in the same league with schizophrenia, at least as far as cognitive dysfunction is concerned. On the contrary, people afflicted with melancholic or manic personalities are often among the most imaginative, the most relentlessly productive, and the most successful among us. For example, Winston Churchill was certainly thus afflicted to some degree, as, less certainly, was Mozart. We should resist the romantic impulse to see ironic causal connections here. Being gloomy or frantic doesn't make anyone wise or creative. But the primary source of the mood disorders is evidently *not* a failure in cognition generally.

The problematic symptoms are straightforward enough. Bipolar disease, once known as *manic-depression*, takes the victim on a roller-coaster ride from highs of frenetic energy and irrepressible excitement for days or even weeks on end, to lengthy lows of lethargy, disinterest, and gloom, and then back up again. These exaggerated mood oscillations are irregular in their cycle, uncontrollable by the victim, and disconnected from external affective (i.e., emotional) circumstances. They are also severe enough to produce behavior beyond the bounds of normal caution, foresight, and restraint, especially in the social domain and especially during the manic phase.

The unipolar disorder, usually called *major depression*, is less colorful but no less cruel. Independently of one's actual life circumstances, a recurrent or chronic pall falls over every aspect of one's daily life. Favorite activities come to seem empty or burdensome. Fatigue enfolds the soul, and feelings of worthlessness dissolve the ego. Sleep brings no relief, tears are never far from the surface, and thoughts of death and suicide are constant intrusions. Major depression is easily the most common of the major forms of mental illness, striking one person in twenty at some point in life. And it is deadly serious. Despite the fact that most depressives grimly soldier on regardless, with their secret burden mostly hidden, one in five of its truly chronic victims eventually commits suicide.

William Styron's powerful little book *Darkness Visible* evokes the character of major depression as experienced by one of its more articulate victims, Styron himself. And Peter Kramer's best-selling book, *Listening to Prozac*, explores the disorder from the point of view of a practicing psychiatrist and thoughtful social commentator. Both books raise compelling philosophical issues best addressed in our closing chapter. For now, let me say only that our understanding of the basic causes of the bipolar and unipolar mood disorders is no better, perhaps worse, than our understanding of schizophrenia. Through sheer blind luck, we stumbled early onto a relatively innocent drug that effectively muffles the wild swings of manic depression: *lithium salts*. And through some informed and determined pharmacological sleuthing, we recently lucked upon a benign countermeasure to major depression: *fluoxatine*. (That is its chemical name, although it is better known by its trade name, Prozac.) In neither case do we understand why each drug relieves the relevant symptoms, although in both cases we understand the initial neurochemical effect. Fluoxatine, for example, inhibits the synaptic end-bulb's reuptake of a common neurotransmitter called *serotonin*, with the consequence that the liquid medium of every serotonergic synaptic cleft maintains a more abundant level of that neurochemical. But why this should lift a crushing depression remains a puzzle. Fluoxatine may modify certain dimensions of personality, but it has no euphoric effect on normal persons. And in any case, fluoxatine enhances the serotonin supply within hours, whereas the patient's depression takes a week or two to lift.

All we can be sure of is the presumptively neurochemical nature of both afflictions. Plainly there is a genetic component or vulnerability to both of them, since both run in families, often over many generations. Equally plainly, there is an environmental component to both, especially major depression, where chronic stress and its resulting high levels of the hormone *cortisol* are statistically prominent as background triggers of depression. At bottom, we presume, these factors come together at a neurochemical nexus yet to be grasped.

Humans, it is interesting to note, are not the only creatures to respond to serotonin enhancers such as chlorpromazine. A recent set of experiments on a population of Vervet monkeys found a robust positive correlation between their brain serotonin levels and their rank within the pecking order of their immediate social group. The dominant or "alpha" males and females had the highest levels, and the "omega" citizens the lowest.

What is going on here? It isn't clear. The first study tested the monkeys as it found them, without manipulating either their social situation or their neurochemistry. In order to explain that positive correlation, one might be tempted to guess that the lower one's ranking, the more subject one is to exclusion, bullying, frustration, and deprivation—in short, to chronic stress—and thus to high cortisol levels, and thence to low serotonin levels, which are associated with depression.

On this assumption, it is the monkey's social ranking that determines its serotonin level. But now consider the reverse hypothesis. In a subsequent experiment several non-alpha monkeys were given fluoxatine, which artificially elevated their serotonin levels; and several alpha monkeys were given serotonin antagonists, which artificially lowered their serotonin levels. The surprise is that, behaviorally speaking, the two classes of monkeys gradually exchanged their social status. The original non-alphas came to behave like alphas, and the several monkeys they displaced retreated to a more modest level of confidence and self-promotion. Here it looks as though the serotonin levels are determining the character of the monkey's social behavior and position, not the other way around. And these behavioral changes were produced in *normal* monkeys, not in monkeys already suffering from major depression.

This finding agrees with the impression that psychiatrists have of the effect of serotonin enhancers, especially fluoxatine, on their human patients. It has the slowly emerging effect of elevating people's social confidence, of enhancing their willingness toward social interaction, and of quelling their fears about its possible outcomes. The effect on most genuine depressives is just to return them to their prior levels of personal and social functioning. But in some patients, as Kramer reports at length, there is a dramatic transformation in affect and behavior, a flowering that invites description as the birth of a new personality.

That the social structure of human communities—offices, shops, factories, clubs—might be largely dictated by something so arcane and socially irrelevant (?) as our scattered serotonin levels is something that compels pondering. That one's social demeanor might be casually enhanced or fine-tuned by low-impact chemical tailoring is food for thought also. But all of these issues must be deferred to the last chapter. For now, I ask the reader's patience: I am still trying to construct a conceptual framework adequate to their eventual discussion.

Social Dysfunction

As we saw in the section on moral perception and moral understanding, effective social skills and stable social integration are crucial to the emotional economy and general flourishing of any normal human being. Almost any deficit here will exact a monstrous price from the deprived candidate, especially over the course of a lifetime. The range of possible deficits, both subtle and grave, is enormous, as is the still larger range of possible social consequences: enough to keep dramatists and novelists exploring their portrayal until the end of time. This is a domain of phenomena where our understanding and control will always be limited by the ever-retreating horizon of relevant social details and compounding dynamical complexities. Conceding this, however, does not mean we should flee or spurn such scientific understanding as may still be possible. On the contrary. Here, if anywhere, the price of continued ignorance is real pain for real humans, and each increment of new understanding may yield compounding social benefits. Let us scout the area.

The earliest and potentially the most catastrophic form of social dysfunction is *infantile autism*, a condition that emerges sometime in the first three years of the victim's childhood. In the prototypically severe case, the preverbal infant does not seek or find pleasure in the normal sorts of child-parent interactions: neither physical interactions, as in holding, touching, and stroking, nor social interactions, as in peek-a-boo, prelinguistic verbal exchanges, and the usual forms of social play. The child may actively resist attempts at physical contact and shrink from inducements to social interaction, if they respond at all. As you might expect, this is extremely hard on the affectionate parents.

Such children behave as if they have no conception of what a *person* is, no appreciation that people are anything distinct from any other physical objects. The rest of us might as well be lampposts or tree stumps, for all we can command these children's interest or attention. They behave as if they were alone, so utterly and completely alone as to lack any conception even of their own isolation. Their language development is feeble or absent. Their motor behavior is meager, stereotyped, and repetitive: they may rock back and forth for hours, visually fixated on trivial objects. The universe for them, apparently, *has no* social dimensions.

We have encountered agnosias before in a variety of perceptual domains, loss of facial recognition, for example (prosopagnosia), and we occasionally encounter anosognosias (unawareness of deficit) to accompany them. With severe autism we have both of these cognitive deficits for the entire range of psychological and social phenomena. Whatever subsystems in the normal brain learn to represent the existence and activities of "other minds"—the very subsystems that allow us to interact with those other individuals as one mind among many—are neural systems that do not develop normally in the autistic child.

This teaches us, at a minimum, that there *are* specialized subsystems for psychological and social representation, systems that can suffer isolated damage. Autistic children are often mentally retarded in ways beyond their social deficit, but often they are not retarded at all in other respects. Occasionally they display plainly superior abilities in certain domains, such as drawing or mechanical work. Moreover, the deficit in social and psychological representation varies dramatically across individuals, from the hopeless to the hardly noticeable, at least in brief encounters. The portrait painted above is of the dark end of the spectrum. That spectrum does have an opposite end, which brackets many cases in between. For example, one autistic individual earned a Ph.D., is a successful academic with many publications, and has an outside consulting business, although she correctly insists that most of what others see quickly and easily in each other's behavior is still utterly opaque to her. In her case, evidently, the representational deficit is unusually isolated and only partial. Yet evidently she is still missing a specific cognitive space that the rest of us take for granted.

One would naturally hope that MRI scans of autistic brains would throw some light on all of these cases, but nothing dramatic has been reported so far. To the current limit of an MRI's resolution, autistic brains look pretty much normal, save for the subnormal development of a small area within the cerebellum, that large, cauliflower-like structure at the lower rear of the brain (see again figure 6.2). This correlation is puzzling, since conventional wisdom considers the cerebellum to be a motor area. The correlation may be real but incidental to the symptoms of autism, or we may be wrong about the role of the cerebellum. We must hope that systematic PET studies, which remain to be done on autistic subjects, will throw some brighter light on the nature of autism by revealing some well-defined deficits in neural *activity* that are invisible to MRI.

If clear lesions are not evident in autistic brains, they are certainly plain in many other social deficits. Boswell's injured brain you have already seen; and in addition to his other cognitive losses, Boswell shows a curious *affective agnosia* or inability to recognize emotions, specifically, the negative emotions. During the experimental session mentioned earlier, I watched as Boswell was shown a series of dramatic posters advertising sundry Hollywood movies. He was asked to say what was going on in each. One of them showed a man and a woman, in close portrait, confronting one another angrily. The man's mouth was open in a plainly hostile shout. Boswell, without evident discomfort or dismay, explained that the man appeared to be *singing* to the woman!

In another poster with a more opened shot, an angry and determined man is striding away from a house and toward the viewer, with a distressed woman on her knees clutching at his pantleg from behind in a desperate attempt to stay his departure. Boswell explained that she seemed to have fallen and perhaps he was offering his leg in an attempt to help her back up! We were all a little taken aback by the robustness of the pattern shown. Boswell was both charmingly, and alarmingly, unable to see the most obvious hostility, anger, anguish, or entreaty, even as depicted in these highly charged posters.

There are many neurological cases that invite description, each different in its internal lesion, and in its consequent social agnosia, social apraxia, or personality change. It is the brain's frontal cortex, and to some degree its temporal lobes, that are most frequently implicated in such losses. But no narrow localization or simple map emerges, and in retrospect it would be surprising if it did. Human social cognition is at least comparable in its subtlety and complexity to human physical cognition, and in both cases the neural networks involved have scores or even hundreds of distinct neuronal layers, each contributing its small chorus to the collective cognitive performance. Teasing out the coding responsibilities and transformational significance of each of those layers is something we can now hope to do, but doing it for the whole brain will take us decades, at least.

The preceding discussion has focused on social dysfunctions arising from brain abnormalities, either structural or chemical. From the point of view of society at large, however, the more common and more pressing examples of social dysfunction may arise in basically normal brains, brains for whom the long process of childhood *socialization* has been degraded or pathological. We are not talking about mere bad manners here. We are talking about the ways in which children can fail to learn to enter into and become a flourishing part of the practical, cognitive, and emotional economy that surrounds them.

The process of human enculturation is not simple and it is not short. Accordingly, given the normal distribution of cognitive abilities across the human population, it is no surprise that the success curve is roughly bell-shaped. Wise social policies and practices, however, can hope to shift the entire curve toward the "success" side of the graph, much to everyone's benefit. Equally, unwise social policies and practices can permit or encourage the entire curve to slide in the opposite direction, much to everyone's detriment, and most especially to the detriment of those who find themselves at its "failed" end.

These reflections currently have a bite to them that would have been absent forty years ago. A nation that is watching a large economic underclass slowly disintegrating, as a coherent society, under the influence of family breakdown, educational collapse, false heroes, drug addiction, organized crime, and nightly gang warfare is a country that must look to its various institutions of socialization and contemplate their sometimes disastrous performance. Worse still, whatever shortcomings have brought us to the present sorry state have yet to exact their full price: an entire generation is currently being socialized within the civil chaos described. The momentum of our failure is not yet spent.

Our obligations here are doubly pressing, because innate cognitive talents are distributed quite normally across that large and diverse population. We cannot write them off as just the inevitable trailing edge of the bell curve. And there is more involved here than just a concern for the current victims. The very stability of that overall social-success curve is a function of its position, and of its shape. No society can isolate itself forever from social disintegration at the levels that now exist.

Therapies: Talk versus Chemical and Surgical Intervention

Our quick tour through the many dimensions of cognitive and emotional dysfunction makes it plain why the practice of psychiatry has changed so profoundly over the past thirty years. The familiar caricature of the bearded and monocled Freudian analyst probing his reclining patient for memories of toilet training gone awry and parentally directed lust is now an anachronism, as is the professional practice of that mostly empty and confabulatory art. How such an elaborate theory could have become so widely accepted—on the basis of no systematic evidence or critical experiments, and in the face of chronic failures of theraputic intervention in all of the major classes of mental illness (schizophrenia, mania, and depression)—is something that sociologists of science and popular culture have yet to fully explain. In retrospect, it is amazing. Perhaps the short answer is just that the vocabulary and the assumptions of Freudian theory allowed us all to tell highly arresting and engaging stories about one another, stories that served a variety of important social purposes, even if the alleviation of major mental illness was not among them.

A longer answer would include the following crucial fact. Freud's theory attempted to redeploy the central family of *commonsense* cognitive prototypes—beliefs, desires, fears, and practical reasoning—in a new domain: the Unconscious. The abnormal behavior of the mentally ill was thus to be explained in familiar and commonsense terms. The only difference was that the beliefs, desires, fears, and so on that figured in the new explanations were *unconscious* beliefs, desires, and fears. Freud's pschyoanalytic theory thus had an immediate intuitive appeal: its basic explanatory prototypes were already familiar; indeed, they were second nature to everybody. To apply the theory successfully to an individual person, however, required gaining *access* to that individual's unconscious beliefs, desires, and fears. This was not easy. Only the trained analyst could reliably unearth these final but crucial explanatory premises. Thus the rationale for a professional analytical priesthood, and thus the initial plausibility of the overall explanatory framework. It was just commonsense psychology relocated one level down.

It was also dubious in the extreme. The problem was not Freud's postulation of unconscious cognitive processes. Not at all. The vast majority of our cognitive activities take place at levels well below the conscious level. Rather, the problem was Freud's assumption that the *causal structure* of those unconscious cognitive activities is the same as the causal structure of our conscious cognitive activities, as represented in our commonsense prototypes for beliefs, desires, fears, and practical reasoning. The problem was Freud's attempt to redeploy the familiar prototypes of *commonsense psychology* as a general model for understanding our unconscious cognitive activities as well, especially the ones that produce pathological behavior.

As the preceding chapters of this book already indicate, those underlying cognitive activites are exceedingly unlikely to have such a sentence-like and inference-like structure. On the picture that has been unfolding in these pages, the basic unit of animal and human cognition is not the sententially expressible state such as *believes that P*, *desires that P*, *fears that P*, and so forth. Rather, it is the *vector of activation levels* across a large population of neurons. Furthermore, the basic unit of cognitive activity is not the rule-governed *inference* from one sentential state to another. Rather, it is the *transformation* of one activation vector into another activation vector. Unconscious activity is there in abundance, but Freud's guess as to its causal structure was not remotely correct.

The chronically feeble explanatory and theraputic record of Freud's psychoanalytic technique is therefore no surprise. In confronting the entire range of psychological dysfunctions, we have done far better by looking for structural failures or abnormalities in the brain, for functional failures in its physiology, for chemical abnormalities in its metabolism, for genetic failures in its original blueprint, and for developmental hitches in its maturation.

I may seem to be arguing here in favor of a wholesale replacement of talk therapies with chemical, surgical, and genetic therapies. That is not my purpose. My first aim is only to highlight the poverty of one major *system* of talk therapy. And my second point is to urge the importance of our getting straight about what kinds of therapies are appropriate for what kinds of psychological deficits. There is no essential conflict here; only a question of properly dividing up the work. If we take seriously our earlier speculation about the prominent role of defective *socialization* in the production of psychological deficits, then there will always be a central place for systematic conversation and social role playing in the theraputic process. Extended human interaction is the essential locus of successful socialization for anyone. We cannot socialize people just by administering drugs. Drugs or surgery might enable the process, but only social interaction can actually provide it. On the other hand, neither can we fix a genuinely broken brain just by talking to it. A deeper understanding of how biological neural networks do their work will help us better to address dysfunctions at all of these levels. And that, to return to our opening theme, will reduce pain and suffering for everyone.

II Exploring the Consequences:
Philosophical, Scientific, Social, and Personal

Let us make no bones about it. Consciousness *is* puzzling. The rest of our common experience contains no obvious analog, no remotely parallel phenomenon, no clear and evocative model that promises some useful grasp of its essential nature. Consciousness thus appears unique and, to many minds, beyond scientific explanation. Or anyway, beyond purely *physical* explanation. Consciousness, it has been argued, is essentially a *subjective* phenomenon, accessible only to the creature that has it, while anything that is truly physical—one's brain activity, for example—is doomed to be *objective* in nature, that is, to be accessible to many people from many points of view. Conscious phenomena, it is often concluded, can hardly be identical with mere brain phenomena; and the objective science of the latter cannot hope to explain the ineffably subjective character of the former. This view may be right, but I am inclined to the opposite opinion. Let me explain why.

Some Cautionary Parallels

We have confronted comparable mysteries before, and more than once. The historical examples are worth recalling. The first-century astronomer Ptolemy wrote off the possibility of any real scientific explanation of the nature and motions of the stars and planets on grounds that they were too remote and inaccessible to human understanding. We could aspire only to describe what little of those motions we could see. Physics, he said, would never capture their true nature or underlying heavenly causes. Those were inaccessible from our earthly perspective.

A similar idea about the heavens was urged by the mathematician, historian of science, and positivist philosopher Auguste Comte as recently as the early nineteenth century. Citing their unthinkable remoteness from us, he ruled out as impossible our ever knowing the physical constitution of the stars.

The point is not that these men were fools. Quite the contrary. Ptolemy was the greatest astronomer of antiquity, and Comte was a hard-nosed and deeply learned defender of scientific method. The point is that even a brilliant thinker can come to assume that what transcends his imagination transcends discovery by science.

By Comte's time, of course, Sir Isaac Newton had already shown that Ptolemy's counsel of explanatory despair was premature. The sun and planets, it turned out, were all made of matter, had mass, and moved as they did because of gravitational forces. Comte's ideas about our cognitive limitations were likewise premature. For within twenty years of Comte's claim, astronomers had discovered the many emission and absorption lines present in the spectrum of the light arriving from any star in the heavens, the sun included. The trick was to spread that light into a "rainbow" by directing it through a prism. Careful observation of that rainbow revealed that the color distribution of the arriving light is not uniform: it contains some bright lines that stand out from the background, and many dark lines where there is no light at all. The spectral placement of the brighter lines (the emission lines) constitutes an unambiguous fingerprint of the natural elements whose dancing electrons originally emitted that starlight. And the darker lines (the absorption lines) form an equally lucid fingerprint of the gaseous elements through which the light has traveled on its long journey to Earth. After astronomers learned the relevant fingerprints from terrestrial examples, the constitution of any star's photosphere could be read off such spectral-line patterns directly.

In Ptolemy's case, the inaccessible, unknowable cause of the planetary motions was in fact the very same force that held his own feet squarely against his ancient observatory floor. Ironically, as it turned out, he was in vital and intimate contact with that force every minute of his life. Naturally enough, it went utterly *unrecognized* by Ptolemy, for he lacked the conceptual framework that Newton would later construct.

Ptolemy, learned Aristotelian that he was, thought of any object's "gravity" as an intrinsic feature of that object, a feature like its shape or its color. As he understood things, it was not a force at all, let alone a force that emanated from the sun and every planet, a force spread throughout the heavens. Newton's framework was therefore revolutionary, for it would have partitioned parts of Ptolemy's neuronal activation space in a new and radically different way. Newton's framework, in contrast to Aristotle's, would have made it possible for Ptolemy to recognize what was endlessly tugging at his own body.

Comte's case was comparably ironic. The information "forever inaccessible" was in fact flooding continuously into his eyes and over his body whenever he stood in direct sunlight or starlight. He was literally awash in it for most of his life. Naturally enough, that spectral information went utterly *unrecognized* by him, because he did not understand the structure and the sources of light; nor did he suspect the rich information that it contained. He lacked the conceptual framework necessary to appreciate what was going on. Even if someone had put starlight through a prism for him, the pattern would have meant nothing to Comte. Like Ptolemy before him, he wasn't lacking informational contact with the mystery at issue: he was lacking the proper concepts with which to grasp it.

Perhaps we should not be too impressed, therefore, by the puzzling nature of consciousness. The appearance of unique mystery and permanent inaccessibility to standard science may reflect only our own ignorance and current conceptual poverty, rather than any special metaphysical status possessed by consciousness itself.

A final and fully contemporary example will underscore this point. In the middle-to-late 1950s, the nature of biological *life* was a topic of vigorous conversation, both in academic circles and in the general public. James Watson and Francis Crick had only recently (1953) sleuthed out the molecular structure of DNA, the genetic material tucked away in the nucleus of living cells. With the physical structure of DNA finally made clear, its all-important functional properties were slowly but steadily being revealed by chemical research. A purely materialist, reductionist account of the nature of life—of self-replication, of genetic diversity, of evolution, of protein synthesis, of developmental and metabolic regulation—seemed to many scientists to be all but in hand.

Outside of molecular biology, the prevailing attitude was quite different. My parent's friends, my high-school classmates, and my teachers were almost unanimous in the idea that life could never be explained in such a fashion. Even my wife's high-school biology teacher shared this conviction, and urged it on his classes. This "vitalist" position held that there exists a nonphysical life force or spark of life that God introduces into certain fortunate bits of what would otherwise be dead matter, a nonphysical spark that is responsible for the behavioral syndrome characteristic of living things.

There was some uncertainty, among vitalists, as to whether God introduced the spark of life anew to each newborn creature, or whether, once divinely introduced long ago, the spark was somehow passed on from parent to offspring. But rejection of the reductionist program was almost universal. Most people insisted that they simply could not imagine how such an explanation could ever succeed. "How could intrinsically *dead* matter, however it might be cobbled together, ever give rise to *life*?!" was the show-stopping challenge. In the absence of a detailed reply, the challenge seemed to dictate the response, "It cannot."

Correcting for the advantage of hindsight, we must sympathize with this opinion, at least to some degree. For it was indeed either difficult or impossible to imagine how life could be exhaustively explained in molecular and energetic terms, especially if one didn't know any biochemistry or chemical thermodynamics. Certainly our ordinary experience found, in the nonbiological realm, no obvious analogs or evocative models that promised a useful grasp on the nature of life. Spreading crystallization, as on any winter windowpane, provided a distantly possible analog for growth, perhaps; and a candle-flame a conceivable analog for stable structure and metabolism. But neither prototype was convincing. One had only to walk through a forest at sunrise to be struck by their poverty.

As with the two historical cases, the argument here was compelling, but at bottom mistaken. One's stumped imagination is a poor predictor of future scientific discoveries. In my lifetime we have come to know that the first part of the answer to the "show-stopping challenge" must run as follows. Matter itself is neither intrinsically alive nor intrinsically dead. Rather, certain complex *organizations* of matter will be alive if they function in certain ways, and dead if they fail thus to function.

The second part of the answer must do more than merely disarm a bad argument. It must actually supply the promised descriptions of the molecular organizations that make life possible, and the chemical functioning that makes life actual. Here the task belongs largely to the discipline of molecular biology, whose task it has been to reconstruct, in biochemical terms and in a unified and revealing way, all of the central behaviors displayed by living things. This, by and large, it has done.

And much more, besides. In the forty years since DNA's zipper-like double helix was revealed, biologists have discovered and explained more about the behavior of life processes than they knew was there to begin with. And since the mid-1980s we have gained a detailed control over those processes that was undreamt of before the mid-1950s. (For example, we can now isolate a crucial snippet of human DNA, splice it into the DNA of an *E. coli* bacterium, let that altered molecule self-replicate in nutrient culture some twenty-five or thirty times to yield hundreds of billions of daughter cells, and then sit back and watch them all synthesize large quantities of chemically perfect human insulin for delivery to human diabetics.) Biological life has turned out to be an intricate but purely physical phenomenon. Might consciousness have a similar fate in store?

As a preliminary, let us agree that trying to decide substantive theoretical questions on the basis of what we can or cannot imagine is a dubious undertaking, especially if those questions lie at the edge of our current understanding. The fact that some thing, *x*, is mysterious to us is a fact about *us*, a regrettable fact about *our* current cognitive state. It is not a "telling" fact about *x*, a fact from which heavy-duty metaphysical conclusions might be drawn.

To be fair, however, neither can substantive theoretical questions be decided just by citing some carefully chosen examples from the history of science, examples that may, or may not, be genuine parallels to the case at issue. We may rightly seek instruction from our intellectual past, but each new theoretical issue must ultimately be decided on its own merits. Let us therefore turn to examine those merits. The point of the historical examples was only to form a dialectical counterbalance to our initial puzzlement where consciousness is concerned, to level the dialectical playing field. Onward now to the issues themselves.

Is Consciousness a Brain Process? Leibniz's View

There is a tradition in philosophy that goes back at least to the great mathematician and philosopher Gottfried Leibniz, a tradition whose adherents find conscious phenomena—thoughts, desires, sensations, emotions, and so forth—to be obviously and fundamentally different from physical phenomena. In *The Monadology*, his principal metaphysical treatise, Leibniz performs a *Gedanken-experiment* or "thought experiment" relevant to this issue. He has us imagine that we are shrunk to the size of the smallest mite, thence to enter into the machinery of the brain as a man might enter a giant mechanical mill, one filled with levers, pulleys, gears, and all of the other intricacies to be contrived within purely physical

Figure 8.1 The philosopher-mathematician Leibniz, shrunk to the size of a mite, looking for thoughts and sensations inside the great mechanical mill of the human brain.

machinery (figure 8.1). However carefully we might examine that vast mill's mechanical economy, claimed Leibniz, it is obvious that we would never catch therein the slightest glimpse of a thought, or a desire, or a sensation. Those phenomena, he was thus assured, must belong to a quite different order of reality.

Leibniz's argument set the pattern for several similar arguments from more recent philosophers, arguments we are about to examine. But the prototype, at least, is plainly an argument from ignorance, not substance. Not that Leibniz was wrong about what we would recognize. It is indeed profoundly unlikely that you or I, shrunk this moment to a mite and turned loose inside the brain, would ever recognize, in its ongoing physical economy, a thought or a sensation as it came and went.

Leibniz fails to note, however, that this recognitional failure would be just as likely even if thoughts and sensations *were* identical with some vast configuration of the brain's physical elements. Recognition would be unlikely because, mitelike though our physical perspective might then be, we would still lack the *understanding* necessary to appreciate the complex activities now visible before us. Putting untrained people inside the brain is all well and good, but what they recognize or fail to recognize will be as much a function of their own prior knowledge and training as it will be a function of what is objectively there to be seen. Leibniz simply assumes, without question, that the expected failures of perception will reflect the absence of the target phenomena rather than the absence of the ability to recognize them. That assumption, however, is just the original point at issue in thin disguise. Leibniz is begging the question.

This does not mean that Leibniz's anti-materialist position is wrong, or that materialism has triumphed. It means only that this particular argument *against* materialism is unsuccessful. In other words, it remains possible, even granting Leibniz's story, that the taste sensation of a peach is identical with a four-element activation vector in the gustatory pathways. And it remains possible that, should you and I happen to know what vectors constitute what sensations, and should we happen to know where and how to look for those activation vectors, then we might recognize those sensations, from our mitelike perspective, as they go by. A well-informed observer could catch what an untrained observer could not.

Because Leibniz's argument does have an intuitive appeal, an analogy may help to reveal its basic logical flaw. Consider a deliberate analog to Leibniz's argument, as it might have been deployed in the now-settled dispute concerning biological life. Suppose that my wife's biology teacher had argued, back in 1952, as follows.

Suppose you were shrunk to the size of a hydrogen atom, thence to enter into the human body, into the secret recesses of its chemical economy, through the cell wall and into the cell nucleus, even into the crooks and crannies of the large molecules themselves. However closely you might watch these molecular structures folding, unfolding, hooking together, unhooking, and drifting aimlessly around in the soup, it is obvious that you would never observe the impulse *of life that urges its growth; you would never observe the* telos *of life that knows and guides its species-specific development; you would never observe the* life force *itself, nor even its departure, should the creature in question die. You could observe only molecular motions, or the cessation of such motions. It is therefore obvious that the essential features of life, as opposed to the physical or chemical matter that embodies it, must belong to a quite different and nonphysical order of reality.*

Here once again we see ignorance parading as knowledge. Certainly Pat's biology teacher, were *he* sent on this fantastic voyage, would fail to observe all of the things he lists, exactly as he predicts (figure 8.2). But that is because he has little or no idea what to look for, no clear idea how to recognize the objects of his search even if they were staring him in the face, as of course they would be, plus or minus some romantic misconceptions on his part.

The "impulse to growth" is there in the zipper-shaped DNA molecule's capacity for self-replication, protein synthesis, and programmed cell division. The so-called "telos" that guides specific development is there in the DNA's long internal structure. It is written in the alphabet of nucleic acids; it is read out in a coherent sequence of synthesized proteins; and if sufficient nutrients and energy are available, the result is a continuing chemical metabolism within a coherent and lasting physical structure.

And yet that chemical economy is extraordinarily intricate. The genetic message hidden in the DNA is some billion letters long. The sequence by which it is read out can take years, and it makes the running of the world's most complex computer program look like a game of tic-tac-toe by comparison. In the face of all this, the scientifically untrained micro-Lilliputian tourist will recognize little or nothing of what is going on, just as the thought experiment claims. But that is because the tourist is both ignorant of the relevant concepts and untrained in their application, not because the whole biological show is being run by some nonphysical agency. In this case, at least, we know perfectly well that it isn't.

Of course, there is no guarantee that the case of Consciousness will turn out to be like the case of Life. That is for our unfolding research to tell us, one way or the other. However, we can be sure

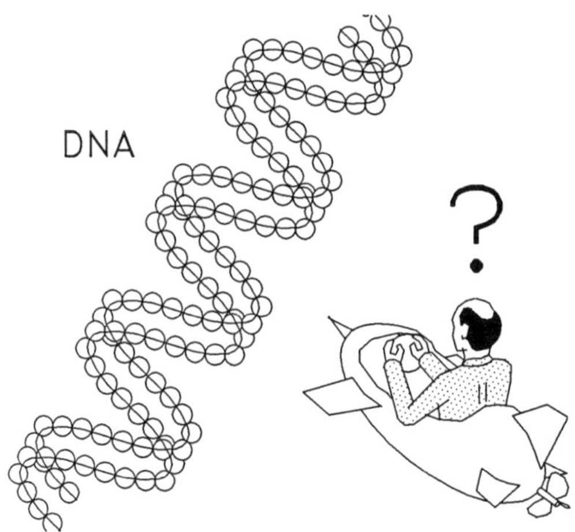

Figure 8.2 Pat's vitalist high-school biology teacher, shrunk to the size of an atom, looking for the *life force* or *spark of life* within the molecular structures of the cell nucleus.

that a thought experiment such as Leibniz's teaches us nothing, either one way or the other. It exploits our current ignorance rather than our understanding. And it covertly assumes what it is trying to prove. Let us see if modern philosophers can do better.

The Elusive Contents of the First-Person Perspective: Nagel's Bat

Some twenty years ago, in a paper engagingly entitled "What Is It Like to Be a Bat?," the New York University philosopher Thomas Nagel articulated an argument somewhat similar to Leibniz's. This time the location for the thought experiment is the brain of a bat, a case deliberately chosen for the presumably alien nature of the animal's sensory experience. Bats, you will recall, locate nocturnal objects by auditory echolocation, not by vision.

Nagel's claim is straightforward and prima facie plausible. He claims that no matter how much one might know about the neuroanatomy of a bat's brain and the neurophysiology of its sensory activity, one would still not know "what it is like" to have the bat's sensory experiences (figure 8.3). One would still not know what those experiences are like from the bat's first-person perspective, from the perspective he has as their unique subject.

Here once again a gap appears to open: between the physical reality of the biological brain and the psychological reality of first-person conscious experience. Exhaustive knowledge of the former

Figure 8.3 Nagel's bat and its accompanying mystery.

does not, apparently, give you exhaustive knowledge of the latter. Accordingly, Nagel concludes that conscious phenomena cannot be given a purely physical explanation.

This may seem to be just Leibniz's question-begging argument again, this time inside a bat instead of a human. But it isn't. There is a crucial difference that makes it more interesting. In contrast with Leibniz, Nagel does not have to say that the neuroscientifically trained observer viewing the bat's brain must *fail to recognize* the bat's unfolding mental states for what they are. The observer may indeed be able to read them off the specific neural activities displayed in the bat's brain. Nagel's point, I believe, is different: even if we could track the bat's experiences in the way supposed, by tracking their neuroactivational patterns, we would still not know *what they are like* from the unique perspective of the creature that has them. Their intrinsic character as felt experiences would still be unknown to us. Purely physical science, accordingly, appears to have some limits, and it reaches them at the subjective character of the contents of consciousness.

Nagel's compact argument is a prominent flag around which much antireductive opinion has rallied. Does it really show that the explanatory aspirations of modern neuroscience are vain? Does it really show that there is a *nonphysical* aspect to conscious states? Let us see.

Unquestionably, the bat has a peculiar access to exactly his own sensations that any external human scientist lacks. More broadly, each one of us has a peculiar access, to exactly one's own sensations, that no other creature has. This is because each one of us, the bat included, enjoys a unique set of intimate *causal connections* to the sensory activity of one's own brain and nervous system. This means that each individual gets information about the moving tapestry of his own sensory activity via a specific set of neuronal pathways that only he has. Others have qualitatively similar pathways, of course, but they form connections between *their* sensory activities and the rest of *their* brains. Each set of such connections is always within-brain, or within-body.

What this means is that each creature has a way of knowing about its *own* sensory states that no other creature has. Others can know about your sensory states by inferring them from your circumstances or behavior, or by peering into your brain with electrodes or PET scans, perhaps. These are alternative ways of knowing about your sensory states. But other people cannot know them via the individual informational pathways by which *you* know them, because only you possess exactly those pathways. They are the pathways that make up your own brain and nervous system, the pathways that constitute your own hierarchy of neural networks with your own configuration of synaptic weights and your own partitions across your own activation spaces. In sum, you have internal representational resources for your own sensory and other cognitive states, and you have causal connections with those states that others do not have.

Does the undoubted existence of this unique way of your knowing about your own internal states mean that there is something nonphysical about those states, something that must transcend representation within physical science? Perhaps. But not obviously. Consider several analogs, all of them universal and familiar.

By way of an axonal network called your *proprioceptive system*, you have informational access to the physical configuration of your own body and limbs. That information comes from the millions of sensors in your muscles, sensors that convey tension information to the brain. Nobody else can know the configuration of your body in this particular way. Only you. Because only your brain enjoys the relevant causal connections to your body. Others must use other means to know your bodily configuration: they must see it, or feel it with their hands, or photograph it, and so on.

On the face of it, we have here the same epistemological asymmetry, the same divergence in ways of knowing, that we saw before. Here, however, the *object* of knowledge is exactly the same from both perspectives, the subjective and the objective, and it is something paradigmatically physical: the configuration of your body and limbs. There is nothing supraphysical, nothing beyond the bounds of physical science here.

This example portends a multitude. You have your own causal access to the fullness of your bladder, and of your bowels. No one else knows their state in quite the way that you do. You have your own causal access to the acidic state of your stomach. Others can detect it, perhaps, but no one knows it as you do. You have your own causal access to the micromuscles in your skin, the muscles that make your skin crawl or your hair stand on end. Others may see your hair bristling or infer from the circumstances that your skin is crawling, but none of them can know it in the direct way that you do. Others can hear that your lungs are congested with a cold, but fortunately no one else has your sorry perspective on your pulmonary status. Others may notice that your face is flushed (that your subcutaneous blood vessels are dilatated), yet no one else knows the heat of that blush in the way your deeply embarrassed self does. Others may hear in your speech that your throat muscles are cramped with fear or anger, but no one will know your esophageal tightness as you do.

Such examples can be tripled, quadrupled, and more, but these eight will serve to make the point. The existence of a proprietary, first-person epistemological access to some phenomenon does not mean that the accessed phenomenon is nonphysical in nature. It means only that someone possesses an information-carrying causal connection to that phenomenon, a connection that others lack.

The point bears underscoring. Notice that Nagel's focal point about the apparent limits of physical science can be made just as plausibly in these eight wholly physical examples. Observe. No matter how much a scientist might know about the current skeletal and muscular configuration of your body—a sprinter's starting crouch, for example—he will not thereby know that configuration in the peculiar way that you know it. No matter how much a scientist might know about the current state of your bladder, down to the last stretched cell and cramped muscle fiber, he will not know it in the way that you know it. No matter how much a scientist might know about the current state of your facial capillaries, he will not know them in the way that your embarrassed self knows them. And so on, for the other examples as well.

Does the correctness of each of these statements mean that the bodily phenomena involved are somehow beyond the explanatory reach of physical science? Clearly not. Those phenomena are paradigmatically physical. But it does mean something. It means that each person has a self-connected *way of knowing* about his own current physical condition, a way of knowing that will function successfully and independently of what that person can see or hear, independently of whatever high-tech scanning devices he may command, and independently of whatever book-learned scientific knowledge he might or might not possess. This peculiarly self-focused way of knowing about one's own internal state is profoundly important, and every creature from a jellyfish on up possesses it in some degree. It is a part of any creature's internal system of bodily regulation, and it is essential for one's bodily survival.

But while genuine, important, and almost universal throughout the animal kingdom, such "auto-connected" ways of knowing have, as the *objects* of knowledge, exactly the same robustly physical things and circumstances as are occasionally known, through "heteroconnected" ways of knowing, by other individuals. The difference between my knowledge of my facial blush and your knowledge of my facial blush lies not in the thing known, but rather in the manner of the knowing: I know it by an autoconnected means (my somatosensory system), whereas you know it by a heteroconnected means (your visual system). The blush itself is as physical as you please.

Note finally that, in the examples cited above, there is a smooth continuum of cases that leads steadily "inward" from things well known and easily detected to things progressively less well known and more difficult to detect, save by way of one's autoconnected pathways. There is no reason to expect, however, that this spectrum from knowledge to relative ignorance should reflect a hidden discontinuity at some point where physical objects of knowledge are suddenly replaced by nonphysical ones. But that is precisely what Nagel's conclusion requires.

Let us now return to the internal states originally at issue: the sensory experiences of the bat. Certainly the bat knows about flying insects in ways that I do not, because it has special causal connections to flying insects that I do not. (I cannot echolocate flying insects.) And certainly the bat knows about its own bodily states, including its sensory states, in ways that I do not. (I am not autoconnected to that bat.) And certainly I will not *acquire* its special ways of knowing simply by learning a ton of neuroscience, even if it tells me everything there is to know about the brains of bats. All of this is true.

But nothing in these facts entails, indeed it no longer even suggests, that something about the bat's sensory states transcends understanding by the physical sciences. The intrinsic character of those sensory states will indeed be discriminated and represented by the bat, using its autoconnected pathways, in highly specific ways. And our collective scientific enterprise will not detect or represent them in those highly specific and proprietary ways, although it will indeed both detect them (with microelectrodes) and represent them (in the language of science). But the states represented, the bat's sensory states themselves, are presumably the very same states in each case. As before, the difference lies not in character of the thing known; it lies in the distinct manner of the knowing.

If one hopes to argue, then, that mental states have nonphysical features, one needs a better argument than Nagel's. It is of course possible that mental states do have nonphysical features. And it remains possible that one's autoconnected epistemic pathways are precisely what detect them, which is essentially what Nagel is insisting. These ideas are certainly not impossible. Quite the contrary. But their credentials as default assumptions have now evaporated. The mere existence of autoconnected epistemic pathways, which almost every creature possesses, should no longer even suggest the existence of nonphysical features. If they do exist, it is the burden of some other argument to spotlight them.

In fact, the situation for Nagel's picture is slightly darker than this, because even if such nonphysical features were to exist, why should one's autoconnected pathways pay any attention to them? Those pathways are themselves entirely physical. How could they interact with any nonphysical goings-on? In any case, it is far more likely that those pathways arose, under the normal selective pressures of biological evolution, so as to integrate all relevant aspects of our internal *physiological* activities, both sensory and motor. Nonphysical properties are not a solution to anything, even where one's self-knowledge is concerned. The existence of one's autoconnected epistemic pathways, their origins, and their current cognitive functions are all intelligible, without remainder, on purely physicalist assumptions.

Sensory Qualities Once More: Jackson's Neuroscientist

In 1983, the Australian philosopher Frank Jackson published a different version of Nagel's thought experiment, located this time in a human's brain instead of a bat's. It has an especial appeal for this reason, and its hero has become at least as popular as Nagel's bat.

The hero of the thought experiment is a neuroscientist named Mary. Mary is special in two respects. First, she has been raised in such a fashion that her visual experience is limited to what the rest of us would see in an old-fashioned black-and-white movie. (You can fill in this rather awkward part of the story in several ways. I prefer the version where Mary's eyes have high-tech chronic implants that flatten any spectral diversity in the incoming light. The only energy variations that get through to her retina are uniform across the entire spectrum. That will yield the desired result.)

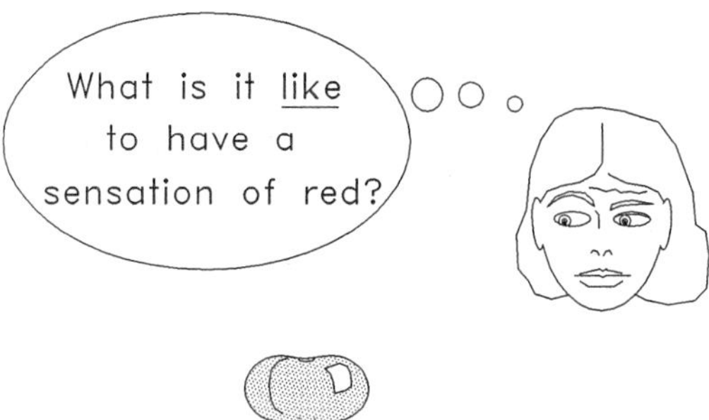

Figure 8.4 Jackson's "omniscient" but color-blind neuroscientist pondering her experiential deficit.

She has therefore never seen the color red as the rest of us have. She does not know what it is like to have a sensation of red.

Second, Mary is special in having become a great neuroscientist, despite her artificial color-blindness. In particular, she has learned everything there is to know about the nature of the human visual system and about the way in which the brain discriminates and represents colors. Despite this exhaustive neuroscientific knowledge, says Jackson, there remains something that Mary does *not* know: what it is like to see red, what it is like actually to have a normal visual sensation of red (figure 8.4). This deficit is clear, because Mary will certainly *learn* something if her optical implants are removed, her color vision is set free, and she is presented with a ripe tomato. She will then learn, at long last, what it is like to see red, to have a normal visual sensation of red. (I will here ignore the developmental brain damage that would surely attend the chronic color deprivation ascribed to Mary. Adulthood would be too late to set her free. By then her neuronal resources for color vision would be severely atrophied. But this would spoil a good story. Let us suppose they would survive.)

Jackson concludes from this, much as did Nagel before him, that there must be limits to what physical science can tell us about the contents of conscious experience. And because physical science leaves something out, he concludes, there must be a nonphysical dimension to one's conscious experience.

A few moments' reflection will reveal the same conflation that we saw in Nagel's argument—a conflation between different *ways of knowing* on the one hand, and different *things known* on the other. Mary's deprived condition has indeed kept her from ever knowing, via her auto-connected epistemic pathways, a sensation of red. No amount of neuroscientific book learning on her part will ever constitute a representation-of-redness *in those pathways*, for those pathways are inactive, cut off from their normal source of stimulation. Any representations of redness on Mary's part must reside in quite distinct neural pathways elsewhere in her brain, the ones that get trained up when she learns such things as theoretical neuroscience. Accordingly, if and when the veil of her optical implants is ever lifted and she is presented with a ripe tomato, then she will indeed come to know the sensation of red in a way that she has never known it before, in a way that finally exploits her auto-connected epistemic pathways.

Once more, however, the genuine occurrence in Mary of that special, prescientific way of knowing does not entail that something nonphysical is what gets known. The object of Mary's auto-connected knowledge is one of her own sensory states, a kind she has never been in before, according to Jackson's story. Even so, it is a kind of state with which she is scientifically quite familiar, a 70-20-30-Hertz coding triplet across the neurons of area V4, perhaps. That sensation is indeed new to her auto-connected sensory experience, but she's seen it a thousand times before in the auto-connected pathways of others. And it is the same thing in her as it is in all of the others: something physical.

There is a general lesson to be drawn here beyond the deserved deflation of two anti-reductionist arguments. It is crucial to bring it out. An assumption common to many thinkers, not just to Nagel and Jackson, is that the neuroscientific, computational, physicalistic approach to human cognition is in some essential way hostile to the notion of consciousness, and to the unique, first-person perspective that any creature has, onto itself and onto the world at large. Although the assumption is widespread, nothing could be farther from the truth. The explanation of consciousness, both animal and human, is one of the central hopes of current research in cognitive neurobiology, as we will see shortly. And reconstructing the intricacies of each creature's unique cognitive perspective on the world is part of the lasting explanatory obligation that cognitive neurobiology is eager to accept. How realistic these hopes are is still a matter of dispute. But there should be no disputing that they are now among the hopes that neuroscience holds dear. Before pursuing them, let us examine one last anti-reductionist position.

Mentality Without Reduction: Searle's Hybrid Position

One does not have to be an old-fashioned Cartesian dualist in order to reject the reductionist aspirations of modern neuroscience. That is, one does not have to maintain that there exists a distinct substance or thing, an immaterial mind or soul, that is the true self and the true subject of all conscious states. There is a theoretical option that lies between this old view and the neuroscientific view that all mental phenomena are at bottom purely physical in nature. In his recent book *The Rediscovery of the Mind*, the UC Berkeley philosopher John Searle attempts to articulate and defend just such a hybrid view. Searle differs from earlier anti-reductionists in insisting that sensations, thoughts, and mental phenomena in general are one and all *states or features of the brain*. Searle wants no truck with any form of substance dualism. The brain itself is the proper locus or subject of all mental activity.

On the other hand, he argues, those mental states and activities are not themselves *physical* states of the brain. They are not identical with, and are not reducible to, but rather they are metaphysically distinct from the intricate physical states of the brain that neuroscience quite properly deals with. According to Searle, mental states form a distinct and novel class of phenomena, with their own peculiar properties (such as meaning and intentionality) and their own peculiar modes of behavior (as displayed in reasoning and deliberation). In vain would we try to reduce them to merely physical phenomena.

What, then, is the relation between the brain's physical states on the one hand, and its mental states on the other? The relation is causal, says Searle. Mental states are not identical with brain states, as the reductionist would have it. Rather, one's brain states *cause* one's mental states, and vice versa. The central aim of a scientific theory of the mind, accordingly, should be to come to understand the special nature of mental phenomena, especially features such as meaning. And a secondary aim, says Searle, should be to figure out how it is that these nonphysical features of the brain causally interact with its purely physical features.

This, in sketch, is Searle's "conservative modern" position concerning the status of mental phenomena. It is "conservative" in that it attempts to stand firm on the independent reality and distinct metaphysical status of mental states. And it is "modern" in that it relocates them as (nonphysical) features of the brain and as proper subjects for scientific study.

Searle's position is also unstable, some will say, in trying to have it both ways. He has one foot on the dock and the other in the dory. If one is prepared to construe all mental states as being states of the physical brain, and if one is further prepared to bring their study within the realm of normal science, then why insist that mental states are nevertheless *non*physical, that they are distinct from and irreducible to the brain's physical states?

Searle, some will say, sounds too much like Pat's 1950s biology teacher. His words still echo in our ears: "Yes indeed, the properties associated with being alive are all properties of the physical body, and they are proper subjects of scientific study as well; but they remain distinct from and irreducible to the body's physical and chemical features!"

As far as achieving a unified scientific world view is concerned, John Searle is in for a dime, but not for a dollar. What is his motivation for this half-way position?

Searle is forthright in answering. The arguments of Nagel and Jackson, he believes, show that mental states cannot be identical with any physical states of the brain. These are the two arguments we examined several pages back, concerning first the bat and then color-blind Mary. As we saw, however, those arguments show no such thing. They show only that each of us has a proprietary and prescientific *way of knowing* about the occurrence and character of one's own internal states. They do not show, or even suggest, that those internal states must be nonphysical or beyond comprehension by the physical sciences.

In rejecting the possibility of identifying mental states with brain states, Searle offers a brief argument of his own.

Suppose we tried to say that pain is really "nothing but" the patterns of neuron firings. Well, if we tried such an ontological reduction, the essential features of the pain would be left out. No description of the third-person, objective, physiological facts would convey the subjective, first-person character of the pain, simply because the first-person features are different from the third-person features.

But this argument establishes its conclusion by the simple expedient of assuming as its premise (namely, "the first-person features are different from the third-person features") a thinly disguised restatement of the very conclusion it aims to establish (namely, "a pain and its subjective features are not identical with a brain state and its objective features"). Searle's brief interjection about what certain descriptions can or cannot "convey" is just more Nagelian and Jacksonian smoke screen creeping distractingly back into the picture. What remains beyond that is a stark example of what the Greeks called begging the question, and what we moderns call assuming what you are trying to prove. Whether or not the qualitative mental features that one discriminates by subjective or autoconnected means are identical with some objective features of one's brain, features that might eventually be discriminated in some objective or heteroconnected fashion, is exactly what is at issue.

Why, one might ask, is Searle so confident in his conviction that the qualitative features of his sensations cannot be physical in nature? His explanation is that one has direct and unmediated knowledge of the character of one's own sensations. In the case of physical things, he says, there is a legitimate distinction between appearance and reality. But in the case of the mental, the distinction disappears; it cannot be drawn; here, within the mind, the appearance *is* the reality and vice versa. One cannot be wrong about the nature of the contents of one's own mind.

This doctrine about the infallibility of introspection is familiar to contemporary philosophers, as a hangover from an earlier and more ignorant time. It has by now been so thoroughly discredited that it is plain curious to find a philosopher of Searle's prominence still clinging to it. The myth is easily seen through, and the distinction between what is the case and what one takes to be the case is easily drawn, even within the mind.

To begin with, consider one's desires, fears, and jealousies. We are not only unreliable in appreciating some of our own desires, fears, and jealousies, we are famously unreliable about them. Clearly then, we are not infallible in our judgments about all mental states. One can misapprehend one's own desires and fears.

Even in the case of our own sensations, we may misapprehend or misidentify them for a variety of familiar reasons. If one's attention is strongly *distracted* by some other matter, for example, then the reliability of one's judgment about the character of one's fleeting sensations will be reduced, just as it would be reduced anywhere else. Alternatively, if one has strong *expectations* about the kind of sensation one is about to feel, then there will be a measurable tendency to misidentify sensations, especially sensations similar to the kind expected, as being instances of the kind expected. Once again, if we artificially produce in you a variety of distinct sensations—brief color sensations in a darkened room, for example—of progressively shorter and shorter *temporal duration*, the reliability of your identifications (as judged by their coherence with the sensation's optical cause) will be inversely proportional to the sensation's duration.

Finally, and most important of all, there is a way in which we can be wrong, not just occasionally but systematically wrong, about the nature of our inner states. *We can have a false or superficial conception of their essential character to begin with*. If we do, then the very concepts we bring to the business of apprehending our internal states are a source of chronic error. This is a real possibility that Searle does not even consider, as we saw above. But this is precisely the possibility at issue when neuroscience proposes to reconstruct the phenomena of consciousness.

What will ultimately decide this issue is not whether our subjective properties intuitively seem to us to be different from any neural properties. How things seem to us too often reflects only our own ignorance or lack of imagination. Whether or not mental states turn out to be physical states of the brain is a matter of whether or not cognitive neuroscience eventually succeeds in discovering systematic neural analogs for all of the intrinsic and causal properties of mental states.

Remember the case of visible light, to choose one of many historical parallels. From the standpoint of uninformed common sense, light and its manifold sensory properties certainly seemed to be utterly different from anything so esoteric and alien as coupled electric and magnetic fields oscillating at a million billion cycles per second. And yet, the intuitive impression of vast differences notwithstanding, that is exactly what light turns out to be. Using the resources of electromagnetic theory, we can reconstruct, in a unified and revealing way, all of the intrinsic and causal properties of light, such as its traveling at 300,000 km per second, its refraction, its reflection, its polarizability, its splitting into distinct colors, and so forth.

In this way, visible light and a host of its nonvisible cousins (radiant heat, radio waves, gamma rays, X rays) have all been successfully identified with (i.e., reduced to) electromagnetic waves of appropriate wavelengths. Who will be so bold as to insist, just as the neuroscientific evidence is starting to pour in, that mental states cannot find a similar fate?

John Searle, apparently, and he will not be entirely alone. People regularly find it difficult to redeploy an unfamiliar scientific prototype within a domain that has habitually been grasped in terms of well-worn commonsense prototypes. This difficulty—this *conceptual inertia*—can prevent new understanding even after it has become clear to the scientific community that the old prototypes are hopelessly inadequate compared with the new.

Some years ago I stumbled across a marvelous illustration of this resistance to conceptual change in the introduction to *Betty Crocker's Microwave Cooking*, a cookbook published soon after microwave ovens began to appear in every kitchen. Before turning to the recipes, the authors provided a brief but presumably authoritative explanation of how these newfangled devices manage to produce heat in the foodstuffs we put inside them.

The magnetron tube converts regular electricity into microwaves. . . . When [the microwaves] encounter any matter containing moisture—specifically food—they are absorbed into it. . . . The microwaves agitate and vibrate the moisture molecules at such a great rate that friction is created; the friction, in turn, creates heat *and the heat causes the food to cook. (Emphasis mine.)*

The decisive failure of comprehension begins to appear half-way through the last sentence. Instead of asserting that the microwave-induced motion of the water molecules already *constitutes* heat, and gracefully ending their explanation there, the authors benightedly continue to discuss heat as if it were an ontologically distinct property. This raises a problem: how to connect heat with the rest of what is going on. Here the authors fall back on their prescientific folk understanding of one of the many things that can *cause* heat: friction! The result is massively misleading to the innocent reader, who is left with the impression that rubbing two molecules together causes heat in the same way that rubbing your two hands together causes heat. In this confusion, the real nature of heat—which is just the teeming micromotions of the molecules themselves—is left entirely out of the account. Heat isn't *caused by* molecular motion: it *is* molecular motion.

This example illustrates the way in which our folk conceptions can stubbornly persist, even in the face of a clean and established scientific reduction. How much firmer their grip, then, when the relevant reduction is still no more than in prospect? What Searle has proposed, I suggest, is something not too far from *Betty Crocker's*

Theory of the Mind. What Searle resolutely rediscovers is not the mind itself, but only our commonsense, prescientific, folk-psychological conception of the mind. The aim of science, by contrast, is to discover a new and deeper conception. Let us finally turn, therefore, from fighting the repeated counsels of impossibility, and take up instead the positive pursuit of that scientific goal.

The Contents and Character of Consciousness: Some First Steps

If science is to achieve a systematic reduction of mental phenomena to neural phenomena, the demands it must meet are stiff indeed. Ideally, it must reconstruct, in neurodynamical terms, all of the mental phenomena antecedently known to us (plus or minus some antecedent misconceptions on our part); and it should also teach us some things about the behavior of mental phenomena that we did not already know, things that arise from hidden peculiarities of the neural substrate.

These are the same demands that science has occasionally met in other explanatory domains. We say that light is electromagnetic radiation because Maxwell and others showed us how to reconstruct all known optical phenomena in electromagnetic terms, and because Maxwell's new electromagnetic theory predicted the unsuspected existence of radio waves, which were soon thereafter produced experimentally by Hertz. We say that heat is molecular motion, because Joule, Kelvin, Maxwell, and Boltzmann showed us how to reconstruct (almost) all known thermal phenomena in molecular-kinetic terms, and because the new theory predicted such unexpected things as the statistical distribution of smoke particles suspended in a gas, which Perrin and Einstein subsequently verified.

In general, when a more general or deeper-level theory proves itself capable of thus subsuming wholesale the portrait of reality embodied in some earlier theory or conceptual framework, we say that the earlier framework has been *reduced* by the new and more general theory; we say that the phenomena of the earlier framework have been revealed to be just *special cases of* the phenomena described in the new and deeper theory.

The point is quickly illustrated with a familiar example. Here is a list of seven salient features of light, features that we would like to see explained, especially in some unified fashion.

1. Light travels in a straight line.
2. Light travels at 186,000 miles per second in a vacuum.
3. Light consists of waves.
4. Light comes in different colors.
5. The velocity of light varies with the medium (air, glass, water, etc.) in which it travels. It is fastest in a vacuum.
6. Light is bent (refracted) from a straight path when it goes from air into water, and in general, from one transparent medium to another.
7. Light is polarizable. That is, it admits of an orientation in the plane normal to its line of flight, and its transmission will be blocked by polarized glass at an orientation different from the orientation of the light.

Thus the nineteenth century's conception of light: a perfectly serviceable conception, but one whose elements beg explanation. The heroic and more general theory that later explained and reduced this conception was James Clerk Maxwell's theory of electric and magnetic fields, a theory which, on the face of it, had absolutely nothing to do with light. But after he had formulated a set of equations to express mathematically Michael Faraday's earlier discoveries about the mutual effects of electric and magnetic fields, Maxwell realized that any oscillating magnet or electric charge should generate an electromagnetic *wave* spreading outward from its origin in every direction, much like the expanding wave on a pond that is created when a stone is dropped on its surface. From here, the story moves quickly.

Maxwell asked himself how fast these presumed electromagnetic waves would propagate. His own general equations entailed immediately that the velocity of an electromagnetic (EM) wave in a vacuum should be equal to $1/\sqrt{\mu_V \varepsilon_V}$, where μ_V and ε_V are a couple of rather boring constants concerning the magnetic permeability and the electric permittivity of any medium, in this case, of the vacuum. Fortunately, these two features were already quite well known, for a wide range of substances, from many humble experiments on electric and magnetic fields. Maxwell was thus able to plug the known values of μ_V and ε_V directly into the expression just cited, and thereby deduce what should be the velocity of EM waves in a vacuum. A few moment's pencil work gave him the answer: *186,000 miles per second*!

He must have fallen out of his chair. That unusual velocity was well known to science, having been cleverly established more than a century before by astronomers. (They timed the apparent advances and delays in the eclipses of Jupiter's moons from two different points in the Earth's orbit. The distance between the two observation points divided by the observed delay time gives the velocity of the light arriving from Jupiter.) What Maxwell was contemplating, there in his equations, was a spreading wave front, each part of which traveled in a *straight line* away from its source at 186,000 miles per second. The new electromagnetic framework thus yielded immediately the first three of the seven salient features of light listed. Might light simply *be* a form of EM waves? Let us look, as Maxwell did, at the next four features of light, to see if EM waves can explain those features as well.

Since EM waves are waves, then like sound waves, they must have a wavelength, one that varies with the oscillatory frequency of its source and its velocity in the medium through which it passes. Like different pitches in the case of sound waves, different colors of light are just EM waves of different wavelengths. Thus the fourth feature of light.

Since μ and ε vary for different transparent substances, so must the velocity of EM waves in those substances, as also predicted by Maxwell's velocity equation cited above. As we plug in the various values for μ and ε, the equation says that EM waves are fastest in a vacuum and slower in everything else. Thus the fifth feature of light.

Moreover, the exact *amount* by which EM waves must be slower in various substances is exactly the amount needed to explain the well-known index of refraction, a feature already established for many different substances. The EM wavefront is redirected or bent because of the forced change in velocity as it enters or exits a slower medium of transmission. Thus the sixth feature of light.

Finally, EM waves are *transverse* waves. They are like water waves, or the wave that travels along a stretched rope: the part that "waves" does its "waving" in a specific dimension at right angles to the direction of propagation. Their propagation can thus be blocked by a suitably oriented medium (polarized glass) that allows waving in only one dimension. Thus the seventh feature of light.

In these ways, all of the familiar features of light—and many unfamiliar features, too—get explained/reconstructed as natural and inevitable features of EM waves. The most natural hypothesis, therefore, is that light is just plain identical with EM waves. It displays all of the features of EM waves for the simple reason that it *is* EM waves.

Could it happen here? Could such a systematic reduction ever illuminate the mind? Can we reconstruct all known *mental* phenomena in *neurodynamical* terms? Not at the moment, we can't. Not by a long shot. But is there reason to believe that it could happen? Is it a prospect worthy of our systematic pursuit? In the arguments of Nagel, Jackson, and Searle we have seen some of the major negative considerations. Let us now do some exploring on the positive side of the ledger.

Most scientists and philosophers would cite the presumed fact that humans have their origins in 4.5 billion years of purely chemical and biological evolution as a weighty consideration in favor of expecting mental phenomena to be nothing but a particularly exquisite articulation of the basic properties of matter and energy. That is what atoms are. And above them, molecules. And then cells. And then multi-celled organisms. Why not minds?

The same theorists would also cite the now familiar fact that each individual person begins life as a sphere of interlocking protein molecules enclosing a cell nucleus filled with DNA molecules, and that he or she develops from there by a long and intricate *but purely physical* process. These developmental facts, both phylogenetic and epigenetic, lead one positively to expect that mental phenomena are just the systematic expression of suitably organized physical phenomena. It would be modestly amazing if they weren't.

Still, we have been amazed before. Although weighty, these are only presumptions. They make the reductive prospect worthy of pursuit, but they do not settle the issue. That can only be settled by addressing the various mental phenomena themselves. Is there any purchase here for the reductive aspirations of neuroscience?

Certainly there is some. Relevant examples appear in the preceding chapters, and in some quantity. In chapter 2 we explored the vector-coding theory of some of our sensory modalities, and we saw how to reconstruct the space of possible tastes in neuroactivational terms. We did the same for colors, for odors, and for faces. In the case of colors, for example, the activation space account successfully reconstructs the antecedently known similarity relations between colors, their many "betweenness" relations, the limits of our capacity for color discrimination, and the existence of three major forms of partial color-blindness (depending on which one of the three types of retinal cone cells fail to develop normally).

Climbing up from the sensory periphery, we saw how feedforward networks can reconstruct the various phenomena associated with sophisticated pattern recognition, including vector completion, tolerance of noise and network damage, and the emergence, through repeated experience, of conceptual frameworks with a well-defined hierarchical structure. Beyond the apprehension of mere patterns, we saw how to reconstruct, in neural terms, our stereoptic capacity for perception in all three of the universe's spatial dimensions.

Beyond simple perception, the resources available for reconstructing sensorimotor coordination were briefly illustrated. The capacity of recurrent networks to generate coherent temporal sequences of bodily behavior was noted, as was their capacity for the perceptual recognition of temporally extended causal processes. Appealing once more to the more powerful properties of recurrent networks, we were able to reconstruct our celebrated capacity to perceive, comprehend, or interpret the same thing in a variety of different ways. Using this machinery, we could even sketch a possible account of major conceptual advances in the history of science. Moving into the social realm, we watched two model networks recreate the discrimination of human emotions and of grammatical sequences, respectively. Finally, we watched many of these cognitive capacities, in humans, suffer partial injury or total destruction at the hands of corresponding neuronal and synaptic malfunctions.

These are reconstructive steps that cognitive neuroscience has already taken, and they are just salient examples of many additional explanatory reconstructions already in hand. Part I of this book is but a superficial and selective survey of a large and ambitious scientific enterprise, one already well under way. The first results are plainly so encouraging that one may think the matter all but foreclosed: mental phenomena just *are* brain phenomena.

But not everyone sees the situation in this way. Skepticism about the prospects of a neurophysiological reduction is still widespread, and it focuses on a phenomenon not mentioned in the preceding list: *consciousness.* This is the castle keep, the central redoubt, the core essence of true mentality, many will argue, and it has so far escaped any plausible reconstruction in neurocomputational terms. All of the diverse cognitive phenomena listed two paragraphs ago might be realized successfully in some purely physical or electronic network. And yet it is still not clear that such a network, for all its sophisticated capacities, must thereby be conscious. The cautionary lesson is that we should not be too impressed by the many reconstructive successes of cognitive neuroscience, not until those successes include the reconstruction of consciousness itself. Those other successes won't mean a thing, it is said, unless we can begin to reconstruct that most central of mysteries in purely physical terms.

Whether consciousness should thus be made so central and privileged is debatable, but I will not pause to address that issue in these pages. Consciousness is at least a real and an important mental phenomenon, one that neuroscience must acknowledge as a prime target of its explanatory enterprise. Better we should square up to the task, rather than find some principled way to duck it. It will have to be dealt with sooner or later, so let's begin to explore the prospects right now.

If consciousness is our explanatory target, let us try to identify some of its more salient features. Let us get clear on just what it is that neuroscience has to try to reconstruct. This is not a demand for an authoritative definition of consciousness. At this stage, that would be a mistake. Definitions are best framed after we have settled on an adequate understanding of what needs defining. And that is something we won't have until we possess an adequate scientific theory of consciousness. In the meantime, however, we can roughly triangulate our target phenomenon by listing a number of its more obvious and important features. Consider, then, the following salient dimensions of human consciousness.

1. Consciousness involves *short-term memory.*
   Consciousness typically displays a sense of how one's current experience and bodily position figure in time, in the unfolding sequence of events that make up the temporally-extended world. Such a sense requires at least some cognitive grasp of the events that preceded the current moment, and that will require some memory. Some short-term memory, at a minimum.
2. Consciousness is *independent of sensory inputs.*
   One can close one's eyes, plug one's ears, and otherwise set about to minimize or shut down all of the many forms of sensory input, but one's consciousness will not thereby be extinguished. One can daydream about the future, search through one's memories, or address and pursue a complex problem in one's imagination, all without input from the senses. Prolonged sensory deprivation, no doubt, has deleterious effects on the quality and coherence of one's consciousness, as experimental tests have shown. Yet the mere

existence of consciousness, at least for short periods, does not seem to be dependent on one's having any sensory inputs.

3. Consciousness displays *steerable attention.*
Consciousness is something that can be directed or focused—on this topic instead of that, on these things rather than those, on one sensory pathway over another, even if one's external sensory perspective on the world is held constant.
4. Consciousness has the capacity for *alternative interpretations* of complex or ambiguous data.
Once one's attention is fixed, on a particular visual scene, for example, a conscious person is still able to generate and explore competing interpretations of the contents or the nature of that scene, especially if the scene is in some way confusing or problematic.
5. Consciousness *disappears in deep sleep.*
Falling into a deep sleep is the single most common way in which one loses consciousness. We would like to know why one ever loses it, and what happens when one does.
6. Consciousness *reappears in dreaming,* at least in muted or disjointed form.
The sort of consciousness one has during dreams is decidedly nonstandard, but it does appear to constitute another instance of the same phenomenon. We would like to know how it differs, and why it should exist at all.
7. Consciousness harbors the contents of the several basic sensory modalities within a *single unified experience.*
A conscious individual appears to have not several distinct consciousnesses, one for each of the external senses, but rather a single consciousness to which each of the external senses contributes a thoroughly integrated part. How, and in what sense, those parts are assembled is something we would like to understand.

The point of this list, once again, is to give us at least a provisional explanatory target with some structure and substance to it. From here, our aim must be to reconstruct all seven of these phenomena, in a unified and revealing way, using the resources of computational neuroscience. Unexpectedly, a recent convergence in theoretical modeling and empirical brain research suggests a way in which this might be done. A suitably configured recurrent network will display cognitive behaviors that are systematic functional analogs of all seven of these familiar dimensions of consciousness.

Reconstructing Consciousness in Neurocomputational Terms

The modeling results relevant here concern the special properties of recurrent networks. The empirical research concerns the diverse behaviors of an important system of neuronal pathways that connect almost all areas of the cerebral cortex, and subcortical areas as well, to a central area of the brain's thalamus called the *intralaminar nucleus*. The thalamus and its internal areas are phylogenetically very old. They developed long before the evolutionary process began to explore the functional possibilities of adding cerebral hemispheres. At present, in humans and many other animals, one of those subcortical thalamic structures, the intralaminar nucleus, projects long axons that radiate outward to all areas of the cerebral hemispheres. Significantly, it also receives systematic axonal projections returning from those same areas, although the returning pathways originate in a lower neuronal layer of the cortex (figure 8.5). (Recall, in cross section, the laminar character of the thin and wrinkled cortical surface.) The cortical neurons and their many interlayer connections complete the grand informational loop. This overall arrangement of neuronal pathways thus constitutes a large recurrent network that embraces all of the cerebral cortex, and it has a bottleneck in the intralaminar nucleus. (One should probably speak, in the plural, of the intralaminar nuc*lei*,

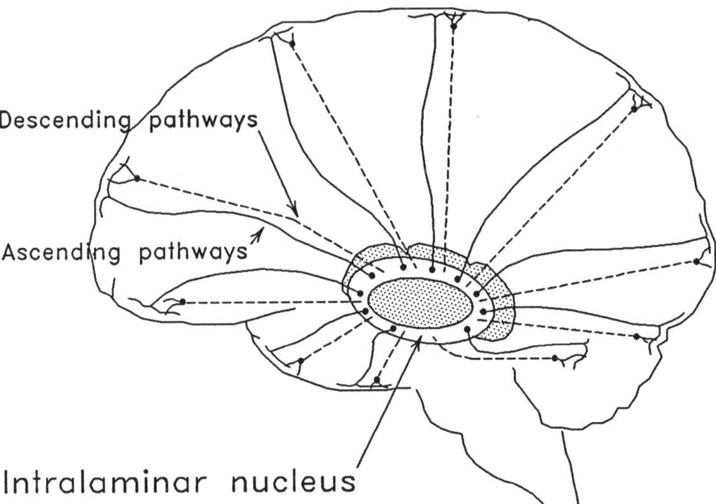

Figure 8.5 The fan-out and fan-in axonal projections that connect all areas of the cerebral cortex with the intralaminar nucleus of the thalamus. The returning pathways are marked with dashed lines. (Adapted from Rodolfo Llinás.)

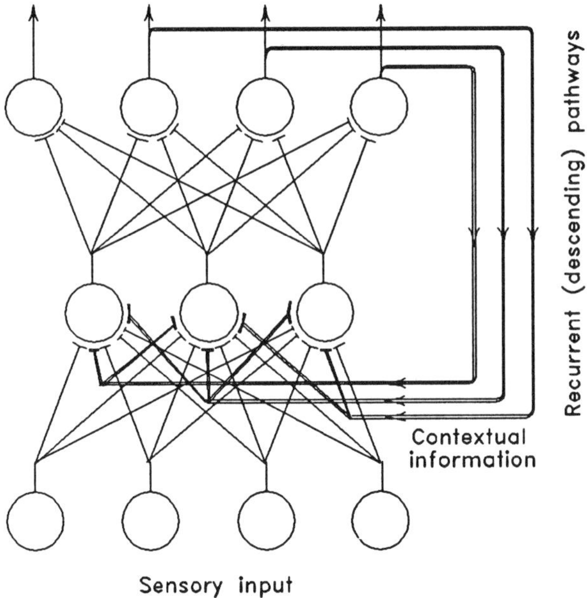

Figure 8.6 A simple recurrent network.

since the relevant area hints at subdivisions. For simplicity's sake, however, I shall stick with the singular.)

We have already seen some of what recurrent networks can do, but let us go back for a moment to one of the simplest examples just to remind ourselves of certain crucial features. We will return to the brain in a moment. Consider the elementary recurrent network in figure 8.6. The first thing to note is that its recurrent pathways bring, back to its second layer, processed information about *earlier* states of that same layer, and they do so continuously. This system contains, therefore, an elementary form of short-term memory. And it will not be limited, in its cognitive grasp of the past, to a single cycle of the network. Some of the information present in the second layer's activation vector two or three cycles ago may still be implicit in the stimulation vector currently arriving there via the recurrent pathways. Such information decays over a number of cycles rather than disappearing after only one. How quickly or how slowly it decays will be a function of details idiosyncratic to each network, such as the ratio of sensory inputs to recurrent inputs at the second layer, and the peculiarities of the network's synaptic-weight configuration. Nor will the decay be uniform: some information will decay quickly while other kinds will be robustly preserved through many cycles. This selective information-holding feature, you may recall, was crucial to the successful coding of grammatical information in Elman's language-processing network in chapter 6. This capacity is an automatic and inevitable feature of any recurrent network. Progressively larger networks, with multi-staged recurrent loops and real-valued coding, will display a short-term memory that reaches progressively farther back into the past.

In sum, a trainable form of short-term memory that is both topic-sensitive and has a variable information-decay-time simply falls out of the structure and dynamics of a recurrent network. It is a natural feature of any such system. Whether such a process truly underlies *our* short-term memory is still an open question, but it is clearly a live explanatory candidate. Let us move on to the second salient feature of consciousness.

Back in chapter 5, while exploring how a recurrent network can generate continuous motor behavior, we noted that such a network has no essential need of sensory inputs, at least as far as its continuous activity is concerned. The coding vectors arriving at its second layer via recurrent pathways can be quite sufficient to sustain continuing activity in the network at large, and the typical result is an ever-unfolding *sequence* of activation vectors at the second layer, a well-defined *trajectory* through the network's activation space. In that earlier discussion, the vectors at issue represented tension configurations of the body's muscle system, and their unfolding sequences represented coherent bodily motions.

But motor vectors are not unique in being generable primarily or solely by recurrent neural activity. All kinds of activation vectors are generable in this way, including vectors that are sensory or descriptive. Given the temporary absence of peripheral sensory inputs, candor requires that we describe these internally generated vectorial trajectories or cognitive excursions as daydreams, fantasies, or passive deliberations; but upon reflection, that is entirely appropriate. It is consciousness that we are here trying to approximate. Let it be noted, then, that continuing cognitive activity in a recurrent network is not dependent on an unbroken stream of external sensory inputs. Its cognitive activity can be self-generated. And let us turn to the third salient feature of consciousness.

Attention is by nature selective: some possibilities are attended to at the expense of others. The third baseman focuses on the batter's swing, determined to recognize immediately and accurately how and where the ball will be launched back into the infield. Other information is suppressed. The anxious mother listens for any sounds from the unwell infant in the next room, determined to recognize any distress immediately. Other kinds of sounds—the rumble of a truck, a distant train whistle—barely register on her. In both cases, a frame of mind is adopted that remains constant over the flux of sensory inputs, a frame-of-mind that tends to enhance the potential recognition of certain kinds of things at the expense of others. The price paid is quite real: while paying close attention to one aspect of a situation, one may well miss events and features that would normally have been recognized. But the payoff is equally real: careful attention yields a local enhancement in cognitive performance, at least on the topic at its focus.

In a neural network, to enhance the chances of a specific recognition being made is to increase the probability that the appropriate prototype vector will be activated by the sensory inputs. Recurrent pathways can and do affect such activational probabilities by slightly pre-activating the relevant neuronal layer in the specific direction of some prototype vector or other (for example, *bunt*, for the poised third baseman, or *choking sound* for the anxious mother). The specific prototype vector temporarily favored in this way is therefore the current focus or object of the network's attention, at least in the functional sense outlined in the preceding paragraph. And such attention is steerable by the network's own cognitive activity, since different recurrent manipulations of the relevant layer will produce different partial pre-activations. Once again, a salient functional analog falls out of the neurocomputational model, this time for steerable attention.

Turn now to our capacity, when conscious, to search for and mull over different cognitive interpretations of a specific and unchanging perceptual circumstance, especially when the circumstance is in some way puzzling or problematic. Here we can be brief, because in the second half of chapter 5 we explored this phenomenon at length, both at the level of mundane perception (recall figures 5.5 to 5.7, the ambiguous perceptual scenes) and at the level of esoteric scientific theorizing (recall figures 5.8 to 5.11, concerning the problematic heavens). A recurrent network has the capacity, once more through its recurrent manipulation of its own cognitive processing, to bring different cognitive interpretations to bear on one and the same perceptual circumstance.

This capacity, by the way, is the complement to our capacity for steerable attention. With that other capacity, one specific and narrowly focused frame of mind is imposed on a constantly changing situation, in hopes of catching certain especially important features, if and when they happen to go by. With our capacity for multiple interpretation, on the other hand, it is the frames-of-mind that we constantly work on changing, relative to a constant problematic situation. But both cognitive phenomena, note well, arise naturally in a recurrent network.

Next on our list is the disappearance of consciousness. Why do we lose consciousness during deep or nondreaming sleep? And why does consciousness reappear during dreaming or so-called "REM" sleep (rapid eye movement sleep)? Here we must turn to some intriguing empirical results unearthed by Rodolfo Llinas, head of the Neurophysiology and Biophysics Department at the NYU School of Medicine. The data concern the behavior of the human brain, and this story finally returns us to the fan-out/fan-in recurrent network displayed in figure 8.5.

The gross anatomical structure or wiring diagram there displayed is derived from postmortem studies of human and other mammalian brains. What is novel is the functional story revealed by Llinás's research. Llinas deployed yet another new and highly sensitive noninvasive technique, *magnetoencephalography* (MEG), to "listen in on" the collective activity of the billions of neurons all over the cerebral cortex. The activity of single cells is not the target of this technique. Such listening, through an area of the skull, to the chorus of neuronal activity just underneath is analogous to listening to the buzz and roar of the crowd in section H-20 during a football game. The undulating noise level is quite audible, although individual voices cannot be distinguished in the general hubbub.

The first discovery relevant here was a small but steady oscillation in the level of neural activity in any area of the cortex, an oscillation of about 40 cycles per second. Llinás found these gentle oscillations at the same frequency in every area of the cortex. Moreover, the oscillations in distinct areas all stood in a constant phase relation to each other: they were all tapping time, as it were, to a common orchestral conductor. This phase-locked activity indicates that in some way or other they must all be parts of a common causal system. The prime candidate for that common connecting system is the structure of recurrent projections shown in figure 8.5, especially since independent research had already revealed that the neurons in the intralaminar nucleus have an intrinsic tendency, when they are active at all, to emit bursts of activity at the required 40 Hz.

So far, so good. Now for the intriguing part. First, during normal waking consciousness, that constant, underlying 40-Hz oscillation is heavily overlaid with large nonperiodic variations in the level of neural activity (figure 8.7a). These reflect the brain's vigorous coding activity over time, and unlike the 40-Hz background oscillation, the character of the local flux is unique to each local area. The actual content or representational significance of those collective shouts is of course indecipherable by the MEG technique: we are listening to large numbers of cells simultaneously. But as in the analogy of listening to the crowd in a football stadium, we can at least detect when something significant has happened. And in fact, during normal waking consciousness, the bursts of activity picked up by MEG are strongly correlated with changes in the subject's perceptual environment, such as lights going on or off, tones being heard, and so forth. The cognitive activity detected at the cortex is plainly an unfolding representation, at least in part, of the subject's unfolding perceptual environment.

Second, since the MEG technique is noninvasive, it can also be used on normal humans during sleep. We can listen in on the same cognitive system while our subject is unconscious. What Llinás found here is displayed in figure 8.7b. During deep or so-called delta sleep, the cortexwide 40-Hz oscillation is still there, although its amplitude is minimal. But the overlaid bursts of presumed coding activity are now absent. The vigorous representational activity evident in that brainwide recurrent system during consciousness has disappeared completely. This large subsystem of the brain, it would appear, is no longer representing anything. It is temporarily out of the representation business. Significantly, the neurons in the intralaminar nucleus are inactive during deep sleep.

Third, during the sleeping subject's occasional periods of REM sleep—that is, during dreaming—the vigorous representational activity reappears. The 40-Hz background hum is once again heavily overlaid by nonperiodic oscillations in the level of collective neural activity. To judge solely from the MEG display, one might think that the subject had once again become conscious (figure 8.7c). But there is a tell-tale difference: while in REM sleep, the brain's representational activity is no longer correlated with changes in the subject's environment. Modest lights can go on or off, and sounds can occur, but these changes are not registered in

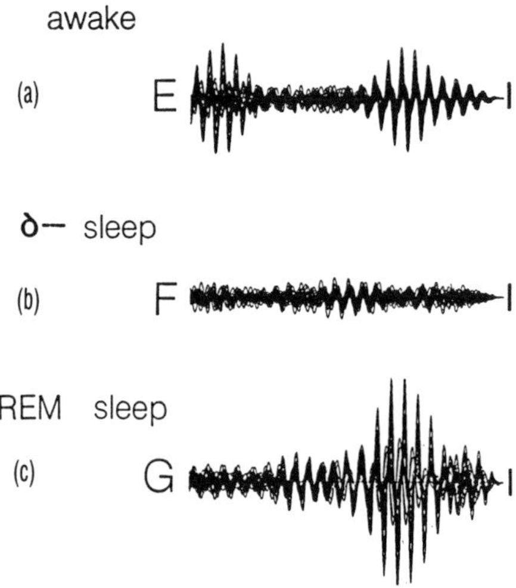

Figure 8.7 (a) Cortical activity during the waking state. (b) Cortical activity during deep sleep. (c) Cortical activity during REM sleep. (Thanks to Rodolfo Llinás.)

the flux of the dreamer's neural activity as they were during the waking state. Whatever representational story is being told, inside that dreaming brain, is being generated by internal factors, not by external perceptions. But the location and general character of that activity are roughly the same as detected by MEG in the waking state.

Our discussion of the first four salient features of consciousness had already given us significant grounds for implicating recurrent networks in the production of typical conscious phenomena. The Llinás results focus our attention on a brainwide recurrent network radiating to and from the intralaminar nucleus, and they give us a suggestive account of the differences and similarities between waking consciousness, deep sleep, and dreaming consciousness.

It should also be mentioned that, in experimental animals and in humans as well, damage to just one side of the intralaminar nucleus produces a *hemi*neglect of everything having to do with the connected side of the animal's body, both sensory and motor. It produces a blanket *agnosia* and accompanying *apraxia* of the sorts discussed in the last chapter. More seriously yet, bilateral damage—damage, that is, to both sides of the intralaminar nucleus—produces a profound and irreversible coma. Consciousness disappears completely. Although far underneath the cortical activity to which it is recurrently connected, the intralaminar nucleus is apparently essential to the occurrence of conscious cognitive activity. We can now begin to see why: the entire recurrent system cannot engage in its complex recurrent activities if that bottleneck part of the system is shut down.

The account here sketched, for the nature of dream activity, may also explain why the actions and episodes in one's dreams are regularly so mundane and prototypical in character. In the absence of the usual control exerted on the recurrent system by sensory inputs, the principal determinant of the system's wandering trajectory through activation space will be the antecedent landscape of temporally structured prototypes already in place. Further determinants, no doubt, are the cognitive and emotional states of the dreamer immediately prior to sleeping, and the low-level activational noise that is intrinsic to any neural system, as suggested by the Harvard psychiatrist Allan Hobson in his instructive and iconoclastic book, *Sleep and Dreaming*. In all, sleep and dreaming fall quite naturally out of the dynamical properties of appropriately recurrent networks.

Finally, the seventh point: why are there several distinct senses but only one unified consciousness? A glance at figure 8.5 suggests a possible answer. There is one widespread recurrent system with an information bottleneck at the intralaminar nucleus. Information from all of the sensory cortical areas is fed into the recurrent system, and it gets jointly and *collectively* represented in the coding vectors at the intralaminar nucleus, and in the axonal activity radiating outward from there. The representations in that recurrent system must therefore be *polymodal* in character. This arrangement is also consistent with the familiar fact that, through oxygen deprivation or anesthetics, one can lose visual consciousness while briefly retaining, for example, auditory and somatosensory consciousness. In such a condition, we may speculate, the recurrent system of figure 8.5 is still functioning, but the loop that includes the visual cortex has lost function slightly ahead of the other loops.

Let us summarize quickly. We have identified a specific recurrent network that should be capable of (1) topic-sensitive, variable-decay-time, short-term memory; (2) steerable cognitive attention; (3) variable cognitive interpretation; (4) cognitive activity independent of sensory inputs; (5) deep sleep; (6) dreaming; and (7) unified polymodal cognitive activity. We understand, in neurocomputational terms, how each of these features can be achieved, and conceivably they are achieved in a real physical structure within your own brain. The suggestion to be considered is that a cognitive representation is an element of your current consciousness if, but only if, it is a representation—an activation vector or sequence of vectors—within the broad recurrent system identified in figure 8.5. Your brain has many other representations, of course, but the story just outlined entails that they are not part of your active consciousness.

The theory is testable, for it entails something we did not already know about consciousness, and which may be false. Anything that cuts either the fan-out pathways from the intralaminar nucleus to the cerebral cortex, or the fan-in pathways returning, should abolish consciousness in the afflicted creature. Partial loss of such connections, to one or other area of primary sensory cortex, should result in the loss of that dimension of sensory consciousness.

I do not know, and you should not believe, that the preceding account is the correct account of consciousness. There is a remote chance, perhaps, that it is. Much more likely, it is only a small and still tangled part of the true account. And most likely of all, it misidentifies entirely the central neurofunctional elements of consciousness. But all of this is beside my true purpose in outlining this stick-figure account. What is central to my purpose is that the story just told is a logically *possible* neurocomputational account of the phenomenon of consciousness. It is a real instance of the general kind of unified and systematic reconstruction of the target phenomena that any adequate explanatory reduction must try to achieve. Whether it is true is a secondary question. But it is a candidate for truth, and its acceptance or rejection will depend on how empirical research continues to unfold, not on how things seem to uninformed common sense, nor on ill-founded arguments a priori, nor on thinly disguised arguments from ignorance. Explaining the many dimensions of consciousness is a daunting task, to be sure, but it is a scientific task that we can already see how to pursue.

The theory-sketch just outlined is not the only speculative sketch in the immediate area. If it fails to help in uniting the empirical data, there are others that may not fail. Francis Crick and Christof Koch hold a related account of consciousness. Theirs is focused primarily on the narrower phenomenon of visual awareness, and they propose that the essential requirement for visual consciousness is neural activity coordinated at a frequency of 40 Hz in layers five and six of primary visual cortex. As it happens, those are the very layers of the visual cortex that interact with the recurrent loop of the intralaminar system of projections, a fact these researchers also regard as significant.

As well, Antonio Damasio has a related view focused on the right parietal lobe of the cerebral cortex, an area that lesion studies reveal to be essential for one's continuously updated concept of oneself as an embodied creature that endures through time. That broad area is also recurrently connected to the thalamus and to other subcortical structures.

Finally, Rodolfo Llinás's view, if I understand it correctly, is essentially the view that I outlined several paragraphs ago, although I think his intention is to locate the contents of consciousness within the layers of the interactively connected primary sensory cortex itself, rather than, as I have speculatively located them, within the much sparser pathways of the grand recurrent loop that connects them all with the intralaminar nucleus.

Indeed, a problem with my suggestion is that the large-scale recurrent loop of pathways from cortex to intralaminar nucleus may be too sparse to carry the rich informational load that consciousness would seem to demand of them. Their function may be that of a mere timekeeper. It may be that I should be looking instead at other grand loops, richer in axonal numbers, that unite the old and centrally placed thalamus with the surrounding cortex. However, the crucial feature of the explanatory account of consciousness offered in the preceding pages is the dynamical properties of *recurrent* networks. It is these properties that do most of the explanatory work. Exactly where such consciousness-sustaining networks might be located in the brain is something at which I am only guessing.

I will not try to evaluate further any of these several neurocomputational hypotheses about consciousness. The philosophically important point is that they all exist, and any one of them might be true.

Return once more to the old issue about the essentially objective nature of physical phenomena and the essentially subjective nature of mental phenomena. We can now see that there is nothing exclusively objective about physical phenomena, since they can occasionally be known by subjective means as well, specifically, by the activity of one's auto-connected epistemic pathways. The physical states of one's brain are no more exclusively *objective* than is the physical matter of one's body intrinsically and exclusively *dead*. It all depends, in both cases, on how the organized physical system is functioning.

Neither is there is anything exclusively subjective about one's own mental states. Although they are typically known by way of one's auto-connected pathways, they can be known by way of other information pathways as well. In fact, they are already so known, even by the standards of current common sense: other people infer my current mental state from my words, from my facial expression, and from my unfolding physical behavior. The core point here is that there is simply no conflict between being objective and being subjective. One and the same state can be both.

I close this chapter as I opened it, by recalling the ironic convictions of the astronomer Ptolemy and the philosopher Comte. The irony in their case was that the "inaccessible" keys to the great mysteries they confronted were in fact central and familiar elements of their own daily experience: gravity in Ptolemy's case, and sunlight in Comte's. But however familiar they might have been, those phenomena went unrecognized and unappreciated for what they were, because neither thinker had the conceptual or theoretical resources with which to fully apprehend them.

I suggest that, where consciousness and other mental phenomena are concerned, we are all characters in our own ironic story. The "inaccessible nature" of conscious phenomena is written clearly in the alphabet of neuronal activity taking place inside one's own brain and nervous system. Moreover, one has continuous access to large parts of that activity right here and now, by way of the brain's auto-connected pathways, and in virtue of the brain's capacity for self-representation. But one fails to recognize the continuing performance for what it is—an exquisite neurocomputational dance—because one lacks the concepts and theoretical resources to appreciate fully what is right under one's nose. Or rather, right behind one's forehead.

The result of that failure is a popular environment filled, at best, with mysterious dualistic hypotheses, and at worst, with despair of ever understanding consciousness at all. But while our situation may be similar to Ptolemy's and Comte's, our attitude toward it need not be. We can aspire to develop the conceptual resources we are missing. We can hope to bring into sharp focus our dull apprehension of the reality that even now lies before our own introspection. The relevant methodology, as so often before, is that of theoretical science. And the relevant theoretical vehicle, to judge by current experimental evidence and explanatory performance, is already in our hands. It is the conceptual framework of vector coding and parallel distributed processing in large-scale recurrent neural networks.

9 Could an Electronic Machine Be Conscious?

The Turing Test and a Bit of Fun

In December of 1993, the annual Turing Test Competition was held in San Diego, graciously and efficiently hosted by the Electronics Division of the General Dynamics Corporation. This is a competition designed to implement the famous test for machine intelligence proposed by the British mathematician and computer scientist Alan Turing back in 1951. Turing was inclined to believe, on abstract mathematical grounds, that an electronic machine with genuine consciousness might indeed be constructed. In the British philosophy journal, *Mind*, he explored this idea for a general audience, and he addressed at some length the question of how we would ever *tell* if we had succeeded in producing such a machine.

Turing's answer was entirely commonsensical, an answer in the same spirit as the old saying, "If it walks like a duck, quacks like a duck, and so on and so forth, then it's a duck." With minds, however, in contrast to ducks, the behavior that the electronic machine must display is paradigmatically *intelligent* behavior. The tinny sound of its electronic voice, the humming and clicking of its disk drives, the ungainly shape of its physical body, its drawing 1500 watts of power from the local electrical mains, and so forth are all strictly irrelevant to the question of whether it has consciousness. To get these and all other distractions out of the picture, Turing proposed that we test any candidate machine as follows.

Put both the candidate machine and a real human being (to serve as a foil) in another room, out of sight and out of earshot of the judges. Set up a two-way teletype arrangement between the rooms so that the judges can communicate freely with both the hidden machine and the hidden human. This narrow informational pathway, one for each hidden candidate, is the only means by which the judges can gain any information about either. Thus, tonal contours in the voice, arched eyebrows, body language, none of these cues are available. The judges must decide—based on a long, teletyped, question-and-answer conversation with each of the two hidden communicants—which is the machine and which is the human.

The judges' questions can probe any candidate's knowledge on a broad range of topics, as well as its emotional profile, its social skills, its political views, and so forth, in hopes of finding some telltale respect in which the machine falls short of human cognitive capacities. If normal human judges prove unable, by this means, to distinguish the machine from the human, claimed Turing, then we can have no rational grounds for ascribing real consciousness and intelligence to the human while denying these same virtues to the machine. In sum, according to Turing, if it passes the Turing Test, it is conscious.

We will discuss the integrity of Turing's behavioral test for conscious intelligence in a moment. I want first to return us to the General Dynamics laboratories, and to a live implementation of such a test. At a new site each year, the Cambridge Center for Behavioral Studies in Massachusetts stages a version of the Turing Test, the Loebner Prize Competition in Artificial Intelligence. Anyone with a suitably programmed computer may enter, to compete against other machine entries, in hopes of convincing the judges that the machine is a human. As Turing specifies, there are also a number of genuinely human foils placed at the other end of their own teletype links with the judges. Their job is to communicate with the judges in as genuinely human a manner as possible. The rules preclude, for example, that the human foil should mendaciously send teletyped messages typical of a badly programmed or malfunctioning machine. That would simply confuse things. We want to make the test as hard as possible for the artificial machines entered in the contest. We want the human foils to set a high standard of intelligent behavior for the machine entrants to try to live up to. That way, their success will mean something.

It must be pointed out that the Loebner competition differs from the original Turing test in two important respects. First, each teletyped conversation is restricted to a single topic established long before the contest—baseball, say, or cooking, or politics. This restriction makes it much easier on the programmers who are trying to make their machines come plausibly to life. They are spared the necessity of putting into their machines a data base equal to the whole of a normal human's knowledge of the world. They can expect to get by on only a restricted part of it, as long as they can program their machines to handle that restricted information in the same ways that a human would.

A corresponding restriction is imposed on the judges. They must restrict their probing questions to the specific topic designated for the candidate entity at the other end of the teletype line. And a corresponding restriction is imposed on the hidden human foils. They must restrict their conversational contributions to the topic assigned them. They are not allowed to distinguish themselves from the machine contestants by displaying any knowledge outside the narrow topic designated.

The second difference from Turing's format concerns the criterion used for determining the winner of the contest. At this year's competition there were eight entrants, four machines and four humans, although one machine had to withdraw at the last moment and so a bench-warming human quickly took its place at a hidden teletype terminal. Three machines and five humans then, eight candidates in all. This means that there were eight terminals in the hidden room, each one connected to a distinct terminal in the judges' room, one of eight, each with its proprietary topic posted above the display screen. (The terminals, of course, were all modern CRT displays, not old-fashioned teletype machines.)

The judges, also eight in number, worked separately and independently. Each judge was allowed a carefully timed total of fifteen minutes' conversational interaction with each of the eight candidates at the other end of the teletype links. After each such round they would all shift to a new terminal fronting a new candidate and topic, and then repeat the questioning process. They did not know how many of the eight candidates were computers or how many were humans. That was part of what they were supposed to find out. Eight rounds and about two and a half hours later, the judges were required to rank the eight terminals in decreasing order of the "apparent humanity" of the unknown entity they had encountered at the other end of the link. The "best machine" was simply the one that received the highest aggregate ranking from the assembled judges.

Notice that, for a machine to win this contest, it did not have to fool any of the judges into believing that it was human. It didn't have to outperform any of the human foils: only the other machines. As far as the prize money was concerned, its only competitors were its fellow programmed computers. Even so, for interest's sake, the judges were asked to draw a line through their rank ordering at some point, with the probable humans above that line and the probable machines below it. And in past competitions, some of the entrant machines did succeed in fooling several of the judges into believing that a human was at the other end of the communications link.

This year the contest organizers sought a tougher breed of judges in order to steepen the slope that the "artificially intelligent" machines would have to climb. Accordingly, eight science journalists from several national magazines, newspapers, and television networks were lined up to serve as the judges. These people are professional interviewers, experienced probers, sufficiently cunning to pose a real test for the machines. And sufficiently cunning to break or bend the rules described earlier unless someone kept a close watch on them. Enter a cadre of flinty-eyed referees, including your humble servant. A handful of local academics and technical people who work in AI and related fields were invited to the competition to keep the judges honest in their questioning, and to keep the human foils honest in their replies. The rules, recall, prohibit any questions or answers outside of the candidate's assigned topic of conversation.

At a pre-contest meeting, the Tufts University philosopher Daniel Dennett, current chair of the Prize Committee, outlined the procedures to be followed by the judges and referees. (Dan has assisted the proper staging of this contest for several years, and is one of the major reasons for its success.) We referees drew lots for where each of us would be stationed. Expert Systems software engineer George Lowe and I drew the hidden room. We were to oversee the human foils. The other referees were stationed in the large and plushly carpeted judges' room. George and I were initially disappointed in our lot, since we thought we would be missing the Real Action in the o‰cial judging arena. But the truth is, we were lucky. The real fun took place in the hidden room.

Upon entering, we were appalled. In contrast to the lush and spacious judges' room, we found ourselves in a boiler room, a sweatshop, a cramped back room with barely the space for eight display terminals cheek-to-cheek against the outer walls, plus chairs to seat their operators. But the company! Five sparkling folks between nineteen and thirty-seven, all employees of GDE Systems, all quite different, and all of whom had volunteered for the indignity of two and a half hours at a computer terminal trying to convince some naive media mavens that they were human.

And, let us not forget, there were also three unmanned computer terminals, terminals that were slaved by modems to the real contestants: the artfully programmed machines of the three aspirants to the Loebner Prize. These three computer displays were lined up against the wall along with the other five, but they had empty seats in front of them. With a bit of head turning, George and I could watch all eight displays at once. Neither did we miss, as at first we had feared, the distant judges' probing of the eight communicants. The complete conversation at each of the eight terminals in the judges' room slowly crawled across its counterpart display in our cramped hidden room. George and I were the only people in the entire building in a position to follow all eight of them at once.

Once the contest was started and the exchanges began, the hidden room thrummed with activity. I felt as though I were Leibniz's tiny mite set loose inside a room-sized artificial brain, there to watch its incoming sensations and outgoing volitions alternate on each of the eight dancing display screens. Each human foil was soon consumed by the task at hand, and the three machine displays chugged implacably away, generating their own replies to the incoming questions displayed onscreen. With the clicking of so many keyboards it was never entirely silent, and every few minutes one or other of the humans would whoop in amusement, or mutter in amazement, at the most recent question from one of the judges. The lunch-time sandwiches arrived and were chaotically distributed while the typing continued apace. A steady flux of Diet Cokes did the same. All the while, the judges' questions inched slowly downward over all eight screens, struggling to distinguish the five shining faces from the three buzzing programs.

After a time, George and I began to recognize the interrogational style of several of the distant judges as they moved from terminal to terminal after each round. We also began to pick up on the strikingly different cognitive styles or dialectical strategies of the three competing programmed machines. One of them had as its topic, Bad Marriages, and it was rather insipidly therapist-like, constantly asking vapid questions of the current judge as if it were trying to dodge the obligation to give substantive answers to the questions that had already been put to it.

This is a strategy that entrant programmers have frequently employed in this contest. The longer the judge is kept busy trying to answer the machine's questions, the less time that the judge will have to pose awkward and potentially unmasking questions to the machine. A second machine entrant, whose topic was Liberals versus Conservatives, employed a rather aggressive version of this turn-the-tables strategy, using political invective to provoke its corresponding judge. The third machine entrant, with the topic Pets, seemed to have an unusually large data base, but its skill in generating a plausible back-and-forth of relevant comments was very limited. The truth is, none of the entrants was worth a damn, at least as examples of artificial *intelligence*. George and I, with the smugness of professionals with inside information, rolled our eyes at the transparency and clumsiness of the programs being run by the several machine entrants.

The human foils too displayed quite different cognitive styles, in their case, spontaneously. One young fellow, whose topic was Abortion, was careful, logical, and precise: a man of few but well-chosen words. The human next to him had the topic Custom Cars, and this fellow gave long descriptive answers to the judges' questions, answers filled with mountains of arcane technical details, easily ten times the length of the abortion answers being typed to his immediate left. At one point, eyeing his talkative neighbor with envy, the abortion fellow turned to me and said softly, "I'm afraid the judges are going to think I'm just a computer." "Don't worry," I whispered. "Your topic requires a real comprehension of the judges' arguments and objections, and it demands a real ability to generate dialectically relevant replies. Your answers are the most obviously human in the room." Marginally reassured, he went back to his typing. I'll return to this human in a moment.

The other three human foils were confined to the topics, Cooking, Martial Arts, and Baseball, respectively. We needn't have worried about the honesty of the human foils: they were fiercely honest in all of their exchanges. They stuck to the topics assigned them, and they quickly settled into a curt "Please return to the topic" as the standard response to the frequent transgressions by the media judges.

The eight judges, on the other hand, were borderline scoundrels throughout. To a man and to a woman, they pushed the limits of the specified topic repeatedly. What out-of-bounds questions the referees in the judges' room didn't catch, George and I, and the human foils, had to catch in the hidden room. Fair enough. The limits weren't very well defined and the judges were pros, determined to exploit any advantage. In the end and on the whole, the typed exchanges were fair.

What were the results? The machine with the Liberals versus Conservatives program edged out the other two machine contestants, by no very great margin. But barring a tie, a machine winner was guaranteed by the rules. What is more interesting is that not one of the eight judges was fooled into thinking that any of the three machine entrants was a human. In this respect, the judges batted 1.000 and the programmed machines batted .000. Even with the helpful restriction to a single topic of conversation, every last machine entrant failed this Turing-like test with every last judge.

Pretty good judges, you might think. But the preceding fails to tell the whole story. Although none of the judges mistook a machine for a human, five of them mistakenly identified one of the human foils as a machine! Indeed, two of the sternest judges dismissed as mere machines not one but *two* of the five hard-working humans. Just as he had feared, the young man who had so carefully managed the Abortion terminal was written off as a machine by a clear majority of the judges. Adding insult to injury, one judge went so far as to rank him *behind* one of the machine entrants. But this result tells us more about the judges than about the young man. His personal style—brief to a fault, simple sentences, lucid logic—happened to fit the public's stereotypical or prototypical image of how a computer is supposed to behave. And that superficial image evidently had a strong grip on a majority of the judges. But not on all. For example, one of the two women judges ranked my young man as the most obviously human of all the communicants. And the one media judge with a degree in psychology ranked him second.

The one other human unfairly ranked as a machine was the fellow conducting the discussion on Martial Arts. He, I think, was a victim of the fact that none of the judges knew anything at all about the subject, were unable to ask probing questions, and were intimidated by his answers, many of which were filled with unfamiliar vocabulary. But this is just a guess.

I wish to suggest only two lessons to be drawn from this story. The first is that, although the flourishing industry of classical program-writing AI continues to produce many startling and welcome functional systems, anything remotely like real human intelligence is not yet among them. Or anyway, not among the entrants to our competition. To these eyes, the three entrant computer programs were all written with the aim of "*appearing* to be intelligent just long enough to run off with the Loebner Prize," rather than with the aim of truly recreating human intelligence.

The second lesson is that people, even bright ones, are not as reliable as we might expect at distinguishing real human intelligence from machine simulations, not, at least, if their probing is limited to a teletype link. And they are unreliable even when the machine simulations are quite poor. Which re-raises our earlier question about the integrity of the test proposed by Alan Turing. Is it a test of any real significance? I am going to argue that it is not, and I will try to show that tests of real significance must lie elsewhere.

The Defects of the Turing Test, and the Need for Real Theory

Turing's narrowly behavioral test gains its appeal from two sources. First, it focuses exclusively on empirically accessible data—the output of the candidate system's teletype. Inaccessible metaphysical, computational, and neuronal matters are thus deliberately pushed aside. And second, it evaluates those empirical data by comparison with the behavior of a paradigm case of intelligence—a human being. The candidate system's teletyped behavior must be indistinguishable from the teletyped behavior of *a human* in the same situation.

Criticisms of the Turing Test are legion. Most of them complain that the test is in some way or other too lenient, that it will allow into the fold of intelligent creatures things that are not genuinely intelligent at all. The background worry is that convincing verbal behavior over a teletype link is something that might be produced from a variety of different causes, none of which has anything essential to do with real conscious intelligence. Pressure is thus applied to broaden the test in some way: to include a wider range of types of behavior, perhaps, and thus to stiffen the conditions for admission. Here, alas, it has always been unclear exactly how to broaden it, for it is unclear exactly what types of behavior are relevant to the possession of conscious intelligence.

Other complaints point out that as it stands, Turing's Test is too exclusive, since intelligent creatures without linguistic competence are doomed to fail his linguafocal test. This includes prelinguistic children, conscious human adults with localized aphasia, most of the higher animals on the planet, and all intelligent aliens who don't communicate by human language. Well, perhaps we weren't supposed to interpret Turing's Test as imposing a necessary condition on conscious intelligence in the first place. But if it isn't a necessary condition on intelligence, and it isn't a sufficient condition either, why are we bothering to discuss it?

Whatever its merits or demerits as a criterion of intelligence, it is independently clear that we are forced to fall back on "behavioral similarity to a paradigm case" only so long as we lack an adequate *theory* of the paradigm case, an adequate theory of what intelligence is and how it is realized in physical systems. Had we such a theory, we would have no need for the austere behavioral restrictions of the Turing Test, and no need to haggle over its validity. An adequate theory of intelligence would itself make clear the relevant features, behaviors, techniques, or mechanisms that are characteristic of genuine intelligence.

We could then test for those features directly, perhaps by looking inside the candidate system to see what is going on, or perhaps by examining the system's behavior in contexts much richer and more demanding than that of a teletyped conversation. The Turing Test is a test precisely for people who *have no* adequate theory of what intelligence is, or no theory beyond the humble framework of our prescientific folk concepts. Alan Turing was very much in that situation, of course, and so it is not surprising that he was forced to fall back on a stop-gap criterion. But we can now aspire to transcend his situation. The thing to do, plainly, is to develop a theory of cognitive activity and conscious intelligence that is genuinely adequate to the phenomena before us.

The "paradigm case"—the human, or higher animal—is no longer so mysterious as it was in 1950, and its internal structures and activities are no longer so inaccessible to experimental observation. As we saw in the preceding chapters, the several sciences now focused on cognition have given us the conceptual and experimental resources potentially adequate to the construction of a correct theory of human and animal cognition. Such a theory has the obligation to explain a great deal more than the capacity for a coherent teletyped conversation (not that this latter is trivial). And the empirical constraints on the theory will be commensurately greater as well. For starters, the theory must be adequate to the much wider range of input-output behaviors that any real animal displays. More important still, it must be adequate to the internal computational realities of the system that produces that behavior. It must cohere appropriately with the kinematical and dynamical features of the biological brain. And it must be able to account for fundamental features of cognition such as learning, perceptual recognition, and conceptual change.

Had we such a penetrating theory, to repeat, we could finally approach with some authority the question of whether any candidate system, natural or artificial, was truly intelligent. This approach, note well, contrasts starkly with Turing's in the following respect. It makes the complex *causes* of intelligent behavior the primary focus of concern, rather than just the observable behavior that those causes produce. Instead of pushing "inaccessible metaphysical, computational, and neuronal matters" deliberately aside, it seeks to gain an understanding of precisely these newly accessible matters. And it seeks to apply that new understanding in order to answer the question still before us: could an electronic machine think?

Building an Artificial Brain

For the sake of exploratory argument, let us assume something that we do not yet know. Let us assume that the conscious intelligence displayed by humans is achieved within the sorts of vector-coding and vector-processing networks that we explored in the preceding chapters. This includes recurrent networks and systems of such networks. Let us also assume that our diverse forms of cognitive competence are acquired by a process of synaptic weight adjustment that partitions our diverse neuronal activation spaces into hierarchies of prototype categories and prototype sequences; into a conceptual framework, that is, that responds to perceptual input, permits deliberative exploration, and directs behavioral output.

If this is how we humans achieve our intelligence, is it possible that an electronic machine might achieve the same thing? On the face of it, the answer is yes, at least in principle. For it is clearly possible to construct electronic implementations of the sorts of networks that in us are implemented biologically and neurochemically. In fact, some first steps in this direction have already been taken.

A celebrated example is the silicon retina created by Carver Mead and his doctoral student, Misha Mahowald, at Cal Tech in Pasadena. Back in the 1960s, Mead was one of the pioneer developers of integrated circuits. This is the technology by which we can etch, on small silicon chips, microscopic versions of the electrical circuits for classical digital computers. That technology, I think we would all agree, has changed the modern world. But it may be that the revolution it has created is not yet spent, nor even fully launched. Mead and his co-workers have now begun to exploit that same technology in order to etch, on small silicon chips, electronic analogs of *biological* neural networks. A silicon analog of the human retina is one of their early successes (figure 9.1).

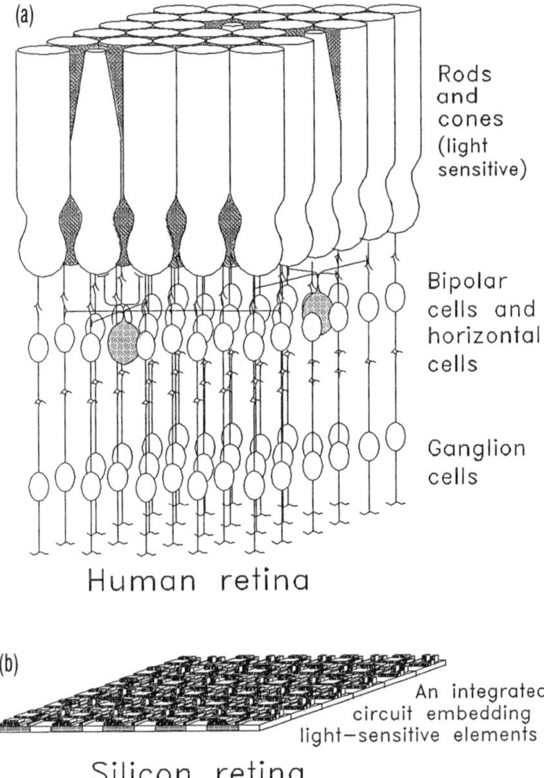

Figure 9.1 (a) The multilayer neural network that constitutes the retina of the human eye. (b) An electronic recreation of the retinal network, this time in a multilayer silicon chip. It has 50×50 cones. (Adapted from Carver Mead.)

One might suppose that such a step had already been taken, several decades ago, with the invention of the television camera. After all, that familiar technology generates a sequence of image vectors by electron-scanning a photosensitive surface. Quite so. But the eye's retina does far more than this. The retina is not a pure photosensor. It is also a multi-layer data-processing computer. As was briefly mentioned at the close of the sections on stereo vision, by the time the original optical information at the photosensors reaches the ganglion cells for transmission to the LGN, it has already undergone several stages of sophisticated processing. The retina's output is thus very different from the output of a TV camera. Mead's achievement lies in recreating these internal computational activities in semiconductor dress.

What are they? What do they do? Perhaps the first thing to mention is that the initial sensor elements, the cone analogs, are part of a recurrent circuit that continuously adjusts their sensitivity to accommodate wide swings in the level of ambient light. The silicon retina thus functions effectively both in dim moonlight and in bright sunlight, just as a real eye does.

Moreover, the bipolar-cell analogs in the layer just underneath the photosensitive cones don't care much about absolute light levels anyway. Instead, they respond to the *difference* between (1) the light level reaching the cone just above them, and (2) the average of the light levels reaching all of the other cones in the immediate area, as computed and reported by the extensive system of the horizontal-cell analogs. In sum, in both the real and the silicon retinas, the bipolar cells compute *delta*brightness levels across the retinal surface and then pass this information forward. Collectively, the bipolar cells are actively looking for structure within the retinal image, for borders or outlines that might indicate something important.

The network is also configured to make the bipolar cells sensitive to structure across time, both to changes in the brightness level reaching any given cone, and to changes in the structure-of-brightness-levels that the bipolar cells have already discovered. They are thus especially sensitive to *movements* of the potentially important edges and outlines already grasped.

Several years ago and shortly after its development, I had the opportunity to play with this silicon network for a few minutes (figure 9.2). Mead had brought it with him to a local interdisciplinary gathering. He had mounted the postage-stamp sized

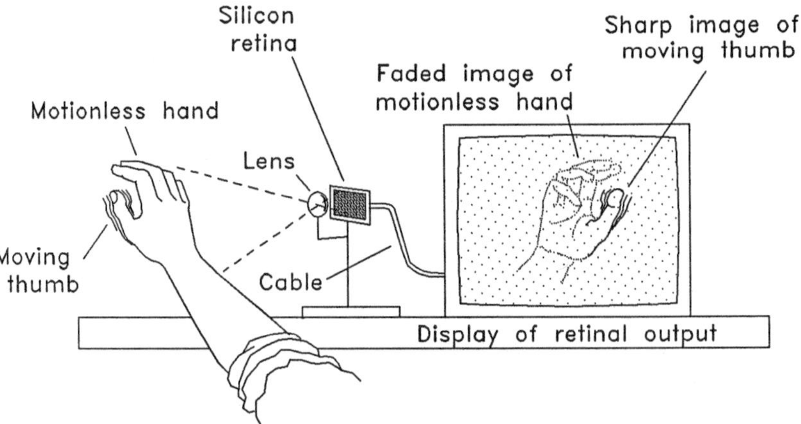

Figure 9.2 Carver Mead's silicon retina detecting the structure and motion of local objects.

retina behind a lens to form an artificial eye, and had connected the retina's vectorial output to an adjacent video display so that one could see its highly processed outputs directly. When I moved my hand in front of the eye, a bright image of my hand moved into view on the video display. As I held my hand still, however, I watched its video image slowly fade as the screen assumed a uniform gray. This is the result of the delta-brightness detectors' gradual adaptation to an unchanging scene. If the human eyeball is artificially immobilized on a static scene, a similar fadeout occurs. This tendency to fadeout is less noticeable in a real eye, because its cones or "pixels" are so very tiny—roughly one micron, or one millionth of a meter—that even micromotions are enough to counteract the slow adaptations. By contrast, the cone analogs on Mead's silicon retina, although small, are still 4000 times larger than a real cone. Unless the image falling across them is moved substantially, the image slowly fades.

It fades because the delta-brightness detectors become adapted to the highly specific image now immobilized on the photoreceptors. Their response profiles have become temporarily deformed, as it were, in such a way as to regard the highly structured but motionless image as if it were a completely blank image. Hence the uniform gray on the video screen. But that image-specific adaptation can be made instantly visible if we now present to the retina a genuinely uniform input image.

When a blank piece of paper was suddenly interposed between the artificial eye and my now motionless hand, a rich *negative* image of my hand instantly appeared on the screen, an image that itself began to fade. This is the analog of what we call, in the human eye, an "afterimage." Notice that, in the case of the silicon retina, what is crucial for producing that negative afterimage onscreen is that the interposed sheet of paper be completely *uniform*. It does not matter whether it is black or white or gray, as long as the brightness levels are constant across its surface. It is only against such a constancy that the localized adaptations in the silicon retina can be effectively revealed.

I cannot bring Mead's retina to you, but you can observe the same phenomenon in your own retina. We all know how to fixate on a high-contrast scene for thirty seconds, and then close our eyes in order to see a negative afterimage against the surrounding blackness. But closing one's eyes is quite unnecessary, and a black background is not essential. The next time you do this, don't close

Figure 9.3 (a) What the silicon retina was looking at. (b) How the silicon retina represents the portrait of Lincoln. (c) How its representation fades over time if Lincoln's image is held constant on its sensory surface. (d) How the retina's time-induced adaptation to Lincoln's image is suddenly revealed, as an afterimage, when the retina is then shown a surface of uniform brightness. (Thanks to Carver Mead and *Scientific American*.)

your eyes at the end of the thirty seconds. Instead, quickly relocate your gaze onto a smooth and uniformly colored surface—any color, any brightness, as long as it is uniform. Your afterimage will appear just as plainly against that background as it does against the back side of your eyelids. A summary of these points concerning motionless images is shown in figure 9.3.

Return once more to my hand's faded image on Mead's video display. If I then wiggled only my thumb, an image of just my thumb would instantly reappear onscreen. Once the thumb was motionless again, its image would start to fade. If my entire hand moved, its full moving image would instantly reappear. The silicon retina, it was plain, is an extraordinarily fast and selective detector of *bodies-in-motion.* It extracts structure within the arriving optical image independently of external brightness levels, and it gives

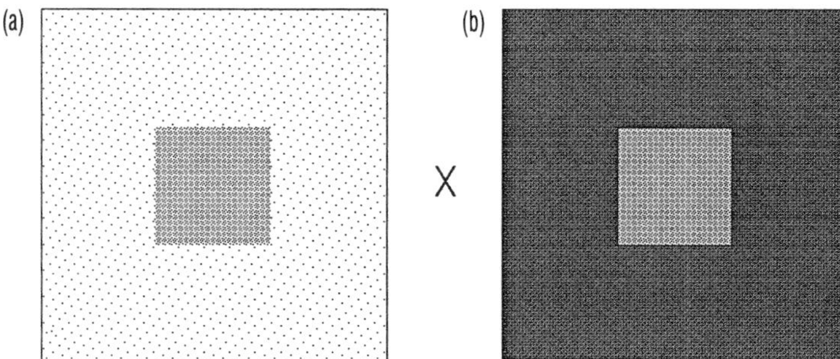

Figure 9.4 A familiar brightness illusion. The inner square of (a) appears darker than the inner square of (b), despite the fact that they have exactly the same absolute brightness level. The effect is best seen if you fixate your gaze on the X.

highly selective representation to exactly those objects in the environment that are moving relative to the line of sight. All of this is accomplished in the first three neuronal layers, before projection to any downstream system such as a brain.

It should be no surprise that biological retinas have a fierce concern with detecting bodies in motion. 600 million years ago, before significant brains had made their evolutionary appearance, motion detection may have been the eye's single most important function. What is more remarkable is that Mead's meticulous semiconductor reconstruction of the micro-network within the retina should reproduce so faithfully some of the retina's major *functional* features. Neither does that fidelity end here. The silicon retina is subject to several of the same illusions to which human vision is subject, something we should expect if the silicon model has indeed captured the functional tactics of the biological retina. A full survey would deflect us from our purpose, but you can see one of them for yourself in figure 9.4.

Recall one last time that the bipolar cells are concerned with representing the *changes* in brightness levels across the image, at the expense of accurately representing the *absolute* brightness levels at any point in the image. Because of this fact, the retina runs into a bit of trouble when it has to evaluate the very same thing against two different backgrounds. As figure 9.4b illustrates, against a black background, a gray square gets represented as "pretty bright." But figure 9.4a shows that, against a light background, that identical shade of gray gets represented as "pretty dark." Such minor illusions, however, are insignificant relative to the payoff of commanding any scene's internal structure, whether lit by dim moonlight, bright sunlight, or anything in between. That tradeoff is a bargain.

I have spent some time on Mead's silicon network because it is so accessible, and because it is so cleanly prototypical of the class of networks we can look forward to. There are other silicon networks we might explore—Mead also has a functioning silicon *cochlea*, for example—but the silicon retina will serve as an adequate exemplar. What we now must address is whether such electronic reconstructions of the relevant neuroanatomy (physical structure) and neurophysiology (physical activity) might be achieved for other parts of the brain and nervous system, and even for the brain as a whole.

Mead himself gives an unqualified positive answer: "By the mid-1980s neuroscientists had learned enough about the operations of nerves and synapses to know that there is no mystery to what they do. In no single instance is there a function done by a neural element that cannot, from the point of view of a systems designer, be duplicated by electronic devices." Mead's position may be a slight overstatement of the case. The biochemical dimensions of neural activity, as discussed in chapter 7, are highly intricate. Recreating all of them electronically is going to be a long and complex process.

Still, the length or complexity of the process is not really the issue. Our question addressed the sheer possibility of an electronic implementation of the cognitively relevant functions of the entire human nervous system. The success of Mead's retina and cochlea illustrate that the job can be done for the sensory periphery. The success of the networks explored in earlier chapters—networks for faces, emotions, stereo vision, grammar, and so on—suggest that it might also be done for many of the higher centers of the brain.

There is no question that the artificial networks explored earlier could all be realized on silicon chips, for example. In fact, it is extremely important that we get such successful networks out of their clumsy programmed incarnations—as mere simulations within a classical, discrete-state, serial machine—and implement them directly, as real hardware networks, in the fashion of Mead's silicon retina. It is important because the central advantages of parallel distributed processing, namely, blinding speed and healthy fault tolerance, have no chance to show themselves within a programmed simulation. Such simulations are easy to produce and they are highly instructive, but they are as slow as molasses, and their reliability is no better than the digital machine running the simulation.

Genuinely parallel implementation is important for the further reason that only then will the values of all of the variables in the network—the excitation levels of the neurons and their axonal projections, the values of each of the synaptic weights, and so forth—only then will they have open to them every point in the mathematical continuum. So-called "digital" or *discrete-state* computing machines are limited by their nature to representing and computing mathematical functions that range over the *rational* numbers, as Pythagoras called them. Classical machines are limited, that is, to computing mathematical functions whose inputs and outputs can be expressed as *ratios of whole numbers.*

This is a potentially severe limitation on the abilities of a digital machine, because the rational numbers form only a tiny and peculiar subset of the continuum of real numbers. Therefore, functions over real numbers cannot strictly be computed or even represented within a digital machine. They can only be approximated. Any functional relation that lies beneath a given machine's built-in level of approximation (ten decimal points of accuracy, say, or twenty) is a function beyond that machine's comprehension. A real neural network, by contrast, does not have this limitation. Its non-classical computations range over the full range of real numbers, not just the rational ones.

In all, implementing our model neural networks in real hardware and in genuinely parallel form is something that brings solutions, not problems. Real neural nets bring computational speed, functional persistence, and computations over the true mathematical continuum. They also bring something else that wants noting. The silicon retina, for example, is a computational system that responds in real time to real light. It is the kind of system that is already causally embedded in the real world, rather than only tenuously and occasionally connected to it by way of a keyboard or a floppy disk.

And yet, would such an artificial silicon brain, lodged in a robot body, be truly *conscious*? To this question our considered answer must depend on the details of the silicon brain in question, and on the details of the theory of consciousness that we hope to settle on in the next decade or two. An answer at the present time can be at best conditional, but it is clear. If something like the theory of consciousness sketched in the preceding chapter is correct, and if Mead's confidence in the functional versatility of electronic media is well founded, then it rather looks as if it will be possible to construct an electronic machine that is as truly conscious as you or I. So far, that dramatic possibility remains wide open.

But not to all eyes. Several prominent thinkers have fundamental reservations about the prospects at issue. Before proceeding, we need to give them a hearing.

Some Principled Objections to Machine Intelligence

In recent years, skepticism concerning the prospects for machine intelligence has centered on three main topics. The first is the matter of the meaning or semantic content of human mental states such as thoughts, beliefs, and desires. The second is the question of whether a computer can ever recreate the full human capacity for doing mathematics. And the third is our old friend, the problem of the qualitative character of conscious experience. Let us take them in turn.

John Searle has a much-discussed view concerning the nature of meaning or semantic content. He claims that genuine meaning is intrinsic to the conscious states of humans, but is simply absent from the states of an electronic computer. The computer's states have, at most, a secondary or "as if" kind of meaning, a kind that arises in the first place only because we humans find it useful or convenient to *interpret* its states as representing these numbers, that situation, or those propositions. Its states do not have intrinsic meaning, argues Searle, any more than the various configurations of beads on an abacus have intrinsic meaning. Moreover, no form of manipulation of those beads will give their configurations any intrinsic meaning, whatever else it might give them. Similarly, no form of manipulation of the computer's states will give them any intrinsic meaning either, whatever else it might give them. The programmed manipulation of physical things, he concludes, is powerless to produce genuine or intrinsic meaning.

It is conceivable that Searle is right about the nature of meaning, but his semantic theory is only one of many such theories, and it is not the most compelling. Even if his semantic theory is true, it is unclear that a massively parallel silicon brain is doomed, like the abacus, to lack states with intrinsic meaning. If high-dimensional activation vectors can have intrinsic meaning within the human neural architecture, then why can't their vector analogs have intrinsic meaning in a silicon recapitulation of that architecture?

Searle has no convincing reply here. In fact, I believe he is willing to contemplate the possibility that the silicon analogs might have intrinsic meaning, so long as the silicon brain is sufficiently similar to the human brain. His main argument against intrinsic meaning in computers is directed against classical programmable machines. That argument has no purchase against the position I am here defending, since it is massively parallel computers that are here at issue. They are simply not engaged in the business of manipulating symbols by reference to stored rules.

Searle's semantic theory is dubious in any case. It is doubtful that there is any such thing as an "*intrinsic* meaning", a meaning that a state has utterly independently of the relations that it bears, or fails to bear, to other states and to the external world. If meaning could be thus disconnected and intrinsic, then it should be possible for a physical system to have exactly *one* internal state, a state with intrinsic meaning—e.g., "Justice is being poorly served in Bosnia" —but have no other meaningful states at all. Although possible, perhaps, this is not very plausible. It seems rather like insisting that some person could be correctly described as "the Junior Senator from California" without there also existing a vast network of other elected positions, legislative institutions, administrative offices, political divisions, electoral procedures, registered voters, and some good hard real estate next to the Pacific Ocean.

A more promising and less mysterious approach to semantic theory locates meaning in the idiosyncratic set of causal and inferential relations that a given cognitive state bears to all of the other states of the person, and to aspects of the external world. This relational approach embraces a variety of quite different semantic theories. They vary according to which relations they regard as the semantically essential ones. But all of them are at least compatible with the idea that the physical states of an artificial neural network can possess genuine meaning, because they all allow the possibility that physical states might enjoy the relations deemed semantically essential.

The context of parallel networks and their special style of cognitive activity may even help to expand our understanding of the nature of meaning. Meaning, in its prototypical sense, is a feature of words, sentences, and perhaps also thoughts and beliefs. It is possible, however, that these cases of meaning are just the tip of a large iceberg, just high-level instances of a more general phenomenon displayed in computational states far below the familiar linguistic level. In the opening chapters of this book we saw how training on a large population of examples produced an organized structure of concepts or categories across even the most elementary of activation spaces, and we saw how those learning-sensitive categories played an active role in complex discriminatory behavior. It is hard to resist the impression that we were there watching the earliest and simplest forms of semantic significance or meaning. Rather than being at odds with a neurocomputational account of cognition, the phenomenon of meaning may be best explained from within it. There is no compelling case against machine intelligence here.

In a recent book entitled *The Emperor's New Mind*, the Cambridge mathematician Roger Penrose raises the second of our three issues. Can the sorts of algorithmic procedures executed by a standard computer program account for the full range of human knowledge and competence in mathematics? Penrose answers No, and I am strongly inclined to agree with him, although not for the same reasons. Penrose, like many others, cites Godel's theorem concerning the incompleteness of any axiomatization of arithmetic. This famous theorem establishes that no finite set of algorithmic procedures can generate *all* arithmetic truths. There must always be some arithmetic truths, truths that are comfortably provable by means that lie outside the particular algorithmic system at issue, truths that are unprovable from within that system. No machine implementation of that algorithmic system, therefore, can establish all the arithmetic truths that we humans can. Penrose, like many others, takes this as showing that human knowledge of mathematical truths cannot be fully explained in terms of our using algorithmic procedures.

However, Penrose's is a minority interpretation of the Godel result. The standard and widely accepted reply is that, if Godel is right, then humans too must have comparable limitations, in that there must exist arithmetic truths that lie beyond *our* peculiar armory of algorithmic procedures, truths that some superior being with an even larger armory might be able to prove where we could not. It is no surprise then that we can prove more than a machine whose armory is limited to Peano's classical axioms and a handful of rules. Godel's result shows that, where mathematical knowledge is concerned, humans are not limited to just *one* set of algorithmic procedures. But that is still consistent with the assumption that algorithmic procedures of some kind or other underlie all of our scattered mathematical knowledge, such as it is.

The standard reply, I believe, is correct. For all that Godel's theorem shows us, it is still possible that human knowledge of mathematical truths is algorithmic. The ranks of the orthodox thus resume their complacency. But that orthodox algorithmic assumption is just one possible explanation of our mathematical knowledge, and it is starting to look threadbare in any case. It would be worthy of reexamination even if Godel's proof had never been achieved. Penrose wishes to defend the competing hypothesis that humans possess a *non*algorithmic capacity for recognizing mathematical truths, a form of "insight" that does not depend on the rule-governed manipulation of physical symbols in a discrete-state procedure. On this point, I think it quite evident that Penrose is correct. Let me try to defend this claim.

First, I must distance myself from Penrose's positive theory of where that nonalgorithmic capacity resides. He locates it in the domain of quantum mechanics, indeed, in a still-conjectural domain of quantum gravitational effects, all taking place inside our heads. The idea is to exploit the unusual properties of wave superposition and wave collapse as described in quantum theory. Everyone will agree that the process of wave superposition and subsequent collapse into a classical state is a nonalgorithmic process. Penrose suggests that such processes might embody nonclassical computations, the very computations we need in order to account for "insight" in the realm of human mathematical knowledge.

I find this extravagant. Although these quantum processes are surely nonalgorithmic, there seems nothing specific to recommend them as performing recognizable *computations*. There is no recognizable pathway by which *information* about some macroscopic mathematical problem—a complex quadratic equation before my eyes, say—can effectively make it down to the level of superposed quantum states, through the computational bottleneck of a wave collapse, and then back up again to the classical level in such a fashion as to help me recognize the messy equation before me as just another instance of the familiar quadratic form. Third, such processes in the brain as we can experimentally implicate in the information-processing business are all at a *scale* of mass-energy exchange that is far above the quantum level and squarely within the classical domain.

Thus my rejection of Penrose's positive account of nonalgorithmic processes. But there is a fourth and final reason. *One need not look so far afield as the quantum realm to find a rich domain of nonalgorithmic processes.* The processes taking place within a hardware neural network are typically nonalgorithmic, and they constitute the bulk of the computational activity going on inside our heads. They are nonalgorithmic in the blunt sense that they do not consist in a series of discrete physical states serially traversed under the instructions of a stored set of symbol-manipulating rules. Nor must all of them be usefully or relevantly approximatable by any physically real algorithmic mechanisms. Instead, they are analog processes, their elements and activities are real-valued, they unfold in parallel, and they unfold in accordance with natural laws rather than at the behest of stored rules. What Penrose deems essential to account for human mathematical cognition is already present as a hallmark feature of neural networks, in both their biological and semiconductor incarnations.

Initially at least, the suggestion that some unspecified form of "insight", one arising from nonalgorithmic processes, might be responsible for some of our mathematical knowledge is a suggestion sure to raise skeptical hackles in almost everyone. But the form of insight need not remain unspecified, and the nonclassical processes are easily identified. Let me give an example to help demystify both aspects of the suggestion.

As a regular teacher of formal logic classes for many years, I can recognize at a glance that the formula

$$(A \,\&\, B) \rightarrow ((C \vee {\sim} D) \rightarrow (A \,\&\, B))$$

is a tautology, a logical truth, a theorem of the propositional calculus. Now, there are algorithmic procedures for deciding whether or not any given formula is a tautology, and in a minute's computation, they will certify the displayed formula as such. But that is not how *I* recognize that this formula is a tautology. I recognize it at a glance, because I can see that it is an instance of the general pattern

$$\mathbf{P} \rightarrow (\mathbf{Q} \rightarrow \mathbf{P}),$$

which is one of the three basic axioms of the propositional calculus. You can see it too: $(A \,\&\, B)$ plays the role of **P**, and $(C \vee {\sim} D)$ plays the role of **Q**. That's it. For me and thousands of other logic teachers, the bold-face formula has become a familiar prototype, a central pattern with many and varied possible instances, all radiating outward in my activation space along certain dimensions of relevant similarity to which I have been trained by long experience at the scratch pad and blackboard.

This capacity for pattern recognition is crucial to being a successful logic teacher, or a logic student, for that matter. If the want of it had forced me to execute a laborious algorithm every time I was interested in whether some formula on the blackboard was a tautology, my students would have lynched me years ago. Fortunately, this humdrum insight into logical structure, this capacity for activating relevant prototype vectors, makes algorithmic plodding largely unnecessary for most logic problems below a certain level of complexity. That is, one falls back on the effective procedures of an algorithm only when one's pattern-recognizing skills are defeated by the complexity of the problem at hand. This falling back on the rules happens often, at least to me, but it is plain that logical comprehension neither begins nor ends with algorithmic procedures.

The same is clearly true in logic's next-door neighbor, mathematics. If one is looking to integrate various formulas or to differentiate them, if one is looking for solutions to polynomial or differential equations, one confronts a similar cognitive task and deploys cognate resources. A calculus teacher at the blackboard is also a nonalgorithmic pattern recognizer, despite her regular recourse to rules. That extra talent is crucial. Prototype activation is almost certainly important for mathematical exploration as well, that is, for research into unfamiliar territory. There the aim is to stumble across novel deployments of mathematical prototypes already in hand, or to develop new prototypes by repeated encounters with novel problems, or both. Simply grinding away at algorithms already in place is not the only way, and certainly not the most promising way, to make conceptual advances in mathematics.

It should be mentioned, if only in passing, that humans are typically very bad at doing mathematics, and most especially we are bad at doing the computational or algorithmical aspects of it. Ask us to add a column of random four-digit numbers, a column thirty numbers high, and ten minutes later we will present the wrong answer at least half the time. A classical computer, on the other hand, will get it right every time, and in less than ten milliseconds.

The shoe is on the other foot, however, if the development of new mathematical concepts and the achievement of fundamental mathematical insights are the skills at issue. Here it is the human who seems to have the deeper capacity, and the classical computer that seems to be the stick-in-the-mud. This is roughly what we should expect if the human is a massively parallel prototype activator, and the classical machine is a high-speed serial algorithm executor. Our assembled skills overlap, but our computational fortes are quite different. They are configured to explore different but complementary aspects of mathematical space.

I have made the situation concerning mathematics seem simpler than it is, and I hope my distortions are not crucial. My aim, however, has not been to peddle a new epistemology for mathematics, although it will be evident that I hope for one. My aim has been a fast evaluation of the prospects for network-style machine intelligence against the problematic case of mathematical knowledge. Significantly, the principal objections from this quarter are all aimed at classical computing machines, and not at neural networks. In addition, the peculiar cognitive capacities of neural networks may help us develop a realistic solution—more realistic than Penrose's quantum gravity hypothesis, anyway—to some of the problems that confront the classical or algorithmic model of human mathematical knowledge. Once again, there is no compelling case against machine intelligence.

The third of the principled objections to the possibility of genuine intelligence in a machine concerns sensory qualia. The problem is to find a plausible home for them within a purely physicalistic framework. We have already defeated the negative arguments of Nagel and Jackson, so there is no need to readdress them. But one more awaits discussion.

The negative argument here addressed was authored about fifteen years ago by the MIT philosopher Ned Block. Block had no dualistic axe to grind in presenting the argument. He was merely worried about an apparent problem with the form of materialism dominant at the time, the position called functionalism. Functionalists argued that the essence of conscious intelligence lies in the "software," in the abstract computer program, in the set of algorithmic procedures, that each normal human implements in his or her biological "hardware." This position was almost universal among both philosophers and AI researchers at the time. For them, the critical part of creating true intelligence in a machine was simply a matter of writing out the program that normal humans implement, or, equally acceptable, a program that is input-output equivalent to it. The machine that ran these programs mattered little. This, you will recognize, is the now classical approach to which this book stands opposed.

Block's worry was simple. One could make, or anyway, imagine making, some rather unusual implementations of the human program. (Let us assume for a moment that such a program exists.) In particular, we can imagine organizing the entire population of China into executing that program by means of special cards that they have, rules that they follow, and interactions that they engage in with one another, and with a single robot body over which they have collective radio control. It would be an exceedingly *slow* implementation of the relevant program, conceded Block, but strictly speaking it could implement the same vast input-output function implemented in a human. Even so, Block insisted, it is not remotely plausible that this sprawling social system, considered as a single individual thing, would thereby have sensations with internal qualitative characters of the same sort that we have. Although the algorithmic requirements might all be met, sensory qualia would still be absent from this system. Functionalism, therefore, must be missing something important about the nature of conscious intelligence.

And so it is. It is missing an adequate account of what takes place *inside* a cognitive creature such as a human. Functionalism cared relatively little about exactly what processes take place inside us, so long as they implement the right input-output function. And even then its presumption about the nature of those processes was mistaken: it portrayed them as algorithmic to the core.

Fortunately, classical functionalism is a burden that materialism no longer has to shoulder. We have learned that it does matter what physical processes take place inside us, and that they are not just executing a program. Most of the major features of human and animal cognition arise not because of any program we are running. They arise because of the peculiar physical organization of the nervous system, because of the peculiar way in which information is physically coded, and because of the physically distributed means by which that information gets transformed.

Once again, and for the third time in this section, a major argument against materialism turns out to be, at best, an argument against a highly specific version of materialism: the version that portrays cognitive activity as the rule-governed manipulation of discrete physical symbols.

And once again, the neurocomputational alternative promises to provide some solutions where the older view provided only problems. As we have already seen, the character of sensory vector coding and the structures within a given sensory vector space give us an opening grip on the problem, and considerable resources with which to address what remains.

Mead's silicon retina attests to the rough accuracy of our current theories about sensory coding and sensory processing in the biological retina. The electronic version displays an intricate dance of qualitatively distinct representational behaviors, a dance that faithfully mirrors our own phenomenological experience in the same circumstances.

No one claims that the silicon retina is conscious, of course. Its representations will not be a target of or a part of something's consciousness until it is embedded in a larger cognitive system, until it conveys those representations to a recurrent system of the sort, perhaps, that unites the cerebral cortex to the intralaminar nucleus of the thalamus. But the same is true of the biological retina. It is not by itself conscious. And unless the brain is conscious at the time, the qualitative dance at its retina cannot be a part of that consiousness.

Could an electronic machine be conscious? It rather looks that way. Will it happen soon? Probably not, although small steps will continue to be taken. Will that technology change things profoundly, at least in the long run? Almost certainly yes, but that is a topic for the final chapter.

Intelligence Differences: Between Individuals, and Between Species

One of the themes that emerged from part I of this book was the large number and the great diversity of distinct cognitive talents that are normally knit together to make up the intelligence of a real human. We saw this in the diversity of artificial networks that have been built to imitate one or other small aspect of human cognition, such as the ability to recognize faces, to read printed text, to see in three dimensions, to generate locomotion, to discriminate sounds, to discriminate emotions, and to discriminate grammatical sentences. We saw it again in the great variety of severe but isolated cognitive deficits that typically result from localized damage to various parts of the living brain.

This diversity illustrates that intelligence is not a one-dimensional commodity, something that varies only from greater to lesser. Rather, the intelligence of any human has many dimensions, and in a normal human population the scattered variation in cognitive ability within each of those dimensions will be considerable. To use a now-familiar term, intelligence is itself a *vector*. One's intelligence cannot be defined except by specifying one's idiosyncratic pattern of abilities across all of its many elemental aspects. This means that intelligence—like tastes, colors, and odors—comes in many different flavors, and it may be of interest and value not just for its occasional sheer overpowering brilliance, but also for the peculiarly charming, local, unusual, creative, task-appropriate, and endearing forms that it may take.

What is it that yields diversity, across individuals, in any one of these constituting dimensions? Why are some people better than others at recognizing facial emotions, for example, or geometrical relations? What is different about their emotion-recognition or spatial-relation networks that explains the difference in their cognitive performance?

In artificial networks, at least, we understand quite well some of the main factors involved. If a network has too few neurons at any one of its several layers to code all of the information relevant to its task, then its performance will suffer accordingly. If a network's collective synaptic connections are too sparse to sustain a good approximation to the vector-to-vector transformation desired, it will be outperformed by a more richly connected network. And if a network is trained by an inefficient or inadequate learning procedure, its performance will fall behind that of other networks no matter how adequate its cell distribution and connectivity.

In extreme cases, the real world shows us clear analogs of the first two forms of deficit. For example, Alzheimer's disease, an affliction of the aged, involves the slow degeneration and eventually the near disappearance of almost all cognitive functions—perceptual, affective, and deliberative. Postmortem examination of the brain of an Alzheimer victim reveals plaques and tangles throughout the gossamer web of his or her neural organization. It reveals widespread neuronal death and systematic corruption of synaptic connections. Korsakoff's syndrome, which results from chronic alcohol abuse, also shows a broad-band degeneration in cognitive function, especially in memory. The postmortem brains of chronic alcohol abusers show some focal neuronal loss in the thalamus, and a reduced number of synaptic connections between their neurons elsewhere. These are pathological cases, of course, but they do illustrate that comparative deficits in one's neuronal population, and/or one's interneural connectivity, exact a price in lower levels of cognitive performance.

On the efficiency of one's learning procedures, it is difficult to say anything useful at this point, since we still understand so poorly what those procedures are. What little we do understand suggests that the process of synaptic modification comes in several different forms, suitable for the acquisition of different cognitive skills, perhaps, or for training distinct networks within the brain as a whole. Our initial diversity in the dimensions of intelligence thus divides yet again.

Finally, there is a relentless internal competition taking place within any normal brain, both during its purely developmental phase in the womb and early childhood, and in the processes of learning throughout one's adult life. As the prenatal neurons form and differentiate, as they migrate to their proper anatomical place, as they project their growing axons toward their distant targets, and as they form and reform thousands of synaptic connections at their axonal destinations, they are always in a complex competition with each other for nutrients, space, connectivity, and information.

Since the available resources are finite, the above-average success of one group of neurons is typically purchased at the slight expense of some other group. Even if the brain's development is perfectly healthy, therefore, both in the total number of its neurons and in the richness of their connectivity, the natural ebb and flow of neuronal competition guarantees considerable variation across people in the profile of the cognitive abilities that result. No one's brain turns out exactly like anyone else's.

When we turn to the obvious differences in intelligence between humans and various nonhuman animals, we must keep in mind this fundamental point that intelligence is a high-dimensional vector rather than a one-dimensional magnitude. The point emerges most clearly when we recall that, in some cognitive domains, other creatures are a good deal more intelligent than humans. For example, a bat is far better than we are at reconstructing, from acoustic inputs, the distribution of objects and obstacles in three-dimensional space. (Incidentally, and despite what one might think, we do have some faint capacities here. Imagine walking blindfolded through a spacious, marble-floored art gallery. The character, timing, and incoming direction of one's sharply echoed footsteps are already sufficient to bring one up short of walking smoothly into a wall.)

The bat's advantage here may be dismissed as merely perceptual rather than cognitive, but this claim will not stand scrutiny. The bat's profound advantage is as much a case of intelligence as it is a case of mere perception, for human ears and the bat's ears differ little in their physical construction. We both have good old mammalian ears. The bat's main cognitive advantage lies elsewhere, farther along in the information-processing hierarchy and well into the domain of repeated vector transformations. The bat's brain *is* exercising intelligence on its auditory inputs. And in making spatio-cognitive use of that peripheral information, the bats have us beaten.

Bats also have a major cognitive advantage over humans where the intricacies of flying are concerned. Dismissing this as mere motor control is once again uncomprehending. Flying is at least as complex a skill as is bipedal locomotion or manual manipulation. All such skills are learned, and all of them are thoroughly integrated into our second-by-second practical reasonings. From early spring until late fall here in La Jolla, I watch brash young humans daily launch themselves off the local cliffs that front the ocean.

With long practice, these hang-glider pilots do achieve a pale and distant reflection of the bat's exquisite skill. I presume it must be delightful to pursue the bats' skills in this way, but humans lack the innate equipment ever to match them. Aerial navigation is indeed a species of intelligence, and once again the bats are our betters.

Finally, and to drive the point home, the business of *coordinating* one's sophisticated auditory input with one's sophisticated aerodynamic motor output, as the dullest of bats can do, is a cognitive skill of high order, a skill of which humans are completely innocent, unless hang-glider pilots have recently taken to flying through marble-floored art galleries in the pitch dark, squeaking throughout. Here is a transparently cognitive skill, a skill more distinguished in the bat than in any bird, a skill that is completely lacking in the typical human.

Choose your nonhuman creature, and chances are that we can tell a similar story about its proprietary cognitive skills. Recall from chapter 2 the discussion of olfactory coding in dogs and their whopping advantage over humans. Dogs and many other animals have an extraordinary access to the rich phenomena within olfactory space, including their temporal and causal features, most of which are beyond human ken. Certain sharks have access to "electric space" with their electrosensitive snouts. They root in the sand for electronically signatured food hidden at various depths beneath the ocean floor, and they search with a systematic intelligence that is alien to our own.

I here choose more sensory examples because their alien nature is plain and because the human deficit is indisputable. But beyond these obvious cases, we must expect sundry cognitive specializations at all levels of the processing hierarchy within nonhuman brains, specializations that we may lack entirely, or possess in comparatively feeble form. In either case, we will be looking at dimensions of intelligence where the animal's cognitive ability exceeds any human's, sometimes by a wide margin. When comparing the intelligence of humans with the intelligence of some nonhuman species, therefore, what we need to do is to compare the two *vectors* of cognitive abilities characteristic of each. We need to compare two complex patterns or profiles, profiles that overlap to some degree, although never completely. And we need to compare them with some humility in the face of what many nonhuman animals have achieved.

Is Language Unique to Humans?

We humans have our own cognitive specializations, and clearly one of them is language. No need to be humble here. Where language skills are concerned, we are the most successful species on the planet. In fact, it is the orthodox opinion among psychologists and linguists that we are the *only* species with the capacity for language.

There is room to doubt this latter claim, in two important respects. First, many other species display what appears to be a systematic means of communication that is specific to that species. Among the larger mammals, the dolphins, whales, and Vervet monkeys are salient examples. The two marine mammals use an acoustic system quite different from the human system, both in their mechanisms of sound generation and in their mechanisms for sensing sound. Their curiously rounded foreheads, for example, constitute an acoustic "lens" that gathers and focuses incoming acoustic energy. There is no doubt that dolphins use these gifts to communicate with each other, although the character of that communication remains hidden from us. Beyond communication, dolphins use their acoustic gifts for echolocation and echo-"palpation", and they are sensitive to subtle phase shifts and other temporal phenomena to which humans are deaf. Underwater sound is different from atmospheric sound in many ways. For starters, it travels much faster and its wavelengths are longer. The dolphin's audition has evolved to exploit these differences, as has its vocal apparatus. This makes the semantically and grammatically relevant structural features of their "speech," should there be any, difficult for us to recover.

The Vervet monkeys, by contrast, are much more accessible to us sensorily, and field studies have revealed a native vocabulary of perhaps a dozen distinctive sounds, all of which have a semantic content that is stable across a diversity of social uses. Vervets live in the high canopy of the tropical forest, however, so yet again it is difficult to become intimate with them in their natural cognitive setting. All three of these species are profoundly social, but we humans are ill equipped to participate in their social institutions or appreciate their intricacies. As long as the nature and complexity of these alien systems remain opaque to us, we cannot be certain that they differ from human language in kind rather than just in degree.

A second worry concerns the ability of our closest evolutionary neighbors, the other great apes, to learn some form or subset of a genuinely human language. The chimps, orangs, and gorillas, unfortunately, lack the necessary vocal apparatus to articulate the sounds of human language. Whatever their cognitive capacities may be, it is not anatomically possible for them to command a spoken language. Early researchers therefore turned to human sign language, the language of hand configurations and movements, as the target skill for a chimpanzee to learn. That sign language is fully as complex as our spoken language, so it is an equally worthy target. And all of the apes have highly developed manual capabilities, so a failure to learn would imply a cognitive rather than just an anatomical deficit.

The early results appeared positive. Washoe, a young female chimp, lived with the psychologists Alan and Trixie Gardener in a deliberately natural domestic setting. She learned a vocabulary of over a hundred signs, and would sometimes combine them in two- and three-word sequences, some of them novel. But skeptics were unsure whether her use of signs was driven by genuinely semantic considerations, as opposed to mere stimulus-response connections that her training had established. More important, they were unimpressed by her grammar. Washoe's command of grammatical structure, her capacity for exploiting appropriate combinations of words remained rudimentary, at best. She never approached the eager fluency of a human child.

A second chimp, a young male, waggishly named "Nim Chimpsky" in honor of the MIT linguist Noam Chomsky, was also trained in the use of sign language, this time by the behaviorist psychologist, Herb Terrace, and under the more carefully controlled experimental conditions of a laboratory. Nim also learned a substantial vocabulary and lived up, more or less, to the standard that Washoe had set. But in the end he served only to strengthen the skeptical worries, for he showed the same limitations as Washoe. Terrace was not able to induce in Nim any behaviors that could not be explained by factors well short of the truly generative capacities that were assumed to underlie the human command of grammatical structure and real meaning. For these reasons, among others, the initial claims of language capacity in nonhuman apes began to fall into disrepute.

There they have remained, although a new generation of linguistic research at the Yerkes National Laboratory in Atlanta is already in the business of reconstituting the debate. This research focuses on the rather endearing pygmy chimps or Bonobos, and the linguistic system in question is an artificial system of visually distinct and easily manipulable physical symbols. Roughly 200 of these smallish symbols, in various shapes and colors, are permanently positioned on a largish grid laid out on a sort of portable electronic slate board. The animal activates any given symbol simply by pressing on it. This system reduces the ambiguity often encountered with vague or poorly gestured hand signs, and it gives us a much more objective grip on what combinations the animal has or has not produced. As in the earlier studies, the animals are trained to use these resources in their daily practical lives. The slate boards go with them everywhere.

Sue Savage Rumbaugh and Duane Rumbaugh and their co-workers at the Yerkes laboratory are the principal researchers on this project. After a decade of work, they report language-like behavior in the pygmy chimps substantially beyond what Washoe and Nim displayed, both in functional vocabulary and in grammatical sophistication. One of their most accomplished animals, an older male named "Kanzi", also shows an unexpected appreciation of *spoken* English beyond its considerable skills with the artificial symbol system. There is nothing wrong with a chimpanzee's ears, after all, and Kanzi, who has been immersed in an active Anglophone environment all his life, has shown an apparently systematic ability to follow complex English-language instructions. Some of these instructions are novel to him. They are instructions that he has never heard before, such as, "Kanzi, go and get the ball that is outdoors and bring it to Margaret." Kanzi did exactly that, passing on the way a second ball that was indoors. Sue Savage Rumbaugh videotaped this episode and many others. Kanzi's responses are impressive.

Kanzi's comprehension skills merit a great deal of further discussion, but these points about comprehending spoken English deflect attention from the quite different and more easily controlled research on the chimps' command of the artificial symbol system. Here the results are robust across several animals, although their significance remains ambiguous. Are the chimps showing an elementary command of the same sort of systematic capacity that underlies human language? Or are they merely stretching to the limit their nonlinguistic cognitive capacities in a hollow mock-up of even the first few layers of the genuinely systematic human capacity? I don't know. Neither, I think, does anyone else.

Why does it matter? What hangs on whether chimpanzees can learn, if only feebly, a generative linguistic skill? At least two things. The first is the fate of the currently dominant theory of how we *humans* command language. This is Noam Chomsky's celebrated view that human brains, and only human brains, contain a special "language organ," a neural subsystem with the unique and genetically innate capacity for manipulating the kinds of recursive grammatical rules that characterize all human languages. It is a consequence of this view that no other animals should be able to learn the sorts of linguistic skills that we learn. Almost any positive results from the ape-language research would be a direct threat to that view.

A second and closely related issue concerns the role that language-like computational skills play in the production of consciousness. Some theorists, most notably Dan Dennett, think that serial cognitive processes—of the kind displayed, for example, in discursive speech—are constitutive of the very special style of consciousness that humans and only humans possess. Dennett sees a gulf fixed between human and animal consciousness, and language-like cognitive processing is what is said to make the difference between them. If Chomsky is right about the capacity for language being unique to humans, and if Dennett is right about language-like processing being the essence of human consciousness, then the consciousness of humans must differ from that of the nonlinguistic animals not just in degree, but in fundamental kind.

I wish to question both premises of this argument. Let us address Chomsky first, and let us focus on his claim that the human brain is unique in having a "language organ" that is computationally devoted to the application and manipulation of abstract grammatical rules. A number of empirical facts sit poorly with this claim.

One might expect that lesion and other localization studies would reveal such a specialized brain area, and this was indeed the interpretation first put on the significance of Broca's area (see again chapter 7). It looked as though it might be the postulated "grammar box." But further research reveals a different picture. As the Damasios and others have shown, our linguistic capacity is distributed rather more widely across the brain. For grammatical comprehension, as opposed to production, Wernicke's area is at least as important as Broca's area, and the two areas are separated by two or three inches and a major lobal boundary. As well, distinct lesions along the entire length of the temporal lobe, from its boundary with the occipital lobe and forward across the boundary into the frontal lobe, knock out distinct grammatical parts of speech, as indicated in figure 7.4. Broca's area emerges as implicated primarily in our command of verbs in particular rather than of grammar in general. If there is a proprietary language organ, it is scattered across much of the brain's surface, and it resides in areas for which many non-human animals have clear anatomical homologs. If we have such an organ and they do not, the difference has yet to show up in our respective brain anatomies.

Let me now change gears. The existence of bilingual and multilingual speakers among humans is a prima facie problem for the language-organ hypothesis: do such people develop two, three, or even more language organs? By itself, this need not be a serious objection. After all, one and the same language organ may be able to command several distinct languages: we need only think of the multilingual person as having *one* complex language that contains several highly distinct styles of speech: an English style, a French style, and so forth.

The problem of multiple and distinct language organs reemerges, however, when we contemplate the empirical fact that a "reversible brain lesion" can render a bilingual subject wholly aphasic in one of his two languages, and yet leave his other language unaffected. There are indeed such cases. During surgical exploration, for example, a bilingual Greek-American would lose his native Greek when certain left-brain areas were artificially inhibited, but his learned English remained unaffected. Artificial inhibition of a nearby brain area had exactly the reverse effect. If language organs really exist, these clinical cases suggest that bilinguals must have at least two of them, spatially distinct, separately functional, and both of them on the same side of the brain.

Confusion mounts when we contemplate a further fact: if a normal human infant suffers brain damage such as to preclude the left-brain structures' normal assumption of their linguistic capacity, then the corresponding areas on the brain's right side typically take over the task. Normal language competence does develop, but it is embodied in the right-brain structures instead of the left. Apparently the right side of the brain contains a language organ also—a potential one, at least—an organ that assumes non-grammatical duties unless fate should happen to call on it.

Do all of us then have *two* language organs, one on each side of the brain? In some sense, plainly we must, although the original description, "language organ", has now become problematic. The point of the language organ, after all, was to be computationally devoted to the application and manipulation of abstract grammatical rules. Clearly the right-brain structures are *not* so devoted, for in the vast majority of humans, those structures never assume their clear linguistic potential: they end up performing a variety of quite different cognitive functions. The right-brain anatomical counterpart to Broca's area, for example, is an area that is standardly implicated in our capacity for fine-grained *manual* manipulation. For something that was supposed to be hard-wired for grammatical duty, the right-brain "language organ" proves to be as plastic functionally as it is scattered anatomically.

The same deflationary judgment must be held of its more commonly linguistic mirror image on the left side of the brain. For there are many left-handed people, without brain damage on either side, for whom the cortical location of linguistic and manual skills is precisely the reverse of the statistically more common arrangement described earlier. If there is a unique, anatomically distinct and hard-wired language organ in the human brain, it is a very elusive customer.

There is a standard objection often raised against Chomsky's claim of a sharp discontinuity between the computational equipment of humans as against the other primates. I will not press the objection, but it merits a mention. From an evolutionary perspective, a sudden leap to having a full-fledged language organ, from having no such organ at all, seems highly unlikely, especially given our close genetic proximity to the other great apes and the comparatively short time span since our evolutionary paths diverged (not more than 5 million years ago). It is much more likely, runs the objection, that humans at some point learned to make full or novel use of a computational capacity that all of the higher primates possess, at least to some degree.

This contrary idea that language involves the special use of a fairly *general* cognitive capacity receives independent support from research on artificial neural networks. Elman's success in producing grammatically competent networks shows that no very special or proprietary neural architecture is necessary for the acquisition of grammar-like skills. The plainest of plain vanilla recurrent networks prove capable of handling at least an elementary generative grammar. The successful model networks are not even very large: only 200 neurons or so. Yet their architecture is capable of learning many grammars other than the specific one taught them, and that same architecture could have been put to an endless variety of uses quite different from the narrowly grammatical use to which it was in fact put. If something highly special is required, in the nature of hard-wired computational structures, in order to sustain grammatical competence, the artificial network models certainly don't show it. In fact, they show just the reverse: even the simplest realistic neural structures have the generative capacity in question.

Neither is language the only generative capacity that humans possess. Humans can learn, with suitable training, to perform music. And they learn not just to read music, but to improvise or "ad lib" fluently, coherently, and at arbitrary length on an underlying but well-defined chordal theme. Humans can learn geometry, and they learn to spin out proofs indefinitely, proofs of ever more complex geometrical facts and relations. Humans can learn arithmetic, and they learn to generate sums, multiplications, divisions, and so forth, of arbitrary length. As with language, nonhuman animals do not participate in these activities either. Must we therefore postulate within us an innate and proprietary "music organ," a "geometry organ," and an "arithmetic organ" to accompany our "language organ"?

If not, then what special claim has language to a computational organ all to itself? Perhaps a claim derives from the fact that *any* normal human infant will learn language if raised in a linguistically active social environment. But equally, any normal human infant will learn music, or geometry, or arithmetic, if raised in a social environment that is suitably active in the relevant activity. If there is a fundamental difference here, it is once again elusive.

None of this shows that Chomsky's hypothesis must be wrong. But if your confidence is wavering, it has my own confidence for company. Especially when Sue Savage Rumbaugh's pygmy chimps demonstrate a systematic combinatorial capacity at the artificial symbol board, regularly putting together quick sequences of four or five words. And especially when Kanzi shows, in addition, the ability to respond appropriately to such novel verbal instructions as, "Kanzi, put the key in the fridge," "Kanzi, take off my shoe," and "Kanzi, give the dog a shot" (the dog was a stuffed toy but the hypodermic was real, and Kanzi took its cap off before using it). The hypothesis that the human linguistic capacity resides in largely standard computational brain structures, and differs from that of nonhuman animals only in degree, remains very much a live hypothesis.

Dennett's Language-Centered Theory of Consciousness: A Critique

We turn now to Dennett and to a theory of human consciousness quite different from those sketched in the last chapter. Dennett is well aware, as is everyone else in recent years, that the architecture of the brain is that of a massively parallel computing system. It does not have the structure of a classical, discrete-state, programmed serial computer, and for the most part it does not behave like one either. And yet the massively parallel human brain is still capable, to a degree, of *simulating* the typical behavior of a serial machine. For example, we can both produce and understand the complex strings of symbols of a language; we can perform deductive operations on such strings with some facility and reliability; we can do recursive arithmetic operations such as addition, multiplication, division, and so forth. When we do such things, according to Dennett, our underlying parallel neural architecture is realizing a "virtual" computing machine, whose activities are now of the classical, discrete-state, rule-governed, serial kind.

What Dennett is adverting to here is the general capacity that your standard, serial, desktop computer has to become a "word-processing machine" if you load it with your WordStar program, a "flight-simulator machine" if you load it with your Flight Simulator program, a "tax-calculating machine" if you load it with your TurboTax program, and so forth. Depending on the program it is running at the moment, your desktop machine becomes a specific "virtual machine"—a word processor, a flight simulator, a tax calculator, or what-have-you. If we program it appropriately, it will even simulate the behavior of a massively-parallel *neural* network, which is how most of our research on that topic is still done.

Similarly, says Dennett, a real, massively parallel hardware neural network can, with suitable setting of its many synaptic weights, simulate the computational activities of a discrete-state serial machine (figure 10.1). Turning the tables on the usual practice just mentioned, a parallel machine can sustain a virtual machine of the classical serial kind. This, according to Dennett, is what human brains do when they learn a language. They acquire the capacity, absent in nonhuman animals, to represent and process information

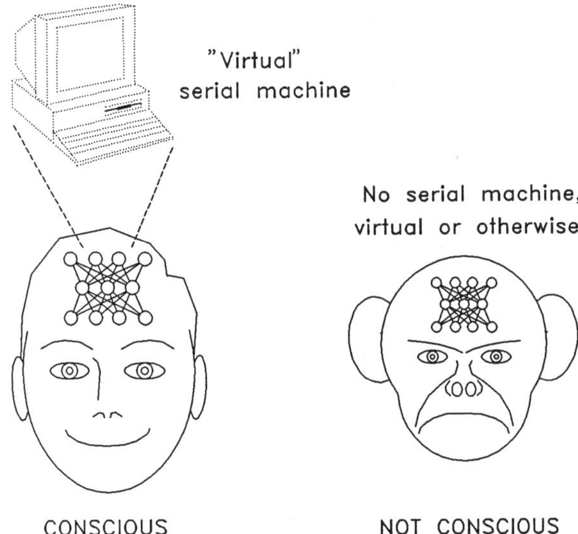

Figure 10.1 Dan Dennett's theory of human consciousness. The massively parallel human brain has its synaptic weights configured so as to realize a "virtual" computer of the discrete-state, serial-processing kind. The activities of that virtual computer—the Joycean machine—constitute the human's stream of consciousness. The brains of chimpanzees and other animals, however, are not capable of realizing a virtual machine of this special kind, so they lack the special kind or level of consciousness that humans have.

in a structured sequence of rule-governed representations unfolding in time.

It is *this* unfolding sequence of representations, *this* broadly linguistic stream of activity, that constitutes, according to Dennett, the stream of human consciousness. It is this "virtual (James) Joycean machine", realized in and sustained by parallel hardware, that generates the stream of activity that we humans call consciousness. Since animals do not and probably cannot learn these discrete-state, serial, recursively rule-governed, broadly linguistic sorts of activities, they do not and probably cannot have consciousness of the special sort enjoyed by humans.

Thus Dennett's view of consciousness, as advanced in his recent book, *Consciousness Explained.* I think it is deeply confused, in ways I will try to explain, but its central mistake is easily stated and it embodies a profound irony.

The prototype of language-like activity has exercised an iron grip over all theoretical attempts to account for human cognition since Aristotle. But it is a *false* prototype for cognitive activity, even in humans. Here in the closing decades of the twentieth century, we have finally unearthed and have begun to explore the power of a very different prototype: distributed vectorial processing in a massively parallel recurrent neural network. It is now beyond serious doubt that this is the principal form of computational activity in all biological brains, and we have begun to see how to explain the familiar forms of cognitive activity with the strikingly novel and fertile resources that this new prototype provides.

But just as we are in the process of displacing that older prototype with this new and better one, Dennett (1) attempts to pull that failed prototype back into the spotlight, (2) makes it the model for human consciousness, (3) gives parallel distributed processing a cursory pat on the back for being able to simulate a "virtual instance" of the old linguistic prototype, and (4) deals with his theory's inability to account for consciousness in *non*linguistic creatures by denying that they have anything like human consciousness at all.

This package strikes me as uncomprehending of the independent explanatory virtues of the aspiring new structural and dynamical cognitive prototype: recurrent PDP networks. One might as well propose the discredited "vital spirit" as a substantive explanation for the phenomenon of Life, and then cite, as support for this theory, the ability of DNA molecules to simulate a "virtual vital spirit" in their assembled causal properties.

The preceding is a prejudicial or question-begging description, of course. It is conceivable that Dennett is right in all four of the moves numbered above. And my deflationary analogy may be inapt. Let us see.

We may begin by reminding ourselves that when we simulate a parallel neural network on a suitably programmed serial machine, all we get from the serial machine is the abstract input-output behavior of the network being simulated. The serial machine is never involved in any genuinely distributed coding or genuinely parallel processing. Its innards remain true to their discrete-state and relentlessly serial form. (That's why the simulations are so frustratingly *slow* at simulating parallel procedures.)

The lesson illustrated in this example can be generalized. When we say that some classical machine **M** has been programmed to sustain some special-purpose virtual machine **V**, *nothing* is implied about the internal computational processes of **M** and how they might resemble the internal processes of the target machine being simulated, except that they somehow manage to produce the same input-output behaviors.

The same qualification must be made when we address simulation in the opposite direction, when we address, that is, the ability of a parallel machine to realize a virtual serial machine. Here also, a successful simulation implies only that the relevant input-output behavior has been achieved. And this success implies nothing about the internal computational activities of the parallel machine doing the simulation. In particular, it does not imply that the parallel machine is engaged in any discrete-state, rule-governed, serial procedures.

Dennett's account of consciousness, however, appears to require the genuine article, and not just its superficial input-output simulation. The parallel system of the brain must realize genuinely serial computational activities, else the required Joycean stream of consciousness will be strictly absent. Dennett's discussion of "virtual machines" and "simulation" is therefore not to the point. To get what his core theory requires, Dennett needs to find *real* serial procedures within the biological brain.

One of the motivations behind Dennett's approach to consciousness, I surmise, is his appreciation that human consciousness typically involves the well-behaved unfolding of cognitive structures over time. Here, of course, I agree with him. But Dennett is still imprisoned, apparently, by the conviction that classical, language-like computational procedures offer the best hope of accounting for that temporal unfolding. Hence his strained attempt to pull a classically serial rabbit out of the massively-parallel human hat.

The fact is, there exists a different way, a much more natural and effective way, of accounting for the well-behaved temporal unfolding of consciousness, and it has nothing essential to do with serial computers or language-like processing. The alternative lies in the dynamical behavior of real (not virtual) *recurrent* networks, with their dramatic ability to generate complex representations with a continuously unfolding temporal dimension. We don't need to import classical serial procedures to address the problem at hand. The dynamical procedures of recurrent parallel networks provide us with much broader resources in any case. As Elman's grammatical networks illustrate, those resources can account for narrowly linguistic processing, should a given creature happen to display any. But sustaining language-like skills is not the primary function of those resources in any living creature, not even in humans. And they can account for a broad universe of quite different cognitive capacities as well, including any and all kinds of motor control, and the capacity for recognizing or imagining all manner of causal processes.

Dennett's book contains no discussion of recurrent networks and their special properties, nor does his index contain an entry for that term. (A footnote mention of Gerald Edelman and reentrant pathways is as close as he comes.) It is possible he was then unaware of their anatomical importance and their computational prowess, especially where temporal structure is concerned.

In any case, the structured temporal dimension of human consciousness is not something that needs a classically serial prototype for its explanation. Temporally structured activity is the natural signature of any recurrent network, independently of whatever linguistic skills it may or may not have learned. Moreover, that capacity for weaving temporal structure promises a unitary account of consciousness in all of the higher animals, whether or not they happen to use language. For example, the several neurocomputational accounts of consciousness outlined in chapter 9 suggest, every last one of them, that the higher animals are just as conscious as we are, at least when they are awake. For most of those animals have multilayered cortex, viscerally-connected parietal representations, and widespread recurrent connections between their thalamus and cortex, much as humans do (figure 10.2).

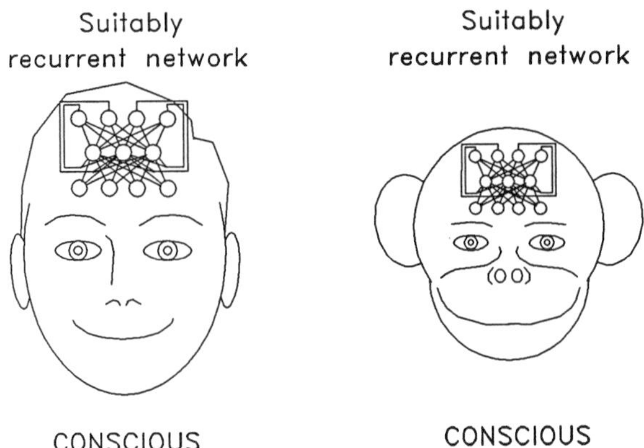

Figure 10.2 Rough parity reestablished between human consciousness and the consciousness of the other higher animals.

Dennett's account of consciousness is not only unfair to animals, it is inadequate to the phenomenon of consciousness as it appears in humans. In chapter 9 we listed seven salient aspects or dimensions of human consciousness to serve as the presumptive target for any explanatory account. Dennett's theory that "consciousness is a virtual serial machine" offers no account of any of them, let alone a unitary account of all seven. It is not just inadequately or improperly motivated, as the preceding paragraphs suggest. It is also inadequate in its subsequent explanatory performance.

Finally, Dennett's account of consciousness is skewed in favor of a tiny subset of the contents of consciousness: those that are broadly language-like. Human consciousness, however, also contains visual sequences, musical sequences, tactile sequences, motor sequences, visceral sequences, social sequences, and so on. A virtual serial machine has no especially promising explanatory resources for any of these things. A recurrent parallel network does.

The Role of Language in Thought and Consciousness

Consciousness, I have just argued, is primarily a *biological* phenomenon rather than a social one. The social institution of language has nothing to do with the genesis of consciousness.

The *contents* of consciousness, on the other hand, are profoundly influenced by the social environment in which any consciousness grows to maturity. And the human social environment includes, as its most prominent element, the language currently in use. Any child growing up in that culture must learn to command the same set of perceptual, causal, and social categories that everyone else already takes for granted. Those categories are systematically reflected in the culture's language, and each child internalizes those categories in the normal process of learning the language.

The result is a child whose armory of prototypes reflects, at least to some degree, the cumulative experience of an entire culture, an experience that reaches thousands of years into the past. A child born into such a culture does not have to begin the long intellectual journey of his many ancestors from scratch. Much of what those ancestors learned about the world—the categories and relations and dynamical processes that were found important—remains reflected, at least in broad outline, in the vocabulary of the language that has long outlived their death. The child still has to learn the relevant concepts or prototypes, of course, and that is emphatically not just a matter of memorizing vocabulary. It is a matter of repeated interactions with the world. But the vocabulary already in place and already at work in the local cognitive commerce forms an abstract template that shapes the infant brain's development by narrowing its search space during learning.

Language thus constitutes a form of extrasomatic memory, a medium of information storage that exists outside any individual's brain and which survives any individual's death. With the appearance of language, the process of learning about the world is no longer limited by what can be acquired in three score and ten years. Hard-won information can be passed effectively from generation to generation, undergoing appropriate modification all the while as each generation makes its own contribution to our unfolding collective consciousness. With the introduction of written language and the permanent records it makes possible, the process is further magnified. For this gives us access to the actual sentences and conversations of our ancestors, and not just the abstract framework in which those conversations were originally framed.

These last remarks introduce a second way in which language makes a profound difference in the contents and quality of human cognition. Putting historical stretches aside, language makes it possible, at any time, for human cognition to be *collective*. It allows a group of humans to address and solve cognitive problems that would prove insoluble to any individual operating alone. Finding solutions need no longer be limited by one person's memory, one person's imagination, one person's intelligence, or one person's perspective. Language allows us to transcend our individual cognitive weaknesses and to conjoin our individual strengths. Figuratively speaking, a shared language and vigorous conversation will turn any group of n people temporarily into a single brain with $2n$ hemispheres. This temporary aggregate is a cognitive system far more powerful, at least for certain tasks, than the mere pair of interconnected hemispheres that makes up a single person.

When we put these two dynamical consequences of language together—the collectivization of cognitive activity, and its extension far beyond a single human's lifetime—we have acquired an extraordinary advantage over any nonlinguistic species. A relatively small advantage in our intrinsic cognitive powers gets twice multiplied by these dynamical consequences of language use, and the cumulative effect over 50 or 100 centuries is a civilization that rules the earth.

Our consciousness, no doubt, has been affected. Humans have become aware of things beyond the ken of any other beast. We think in terms that they will never command. The contents of human consciousness regularly transcend any animal's imagination, and that is a fact to be celebrated, not minimized.

But consciousness itself need be nothing different in humans from what it is in animals, namely, a peculiar and rather special form of cognitive activity that displays, for starters, the seven cognitive features explored in the last chapter: short-term memory, input independence, steerable attention, plastic interpretation, disappearance in sleep, reappearance in dreaming, and unity across the sensory modalities. In these respects, we are little or no different from the animals. Language has led to a profound transformation in the *contents* of human consciousness, and, as we will see, that transformational process is far from over. But the phenomenon, consciousness itself, is a commodity we share with much of the animal kingdom. On the best evidence and theory currently available, the higher animals are just as conscious as we are.

Theoretical Science, Creativity, and Reaching Behind the Appearances

Having emphasized our continuity with the rest of the animal kingdom, it is appropriate for us to resume our exploration of the achievements and techniques that set humans apart. One of these is the institution of theoretical and experimental science. Consider the conceptual and practical edifice that is modern physics, for example. Or modern chemistry. Or modern biology. With these frameworks internalized through long study and practice, a human can command an atomic nucleus, reconstruct a distant stellar interior, fabricate new materials not found in nature, and bring disease after disease under control. How do we produce conceptual structures of the power and magnitude of these examples? How is it that humans manage to "reach beyond the appearances" to gain command of the hidden reality behind? How is such deep understanding created?

There are many myths here, and any commentator runs the risk of adding to them. So be it. If the myth is worthy, perhaps I will be forgiven.

To introduce my story, I take the reader back to 1962, when the academic world saw the publication of *The Structure of Scientific*

Revolutions, by Thomas Kuhn. Kuhn was trained as a physicist, found his passion as a historian of science, and made his principal impact as a philosopher of science. His smallish book, brimming with historical examples, took a few years to catch on, but when it did, it set the philosophical world on its ear. Most certainly, it upset my own Logical Empiricist assumptions.

It had that effect for two reasons. The first was his claim, vividly documented, that past scientific revolutions were not the unambiguous expression of sheerly logical and experimental factors, rationally played out according to a well-defined methodology. Rather, they were the expression of a variety of nonlogical factors as well: social, psychological, metaphysical, technological, aesthetic, and personal. Logic played an essential and undeniable role in settling the outcome of those revolutionary conflicts, according to Kuhn. But it played a relatively small one, a role much exaggerated in the subsequent scientific histories. (Those heroic and neatly logical histories were always written, of course, by the *winners* of the original conflict, or by their intellectual descendants.) The real determinants of a revolution's outcome, argued Kuhn, are not adequately captured by our post hoc reconstructions in terms of "inductions", "confirmations", "refutations", and other purely logical notions.

The second reason for the ensuing controversy was his claim, also well-documented, that the unit of scientific understanding is not the sentence, or set of sentences, but rather the so-called "paradigm", or family of paradigms. A paradigm, as Kuhn used the term, was a concrete example of how-to-understand-something. It was an exemplary or prototypical explanatory achievement to which all other explanations in that field were related, as variations are related to a basic theme. The student who is learning a scientific theory learns, first of all, the prototypical features of the central example, and then learns to extend that understanding, suitably modified, to further examples that radiate out from the central example already mastered. We can see what Kuhn had in mind by looking at the series of examples in figure 10.3.

These illustrate what a high-school physics student would learn in elementary mechanics. Figure 10.3a shows a freely falling body. The ball moves straight downward with increasing velocity. Specifically, the successive distances it falls, in equal increments of time, stand to each other in the ratio of the successive odd numbers. (This is Galileo's old discovery.)

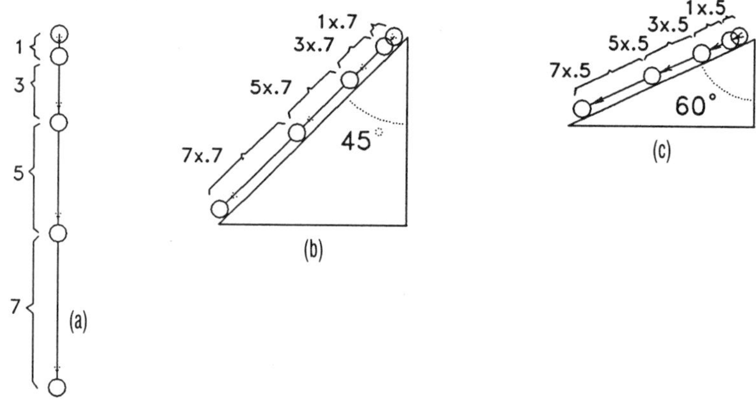

Figure 10.3 (a) A freely falling body: purely vertical case. (b) A body whose fall is constrained by a deflecting ramp at an angle of 45 degrees. (c) A body whose fall is constrained by a deflecting ramp at an angle of 60 degrees.

Figure 10.3b, by contrast, shows a falling body that is not entirely free. Its path is constrained to a specific straight line: the floor of the ramp down which the ball is rolling. Here the successive vertical distances fallen are still in the mutual ratio of the successive odd numbers, but those successive distances are all smaller than their counterparts in 10.3a by a uniform factor of .7, which is the cosine of the ramp's angle of inclination, 45 degrees. The final case, figure 10.3c, shows an even more severely constrained fall. The angle here is 60 degrees, and the resulting successive vertical distances are now only .5 of the corresponding distances in figure 10.3a (because the cosine of 60 degrees = .5). Figure 10.3a now looks like the next two, except that the (nonexistent) ramp's angle in that case is 0 degrees.

Let us now observe a second dimension of variation on this basic theme. Figure 10.4a restates the theme. Figure 10.4b shows essentially the same situation, only this time the freely falling body also possesses some uniform horizontal motion from the outset. The combination of the two motions—uniform horizontal and falling vertical—yields a graceful parabolic path. How wide it is depends on how great is the initial uniform horizontal motion of the falling body, as illustrated in figure 10.4c. The first figure now looks like the next two, except for having a horizontal velocity of zero.

From here a student would be introduced to motion *up*ward under constant *de*celeration. Picture a family of diagrams exactly like those in figures 10.3 and 10.4, except with all of the arrow-

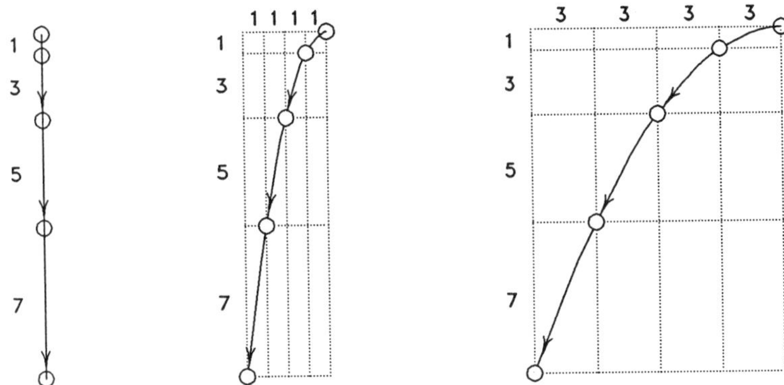

Figure 10.4 (a) A freely falling body: purely vertical case. (b) A freely falling body with a small component of uniform horizontal motion. (c) A freely falling body with a larger component of uniform horizontal motion.

heads pointing up instead of down. From there the range of possibilities would open to include freely falling motion under *non*uniform gravitational force, as instanced in the several planets orbiting the Sun (figure 10.5).

You can see the relevant pattern emerging. Learning a theory is less a matter of memorizing a set of sentences than it is a matter of becoming familiar with the family of paradigms or prototypical causal processes identified in that theory. I could have written explicit mathematical equations under each of the six cases just illustrated, and students are indeed taught those equations. But I have deliberately left them out. Kuhn's point, I think, is that a grasp of these diagramed examples, and of the family trees of similar diagrams that surround them, is more fundamental to a successful student's understanding than is a list of equations.

It is moderately clear that he is right. We are all familiar with the derelict student who, the night before the exam, desperately memorizes the "top five" equations in the textbook, or perhaps writes them on his or her wrist. Students who prepare in this way usually do abysmally on typical exams, where they have to confront a range of diverse applications of those equations, applications that typically involve *modifying* the equations to suit the problem at hand. No wonder the students do so poorly. Far better for them to memorize the *diagrams*, and the dimensions along which they vary. For the diagrams are much more easily "fitted" to a novel problem situation, and one can always reconstruct the appropriate equation(s) from the appropriate diagram in any case.

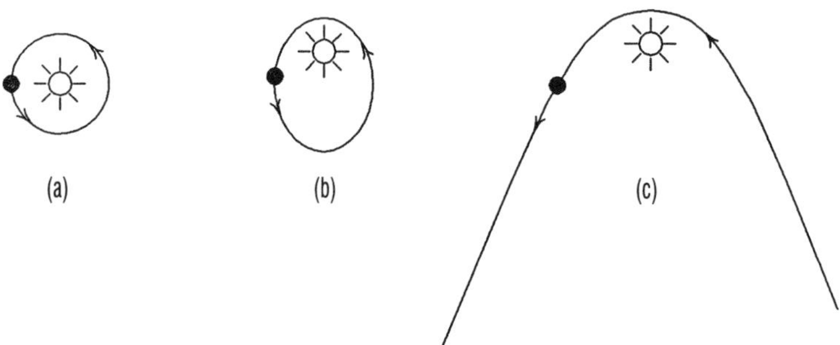

Figure 10.5 Freely falling bodies in a nonuniform gravitational field. (a) The circular case: sunward acceleration is constant. (b) The elliptical case: sunward acceleration is nonconstant, but cyclic. (b) The hyperbolic case: sunward acceleration is nonconstant and noncyclic.

The lesson of this case—elementary mechanics—is that the understanding of someone adept in this theory does not consist primarily in a set of explicit sentences, equations or otherwise. Rather, it consists in a grasp of certain paradigmatic kinds of situations and processes, and of the possible variations on those basic themes. Kuhn wished to generalize this lesson to all scientific theories, to scientific understanding in general. Other theories, other fields, these will use different paradigms. But those different paradigms will there serve the same function, specifically, as basic examples of how to conceive of the phenomena within that theory's domain. Equations and other forms of explicit propositional representation will often be deeply important, but competence in their use is just one aspect of a broader framework of skills—perceptual, conceptual, interpretational, analogical, transformational, and manipulational—which broader framework is the true vehicle of understanding. And such frameworks are always focused, according to Kuhn, on a central family of paradigmatic examples.

Given Kuhn's view that scientific understanding consists in the grasp of and the ability to exploit a paradigm, rather than in the acceptance of a set of sentences, it is no surprise that he also took an unorthodox view of how scientific theories are *evaluated*. This is what got him into trouble.

The orthodox view among philosophers of science was that a theory is to be evaluated by its logical consistency with observation sentences, or by its induction therefrom, or by its confirmation thereby, and so forth—sentential and logical matters, all. Against this view, Kuhn urged a "performance" conception of theory evaluation, a pragmatic rather than a logistic conception. A theory is a vehicle whose virtue lies in its many uses: explanation, prediction, unification, and manipulation of the real world through the many technologies that it makes possible.

Given this pragmatic conception of theories, it is plain that how any given scientist evaluates a theory will depend, at least in part, on what *aims* the scientist has in all of the dimensions just listed, on what the scientist already regards as a pressing problem, and on the generic kinds of solutions that he or she is already disposed to find valuable, useful, or plausible. Inevitably, people differ in these dimensions, and so the evaluation of a theory by the scientific community is almost always a matter of complex social and intellectual negotiation. It is seldom if ever a purely logical matter.

Kuhn's position here was widely seen as letting down the side, as opening the gate to the barbarians, as a slide into relativism, and as an appalling encouragement to the collapse of scientific standards. Whether or not this was true, it was not even remotely Kuhn's intention. In fact, Kuhn is decidedly conservative in his methodological impulses. If science is politics, then he is a staunch Tory, not an anything-goes radical.

In fact, Kuhn was not attacking scientific standards. Rather, he was attacking a false and confabulatory *theory* about the nature of scientific standards, a worthy and nontrivial philosophical theory called Logical Empiricism, a theory that tried to capture all such standards in narrowly logical terms. If one already accepts that orthodox but confabulatory theory, as most philosophers did, then one is doomed to see an attack on it as an attack on scientific standards in general.

But it needn't be so. Once we have seen that a scientific theory is much more than a set of sentences, then we can appreciate that its evaluation must encompass much more than mere logical relations among sentences. Once we are freed from the grip of the orthodox philosophical approach, we can pursue the question of theory evaluation with a fresh eye. We can draw, for example, on our growing understanding of how neural networks evolve their conceptual frameworks, how they change them under the pressures of hostile experience, and how they redeploy them as new opportunities are presented. In the end, we may hope, the result will be a *raising* of our scientific standards, a result firmly grounded in a better understanding of what scientific theories really are and what they really do.

This returns us to neural networks, and to the point of my excursion into the philosophy of science. A *paradigm*, for Kuhn, is clearly an objective counterpart to, or an objectivized version of, what we have been calling a *prototype vector*. And the range of problem-solving abilities that, for Kuhn, constitute a grasp of a given family of paradigms is exactly the range of abilities that arise from training up a neural network to the corresponding hierarchy of internal prototype vectors. At bottom then, a scientist's grasp of a given theory consists not in accepting and manipulating a given set of sentences. Rather, it consists in a family of abilities embodied in the synaptic configuration of the scientist's brain. It consists in a family of abilities encoded as a hierarchy of prototypes and prototypical sequences in the neuronal activation space of his or her brain.

Evidently, and unexpectedly, this independent account of cognition based in neural network research converges smoothly with the most controversial account of scientific cognition proposed in the last fifty years. Viewed from our perspective, here in 1994, Kuhn had it roughly right back in 1962. Our discussion in chapter 5 of the successive cosmological theories of Aristotle, Descartes, Newton, and Einstein was a story that, plus or minus a prototype vector, Kuhn himself might have told. But our current perspective allows us to pursue our topic a good deal farther than Kuhn was able, for it embodies the assembled resources of neuroanatomy, neurophysiology, cognitive neurobiology, and computational neuroscience.

We can now see clearly, for example, that scientific cognition is not different in kind from our ordinary, commonsense cognition. It is distinguished only by its comparative novelty, by its ambition, by the institutional procedures that work to keep it honest, and by its extraordinary pragmatic power. This result is interesting not just for the unification of philosophical understanding that it effects, namely, that science is completely continuous with common sense. It is interesting for the further reason that it holds out the prospect of major cognitive growth for entire societies. Let me explain.

If we—all of us—were systematically to replace our humble commonsense concepts with their more powerful scientific counterparts, even in our dreams and in our daily practical affairs, then each of us would gain a cognitive grip on the world, and a continuing control over it, that far exceeds one's current feeble grasp. In principle, at least, we can all become scientific "adepts". With appropriate socialization, we can all become as completely at home with thermal gradients, voltage drops, spectral emission, coupled oscillators, phase transitions, semiconductors, lactic-acid buildup, hydrogen-ion excess, serotonin deficits, and hyperactive amygdalas as we are at home with anything else. Whether we know it or not, all of these things are regular elements of our daily practical lives already. We might as well know them for what they are. And make practical use of them with what that knowledge brings. Accordingly, what was the exclusive possession of a scientific elite during one age can become the working possession of Everyman in another. Today's esoteric theoretical framework can become tomorrow's thumb-worn common sense. And today's common sense can become tomorrow's forgotten mythology. The scientific enterprise, accordingly, is not just the indulgence of the hyper-curious. It is the leading rung of a ladder the entire human race is climbing.

A second respect in which a network perspective allows us to penetrate more deeply into the cognitive process concerns scientific creativity. Creativity, like intelligence itself, is probably not a single feature or a one-dimensional phenomenon. But one of its salient dimensions is clearly illustrated in the case of major scientific discoveries. It is the capacity to see or interpret a problematic phenomenon as an unexpected or unusual instance of a prototypical pattern already in one's conceptual repertoire. Aristotle saw the sky as a rotating sphere; Descartes saw the solar system as a whirlpool of transparent matter; Newton saw the moon and planets as freely falling bodies with a tangential inertial motion; Einstein saw the planetary orbits as pure inertial motion along a four-dimensional straight line. These are all cases of toying with the figure of a duck until it suddenly re-presents itself as a rabbit, of puzzling over some scattered elements until they suddenly cohere as a man-on-a-horse.

All four thinkers were using their recurrent pathways to explore a range of different activational possibilities. These possibilities—these many candidate prototypes—were already there in the theorist's hierarchy of partitions. But, being prototypes, they were also embedded in a similarity space that includes many nonstandard possibilities radiating out from that central prototype in many dimensions. Recurrent activity arriving at that population of neurons can tilt its cognitive responses, to a chronically problematic input (the night sky, the planetary motions, whatever), now this way, now that, all in hopes of activating something close to a familiar prototype, a prototype that finds a familiar kind of order in the problematic phenomenon confronted.

Any normal human can do this. We all have imaginations. We are all capable of recurrent manipulation of our cognitive response to a continuing input. The unusually creative people among us are simply those who are unusually skilled at such recurrent manipulation, who are compelled to engage in it by a strong sense of delight or entertainment, who are sufficiently learned to have a large repertoire of powerful prototypes whose novel redeployments are worth exploring in the first place (here the matured and slightly older brain will have an advantage), and who are sufficiently critical to be able to distinguish between a merely strained metaphor on the one hand, and a genuinely systematic and enabling insight on the other. Less creative persons, by contrast, would be those who are undistinguished in one or more of these respects, most especially in their skill at recurrent manipulation of their own cognitive activity. In summary then, the suggestion is this. Scientific creativity is the capacity for the novel deployment and extension of existing activational prototypes in the face of novel or problematic phenomena, by means of vector completion and the recurrent manipulation of one's own neuronal populations.

This approach to the nature of scientific discoveries and theoretical breakthroughs also allows us to address the fundamental question that opened this section. How is it that human cognition manages to reach behind the appearances? How do we discover, for example, that light consists of submicroscopic waves? That a gas is a swarm of submicroscopic ballistic particles? That X rays are just an unusual (invisible) form of light? All of these things are well beyond human perception, even with instrumental aids. How then does a neural network such as a human scientist—a network doomed, after all, to be trained on a uniform diet of *observable* phenomena—ever manage to form concepts or prototypes of *un*observable phenomena, or come to apply such concepts so successfully to things beyond its perceptual reach?

The answer, to a first approximation, is that we learn all of our prototypes solely within the domain of observable things. That process of concept formation takes place relatively slowly as one's global pattern of synaptic weights is gradually reconfigured in response to one's ongoing sensory experience. But once those prototypes are in place, a human is in a position to find new and surprising applications of those prototypes, even in perceptually inaccessible domains, by virtue of our built-in capacity for *vector completion* or filling in the gaps.

You will recall from chapter 3 (where we discussed how feedforward networks respond to degraded inputs) that a network trained to produce a certain prototype vector as output will continue to produce such a vector, or vectors very close to it, even when the evoking input vector is missing large amounts of typical information. Once trained, the network is capable of completing the partial or degraded input vector, so long as the input vector retains enough weakly distinguishing features.

This capacity for presumptively filling in information that is strictly missing is a capacity already in evidence with the simplest of feedforward networks, as we saw. (Recall Cottrell's facial network and its reconstruction of Jane's face, despite the broad bar across her eyes.) But the capacity is magnified in the case of recurrent networks, because recurrent pathways can bring presumptive background information to the relevant layer of neurons, information above and beyond what remains in the degraded sensory input. In producing its twice-tentative vectorial outputs, such a network is "guessing," of course, but not entirely in the dark. Sometimes it will guess correctly, and when it does, it can anticipate the causal consequences of things it has not actually observed.

We can illustrate the process, whereby vector completion yields information about unobservable objects, with the case of light. Figure 10.6 shows an instance of the famous Two-Slit experiment. A point source emits light that travels through a pair of narrow slits in a mask. That light strikes a screen on the far side of the mask. If one

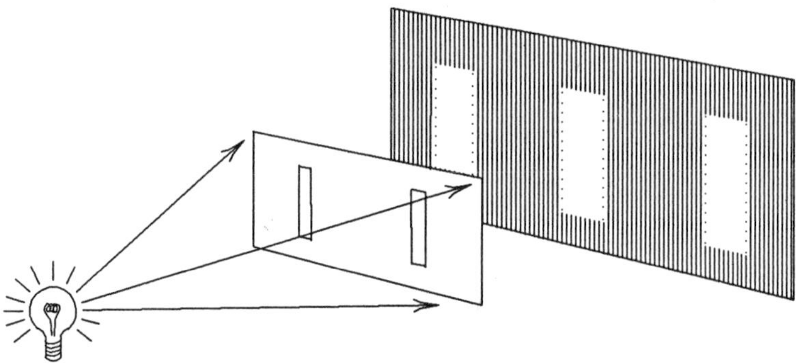

Figure 10.6 The two-slit optical experiment and its actual outcome.

thinks of light as a stream of tiny particles, or as rectilinear rays, then one expects the screen to show exactly *two* bright images: the straight-line projections of the two slits through which the light came.

Surprisingly, for very thin slits in the mask, that is not at all what happens. Instead of two bright lines, the screen displays several lines, the brightest near the center and the fainter to either side. And none of those lines is properly placed so as to be a straight-line projection of either one of the original two slits. All told, the pattern of light displayed at the screen is extremely puzzling. What on earth could produce such a pattern?

Many things. An infinite number of things. Too many to canvass in an exhaustive search. But while viewing the unexpected empirical result of figure 10.6, one very specific possibility might well pop into someone's mind if that someone were already closely familiar with the various ways in which water waves behave. Consider the rather humdrum situation of figure 10.7. Parallel waves approach a sea wall with two gaps in it. After passing through the gaps, each wave crest radiates out in two distinct expanding arcs. Those two arclike waves criss-cross each other to form an interference pattern. Where crest meets crest, the wave height is amplified. Where crest meets trough, the two waves cancel each other. The result, at the second sea wall, is a high-amplitude oscillating wave activity at a number of stable places, separated by steadily quiescent places in between. If you don't live in a port city with sea walls to observe, you can set this up yourself, in miniature, with a

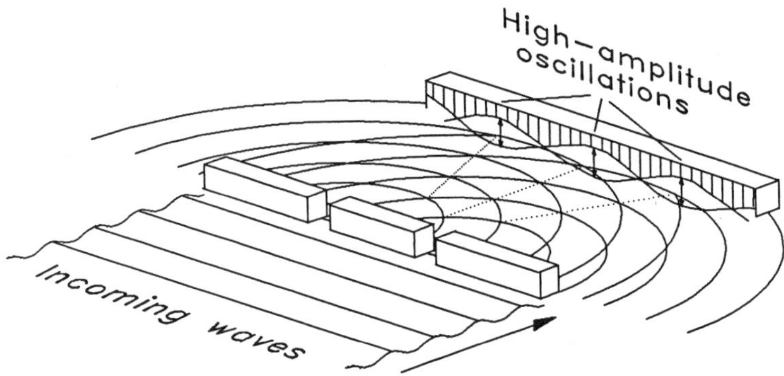

Figure 10.7 The pattern of wave activity produced at an unbroken sea wall by the mutual interference of two incoming sets of arclike water waves. Note the three positions where the water oscillates wildly, separated by positions where it does not oscillate at all.

couple of boards suitably placed in a rectangular cake pan. It works quite well.

When the waves are water waves, they are wholly visible. One can see not only what they do at the final sea wall, one can also see how they interact with one another to produce that pattern. This prototypical example of interfering waves has all of the causally relevant elements out in the open. Nothing is hidden. There need be no problem, therefore, in learning it.

But once that prototype is firmly in place in some scientist's brain, it becomes a candidate for activation in response to the phenomena observed in the optical experiment of figure 10.6. Here things are not at all "out in the open." The nature or constitution of light is hidden from our perception. All we can see is the experimental situation, and the resulting pattern of illumination at the final screen.

That experimental situation, however, is visibly almost identical with the original sea-wall situation, save for its much smaller scale. And, scale once more aside, its visible outcome at the final screen is closely analogous also. It shows a high-amplitude illumination at a number of stable places, separated by areas of low-amplitude illumination in between.

With the parallels laid out this clearly for us, we would have to be thick indeed not to have it occur to us that the puzzling optical pattern observed in figure 10.6 might reflect the underlying fact that light, too, consists of waves! Waves that mutually interfere on the far side of the two slits, waves much smaller than water waves so as to fit the tiny scale, waves in some as yet unknown medium, but waves nonetheless.

Once activated, in large measure by chance, the water-wave prototype has a chance to strut its cognitive stuff. One who commands that prototype is already acquainted with the dimensions along which its real-world instances may vary. In particular, changing the distance between the two gaps in the first sea wall will change the spacing and the positions of the high-amplitude areas at the final sea wall in completely predictable ways. Changing the distance between the two walls will have a similar effect, also predictable. These things are already known. They are part of the background.

Well then! If the water-wave prototype is genuinely appropriate to the optical experiment—that is, if light really does consist of waves—then changing the distance between the two tiny slits in the optical experiment, or changing the distance between mask and screen, should have effects on the pattern of illumination at the screen analogous to those characteristic of the water-wave case.

Charmingly, this is precisely what happens. The prototype's novel application to optical phenomena is systematically vindicated by this prototype-driven experimental probing. The distribution of the bright and dark bands of light vary exactly as do the high- and low-amplitude water wave sites. What began as an analogically inspired guess quickly acquires the status of a confidently held theory. If the manipulative powers that characterized the original prototype carry over successfully into its new domain of deployment, wild horses will not stay our conviction that light must be waves.

A second historical example of redeployment is even easier to grasp, and it reveals even more about the hidden nature of the universe. Specifically, it reveals the fact that any gas is just a swarm of submicroscopic physical *particles*. That is, it reveals that the ancient Greek atomist Democritus was right. It also reveals the dynamical fact that the heat of any gas is just the ceaseless *motion* of the tiny particles that make it up. The faster their motion, the higher the temperature. You can virtually see both of these things in a famous phenomenon called Brownian motion.

The phenomenon itself is initially puzzling. Certainly it puzzled Robert Brown, the nineteenth-century English naturalist who discovered it. It is most easily seen if we blow some smoke into a transparent bottle, seal it, and then observe the tiny smoke particles through a high-power microscope (figure 10.8). After the bottle is left motionless for a time and everything settles down, the tiniest of the suspended smoke particles can be seen to display a ceaseless jittering motion, a nonstop agitation, as if they were being continually battered on every side by implacable but invisible adversaries.

In fact, that is exactly what is happening. A simple analogy will make clear what is going on. Suppose you are riding in the Goodyear blimp, hovering 1000 feet over a football stadium, looking straight down at the field. In the middle of the field is a large billiard table with many billiard balls careening around its surface because a fast game is in progress. The green expanse of the table's surface is easily seen from the blimp, but the billiard balls themselves are too small to be discriminated from that great height: no matter how hard you squint, they remain invisible to you (figure 10.9).

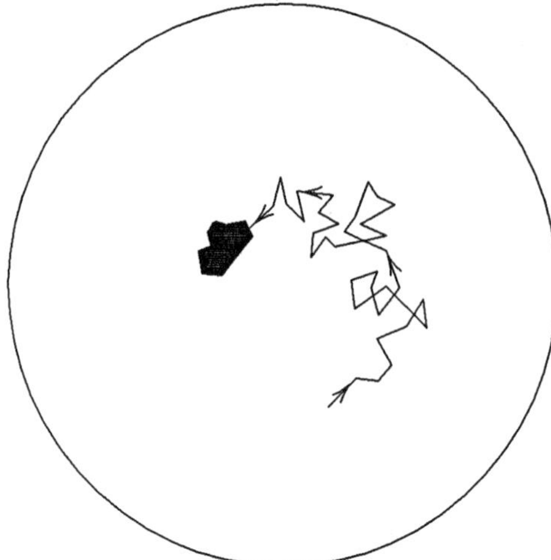

Figure 10.8 Brownian motion: as viewed in a high-power microscope, the particles of smoke suspended in a gas display a ceaseless jittering motion as they are continually battered on all sides by the flying molecules that make up the gas.

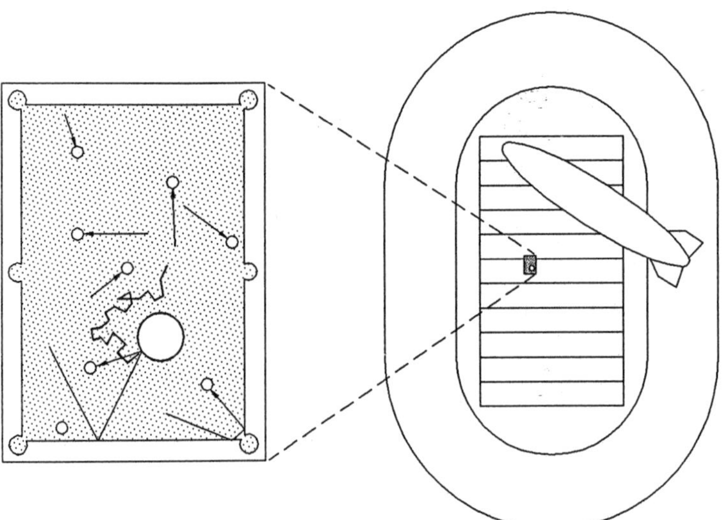

Figure 10.9 A macroscopic analog of Brownian motion: a white volleyball's jittery motion on a table full of moving billiard balls is just visible from a blimp at 1000 feet, although the smaller billiard balls that produce that motion remain invisible.

A single volleyball, however, has also been placed on the table's surface. From the blimp, its white expanse is just barely visible to your eye against the green background. Because the volleyball is in the midst of the busy traffic of moving billiard balls, it will be knocked around the table, now this way, now that way, as the smaller balls frequently collide with it during the course of the game. That ceaseless random jittering motion of the white volleyball will be visible to you from your vantage point in the blimp, even though the smaller billiard balls that produce it remain invisible.

The just-visible smoke particle suspended in a gas is in the same position as the volleyball on the billiard table. The swarm of flying molecules that make up the gas are forever invisible under a microscope: each molecule is much smaller than the wavelength of visible light and is thus incapable of reflecting such light. The smoke particle, however, strikes a perfect medium from our point of view. It is just large enough to be seen in the microscope, yet small enough to be visibly knocked around by the many flying molecules that collide with and bounce off it.

Seeing the dancing smoke particle in a gas as a microscopic instance of a volleyball-on-a-billiard-table is another case of completing a prototype vector, of creatively redeploying a familiar prototype in an unexpected domain. As in the case of the two-slit experiment, the principal actors in this microscopic drama—the molecular particles themselves—remain invisible. But their effects on things visible are sufficiently characteristic to suggest the idea of a larger object adrift in a sea of fast-moving particles that are continually bouncing off it.

As with the interfering-waves prototype discussed earlier, the bombarded-particle prototype involves some standard expectations. If the smoke particle really is suspended in a swarm of tiny ballistic particles, then increasing the average velocity of those molecular particles (that is, raising the temperature of the gas) should visibly increase the agitation of the smoke particle. Those faster-moving molecules, which also bounce off the inside walls of the bottle (as billiard balls bounce off the table's inside rail), should also increase the outward pressure on those glass walls. Charmingly once more, heating the gas produces both of these effects, and in just the amounts expected. Cooling the gas produces the opposite effect. Once more, what began as an analogically inspired guess quickly acquires the status of a confidently held theory. If the manipulative powers that characterized the original prototype carry over successfully into its new domain of deployment, nothing will stay our conviction that a gas must be a swarm of ballistic particles.

With the preceding examples in place, we can appreciate how a dynamical prototype, initially learned "in the clear", can come to be redeployed as the vehicle for understanding and manipulating phenomena whose internal constitution is too small or too inaccessible to be grasped directly by our native sensory systems. Humans can indeed reach behind the appearances, and with some reliability. The vehicle of this achievement is the creative redeployment and extension of existing prototypes by means of recurrent manipulation, vector completion, and subsequent experimental probing. We *can* come to know what light is, what a gas is, what heat is, and many other secrets besides. The trick lies in having some prototypes potentially worthy of redeployment in the first place, and in being relentless in exploring their potential applicability to new domains. Vector completion and subsequent experimental probing will take care of the rest.

Cognitive Progress in the Moral and Political Domain

There is a common and mostly unspoken conviction that the moral and political domain is utterly different from the scientific domain. Scientific principles express objective facts, it is often said, whereas moral and political principles do not. They express only subjective feelings, romantic hopes, arbitrary rules, or the oppression of this week's tyrant, benign or otherwise.

At the close of chapter 6 I expressed a contrary inclination toward Moral Realism, toward the view that moral knowledge is indeed a form of genuine knowledge, and that it embodies an appreciation of complex but objective realities. I will here try to expand on those earlier remarks. In particular, I would like to explore the parallels that unite, rather than divide, our scientific cognition on the one hand, and our moral and political cognition on the other.

Science, it will be pointed out, is an enterprise with a history of dramatic progress. False theories are regularly unmasked, to be replaced by true theories, or at any rate, by theories better than the ones they replace. For we have the ultimate authority of Nature itself, as exercised through the medium of experiment, steering our choice of theories. And we have the centuries-old institutions of science upholding a tradition of honest evaluation: academic societies, annual meetings with public presentations and critical discussions, refereed journals, independent replication of experimental results, competition and cooperation between distinct laboratories, a standard curriculum of initial instruction that remains fluid at its leading edges, and a sequence of rigorous evaluations and certifications that determine academic degrees, academic rank, academic offices, and the distinct powers and responsibilities that go with each. Science, *qua* international institution, is an entity that precedes and long outlives the individuals who pass through it, and it is systematically geared to the business of producing a deeper understanding of the world at large, and a more effective human control over its behavior.

Our knowledge of so-called "right" and "wrong" in the moral and social domain looks flimsy, arbitrary, and subjective when placed in contrast with the results of the relentlessly objective procedures of science. Moral and political convictions are the focus of systematic disagreement and endless squabbles. They are regularly steered by ignorance, prejudice, self-interest, class interest, unbridled emotion, and religious enthusiasm. On the face of it, moral "knowledge" fails to attach to any objective reality in the way that science does.

But these contrasts are superficial and imperfectly drawn. The proper analog for the average person's admittedly confused, narrow, and arbitrary convictions on moral and social matters is not the carefully distilled wisdom of institutionalized science. It is the average person's profoundly confused, narrow, and arbitrary convictions on broadly scientific matters. The fact is, most people are no better grounded in their scientific knowledge than they are in their moral and social knowledge. Think of the average person's convictions about or complete ignorance of the origins of life, the nature of the mind, the history of the human race, the status of a fetus, the origins of the universe, and the prospects for a life after death. Here, also, there is widespread disagreement and endless squabbling. Here, also, the average person's consciousness is shaped by ignorance, arbitrary upbringing, unbridled emotion, and religious enthusiasms. If anything, the average person displays a slightly higher level of moral cognition than of scientific cognition. If we wish to disqualify moral cognition as a form of knowledge, we must look to some other contrasts to bring it down.

If moral cognition is not obviously disadvantaged at the level of the man in the street, neither is it obviously disadvantaged at the level of our lasting social institutions. Nations such as the United States and Britain have a history of continuous constitutional government reaching back over three or four centuries. Other countries have interruptions in their constitutional histories, but the pattern is the same. The relevant legislative bodies have been continuously formulating and reformulating social policy of some sort or other—prohibiting certain kinds of behavior, regulating many others, and positively encouraging others still—in an ongoing response to the unfolding environment and to the observed social effects of policies already in place.

This continuous adjustment of social policy takes place at many levels, from the federal down to the most mundane of municipal concerns. But almost all of it is done in the light of *past social experience*. Policies are adopted, laws are enacted, and the public ends up living a collective life that is shaped by those policies and laws. That collective life may be much the better for those constraints, or it may display unintended cruelties, unexpected costs, unanticipated conflicts with other policies already established, or a host of further disutilities. In addition, a policy that works well at one stage of our economic, technological, or educational evolution may not work at all well at a later stage. What was appropriate and useful in one factual environment may be observably cruel or stupid in another. Our permanent political institutions are in place precisely so as to respond to such discovered unhappiness and emerging injustice, to respond with modified or wholly new social policies and legislation.

As the decades and the centuries roll by, such legislative bodies are the focus of what is clearly a *learning* process: the accumulated legislation currently in force is the reflection of long experience and many adjustments. Furthermore, it sustains a social and administrative practice that is itself under constant pragmatic evaluation. To be sure, there is nothing infallible about this learning procedure, but there is nothing infallible about the parallel learning procedure in institutionalized science either. In both cases, the human cognitive endeavor repeatedly runs afoul of and makes adjustments to the real, objective world—social in the first case and natural in the second. And the result in both cases is an always-imperfect but ever-deeper grasp of how the world works and how best to make our way in it.

This oversimplifies the situation, of course. Occasionally, wise kings are murdered, constitutions are overthrown, corruption rots an enlightened practice, barbarians storm the city, and entire societies backslide into a poorer and darker form of life. Moral progress is not without its setbacks. But neither is scientific progress. The long Dark Age in Europe is testament to that.

These parallels are reinforced when we look past declared social policy and written legislation to the institutions that enforce them, in particular, the judiciary branch of all levels of government. If continuing legislative activity in the social domain corresponds to continuing theoretical activity in the scientific domain, then society's judiciary corresponds very roughly to science's engineers: they both have the job of actually *applying* the current abstract wisdom case by case to the real world, to the social world in the former case and to the natural world in the latter.

As with our institutions of engineering, our judiciary comes to embody an additional layer of wisdom and know-how, a layer beyond what appears in the standard science textbooks or the written legislation. How best to *interpret* the current abstract wisdom, as one attempts to bring it to bear on an endless variety of novel cases, is something that can never be exhaustively articulated in a set of written laws, whether scientific or social. In the latter domain, the burden of such ongoing interpretation is assigned to the judiciary, and their practice here displays an old friend: prototypes, or paradigms.

They are called "precedents" in the legal profession, but they play a role comparable to that played by paradigms or prototypical examples in science. A precedent is an earlier judicial decision on a specific legal issue, carefully written up by the presiding judge and then published in the judiciary's legal record, a record that reaches back several centuries and encompasses hundreds of thousands of cases.

Roe *v.* Wade is perhaps the most famous precedent in the present legal environment: this was the original court decision, subsequently upheld by the Supreme Court, that established a woman's right to an abortion. Brown *v.* the Board of Education is another prominent precedent, one that broke the practice of racial segregation in the public school system. These and other decisions are held up as "just applications of the law". Legal issues judged to be relevantly similar to them are subsequently decided in similar ways.

The point of such a record is manifold, but two elements stand out immediately relative to our concerns. First, such a record encourages, and helps make possible, *consistency* in the law's application, over individuals and over time. Barring special circumstances, any case currently before the bench must be decided in a fashion consistent with past judicial decisions about relevantly similar cases. Here we are, once again, watching cognitive creatures—lawyers and judges in this case—attempting to apprehend a wide variety of real-world cases as instances of some antecedent prototype, cases that resemble and differ from the prototype along many different dimensions. They are then dealt with accordingly.

We also see something else that we see in science: the occasional *challenge* to an existing prototype and its subsequent modification or replacement by a new prototype. If a judge comes to perceive a flaw of some sort in an existing precedent, perhaps because the special details of the case currently before the court bring them into unexpected focus, then he or she may choose to challenge that precedent. The judge may decide the present case in a way that changes or extends the written law's usual interpretation. The judge may then enter this new precedent into the judicial record, a precedent that other judges may then invoke or ignore, as their own cases and their own best judgment inclines them.

In the long run, this accumulated sequence of judicial precedents and subsequent overriding precedents amounts to another learning process beneath the obvious legislative level. It embodies the accumulated and self-modifying wisdom of an institutionalized judiciary that is far older and has had a far broader experience of cases than any individual judge who might fleetingly hold one of its offices. And once again, what the judiciary learns by this process is how best to understand and deal with a problematic world, in this particular case, the world of socially unacceptable human behavior.

These examples—legislation, and judicial precedent—provide a framework of social governance that still leaves a great deal to the discretion of individuals. The realm of socially-enforced law encodes only the most serious of our collective convictions about appropriate and inappropriate behavior. Beneath that realm there is a similar body of shared understanding, a similar framework of social-recognitional and social-behavioral skills that we expect our fellow citizens to command. Furthermore, there are similar appeals to standard positive and negative prototypes against which everyone's behavior is regularly judged: being someone others can count on, spreading oil on troubled waters, resisting unfairness to others even at personal cost, refusing to exploit the chronic or fleeting disadvantage of others, recognizing the legitimate aspirations of others, cooperating with others for collective gain, and so forth.

This is the domain of common public morality. Here, too, there is evolution over time, although its development and application has little of the careful and deliberate character found in the law. Even so, we manage to make moral progress. Sometimes this is because public morality simply follows the ever-developing law. But sometimes it is because public morality, in response to its far broader and more finely grained experience, runs ahead of the law and the law has to struggle to catch up.

Someone might well ask at this point, "What about humanity's great religions? Are they not also historical institutions that hold up models of worthy and unworthy behavior, models that shape our lives accordingly?" They are indeed, and very powerful, too. Moreover, those institutions will no doubt endorse my claim that moral knowledge is real knowledge. Their grounds for this claim, however, will be very different from mine. In these pages I have been attempting to support this claim by highlighting the unfolding process by which we *learn from our mistakes*. Moral knowledge, broadly speaking, is real knowledge precisely because it results from the continual readjustment of our convictions and practices in the light of our unfolding experience of the real world, readjustments that lead to greater collective harmony and individual flourishing. If this is the way one wishes to argue for the rough objectivity of moral knowledge, then the world's great religions, the Western ones anyway, are poor examples to help one do it.

The reason is simple and not without some irony. In order to purchase a compelling authority for their respective catechisms, Christianity, Islam, and Judaism all claim a divine origin for the moral wisdom that they contain. Their moral laws are held out to us as the revealed truths or irrevocable commands of God. Putting aside the awesome presumption of those who would speak for God Himself, the tactical gain purchased by the claim of divine authority eventually matures into the profound *liability* of not being able to change the relevant body of law. Their dubious claim to authority returns to haunt these institutions. It returns as the awkwardness or complete inability to *learn* from mankind's subsequent moral and social experience. For if those religions have already been given

God's final word directly from God Himself, how can they subsequently claim to find fault with it?

This situation is worse, I think, than mere irony: it is a continuing tragedy. Some of the most powerful institutions on the planet, for preserving and teaching such moral wisdom as humanity had already achieved ten or twenty centuries ago, have now become the principal barriers to the wholly natural processes by which humanity might ascend to still higher levels of moral understanding.

While important, perhaps, these remarks on religion are a digression from my main purpose, which is to outline a more modest authority for moral knowledge; namely, the imperfect but very real authority of our collective social experience. Let me conclude this section by returning to that theme. Focus now on the single individual, one who grows up among creatures with a more or less common human nature, in an environment of established social practices and presumptive moral wisdom already in place. The child's initiation into that smooth collective practice takes time, time to learn how to recognize a large variety of prototypical social situations, time to learn how to deal with those situations, time to learn how to balance or arbitrate conflicting perceptions and conflicting demands, and time to learn the sorts of patience and self-control that characterize mature skills in any domain of activity. After all, there is nothing essentially moral about learning to defer immediate gratification in favor of later or more diffuse rewards.

So far as the child's brain is concerned, such learning, such neural representation, and such deployment of those prototypical resources are all indistinguishable from their counterparts in the acquisition of skills generally. There are real successes, real failures, real confusions, and real rewards in the long-term quality of life that one's moral skills produce. As in the case of internalizing mankind's scientific knowledge, a person who internalizes mankind's moral knowledge is a more powerful and effective creature because of it. To draw the parallels here drawn is to emphasize the practical or pragmatic nature of both scientific and broadly normative knowledge. It is to emphasize the fact that both embody different forms of *know-how*: how to navigate the natural world in the former case, and how to navigate the social world in the latter.

This portrait of the moral person as a person who has acquired a certain family of cognitive and behavioral *skills* contrasts sharply with the more traditional accounts that picture the moral person as one who has agreed to follow a certain set of *rules* (e.g., "Always keep your promises", etc.), or alternatively, as one who has a certain set of overriding *desires* (e.g., to maximize the general happiness, etc.). Both of these more traditional accounts are badly out of focus.

For one thing, it is just not possible to capture, in a set of explicit imperative sentences or rules, more than a small part of the practical wisdom possessed by a mature moral individual. It is no more possible here than in the case of any other form of expertise—scientific, athletic, technological, artistic, or political. The sheer amount of information stored in a well-trained network the size of a human brain, and the massively distributed and exquisitely context-sensitive ways in which it is stored therein, preclude its complete expression in a handful of sentences, or even a large bookful. Statable rules are not the *basis* of one's moral character. They are merely its pale and partial reflection at the comparatively impotent level of language.

If rules don't do it, neither are suitable desires the true basis of anyone's moral character. Certainly they are not sufficient. A person might have an all-consuming desire to maximize human happiness. But if that person has no comprehension of what sorts of things genuinely serve lasting human happiness; no capacity for recognizing other people's emotions, aspirations, and current purposes; no ability to engage in smoothly cooperative undertakings; no skills whatever at pursuing that all-consuming desire; then that person is not a moral saint. He is a pathetic fool, a hopeless busybody, a loose cannon, and a serious menace to his society.

Neither are canonical desires obviously necessary. A man may have, as his most basic and overriding desire in life, the desire to see his own children mature and prosper. To him, let us suppose, everything else is distantly secondary. And yet, such a person may still be numbered among the most consummately moral people of his community, as long as he pursues his personal goal, as others may pursue theirs, in a fashion that is scrupulously fair to the aspirations of others and ever protective of the practices that serve everyone's aspirations indifferently.

Attempting to portray either accepted rules or canonical desires as the basis of moral character has the further disadvantage of inviting the skeptic's hostile question: "Why should I follow those rules?" in the first case, and "What if I don't have those desires?" in the second. If, however, we reconceive strong moral character as the possession of a broad family of perceptual, computational, and behavioral skills in the social domain, then the skeptic's question must become, "Why should I acquire those skills?" To which the honest answer is, "Because they are easily the most important skills you will ever learn."

Neural Representation and the Many Forms of Art

The cognition and creative skills of the artist form another domain that is commonly contrasted with the "cold, hard" cognition of the natural scientist. As we have already seen, such a view fails to recognize the excitement and the creative insight of the successful scientist. It also fails to recognize the keen-edged cognition and highly organized skills of the outstanding artist. From the point of view of brain function, these two triumphant human enterprises are not remotely so different as is commonly believed. Let me outline why we should reconsider this ancient prejudice.

The musician or composer, the painter or graphic artist, the novelist or playwright, the dancer or choreographer, all ply trades that require enormous amounts of learning or practice. And what all of them learn is a family or system of prototypical performances or productions, prototypes that form the basis for almost all of the artistic work they do. Those prototypes constitute fertile themes such that almost all subsequent work is an exploration of their possible combinations and variations.

The point is easily seen in music, especially in one of its most mundane instances: the hopeful teenager learning to play "popular" guitar. The infamous three chords—usually C, F, and G7th—all too often exhaust the basic repertoire of the neophyte. They can be played in a variety of useful sequences, however, perhaps the most common of which is the so-called "twelve-bar blues"—for example: C,F,C,C7; F,F,C,C; G7,F,C,G7—a twelve-bar chord sequence that is repeated over and over again as the background for some voiced melody or other, which melody defines the composition. Any specific blues will consist of some twelve-bar sequence of notes, a sequence always in harmony with the changing chords in the background.

Despite the simplicity of a blues, there are tens of thousands of distinct compositions within this prototypical volume of musical space. The twelve-bar pattern at issue underlies such original rock classics as Bill Haley's "Rock Around the Clock," "Shake, Rattle, and Roll," and thousands of copycat rock tunes. It also underlies thousands of more challenging classics within both traditional and modern jazz, such as "Billie's Bounce" (Charlie Parker), "Swingin' Shepherd's Blues" (Moe Koffman), and "Blues and the Abstract Truth" (Oliver Nelson). In jazz, however, the twelve-bar chord sequence more typically contains minor rather than major chords: the chronically flatted third of those minor chords is part of what gives it its bluesy character. Endless gold remains in both these veins.

The neophyte guitarist also learns that this same abstract pattern can be played in every musical key, so he must also master the chord sequences for a blues in F, a blues in B♭, a blues in G, and so forth. (The more general prototype, therefore, is 1,4,1,1; 4,4,1,1; 5,4,1,5, where the number indicates the chord's place in the key scale at issue.) The same patterns are learned by the neophyte pianist or keyboard player, and by the player of any single-voiced instrument who wishes to produce the extemporaneous compositions of jazz improvisation. In this latter case, the successful musician produces a new instance of the prototype in every twelve-bar cycle; he is composing on the fly, and without a net.

There are many other prototypical chord sequences, each one the basis for many different songs. Some of these sequences span many centuries. The chord sequence for the gentle medieval ballad "Greensleeves," for example, and the later Christmas carol "What Child Is This?" is also, perhaps surprisingly, the basis for Dire Strait's pounding hit single, "We Are the Sultans of Swing."

Chord sequence and key form two important dimensions of musical space, but there are many other dimensions of comparable importance. Rhythm is a third, and it contains a variety of familiar prototypes. Restricting ourselves just to modern music, we have the march, the foxtrot, the waltz, the polka, swing, the samba, the rumba, the bossa nova, reggae, and a growing list of others.

Phrase structure is a fourth dimension. Not all songs consist of a twelve-bar unit repeated. There are many sixteen-bar songs, such as Gershwin's "Summertime," which are four-by-four rather than three-by-four. And there is also that well-worn favorite of the legendary Tin Pan Alley composers, the thirty-two bar song. This longer format typically has four eight-bar melody units, all identical except for the bridging third unit, which provides eight bars of relief from the cycling main theme (think of Harold Arlen's

"Stormy Weather"). Close to half of the musical hits of the 1930s and 1940s had this same four-by-eight-bar pattern. To be a successful songwriter in that period pretty much required mastery of that format. It was a musical instance of what Thomas Kuhn has elsewhere called a dominant "paradigm". It defined what people expected of a popular song, and in competent hands, its deployment was a good bet for musical success.

This short list of features hardly exhausts the structure of modern musical space, but collectively these four dimensions yield a wide array of familiar musical combinations, and room for many more. As well, some compositions stand out precisely because they subtley *violate* the prototypical patterns in cleverly systematic ways. Paul McCartney's "Yesterday," for example, nicks the old 8/8/8/8 Tin Pan Alley format by using a strangely effective 7/7/8/7-bar format instead. And Paul Desmond's rhythmic landmark "Take Five" (recorded with Dave Brubeck) strides out with a hypnotic *five* beats to the bar—a sort of waltz with a two-beat kicker appended to each triplet.

Other ages and other musical cultures display musical prototypes of their own, to be sure. The examples cited are historically and stylistically parochial. But they illustrate well enough the background claims being made. First, competence in the performance and composition of music requires the assimilation of prototypes, just as does competence in the application of a scientific theory. Presumably these prototypes are represented in the well-trained musical brain by suitable regions or partitions in its neuronal activation space, or more likely, by suitable *trajectories* in the space. Music, like speech, has a temporal dimension, which means that *recurrent* networks must be the engines at work.

Significantly, humans can complete the vectorial sequence of a familiar melody if given a few bars of it, just as we can recognize a familiar but partially hidden face. Evidently, the exercise of one's musical competence, whether in musical production or in musical perception, involves the appropriate activation of internal prototypes. Moreover, the range of one's musical competence will be defined by the specific prototypes one has mastered. That competence is nontrivial. In music, as in science, the trained person can do things and perceive things that are simply closed to untrained hands and ears. And in music, as in science, the creative person is the one who finds novel and effective instances of old prototypes, or generates entirely new ones.

To be sure, the aims of music need not be the aims of science. Perhaps their aims are mostly disjoint. For example, we might see the main aim of music as being the manipulation of the auditory environment for affective purposes. And we might see the main aim of science as being the manipulation of the physical environment for practical purposes. And yet the neural resources required, the coding strategies employed, and the transformational activities displayed are the same in both cases.

Furthermore, these parallels between music and science extend beyond the individual brain and into the social realm. The flourishing of new forms of activity, their condensation around a small set of successful patterns, their widespread acceptance and celebration, their eventual decadence, the scattered emergence of revolutionary alternatives, and the cycle begins anew. We may wonder about "intellectual progress" through such cycles of fashion: does music really make *progress* as science does? I will not pause to pursue it, but even here a strong case can be made on music's behalf, if not so compelling as the case to be made for science.

We began this section by worrying about artistic versus scientific cognition. The upshot of the discussion so far is that, from a neurocognitive point of view, the differences are superficial. This impression is confirmed, I think, if we look beyond music to the other major forms of artistic endeavor.

The graphic arts have their own range of formats: the pencil sketch, the charcoal drawing, the watercolor, the oil, the acrylic. They have their own range of prototypical subjects: the landscape, the portrait, the still life, the cityscape. And they have their own range of standard-but-plastic techniques for constructing images: with lines, with planes, with light and shade, with color, with tiny points, with out-of-focus splotches, and so forth. Once again we see a space of high dimensionality, with widely scattered prototypical hotspots and almost endless volumes still waiting to be explored. Once again we see highly developed *skills* in the application of these techniques and the creative deployment and redeployment of these prototypes. Once again we see vector completion playing a role, especially in contemporary art. Think, for example, of Picasso's various violins and guitars: an *f*-hole here, a hint of parallel strings there, a tuning peg, and voila! Once again, we see a case for progress over the centuries. The manipulation of the visual world for broadly affective purposes has come a long way since the prehistoric cave drawing and the Egyptian frieze.

The same lesson emerges if we look at the several narrative arts: literature, theater, and film. A universal theme such as Faust's deal with the Devil can have many instances, ranging from Esau's mess of pottage in the Old Testament to Dante's *Inferno* to Broadway's *Damn Yankees*. The theme of selling one's soul has a lot of thematic company—the tragic flaw, the abuse of power, the poor waif risen high—but I will spare you further lists. The story here parallels that for music and for the graphic arts. Those with greater knowledge will tell it better than I. Let me point out only that the illustration of general *truths* is here a self-conscious aim of the art. A genuinely successful novel or play is one that captures a universal human theme or lesson in some striking and memorable example of possible human behavior, and it leaves us significantly wiser for the encounter. The representational technique may be somewhat different, but here the aims of art and the aims of science overlap.

The point of this brief survey has been to bring the broad range of human artistic endeavor comfortably into the fold of a neurocomputational account of human cognition. As with the earlier topic of human moral knowledge, my hope is that this new explanatory perspective will serve to illuminate these several artistic endeavors, and to advance their diverse aims. If it gives us a deeper understanding of how humans perceive, interpret, and create, it can hardly fail to advance the cause of human art.

11 Neurotechnology and Human Life

The aim of this concluding chapter is to explore the consequences that a detailed theory of the brain, and the technologies it will inspire, are likely to have on the nature of human life. What will be their impact on the individual's practical affairs? On our social policies? On one's personal and spiritual life? And how will they affect the long-term development of the human race?

Medical Issues: Psychiatric and Neurological Medicine

The first place we will feel the effects is in psychiatric and neurological medicine, the domain of damaged or dysfunctional brains. As we saw in chapter 7, these disciplines already have the shape they have by virtue of the theoretical knowledge we possess and the technologies we command for observing the brain and for intervening, in a benign spirit, in its activities. Developments now coming on line will accelerate their development.

A new brain-scanning technique called FMRI (functional magnetic resonance imaging) will give a real boost to brain research and medical practice alike. With this technique, existing MRI technology is refocused in order to detect localized physiological *activity* within the brain, brain *function* this time, rather than brain structure. FMRI can thus do everything that PET scanning does. It can make visible, noninvasively, the current levels of neuronal activity in various areas of the live, awake, and cognitively active human brain.

But FMRI has two major advantages over PET. First, it does not require the injection of any short-lived radioactive tracers into the subject's bloodstream. More important, it does not require a multimillion-dollar on-site cyclotron (a subatomic particle accelerator) to produce those fleeting tracers immediately before the PET scan is performed. Rather, FMRI is tuned to the natural difference between the oxygenated hemoglobin molecules in one's bloodstream and those that have been *de*oxygenated in order to sustain local increases in neural activity. Like PET, therefore, FMRI tracks neural activity indirectly, by tracking its metabolic precursors and byproducts. But it can do so without elaborate preparation, and without the annoyingly brief time limit imposed on PET by a rapidly fading radioactive tracer.

The second major virtue of FMRI is its improved temporal resolution. A PET scan is blind to a local elevation in neuronal activity if it lasts for less than thirty seconds. Current FMRI will detect such elevations even if they last only one-half second, and the technology has not yet reached the theoretical limit of its temporal resolution. It already provides us with a 100-fold improvement over PET, and it may yet provide a 1000-fold gain. Since most of a recurrent neural network's cognitive activities take place on a scale in the millisecond range, an imaging technique that reaches into that range will allow us to watch real-time neural activity as the conscious subject is engaged in any number of perceptual, cognitive, deliberative, or motor activities. The business of correlating mental states with brain states will reach a new level of spatiotemporal detail.

Beyond FMRI, a second major technique is emerging: magnetoencephalography (literally, "magnetic brain-picturing") or *MEG* for short. Lloyd Kaufmann is its primary author. This is the technique used by Rodolfo Llinás in his research on waking, dreaming, and delta sleep discussed earlier in connection with the problem of consciousness. It works as follows. Wherever there is elevated neural activity, large numbers of electrically charged chemical ions are in oscillatory motion, for these are what make up the electrochemical waves that travel along any axon to convey information to the next population of neurons. Electric charges in motion invariably generate tell-tale magnetic fields. These are what the MEG machine detects.

Like FMRI, MEG is physically and chemically noninvasive. A benign magnetic field is the only thing to enter the brain. But since MEG detects the instantaneous magnetic signature of neural activity, rather than its inevitably delayed metabolic signatures, MEG's temporal resolution is dramatically better. Indeed, it already reaches into the single-millisecond range. That is how Llinás was able to recognize oscillations of 40 Hz at various points in the cortex, and to note that they were phase locked, but phase shifted by as little as one or two milliseconds.

As an observational technique, MEG is wonderful. Its real promise, however, may lie elsewhere. Wherever it can reach into the brain and "feel" the magnetic fields that accompany local neural activity, it can also be used in reverse. It can reach into the brain and create local magnetic fields, of appropriate strength and oscillation, so as to accelerate the millions of chemical ions and thus *produce* neural activity at selected locations in the brain. In short, it can be used for stimulating neural activity as well as for recording it.

The much older technique of inserting a physical microelectrode into the brain allows us to do the same things, but only one cell at a time, and only by first opening the skull. The cost was high and the payoff was low. With MEG, the ratio is reversed. The activation vectors produced by MEG stimulation are hopelessly clumsy, of course: rather like pressing on a piano's keyboard with your entire forearm. MEG will not allow us to generate highly specific vectors within a neuronal population, but it does give us a handle on conscious neural activity that we have never had before.

This will open a new field of cognitive research. For in principle, MEG allows us to stimulate any part of the brain at all—perceptual areas, emotional areas, language areas, specialized cognitive areas, deliberative areas—and then to ask the perfectly conscious experimental subject to *tell* us what forms of mental activity are taking place inside him. As a technique for mapping the functional organization of the human brain, it is almost too good to be true. Early exploration of the MEG recording and stimulation technique is already in process at Llinás's NYU facility.

These new ways of monitoring and manipulating neural activity, especially when used in conjunction with pharmacological modulation of the biochemical soup in which that activity takes place, will eventually give the psychiatrist and the surgeon a much better understanding of the dimensions and mechanisms of normal brain function. This will inevitably lead to better and safer techniques for detecting and fixing *failures* of normal function. And perhaps for heading them off before they ever occur.

Is there a dark side to all of this? Of course there is. Ignorant psychiatrists will occasionally prescribe dangerous drugs. Clumsy surgeons will occasionally damage vital neural subsystems. Confused theory will legitimize some irrelevant and retrograde medical practices. Bureaucratic policy will occasionally attempt to solve chemically what can only be solved socially. Some welcomed cures will prove to have disastrous long-term side effects. A black market in neuroactive drugs and devices will flourish. A subculture of abuse, however small, is inevitable. All of these things will happen. Only their frequency is uncertain.

In the face of these inevitable frustrations we might be tempted to slam the lid on the entire project, research and technology alike. That decision, of course, would have consequences of its own. Wise psychiatrists would be denied the drugs to restore dysfunctional brains. Skilled surgeons would be denied the information necessary for pinpoint interventions. Accurate theory would never sustain a more enlightened medical practice. Bureaucratic policy would frustrate itself trying to solve socially what can only be repaired chemically. There would be no welcome psychiatric cures at all, with or without long-term side effects. And finally, we are *already* up to our ears in a vicious black market of insidious and self-destructive drugs. Without neural research and improved health care, we may never replace them with more benign drugs, nor find treatments that will stop addiction in its tracks.

The problem is one we have faced many times before, ever since the discovery of fire. Any new technology brings the potential for careless accidents and deliberate abuse. In the early stages, when society barely understands the new technology, apprehension and outright fear are the natural reactions. But subsequent public understanding regularly replaces fear with comfort; subsequent government regulation of practice brings confidence; and a subsequent flood of public benefits eventually brings a strong commitment to the new technology. What we need to do with neurotechnology, as with any other, is learn to use it responsibly.

Medical Issues: Neural Networks for Diagnosis and Treatment

So far we have focused on medical problems with the brain itself, but these make up a smallish part of diseases generally. In the not so long run, neurotechnology will have an effect on general medicine at least as great as the effect it will have on neurology. The reason can be summed up in two words: *diagnosis* and *treatment*. They are the essence of the medical profession, and artificial neural networks will soon allow us to reach a diagnosis far more reliably, quickly, and consistently than even the best human diagnostician. And they will recommend finely tuned treatments with greater speed and insight as well. The reasons are as follows.

Most doctors become skilled diagnosticians at least in their own medical subfields. Diagnosis, however, is a skill of enormous complexity. Not everyone reaches the same level of skill, either in speed, reliability, or range of expertise. Even the best people top out at a level far below perfection. Each disease presents itself in so many different forms—depending on its stage of development, and on the patient's age, sex, medical history, genetic background, concurrent diseases, and general health and emotional state—that there is no canonical list of necessary and sufficient symptomatic conditions that will serve to identify it. Most diseases bear a close resemblance, where symptoms are concerned, to a great many other diseases, at least at some stage of their respective developments. In all, trying to see past the collective configuration of 10, or 50, or 200 variable symptoms, in order to choose a specific diagnosis from a list of a 1000 or more possibilities is an exercise in pattern recognition of a very high order.

This is not just a metaphor. A long list of features such as temperature, blood pressure, white blood cell count, skin condition, muscle tone, pupil dilation, pulse rate, pulse strength, blood sugar level, and so on *constitutes* a high-dimensional input vector. And recognizing a specific disease from such a pattern of information is once more a matter of activating a diagnostic prototype vector ("It's spinal meningitis"), one of many to which the doctor has already been trained. It is an "inference to the best explanation" of the pattern of symptoms at issue. It is another instance of the cognitive process by now so familiar to you: vector completion in the face of partial or degraded inputs. A doctor beholds the scattered blobs, as it were, and must try to find the walking dog, the bearded face, or the horse-and-rider implicit therein. Only then will she know what she is confronting, and only then will she know what to expect from it and how to deal with it.

Enter artificial neural networks. Sophisticated pattern recognition despite partial or degraded input is a network's natural forte. We have already seen one case where an artificial network outperforms a human by a wide margin: Sejnowski and Gorman's network for distinguishing sonar rock echoes from sonar mine echoes. Medical diagnosis is another domain where artificial networks are sure to do better than humans.

The reason is simple. The extraordinary range and variation of symptoms within a given disease, and their extensive and variable overlap across distinct diseases, are so great that a single human cannot possibly grasp that vast and convoluted statistical profile in its entirety, nor apply more than a small part of it to real patients even if she did. Real-time human skill here must always fall well short of the ideal, even of the statistical wisdom that is already explicit, let alone implicit, in existing textbooks, medical journals, and research archives. There is simply too much for us to grasp.

A large artificial network, however, can be trained to embody every last decimal point of those accumulated statistics, every last conditional probability, every last arcane symptomatic profile. Crudely, we train up the network on the very large "training set" of existing medical records: on an arbitrary patient's initial symptoms as input and that same patient's final diagnosis as output. Given a large number of medical records, such a network can come to embody the accumulated experience of many thousands of individual doctors.

More important, it can bring all of that wisdom to bear on a real patient almost instantaneously, as soon as we start providing the trained network with the patient's symptoms. We might suppose that in future medical facilities each new patient will be subject to an automatic survey of a canonical set of perhaps fifty biological, personal, and historical variables. This will provide the doctors with a fifty-element vector to present to the trained network. The network will provide, as output, a summary of the patient's condition and a diagnosis of the underlying disorder, if any, complete with a confidence measure. We can even train it to give as auxiliary outputs, in cases of low diagnostic confidence, a list of further tests for the doctors to perform, specific tests that the network has found to be important for splitting the sorts of ambiguities that so far prevent it from giving a firm diagnosis.

Change of a patient's symptomatic profile over *time* is also important for discriminating one disease from another, or for predicting imminent crises. If our diagnostic network has a recurrent architecture, it can learn to handle such temporal information as well, and to refine its successive diagnoses accordingly. A disease, after all, is a dynamic thing, and an ideal diagnostician will track its symptomatic profile over time, minute by minute. A hospital's resident doctors cannot give such close attention to every one of the thousand patients in the building. But a tireless neural network, centrally connected to a thousand sensing devices, can do it easily. Being recurrent in its architecture, it can also recognize unfolding causal processes. It can thus continually update its diagnoses and set off the occasional alarm.

The ultimate point of a diagnosis is to recommend an appropriate treatment, and this, too, can be done by a well-trained network. There is no one-to-one correlation between diseases and treatments, any more than there is between diseases and symptoms. A thousand contextual factors intervene here as well. Once more, our medical records of past patient histories can be put to work on behalf of future patients. If reliable historical information can be made available to the network during its training period, and if reliable contextual information can be made available when it is finally put to work serving real patients, it can shine in the area of treatment proposals just as it shone in the area of diagnosis.

Will such networks make doctors unnecessary? Of course not. Rather, they will become one more tool in the medical profession's armory. The final and appropriate judge of how they should be used—how much trust should be placed in them, and how to arbitrate conflicts between human and network diagnoses—must be the medical profession itself. At first, no doubt, the networks will be clumsy. In time, they will improve. In the long run, they will become indispensable. The proper pace of their introduction and use is for the medical profession to decide.

This technology need not be at all expensive by today's standards. A massively parallel network etched on a single microchip can serve an entire hospital. The various sensors to which it is connected will cost far more than the central chip. Nor need we train every such network. Once we have trained up the first one, we can read out its configuration of synaptic weights and impose it directly on all subsequent chips. As an addition to the armamentarium of modern medical practice, Diagnostic Networks will be as welcome as they are inexpensive.

Legal Issues: The Birth and Death of the Self

A better conception of the nature and ground of the human self is sure to affect the law and the ways in which it is applied. It already has. Most states have for some time counted "brain death"—the cessation of all brain activity as measured by simple EEG (electroencephalography)—as legally equivalent to bodily death. In particular, further efforts to maintain the body are no longer required. It can be allowed to perish.

This is clearly a humane policy, at least to these eyes. With the death of the patient's brain, the valued *self* that it sustained is now utterly and irretrievably lost. But the principle that quite rightly bids us adopt the policy of Letting Go in this case may soon invite its extension to relevantly similar kinds of cases. Consider the case where the brain still shows measurable electrical activity, yet the patient lies in a coma, that deep form of unconsciousness from which no stimulus will produce arousal. These are usually not cases in which the self is irretrievably lost, and we take good care of the individual accordingly, waiting faithfully for the coma to lift.

But in some of these cases, because of new imaging technologies perhaps, we may come to know with moral certainty that the cause of the coma is such that it will never lift, a live brain and some residual brain activity notwithstanding. For example, if the problem that confronts us is massive cell destruction to the patient's thalamus at the center of the brain, and in particular, to the intralaminar nucleus, then we are looking once again at a case where the valued self is wholly and irretrievably lost. A functional intralaminar nucleus, you may recall from chapter 8, is apparently essential for consciousness in all of the higher animals.

Medically and morally, such cases are relevantly the same as cases of brain death. The self we care about is irreversibly gone. But current law makes it awkward or impossible to treat such cases with the parity they almost certainly deserve. The EEG still shows some neural activity, although it has nothing to do with any actual or potential consciousness. Here is a possible instance of where the law needs updating.

Another possible instance, more widespread this time, is the case of advanced Alzheimer's disease, although here we face a serious continuity problem. The most common form of senile dementia, Alzheimer's disease is a gradually degenerative condition that afflicts twenty percent of all people over seventy. In its advanced stages, Alzheimer's disease ends up by stealing all of the self. It does so by gradually and irreversibly destroying the intricate brainwide configuration of synaptic connections that embodies all of one's knowledge, memories, and skills—all of one's capacities for recognition, deliberation, and action. The well-tuned network of the self is slowly corrupted into a dysfunctional mass of microscopic plaques and tangles. The advanced patient loses all biographical memory, ceases to speak entirely, responds with no recognition or emotion to things that go on around him, initiates no behavior whatever, and fails even to feed himself or take care of basic toilet functions. He eventually becomes a statue, staring vacantly into space, comprehending nothing, and caring about nothing.

The valued self, once more, is then irretrievably lost. The body remains, and the brain is still strictly alive, but its astronomical synaptic configuration space is now shrunk to a figurative matchbox. Its hierarchy of prototypical categories has evaporated. Although some active neurons survive, the overall system is no longer capable of coherent transformational activities. The self it once sustained is no longer there.

As with irreversible coma, the parallel with brain death is plain. And a parallel policy of allowing such patients to perish would seem to be in order. The financial and psychological burden on the living is as appalling here as in the other two cases, and such empty human shells consume medical resources that could more humanely be used elsewhere.

But in this case we face a moral and procedural awkwardness we are spared in the case of brain death and permanent coma: *at what point* in the Alzheimer patient's slow decline is the fading self finally to be counted as legally *gone*? The accidents that yield brain death, or permanent coma, typically happen suddenly. With the healthy self so clearly in our memory from only yesterday, the catastrophic contrast with the empty shell now before us is plain. Not so with Alzheimer's disease. Each day is humanly indistinguishable from the day that preceded it. The patient's loving family adjusts its expectations by insensible increments. No clear and merciful event marks out for them the time to let go. Many of them never do.

I have no pat solution to this problem. What is needed is an objective and reliable measure of when the cognitive functions in an Alzheimer's victim have fallen to the same low levels found in terminal coma and brain death. The EEG alone will not suffice, for it gives a falsely optimistic measure of cognitive capacity in Alzheimer's patients. Detectable neural activity does not constitute a thinking self if it lacks the coherent form that only a well-tuned neural network can give to it. Perhaps the newer imaging techniques—FMRI and MEG—can do better. Once more, the law almost certainly needs some amendment, but exactly how it should be amended remains unclear. We need both better theory *and* better technology.

In other cases, the current law may need, not amending, but protection and reaffirmation. I have in mind a second case where continuity poses a serious problem for the law: the time limit on a legitimate fetal abortion. Allowing a normal, newborn, full-term human baby to perish strikes almost everyone as unacceptable. At the other end of the developmental spectrum, the deliberate destruction of an unwanted sperm or egg strikes almost everyone as acceptable. Between these two end points there is much disagreement about where the permissible leaves off and the impermissible begins.

The law itself strikes a rough compromise: abortion in the first six months after conception is part of a woman's constitutional right to privacy. This decision is disputed by a significant minority of Christians, most fiercely by Roman Catholics, who wish to make the moment of an egg's fertilization the cutoff point. Into the historical intricacies of this debate I will not enter. Its general shape was sketched back in chapter 6. I wish only to draw attention to a purely factual premise to be accorded whatever relevance the respective parties might now decide to give it.

The observable fact is, the brain and central nervous system are not yet properly formed in a first-trimester fetus, nor even in a second-trimester fetus. Many of its cellular precursors are there, of course, but they are tiny, immature, and nonfunctional. Most of these neuron-precursor cells have yet to make their long migration through the cellular matrix to take up their final physical positions within the organized brain, and they are still some months away from growing long axons with which to make systematic synaptic connections with other neurons. Moreover, those potential synaptic connections are some months further still from being adjusted by learning into a configuration that will sustain any form of cognition. There is no network *activity* within the first- or second-trimester fetus, because there is as yet no network there.

The potential relevance of this is as follows. If the felt need to protect any fetus from abortion has its basis in a concern to protect and preserve an existing *self*, then that concern appears to be factually misplaced. If the neurobiological account of cognition, consciousness, and the self emerging from current research is even roughly correct, then there can be no self, not even an unconscious one, until the fetus has developed a functional nervous system and has begun to configure its myriad synaptic weights so as to sustain an ongoing history of cognitive activity. Without a neural network in place, there can be no self, neither an emotional self, nor a perceiving self, nor a deliberating self, nor any other kind of self. A first- or second-trimester fetus is many things, to be sure, but an established self it is not. If we presume to overturn Roe *v.* Wade, therefore, we will need some argument other than the standard presumption in favor of preserving a self. In the cases at issue, there is no self.

Legal Issues: Sociopathology and Corrective Policy

Questions of just and humane policy at the beginning and at the end of human life will clearly find more enlightened answers when they are posed in the light of better neuroscientific understanding. By far the largest impact, however, will be on human life between those two points. In particular, we are likely to see a revolution in the ways that society deals with the broad spectrum of pathological social behavior. A neurally informed and technologically sophisticated society will be able to make judgments reliably and do things effectively, where current practice is groping and impotent. Examples of the latter are close at hand.

A question that faces any court of law is the background cognitive, emotive, and deliberative competence and actual cognitive, emotive, and purposive state at the time of the alleged offense. The law draws several crude but highly consequential distinctions, such as that between appreciating or not appreciating the quality of the act; between being sane or insane at the time; between premeditated and spontaneous acts; and between various classes of motives—the base, the innocent, and the praiseworthy.

These distinctions are consequential because strict guilt before the law depends on them, and also because the character and magnitude of the punishment, incarceration, or other corrective policy imposed on the convicted party depends heavily on where the court locates him in this matrix of psychological possibilities. The same physical act may earn 10 years in jail for one person, 2 years in a mental institution for another, and 160 hours of community service for a third, all depending on cognitive and other psychological factors.

Justice and good sense alike demand that distinctions such as these be taken into account, both in evaluating guilt and in measuring out appropriate punishment. But few will deny that courts are deeply unreliable at determining the many dimensions of cognitive, emotional, and social competence in any defendant. And given the high frequency of repeat offenders, few will pretend that our current punitive or corrective procedures do much good. The current mood of the country, at least where repeated violent crimes are concerned, is to forget about attempts at correction and simply lock the offenders away from society for as long as possible.

As I write this, my own state of California signed a three-strikes-and-you're-out bill into law yesterday morning. And this morning's newspaper announced that San Diego's very first indictment under this law had just been filed against one of three armed robbers who held up the supermarket at the foot of my street, just six hours after the bill had been signed by the governor. The felons fled the scene in a car they had "car-jacked" from a terrified motorist just an hour before. By sheer chance, their flight from my supermarket was observed by some FBI agents taking an ice cream break across the parking lot. Ten miles away and twenty minutes later, the three gunmen were surrounded at gunpoint and taken into custody. Some of my favorite check-out clerks are still shaken. An abstract discussion this is not.

Such bills, and I doubt California's will be the last, are the expression of failure: the failure of existing legal and corrective practices to protect the innocent public. These failures are manifestly real, and so the current lock-'em-up-and-lose-the-key reaction must be respected. Indeed, we should probably support it, vigorously if need be. But the expense is appalling, both in tax dollars desperately needed elsewhere, and in wasted human resources, the guards and the guarded alike. One can be forgiven for wondering if the next fifty years might produce a more just, more effective, and less expensive system for dealing with criminal behavior.

The possibilities here are vague and uncertain, so keep your skepticism at a healthy level. On the other hand, our understanding of pathology and our techniques for confronting it are certain to change, and change dramatically. We would be well advised to be at least partially prepared for them. So, with vagueness acknowledged, let us do our best to see past it.

Criminal behavior surely has no single cause or locus in the brain. It can stem from chronic failures in social perception, from an inability to empathize with others, from a contorted emotional profile, from weird and overpowering desires, from chronic deficits in practical reasoning, from the lack or corruption of normal socialization, from sheer desperation, from sheer cussedness, from any combination of these, and from a hundred other things we have yet to appreciate. In its way, the law already acknowledges this diversity by the attention it pays to the cognitive, emotive, and deliberative competence of any defendant.

But as remarked earlier, the law needs to do much better in getting a reliable fix on these matters if it is to make useful decisions based on them. Once again, neurotechnology may give us a hand. Three distinct things need to develop and then come together. First, noninvasive techniques for recording highly localized brain activity need to be brought to a high level of accuracy and convenience. Functional MRI and MEG would seem to be our best bets here. Second, our theoretical understanding of the many dimensions of cognitive, emotive, and deliberative activity needs to be deepened, perhaps even reconceived entirely, in order to square with what these scanning technologies will teach us, both about healthy brains and about handicapped, damaged, and truly pathological brains. Third, we need to deploy artificial networks as well-informed diagnostic aids, not just for ills of the body, as discussed above, but also for failures and pathologies in *brain* function.

The new scanning techniques will allow us to accumulate a large data base concerning individual profiles of brain function, from normals through to violent sociopaths. Those brain profiles can be probed and recorded, for example, during any subject's viewing of a variety of prototypical social, moral, and practical situations as displayed on a TV screen. Once recorded, these neural profiles can be paired with an independent diagnosis of the subject's overall cognitive state, and most important, with a profile of the subject's actual behavioral history, social and criminal. A large number of such pairs will constitute a training set for the sort of diagnostic network we desire, a network that, once trained, will accurately diagnose certain types of brain dysfunction and accurately predict problematic social behavior. As in the medical case discussed earlier, such a psychodiagnostic network can come to embody far more experience than any single human, and bring all of it to bear consistently on the intricacies of each and every case it encounters.

Such a technology would not allow us to do anything we have not already been doing for most of this century. Criminal defendants are regularly remanded for psychiatric evaluation if the court deems it appropriate to the fair conduct of the case at hand. But it would allow us to perform this essential task far more accurately, and thus more fairly, than current wisdom permits.

Being able to distinguish reliably between the truly problematic people and others—those who have merely stumbled into a once-only encounter with the law—will be benefit enough. The legal system can quickly escort the latter folks, appropriately chagrined, back into the social mainstream. But the real benefit of identifying the truly problematic people in this high-tech way is that the specific *nature* of their neurosocial problem can thus be identified, and they will thus become a candidate for possible relief, repair, or continuing modulation.

At this last suggestion, either your skin has begun to crawl or you haven't been paying attention. There is a standard fear in modern society, a fear expressed in novels such as Orwell's *1984* and Burgess's *A Clockwork Orange*, a fear that an evil or irresponsible government might attempt to seize control over our very thoughts, desires, and basic character traits. I agree that this is an appalling prospect, to be resisted as fervently as anything we can imagine. If neurotechnology raises in any way the prospects of this happening, then it is a technology whose use should always remain under close public scrutiny and under firm public control. These sentiments I will take as a given in what follows, and I will not reverse them.

Withal, perspective is still needed. Good and responsible governments have long acknowledged it as their *duty* to help shape at least the basic beliefs of the nation's children by means of an honest and thorough education, and to shape some of their basic desires and character as well. There is nothing essentially sinister here, as long as the agencies involved function in good faith. Moreover, good and responsible people in psychiatric and neurological medicine have long acknowledged it as their duty to try to restore normal cognitive and emotional function to people who have lost it through illness, injury, or other cause. There is nothing sinister here either.

Removing a brain tumor that causes uncontrollable rage in a patient is no different from removing a bullet that causes excruciating pain. Giving serotonin-enhancing drugs for major depression, to compensate for low levels of brain serotonin, is no different from giving insulin for diabetes, to compensate for a shortfall in natural insulin. Giving fluoxetine to suppress obsessive-compulsive disorder (the self-stultifying repetition of ordinary actions such as washing one's hands or checking locked doors) is no different from giving an antihistamine to suppress the body's occasionally overblown immune responses such as inflamed skin and swollen breathing passages. The brain is a physical organ like any other, and it may occasionally need some benign medical intervention like any other.

There is a principle of individual choice operative in medicine generally: no one can be forced to receive medical treatment against his or her will. It is violated only in those rare cases where the patient is properly judged to be mentally incompetent of such a decision. It may also be violated in those rare cases where the patient's illness constitutes an infectious danger to the community of intolerable proportions. But even here, simple quarantine is usually all we forcibly impose. People are mostly reasonable, and are mostly willing to take the required medical measures. Hardly anyone *wants* to be a danger to society.

A similar principle of individual choice should operate in psychiatric and neurological medicine specifically: no one should be forced to receive psychoneural medical treatment against his or her will. Violations of this principle should be considered only when the person is properly judged to be mentally incompetent to make such a decision, or where the danger to the community posed by the individual is of unacceptable proportions. Even here, simple incarceration is perhaps all that we should impose by force. If the person is capable of a rational choice, perhaps the choice between accepting medical treatment and being locked up should remain with him. If he insists on keeping his dangerous sociopathology, then perhaps he should be free to contemplate it, untreated, behind locked doors and barred windows.

This returns us, finally, to the question of the criminal law. Let us be clear about the kind of technology envisioned. First, a noninvasive scan of a defendant's neural activities during various standard sorts of social observations and interactions. Second, presentation of that neurofunctional profile to a standard and approved neural network, previously trained on a large data base of such profiles, in order to get a detailed sociopathic diagnosis, an estimate of future behavior problems, and recommendations about possible treatments. As with medical neural networks generally, a confidence measure will be a part of all such network outputs. This is the technology we are contemplating.

Plainly, psychiatric evaluations of criminal defendants will not cease to be legitimate just because new technologies permit more accurate evaluations and more reliable projections of future behavior. Nor will the court's decisions on corrective measures be any the less just for taking those better evaluations into account. Other things being equal, they will be that much more just.

More to the point at issue, such high-tech evaluations may also help the courts to be more effective at protecting the innocent public. Identifying the truly problematic offenders is the first thing, if only to lock them away. But if diagnostic and treatment technologies improve as projected, then problem-specific neurological interventions may allow us to return a dangerously dysfunctional personality almost immediately to a state much closer to social and psychiatric *normal*, to a state that no longer represents a danger to the innocent public, to a state capable of earning one's own living without incarceration. The savings in purely human costs would be incalculable. More selfishly, think of our tax dollars. If only half of our convicts could be deflected from prison in this way, maintained by cheap pharmaceutical implants perhaps, voluntarily received, we would save many billions of dollars in direct costs each year. It currently costs the taxpayer about $40,000 per year to keep a single person in prison. In total, the federal and state governments spend more on prison costs annually than they spend on all federal and state institutions for higher education combined. Here, if anywhere, is an imbalance that wants fixing.

None of this is imminent. Decades of exploration, both neurological and legal, lie before us still. Such changes will come, but they will likely come gradually. Well and good. Neurotechnology must genuinely earn its eventual uses, and society needs time to become informed and to develop a mature perspective on the new developments. In due course, the public will decide these policy matters for itself, although the initiatives will likely come from the legal, medical, and corrective professions. The thesis of this section is that, as long as we stay informed, there is much more to be welcomed than there is to be feared.

Turbocharged Science: Using Neural Networks for Research

I can be fairly swift here. The preceding two chapters already contain introductory examples of the several techniques to be explored. The brevity of this section is no measure, however, of the depth of the topic here addressed. Science has the power to change the world. Artificial neural networks have the power to change the way we do science.

The first and simplest use of neural networks in research will be as sophisticated pattern recognizers; that is, as sensory devices, as instruments of detection, measurement, and classification. When we think of a measuring instrument we typically think of something like a thermometer or a voltmeter, something that detects and assigns a simple numerical value to a one-dimensional variable such as temperature or voltage. But these homey examples live at the simplest end of the sprectrum. Neural networks will live at the opposite end. Their closest kinship is not with voltmeters, but with the sensory modalities of fully intelligent creatures. They will allow us to detect subtle profiles across variables of very high dimensionality. They will allow us to recognize, almost instantaneously, theoretically interesting or dynamically relevant factors within situations of great complexity. And unlike the natural neural networks of the sensory modalities of biological creatures, they will not be limited to detecting the cosmically narrow data profiles that our local biological evolution happened to find valuable. Rather, they will reach out to the full range of detectable and perceivable realities that Nature affords.

Modest uses of this kind are already in place. At CERN, the major European particle accelerator, and at similar "atom smashers" here in the United States, neural networks have been trained to look past the chaos of familiar vapor trails, trails left by the subatomic debris produced in atomic collisions, and pick out only the signature vapor trail of a very specific hypothesized particle, should that particle happen to emerge from that collision. If one is searching for an elusive subatomic signature, one can save the drudgery, and the unreliability, of a human search through thousands of experimental photographs. One can use instead a trained neural network. It will tirelessly process every photo, pick out the elusive particle's occasional appearance, and ignore everything else. This can speed up the business of theory testing by several orders of magnitude.

It can also allow us to pick out patterns to which the human nervous system is simply not tuned. The mine-rock sonar network of chapter 4 provides one example of this. The sensory modalities of millions of nonhuman animals provide so many more. Canine olfaction, dolphin sonar, eel electrolocation, and other alien windows onto the natural world can be recreated in artificial form for human use. Simply construct an artifical sensory transducer with the same dimensions of external sensitivity as the target animal, feed the resulting input vectors into an artificial network of appropriate form, train the network on the sensory environment of the animal in question, and the same perceptual capacities will emerge, capacities not possessed by humans.

The occasional recreation of existing animal perception, however, will not be the prime focus of this research. The animals, too, have been shaped by evolutionary pressures that are ultimately parochial. Beyond them, there are countless possibilities unexplored by terrestrial evolution, and some of those possibilities will prove to be relevant to human concerns.

Think of a high-dimensional bank of sensors that takes in, simultaneously, the following sorts of information: the current seismic mutterings recorded by a thousand stations scattered across southern California, the current positions of the tidal agents of the Moon and the Sun, the current electrical resistance between a thousand cross-fault pairs of underground locations, the current surface concentrations of rare gases usually in solid solution within underground rock, the current number of sunspots, the current blatherings of Los Angeles psychics (I am making some of this up as I go along), and so forth. Feed all such information, on a continuous basis, into a recurrent network that is slowly being trained on the actual earthquakes that appear in southern California. Such a network, it is distantly possible, might eventually learn to "smell" an impending earthquake before it occurs, by discovering a complex profile in its highly diverse inputs. (The L.A. psychics, and perhaps also the sunspots, will quickly be filtered out of the network's transformational activities, since they are statistically irrelevant, I presume, to the causal processes at work. Alternatively, we may be surprised. In either case, the public will learn something.)

This particular idea may be faulty, since the behavior of the Earth's crust may be deeply chaotic and hence unpredictable, but the general idea is foursquare. Networks have already been trained to process the auditory and electrophysiological profiles of a human heatbeat, and to pick out those people whose cardiographic profile indicates such things as a blood-starved muscle region, a faulty valve, or a potential for rhythmic anomalies. Trained physicians can hear some of these things by listening through a stethoscope, and see some of them by looking at graphic tracings. But a single-purpose recurrent network can pull out dynamical information, implicit in the temporal profiles at issue, to which humans are both deaf and blind. And that information can serve not only to guide individual medical treatment in the here and now; in quantity, it can guide and inspire new scientific theories about the dynamics of the heart.

The point of detecting such intricate and arcane profiles is of course to permit the prediction, and perhaps also the control, of things of interest to us. Complex pattern recognition is an essential part of learning the functional relationships that structure the causal unfolding of reality at large. In many cases, those causal relationships are of a complexity that surpasses any ready grasp by the human brain, but they need not escape the relentless learning of an artificial neural network.

An example much on people's minds these days is the human genome, the entire genetic sequence that defines us all as human. That long definition is framed in the language of nucleic acids. It runs to roughly two billion "letters", all of them strung together as the rungs on the helical ladder of a handful of DNA molecules. Stretched end from end in your hands like a single piece of spaghetti, the relevant DNA makes an invisible string about six feet long. Every nucleated cell in your body contains its own complete copy of that string, safely folded up inside its nucleus. There the information coded in the string directs the chemical activity within its cell, making proteins, shaping metabolism, and occasionally duplicating itself. More to the point, that long genetic sequence is what produced you in the first place. Its g-g-great-great grandparent copy, forged within your original egg, is the author of the long sequence of carefully timed cell doublings and cell specializations that transformed the microscopic egg into a seven-pound infant. And the modest infant into a massive adult.

Here is where things get interesting, because that developmental sequence is what makes you a human rather than a chimpanzee, or a mosquito, or a slime mold. It is what makes you male or female, heavy-set or slender, brown- or blue-eyed. It is also what occasionally misfires in small ways, leaving a legacy of genetic disease: a missing protein, a missing metabolic chemical, an immune deficit, and so forth. These are what yield the host of afflictions such as Tay-Sachs disease, sickle-cell anemia, Huntington's chorea, cystic fibrosis, and various vulnerabilities to specific cancers.

What we would like to know, partly so as to prevent or correct these frustrations, is the functional relation between any individual's original genome, on the one hand, and the final creature, with all its idiosyncracies, to which the genome gradually gives rise, on the other.

That relation, however, must be one of the most complex in all of Nature. We often speak glibly of "the gene for brown eyes" or "the gene for tallness", as if there were a one-to-one correspondence between every human trait and some single gene. But it isn't like that. One's genome contains the instructions for a carefully orchestrated *process*, for a timed sequence of developmental events whose every element is dependent on the biological context provided by all of its neighboring elements. One's genome is less a "picture" of the completed you than it is a set of "instructions" for building you, where the task is at least as complex as building a skyscraper from scratch.

This genetic instruction booklet, unfortunately, is written in a language we do not understand: a sequence of molecular gibberish two billion letters long—GACTAAGACATCTAACACGT . . . , and so on. How can we ever hope to read it with comprehension? That is, how can we gain the understanding necessary to look at a specific genome and *predict* all of the features that it will produce in the completed individual—slime mold or mosquito, chimpanzee or human, hulking male or gracile female?

A feeble but instructive analogy is the task confronting NETtalk, the artificial network discussed in chapter 4. To produce the right phonetic output, NETtalk had to learn the *contextual* significance of the three letters on either side of the central target letter. It was only against that local background that the proper phonetic output could be determined. Might a very large neural network be trained to give, reliably, mature biological traits as outputs, given long sequences of genetic DNA as input? The statistical complexity of the functional relation between one's initial DNA (the genotype) and one's mature biological form (the phenotype) is so great that the problem would appear humanly intractable. But an artifical neural network—a GENEtalk, as it were—might well be able to crack it.

Don't expect this any time soon. Obtaining the vast amounts of information necessary to train such a network must be the first step. The human genome project has the task of fully mapping human DNA, but it is still years from completion, and by itself it will not help much in this task. We will need the genomes of many species before we can undertake the second-generation project proposed.

Still, the idea is appealing. Understanding how specific genomes produce specific creatures will give us a measure of control over the features of the creatures produced. That is a technology, like the technology of brain intervention, that will require of us rather more maturity than we currently possess. Let us make sure we develop it.

The Impact on Our Self Conception

All of the advantages of neurotechnology will pale, I suggest, next to something that is not really technological at all, namely, the increased *understanding* that the conceptual framework of an advanced neuroscience will bring to life within each of us, if only we trouble to learn that new framework. First we must finish building it, of course, for it is still in its infancy. But the ten chapters now behind you provide a tentative sketch of what it might look like—enough, at least, for us to readdress an old philosophical question: How does the mind have knowledge of *itself*?

The traditional answer, popular at least since Descartes, is that the mind knows itself directly and indubitably, both its own general nature and its own current state. The mind, it is often said, is "transparent" to itself: it may be that it has to struggle to achieve knowledge of the physical world outside it, says the tradition, but it has immediate and certain knowledge of the various mental states that make up the flow of its own consciousness.

From the perspective of the last ten chapters, this traditional view is deeply problematic. Indeed, it cannot possibly be true. For it amounts to the claim that neural networks have automatic and certain knowledge of their own cognitive activities. And this claim is simply false. A neural network has no direct or automatic knowledge of anything at all, let alone of its own cognitive activities. Let us quickly remind ourselves of how they work.

As we have seen, for a neural network to have knowledge of any particular domain is for it to have acquired an expertise in discriminating some important and recurring set of features within that domain, and to have acquired some expertise in responding to them in some systematic way. This requires in turn the development of a suitable configuration of synaptic connection weights, one that partitions the network's neuronal activation space into a useful set of categories (see again figures 3.8, 4.19, 4.22, and 4.23). Once those categories are in place, the network can be said to have a general or background comprehension of the domain at issue. And once it begins to activate those categories on appropriate occasions, it can be said to have specific knowledge of the domain's *unfolding* activities.

All well and good. But there is nothing "automatic" about the network's grasp of the target domain, *whatever* that domain might happen to be. Success still requires development of an appropriate configuration of synaptic connection weights. If trained to do so, networks can indeed come to represent some of their own cognitive states and processes; but that achievement will be no different from its achievements in any other domain. It will be the result of a learning procedure, perhaps a long one, here as anywhere else.

Neither will the exercise of that acquired cognitive capacity ever yield "certain" knowledge, as the tradition claims. Nothing ever guarantees that the category or the prototype activated on some occasion must be a correct or an accurate representation of the input reality that led to its activation. Networks are always hostage to the possibility of error. The labyrinth of any real network is always full of noise. Trained nets are good at seeing past noise, but they are never perfect at it. Furthermore, real networks are typically nonlinear in their dynamical behavior, which means that tiny errors at the input layer can occasionally be magnified into large errors at the output layer. Further still, networks can regularly be fooled by a situation that, while different in its real nature, is deceptively *similar* to some familiar input pattern (remember the strong tendency of all networks to assimilate a complex world to its own learned categories). Moreover, a network can accidentally deceive itself by means of its own recurrent pathways. Transient perceptual bias produced by contextual factors or expectation effects, can lead a network to faulty discriminations even in cases where it would otherwise get them right.

Finally, and perhaps most important, there is never any guarantee that the system of prototypes or categories employed by the network is really an *accurate* representation of the reality it attempts to depict. A modest degree of practical and predictive success is no guarantee of the truth of any conceptual framework. For fourteen centuries, Ptolemy's geocentric theory of the heavens served moderately well to predict the observed motions of the stars and planets, but its portrait of the underlying reality was flatly false. We rightly regard any network's success as a *presumption* in favor of the accuracy of the representations it has learned, but for no network is that accuracy ever guaranteed. Some new inputs may always be waiting in the relevant domain, inputs that will upset the prototypes already achieved. And another network, trained on the same inputs, may always come up with a different and superior set of prototypes.

The upshot is that immediate and absolutely certain knowledge is something that is not to be expected from a neural network. Quite aside from the many local perils that attend the local application of a given framework in a specific circumstance, there is the ever-present background peril that the general framework is faulty, inadequate, or suboptimal to begin with. This is true of all neural networks. It is therefore silly to expect such pristine knowledge in our own case, assuming we are indeed just sophisticated neural networks.

One might be tempted, briefly, to suppose that our framework of categories for self-representation is *innate*. That is conceivable, perhaps, but the main issues at stake here would be changed not at all. Whether the framework is innate or not, its application on specific occasions will be no less subject to each of the several perils listed above. And its being innate would guarantee only that evolution has selected it as locally useful, not that it must be an accurate portrayal of cognitive reality. In sum, the assumption of innateness buys us nothing usable in the present discussion.

The assumption is dubious in any case. The genetic specification of synaptic weights is not impossible; like other animals, the infant human does have some innate cognitive capacities such as seeking the mother's nipple by both olfactory and tactile means, but it is difficult for the genome to specify very much of our overall cognitive skills. A mature brain has at least 10^{14} independent synaptic connections, whereas the human genome contains only 2×10^9 base pairs or "letters". Plainly, the bulk of human synaptic configuration must be shaped by postnatal experience of the real world. Moreover, of the small portion that is genetically specified, one would expect to it to be concerned with very basic biological functions, such as suckling, rather than with sophisticated frameworks for apprehending the intricacies of high-level cognition. After all, the infant human doesn't have any high-level cognition at birth, and won't develop any for many months to come.

A better account sees our self-understanding and our ongoing self-perception as gradually learned, and as contingent for their content on the culture in which one is raised. The "training set" that shapes our mature conception of thinking creatures is dominated, of course, by our fellow humans, humans with a matured conception and shared language already in place. We learn our conception of cognitive, emotional, and deliberative activity primarily by applying it to the task of understanding and anticipating the behavior of other people. The rich framework learned in that endeavor can then be deployed in the business of understanding *oneself*, and the depth of self-understanding achieved is much the greater for having been informed by that much larger set of training examples.

It is therefore more accurate to see one's self-knowledge as something that grows significantly with time and experience, and as something that can always be transformed by new information. As it happens, we are now confronting a mass of new information about the brain and its activities, and we face the prospect of a great deal more. Might this new information change the ways we think about ourselves? Might it change the character of human cognitive and social interaction?

Of course it might, and it will. If you have read to this point, the process has already begun. You came to this book assuming that the basic units of human cognition are states such as thoughts, beliefs, perceptions, desires, and preferences. That assumption is natural enough: it is built into the vocabulary of every natural language. And each such state is typically identified by way of a specific *sentence* in one's natural language: one has the belief *that P*, or the desire *that Q*, for example, where *P* and *Q* are sentences. Human cognition is thus commonsensically protrayed as a dance of sentential or propositional states, with the basic unit of computation being the inference from several such states to some further sentential state.

These assumptions are central elements in our standard conception of human cognitive activity, a conception often called "folk psychology" to acknowledge it as the common property of folks generally. Their universality notwithstanding, these bedrock assumptions are probably mistaken. In humans, and in animals generally, it is now modestly plain that the basic unit of cognition is the *activation vector*. It is now fairly clear that the basic unit of computation is the *vector-to-vector transformation*. And it is now evident that the basic unit of memory is the *synaptic weight configuration*. None of these things have anything essential to do with sentences or propositions, or with inferential relations between them. Our traditional language-centered conception of cognition is now confronted with a very different brain-centered conception, one that assigns language no fundamental role at all.

It will be some time before we digest this major shift in perspective, and longer still before we begin to use the new conceptual framework in casual conversations and daily human life. But it will not be as long as some suppose. The reason is simple. These new assumptions, and many more from functional neuroanatomy and cognitive neuropharmacology, will soon be put to work in medicine, psychiatry, child development, the law, correctional policy, science, and industry. Their impact in these areas will not be minor. And as they affect our lives from these many points of the social compass, we will have both the opportunity to learn the relevant vocabulary, and the motivation to participate in the relevant conversations. The new framework, like any other, will gradually work its way into the general population. In time, it will become the common property of folks generally. It will contribute to, or even constitute, a *new* folk psychology—one firmly rooted, this time, in an adequate theory of the brain.

Some of my colleagues find this last idea implausible. They doubt that the vocabulary of a sophisticated science could ever gain general use on the scale at issue. I think they are wrong, and I am encouraged by the following facts about our recent social history. In the middle third of this century, the peculiar vocabulary and special assumptions of Freudian psychology spread through the educated populace like a wildfire. The lexicon of "anal retention", "Oedipal complex", "sexual repression", and a hundred other terms provided a rich resource for gossip and mirth, for criticism and disdain, for self-indulgence and self-rationalization, and for social confabulation across the board. These manifold social functions earned it a popular currency quite independent of its therapeutic success, or the lack of it.

The Freudian framework had faded badly by the early 1970s, but was soon replaced by New Age psychobabble, a pastiche of "primal screams", "inner children", and "getting in touch with one's feelings". As a therapeutic technique, it was several steps down from Freud's. But once more this vocabulary swept through the population, by reason of its serviceability in the same social dimensions earlier served by the Freudian lexicon.

Evidently, getting a new form of psychobabble into general use is not difficult at all. Evidently, the public is eager for such frameworks, eager to the point of embracing nonsense for decades on end. What would happen, let us ask, if a conceptual framework were to come along that had some real integrity? Some real correspondence with the pulleys and levers of our cognitive and emotional activity? Some real insight into the causal connections that animate that activity? It might sweep through the population, for the same superficial reasons as in the two historical cases just mentioned. But if, unlike its hollow precursors, it brought with it a real grip on the structure of cognitive reality, it just might stick. And it just might end up serving a host of practical purposes beyond the superficial ones that motivated its initial entry into the popular consciousness.

Service to our practical purposes is the only justification that will really count in the end. I quite agree that the human race is not about to reconceive its cognitive and affective nature for the sheer scientific fun of it. Any such reconception will have to earn its keep, by enabling each one of us to see more deeply into our social and personal situations, by giving each us a broader range of behavioral responses to awkward or problematic situations, by allowing us to smooth the course of our cognitive and emotional commerce, by helping us to realize our individual potentials, and by making mutual love a deeper and more widespread human achievement.

One's first impulse, perhaps, is to see the vocabulary and framework of a general theory of the brain as something alien and cold. But it will not be alien if it depicts all of us, at last, as we truly are. And it will not be cold if it serves all of the human purposes just listed. The aim of these concluding suggestions, therefore, is not to deny us our humanity, but to see it better served than ever before. Whatever the distractions, we must continue to exercise our reason. And whatever the temptations, we must continue to nurture our souls. That is why understanding the brain is so supremely important. It is the engine of reason. It is the seat of the soul.

Selected Bibliography

The list of articles here provided will allow the determined reader to track down most of the original research reported in this book. The casual reader, however, will be more interested in the many books listed, books now prominent for the past impact they have had on the subject, or for their contribution to scientific and philosophical debates currently in progress. I have chosen these books for their accessibility to the general reader, as well as for their other very considerable virtues. I do not agree with all of them, but in each case they represent work that is important by anyone's standards.

On Artificial Networks

Cottrell, Garrison, "Extracting features from faces using compression networks: Face, identity, emotions and gender recognition using holons," in Touretzky, D., Elman, J., Sejnowski, T., and Hinton, G., eds., *Connectionist Models: Proceedings of the 1990 Summer School*, (Morgan Kaufmann, San Mateo, CA: 1991).

Cottrell, Garrison, and Metcalfe, Janet, "EMPATH: Face, Emotion, and Gender Recognition Using Holons", in Lippman, R., Moody, J., and Touretzky, D., eds., *Advances in Neural Information Processing Systems*, Vol. 3 (Morgan Kaufmann, San Mateo, CA: 1991).

Gorman, R. P., and Sejnowski, T. J., "Analysis of Hidden Units in a Layered Network Trained to Classify Sonar Targets," in the journal *Neural Networks*, Vol. 1 (1988).

Rosenberg, C.R., and Sejnowski, T.J., "Parallel Networks that Learn to Pronounce English Text," in the journal *Complex Systems*, Vol. 1 (1987).

Churchland, Patricia S., and Sejnowski, Terrence J., *The Computational Brain* (MIT Press, 1992).

On Visual Psychology and Physiology

Gregory, Richard, *Eye and Brain: The Psychology of Seeing* (London, Weidenfeld and Nicolson: 1977)

Hubel, David, *Eye, Brain, and Vision*, in the Scientific American Library series (W. H. Freeman & Co., 1988).

Julesz, Bela, *Foundations of Cyclopean Perception* (University of Chicago Press: 1971).

Pettigrew, J.D., "Is there a single, most efficient algorithm for stereopsis?", in Blakemore, C., ed., *Vision: Coding and Efficiency* (Cambridge University Press, 1990).

Mead, Carver, and Mahowald, Misha, "The Silicon Retina," *Scientific American* (May, 1991).

Clark, Austen, *Sensory Qualities* (Oxford University Press, 1993).

On Language

Elman, Jeffrey L., "Grammatical Structure and Distributed Representations," in Davis, S., ed., *Connectionism: Theory and Practice*, Vol. 3 in the series *Vancouver Studies in Cognitive Science* (Oxford University Press, 1992).

Lakoff, George, *Women, Fire, and Dangerous Things: What Categories Reveal About the Human Mind* (University of Chicago Press, 1987).

Pinker, Steven, *The Language Instinct* (G. H. Morrow and Co., 1994).

Savage-Rumbaugh, E.S., Sevcik, R., and Rumbaugh, D.M., Rubert, E., "Symbol acquisition and use by *Pan troglodytes, Pan paniscus,* and *Homo sapiens,* in Heltne, P.G., Marquardt, L.A., eds., *Understanding Chimpanzee* (Harvard University Press, 1989).

Savage-Rumbaugh, E. S., and Rubert, E., "Language Comprehension in Ape and Child: Evolutionary Implications", in Christen, Y., and Churchland, P.S., eds., *Neurophilosophy and Alzheimer's Disease* (Springer-Verlag, 1992).

On Psychology: Moral and Personal

Damasio, Antonio, *Descartes' Error: Emotion, Reason, and the Human Brain* (G.P. Putnam's Sons, 1994).

Johnson, Mark, *Moral Imagination: Implications of Cognitive Science for Ethics* (University of Chicago Press, 1993).

Flanagan, Owen, *The Varieties of Moral Personality* (Harvard University Press, 1991).

Styron, William, *Darkness Visible: A Memoir of Madness* (Random House, 1990).

LeVay, Simon, *The Sexual Brain* (MIT Press, 1993)

Kramer, Peter D., *Listening to Prozac* (Viking, 1993).

On The Philosophy Of Science

Kuhn, T. S., *The Structure of Scientific Revolutions* (University of Chicago Press, 1962).

Churchland, P.M., *A Neurocomputational Perspective: The Nature of Mind and the Structure of Science* (MIT Press, 1989): chapter 9, "On the Nature of Theories: A Neurocomputational Perspective," and chapter 10, "On the Nature of Explanation: A PDP Approach".

Giere, R.N., "The Cognitive Structure of Scientific Theories," in the journal *Philosophy of Science*, Vol. 61, no. 2 (June, 1994).

On Consciousness

Turing, Alan, "Computing Machinery and Intelligence," in the journal *Mind*, vol. 59 (1950).

Nagel, Thomas, "What Is It Like to Be a Bat?", in the journal *Philosophical Review*, Vol. 83, no. 4 (1974).

Jackson, Frank, "Epiphenomenal Qualia", in the journal *Philosophical Quarterly*, Vol. 32 (April, 1982).

Block, Ned, "Troubles with Functionalism", in C. W. Savage, ed., *Perception and Cognition: Issues in the Foundations of Psychology*, Vol. 9 of the series, *Minnesota Studies in the Philosophy of Science* (University of Minnesota Press, 1978).

Churchland, Patricia S., *Neurophilosophy: Toward a Unified Science of the Mind-Brain* (MIT Press, 1986).

Churchland, Paul M., *Matter and Consciousness* (MIT Press, revised edition: 1988).

Churchland, Paul M., "Reduction, Qualia, and the Direct Introspection of Brain States", in *Journal of Philosophy*, vol. 82, no. 1 (Jan., 1985). Reprinted in Churchland, P. M., *A Neurocomputational Perspective* (MIT Press, 1989).

Dennett, Daniel, *Consciousness Explained* (Little, Brown, and Co., 1991)

Penrose, Roger, *The Emperor's New Mind* (Oxford University Press, 1989).

Flanagan, Owen, *Consciousness Reconsidered* (MIT Press, 1992).

Searle, John, *The Rediscovery of the Mind* (MIT Press, 1992).

Llinás, Rodolfo, and Ribary, U., "Coherent 40-Hz oscillation characterizes dream state in humans," in the journal *Proceedings of the National Academy of Sciences*, Vol. 90 (1993).

Crick, Francis, *The Astonishing Hypothesis: The Scientific Search for the Soul* (Scribner's and Sons, 1994).

Damasio, Antonio, *Descartes' Error: Emotion, Reason, and the Human Brain* (G.P. Putnam's Sons, 1994).

Index